MW00850346

PREPARING
TEACHERS
FOR DEEPER
LEARNING

PREPARING TEACHERS FOR DEEPER LEARNING

Preparing Teachers for Deeper Learning
by Linda Darling-Hammond and Jeannie Oakes
with Steven K. Wojcikiewicz, Maria E. Hyler, Roneeta Guha,
Anne Podolsky, Tara Kini, Channa M. Cook-Harvey,
Charmaine N. Jackson Mercer, and Akeelah Harrell

E-Book Case Studies for
Preparing Teachers for Deeper Learning

Preparing Teachers for Deeper Learning at Alverno College:
A Case Study in Creating a Learner-Centered Culture
by Anne Podolsky and Maria E. Hyler

Preparing Teachers for Deeper Learning at Bank Street College:
A Case Study in a Living Laboratory for Developmentally Grounded Practice
by Anne Podolsky and Linda Darling-Hammond

Preparing Teachers for Deeper Learning at High Tech High:
A Case Study in Building a Project-Based Learning Environment
by Steven K. Wojcikiewicz, Charmaine N. Jackson Mercer, and Akeelah Harrell

Preparing Teachers for Deeper Learning at Montclair State University:
A Case Study in Developing Student-Centered Practice through K–12 Partnerships
by Maria E. Hyler, Akeelah Harrell, and Steven K. Wojcikiewicz

Preparing Teachers for Deeper Learning at San Francisco Teacher Residency:
A Case Study in Learning for Transformative Teaching
by Tara Kini and Steven K. Wojcikiewicz

Preparing Teachers for Deeper Learning at Trinity University:
A Case Study in Developing an Inquiry-Based Approach to Teaching
by Roneeta Guha and Steven K. Wojcikiewicz

Preparing Teachers for Deeper Learning at University of Colorado Denver:
A Case Study in Learning to Teach for Social Justice
by Channa M. Cook-Harvey and Jeannie Oakes

PREPARING TEACHERS FOR DEEPER LEARNING

Linda Darling-Hammond
Jeannie Oakes

with

Steven K. Wojcikiewicz
Maria E. Hyler
Roneeta Guha
Anne Podolsky
Tara Kini
Channa M. Cook-Harvey
Charmaine N. Jackson Mercer
Akeelah Harrell

HARVARD EDUCATION PRESS
CAMBRIDGE, MASSACHUSETTS

Copyright © 2019 by the President and Fellows of Harvard College

All rights reserved. No part of this publication may be reproduced or transmitted in any form or by any means, electronic or mechanical, including photocopy, recording, or any information storage and retrieval systems, without permission in writing from the publisher.

Paperback ISBN 978-1-68253-292-8
Library Edition ISBN 978-1-68253-293-5

Library of Congress Cataloging-in-Publication Data is on file.

Published by Harvard Education Press,
an imprint of the Harvard Education Publishing Group

Harvard Education Press
8 Story Street
Cambridge, MA 02138

Cover Design: Ciano Design
Cover Photo: Beth LaFrenier/AMP/Getty Images
The typefaces used in this book are ITC Stone Serif, ITC Stone Sans, and Museo Sans.

CONTENTS

CHAPTER 1

PREPARING TEACHERS FOR DEEPER LEARNING

The best employers the world over will be looking for the most competent, most creative, and most innovative people on the face of the earth and will be willing to pay them top dollar for their services. . . . Beyond [strong skills in English, mathematics, technology, and science], candidates will have to be comfortable with ideas and abstractions, good at both analysis and synthesis, creative and innovative, self-disciplined and well organized, able to learn very quickly and work well as a member of a team and have the flexibility to adapt quickly to frequent changes in the labor market as the shifts in the economy become ever faster and more dramatic.

—New Commission on the Skills of the American Workforce, 2007

[At Bank Street] it's about . . . giving children the tools to be thinkers and to understand big ideas and make connections and be communicators and work collaboratively, or work independently, and have a multifaceted approach to learning and really enjoy it. It seems powerful that you're preparing children to be lifelong learners and be curious. It seems really applicable to life in the twenty-first century, when you're not going to need to rely on a foundation of facts, but more about how to manage the information that is accessible and how to determine for yourself what is interesting, how to ask questions, and guide your investigations.

—A Bank Street College teacher candidate, 2016

I n a world where knowledge and new technologies are growing at an exponential rate, the economy is changing rapidly, and education matters more than ever for individual and societal success, there is an ever-increasing need for well-prepared teachers who can help all children learn for the complex world they are entering.

In the last decade, mountains of reports have been written in countries around the world about the need for more powerful learning focused on the demands of life, work, and citizenship in the twenty-first century. The process of managing decisions and solving social and scientific problems in contemporary democracies is growing ever more complex. In the early 1900s, when our current school system was designed, only 5 percent of jobs required specialized knowledge and skill; today about 70 percent of jobs are "knowledge work" positions that require the ability to acquire and use specialized information, manage nonroutine tasks, and employ advanced technologies. Between 1980 and 2015, the number of jobs requiring high levels of interpersonal, critical thinking, management, and communication skills increased by 83 percent, while the number depending on manual labor or routine skills increased by only 18 percent, and there were many more of the former types of jobs than the latter.[1]

We see this shift as well in the proliferation of difficult decisions that families and communities grapple with every day, and in the increasingly complicated issues that citizens are asked to understand and consider in ballot measures and in elections of public officials. Thriving in such conditions of social and political complexity also requires the ability to acquire and use specialized information, manage nonroutine tasks, and employ advanced technologies, as well as navigate the increased diversity of people and ideas encountered every day.

Furthermore, the nature of work, life, and citizenship will continue to change ever more rapidly. The World Economic Forum report *The Future of Jobs, 2016*, notes that in many industries and countries, the most in-demand occupations or specialties did not exist ten years ago, and the pace of change is set to accelerate.[2] The challenges of a rapidly changing economy are made more complex by global migration, highly visible inequalities, and the increasingly dramatic effects of phenomena like climate change and ever more world-threatening conflicts. This means that twenty-first-century communities and citizens need to forge constructive, democratic relationships and fair resource-sharing strategies in a shrinking and interdependent world.

Thus, the new mission of schools is to prepare students for jobs and ways of life that do not yet exist, using knowledge that has not yet been discovered, creating ideas and solutions for products and problems that have not yet been identified, using technologies that have not yet been invented. Employers and civic leaders have increasingly called for K–12 schools to fulfill this new mission by equipping graduates with "twenty-first-century skills"—the abilities to engage in high-level reasoning, transfer knowledge and solve problems, and understand content and how to apply it.[3] Going even further, young people must know how to research new information and ideas, analyze and evaluate that information, and synthesize it and produce new analyses, ideas, solutions, and products. In doing so, they need to be able to collaborate effectively with others and communicate their ideas in many forms, assess and improve their own work, and be resourceful and persevering in the face of social, political, and scientific challenges.

To meet these demands, virtually all states have enacted more ambitious standards for learning tied to new curriculum expectations and assessments. These standards expect students to master more challenging subject-matter content as well as to think critically, create more sophisticated products, and solve complex problems, rather than merely to perform routine tasks. The standards press for deeper understanding of academic content and for students' ability to apply that content, while acquiring and integrating new knowledge on their own. Learning to do these things requires far more than rote recall of facts or application of rules and algorithms.

Since it is now widely accepted that teacher quality is a critical component of a successful education, it is clear that much of the burden of meeting these new demands will fall on teachers. Yet teachers must do more than adapt their instruction to fulfill the broad vision of a twenty-first-century education; they are also being asked to achieve these goals for *all* children, not just a small minority who have traditionally been siphoned off into gifted and talented programs or advanced courses. At the same time, the very diverse group of students in today's schools has more wide-ranging needs than ever before. Because schools have both expanded the range of students they educate and included more of them in mainstream classrooms, teachers encounter more students with language and learning differences. And as child poverty has grown to the point where a majority of children in public schools now come from low-income families, educators must support learning while also helping children deal with homelessness, food insecurity, and lack of medical care, as well as frequent violence in their communities.[4] Teachers in many communities need to work as professors of disciplinary content, facilitators of individual learning, assessors and diagnosticians, counselors, social workers, and community resource managers.[5]

The need for such teachers is especially great where schools are the critical lifelines for students' success. It may not take much training to teach children who are already skillful learners; who are supported by affluent, highly educated parents whose language and culture match those of the school; and who can afford tutors, summer enrichment programs, and trips to museums and vacations around the world to supplement instruction. But these outside-of-school supports are the exception rather than the rule in most public schools today.

If much is being asked of teachers, then much is also being asked of teacher preparation programs, and in this complex and multifaceted context, the field of teacher education faces a dual challenge. Teachers who are unable to teach in ways consistent with the development of twenty-first-century skills will not succeed in providing their students with the deep, engaging, flexible, and broadly applicable learning experiences associated with those skills. Moreover, teachers who lack the skills to reach *all* students—including students without rich supplementary learning opportunities and supports outside of schools—will not be adequately prepared to meet the goals of twenty-first-century education. Therefore, a vital question confronts teacher educators amid the rapid changes in society and schooling: How can we prepare those who enter the profession to *teach for deeper learning*—and, in so doing, to *teach for equity and social justice* as well?

This book describes seven programs of teacher education that have organized themselves to meet the dual challenge of teacher preparation for both deeper learning and equity. There is much to be learned from these programs, as well as from others like them around the country that are engaged in such work. The programs differ from one another considerably in their surface features—such as size, sector, and type of institution—but they share a deep structure shaped by their common understandings of how people learn and their common commitments to a just society that focus them squarely on preparing teachers to teach diverse learners equitably.

The seven programs' various structures and practices provide useful and concrete examples of how a diverse set of institutions is preparing teachers to meet the demands of twenty-first-century schooling; understanding their various features could be helpful for improving many other programs. However, it is the deep structure they share—their coherent grounding in how children and adults learn and develop, with an insistence that the opportunities for such development be available to each and every student and teacher—that carries the most profound lessons about what it takes to prepare teachers to enable deeper learning for all children.

A FRAMEWORK FOR UNDERSTANDING TEACHER PREPARATION FOR DEEPER LEARNING

Deeper learning, as we elaborate more in this section, is both a new and an old idea, rooted in the findings of research on learning over the past century, yet also aligned with the needs of twenty-first-century students. Classrooms where deeper learning is the goal are ones in which challenging academic content is paired with engaging, experiential, and innovative learning experiences. Such experiences equip students with the skills to find, analyze, and apply knowledge in new and emerging contexts and situations, and prepare them for college, work, civic participation in a democratic society, and lifelong learning in a fast-changing and information-rich world.

What does it mean to teach in ways that prepare children and young people for the twenty-first century? And what does it mean to prepare teachers to teach in these ways? Answering these questions requires us, first, to consider what outcomes we seek—what we expect today's students to know and be able to do. We then must determine what learning experiences can lead to these outcomes, drawing on the rich understanding of learning that has developed over more than a hundred years of research and practice. Next, we must identify what teaching practices produce those learning experiences. Finally, we must examine what kinds of teacher development opportunities enable teachers to engage in these practices, developing the knowledge, skills, and dispositions necessary to bring twenty-first-century learning to all students.

What Educational Outcomes Do We Seek?

Three kinds of student outcomes are embedded in these new expectations and are widely viewed as critically important for contemporary education. These encompass cognitive abilities, social and emotional capacities, and the moral and ethical dimensions of a purposeful life.

The first set of outcomes pertains to *what students can do* with what they know and learn: they must be able to understand concepts deeply enough and have sufficiently developed inquiry skills that they can seek out, understand, and combine knowledge in many ways, and can apply what they know to novel, complex problems in different real-world situations. This means that they need to learn in ways that make content knowledge generative and transferable.

The second set of outcomes pertains to *how* young people approach what they are learning and doing—the set of co-cognitive skills (sometimes called social and emotional skills) that support successful work that is both individual and collective. These include abilities to organize and manage one's own work, to take and use feedback to continually improve it, to persevere and be resilient in the face of setbacks or obstacles, and to communicate and collaborate effectively with many people in multiple ways. These outcomes depend on building students' capacities for self-regulatory and executive functioning, their personal and social awareness and responsibility, and positive mind-sets and beliefs about self and school.[6]

The third set of outcomes pertains to *why* students are learning. We want young people to develop a sense of purpose and personal efficacy that derives from equitable treatment and is powered by a sense of social justice focused on how to improve one's own life and that of others in the community. Taking into account the *why* of learning means paying attention, not only to the needs and interests that students bring to school, but also to how schooling relates to who they are, where they come from, where they want to go in life, and what systemic challenges they may face along the way.

These capacities are increasingly essential to a full, rich, contributing life that also allows for engagement in the modern economy and society. Strong evidence has emerged that opportunities to engage in activities focused on these interrelated aspects of student development result in deeper understanding of core academic content, higher graduation rates, and higher rates of postsecondary enrollment and persistence.[7]

What Type of Learning Leads to These Outcomes?

Clearly, the new demands posed by the rapid expansion of knowledge in today's world and the growing demand for high-level reasoning, communication, and interpersonal skills cannot be met through passive, rote-oriented learning focused on basic skills and memorization of disconnected facts. Neither can they be met with provincial thinking or an inability to engage new ideas and diverse people.

Realizing today's ambitious goals requires dramatically different approaches to learning than those that dominated for much of the twentieth century. Those approaches were shaped by behaviorist theories associated with early work in educational psychology, particularly that of Edward L. Thorndike. In this view, learning was conceptualized as acquiring a predetermined body of knowledge and skills that were transmitted by others, primarily through a process of conditioning. Stimulus-response theory, for example, conceives of the learner as passive and assumes that if a learner's correct response is rewarded, he or she is more likely to repeat the response—that is, to learn.

Although "deeper learning" has gained currency recently as necessary for acquiring twenty-first-century skills, it is not a new type of learning. The underlying ideas harken back to conceptions of education propounded by Jean-Jacques Rousseau in the eighteenth century, Friedrich Froebel in the nineteenth, and John Dewey at the turn of the twentieth century, among others. All of these philosopher educators argued for experiential, reflective forms of education that enable critical thinking and production and expression of ideas, rather than rote learning. Dewey argued that, in contrast to memorizing secondhand information, learning is essentially an active mental process of problem solving and making sense of one's experience through action. Dewey conceived of learning as purposeful, complex, emergent, and inherently social. For Dewey, such learning equips students to perceive and to act upon the world in ever-growing ways, matching their purposes and goals to the materials and situations at hand to navigate real problems and issues.

Others also came to this concept of learning. Close observers of children, such as Maria Montessori in the early 1900s and Jean Piaget and Lev Vygotsky in the 1930s, devoted themselves to understanding how children develop cognitively and concluded that engagement within a social environment is a key to learning. Montessori created methods to help children work both together and independently through practical play and hands-on tasks to reach deeper levels of understanding. She believed that carefully observing children and addressing individual needs and interests would help each child reach his or her potential.[7] Piaget viewed children as independent learners and as having an inherent ability to make sense of the environment they observe and experience, including relationships with others. He noted that children think in fundamentally different ways from adults and their thinking *develops* as they make sense of experiences. Vygotsky saw social experiences and mental processes as deeply connected and interrelated. He concluded that learning and problem solving occur in the interactions *between* a learner and others. Social participation, he argued, does far more than provide external stimulation for thinking; rather, it is actually part of one's own thought process and can help a child develop, as well as express, ideas.[8]

Vygotsky

Research on learning experienced a cognitive revolution in the mid-twentieth century, in which scholars from psychology, linguistics, and anthropology challenged behaviorism with studies examining the mind and how it made meaning, work that became the field of cognitive science. In later decades, learning research took another new turn with the emergence of sociocultural theories as researchers such as Roland Tharp and Michael Cole showed that social and cultural contexts determine learning and that knowledge emerges through social and cultural activity during community participation.[9]

Tharp

Psychologists such as Kenneth Clark and, later, Claude Steele examined the relationship between social contexts and cognition and advanced our understanding of how learning and development can be negatively influenced by stereotypes and deficit views of minoritized cultures. They were joined by researchers like Geneva Gay, Gloria Ladson-Billings, and Carol Lee in discovering protective factors such as affirmation, removal of stereotype threat, and cultural, racial, or ethnic socialization, which can positively shape features of the larger ecology in which learners are situated.[10]

Together, this work gives us a complex and nuanced picture of learning. We know that learning occurs as people try to make meaning of the world and use what they have learned in new situations. Learning occurs through the social interaction of people, problems, ideas, and tools within specific contexts as people get feedback from their actions and about their ideas. It is culturally embedded, developed both neurologically and psychologically through relationships and experiences. That is, each experience influences the possibilities and frameworks for future learning. Usable learning requires conceptual understanding that can be transferred to new and novel situations, and it emphasizes the meaning that students bring to their experiences and the essential role their lives and communities play in providing context, value, and resources for the learning process. Importantly, the work on the relationship between culture and learning has revealed, in the words of Harvard researcher Jal Mehta, "the pluralism of different approaches to learning deeply," as "in every religious or ethnic community there is some tradition through which people learn deeply."[11]

Modern learning theory also emphasizes the situated and social nature of meaning-making, by which "mind, behavior, perception and action are wholly integrated."[12] The science of learning indicates that humans learn more effectively when they are not anxious, fearful, or distracted by other pressing concerns; when the learning is connected to their prior knowledge and experience; when they are actively engaged; and when they have a reason to care about the content they are learning and can use it to deepen their understanding and to solve real questions or problems.

Finally, people's beliefs or perceptions about intelligence and ability—both generally and in relation to themselves personally—affect their cognitive functioning and learning. Identity development is a key part of learning—how people see themselves as learners and where they feel competent matter for where they exert effort and what they believe they can do.

How Can Teaching Practices Create Deeper Learning Opportunities?

For teachers to create these kinds of deeper learning experiences for children, they need to learn a set of principles and pedagogies that will allow them to bring these opportunities alive in the blooming, buzzing classrooms they will create and manage. The National Academy of Sciences summary, *How People Learn*, drew on the learning sciences to identify three fundamental and well-established principles of learning that are particularly important to guide teaching practices:[13]

1. *Students come to the classroom with prior knowledge that must be addressed if teaching is to be effective.* If what they know and believe is not engaged, learners may fail to grasp the new concepts and information

that are taught, or they may learn them for purposes of a test but not be able to apply them elsewhere, reverting to their preconceptions outside the classroom. This means that teachers must understand what students are thinking and how to connect with their prior knowledge if they are to ensure real learning. Children's developmental and learning trajectories vary as a product of the interactions of their attributes and social contexts as well as in their development over time.[14] When students from a variety of different cultural contexts and language backgrounds come to school with different experiences, they present distinct preconceptions and knowledge bases that teachers must learn about and consider in designing instruction.

Teachers who are successful with all learners must have tools and practices to learn about their students' different ways of learning, prior experiences and knowledge, and cultural and linguistic capital. Teachers can learn about the strengths and needs of individual students through techniques such as regular check-ins and class meetings, conferencing, journaling, and classroom surveys, and by meeting with parents as authentic partners to learn about their students' lives and learning strategies and to create more coherent, well-reinforced learning opportunities between home and school. These moves can help create environments where students feel culturally respected as well as emotionally and intellectually safe. Many studies have documented the positive effects of practices like these that foster developmentally informed, meaningful relationships among students, parents, and staff.[15]

2. *Students need to organize and use knowledge conceptually if they are to apply it beyond the classroom.* To develop competence in an area of inquiry, students must not only acquire a deep foundation of factual knowledge, they must also understand facts and ideas in the context of a conceptual framework or schema and organize knowledge in ways that draw connections among ideas and facilitate retrieval and application. This means that teachers must be able to structure the material to be learned in ways that help students fit it into a conceptual map and teach it in ways that allow application and transfer to new situations.

The teaching strategies that allow students to do this integrate core concepts derived from the structure of the discipline with the modes of inquiry specific to the discipline—such as scientific investigation, mathematical modeling, literary analysis, historical inquiry, or artistic performance. Teachers carefully select materials and offer explanations to provide a sense of the big ideas and how they are connected, structuring hands-on inquiries that engage students actively in using the material to make sense of how concepts build on each other and fit together. Teachers use multiple and varied representations of key concepts that make them vivid and accessible, stimulating applications and problem solving of increasing complexity as students' understanding of the domain grows.

3. *Students learn more effectively if they understand how they learn and how to manage their own learning.* A "metacognitive" approach to instruction can help students learn to take control of their own learning by having a set of learning strategies, defining their own learning goals, and monitoring their progress in achieving them. Teachers need to know how to help students self-assess their understanding and how they best approach learning.

Through modeling and coaching, teachers can teach students how to use a range of learning strategies, including the ability to predict outcomes, to create explanations to improve understanding, to note when they are confused so as to seek clarification, to activate background knowledge, to plan ahead, and to apportion their time and attention. Successful teachers provide carefully designed "scaffolds" to help students take each step in the learning journey with appropriate assistance, and these vary for different students depending on their learning needs, approaches, and prior knowledge.[16]

Teachers can support metacognition when they use multiple forms of assessment that reveal aspects of students' understanding for the purpose of guiding instruction and student revisions of their work. These include self- and peer assessments that allow students to evaluate work against criteria or a rubric, as well as exhibitions and other occasions for students to receive feedback and revise their work. Providing time and opportunity for formal reflection and discussion about students' insights builds their metacognitive capacity as well. Teachers can encourage students to elaborate, question, and self-explain, which deepens their understanding of *how* to learn as well as of *what* they are learning.

In sum, effective teaching activates students' prior knowledge, connects to their experiences, scaffolds the learning process, is adaptive to students' needs, incorporates applications to real-world situations, and helps students reflect on and improve their own learning processes. In classrooms teaching effectively for deeper learning, an observer is likely to see students' work on the walls—as well as images and materials—drawing connections to students' lives, experiences, and cultures and tapping learners' passions, identities, and motivations. The teacher creates a positive environment by communicating respect and support for each student, offering culturally responsive examples and materials, and supporting each student's sense of belonging by acknowledging his or her talents, work, and contributions in a variety of ways. The observer sees students engaged in rich instructional conversations that allow them to ask questions, explain their ideas, and probe the ideas of others.

The observer is also likely to see engagement of learners in challenging, inquiry-oriented learning tasks that involve disciplined inquiry and experimentation, using aspects of choice to support student agency. These tasks—which may be structured as projects or problem-based learning—demand analysis, synthesis, and evaluation of ideas in order to produce new products, ideas, or solutions. They are often collaborative, with clear student roles that students have been taught to undertake, designed with multiple entry points and enacted with supportive guidance, scaffolding, and feedback. Students have opportunities to revise their work in response to feedback; this helps them to develop a growth mind-set and confidence in their capacity to improve their competence. They bring an inquiring mind to their work, along with a set of cognitive and psychological tools that allows them to find and use resources—including each other—to figure things out and to solve problems that are motivating and meaningful to them.

HOW CAN PROGRAMS PREPARE TEACHERS TO TEACH FOR DEEPER LEARNING?

If teachers are to be able to teach in ways that reflect the outcomes we desire for students, which are informed by historical and current understanding of the workings of learning and are consistent with practices that can support deeper learning, then teacher preparation has a high bar to meet. Teachers must learn how to teach ambitious subject matter in ways that support higher-order thinking skills and students' abilities to transfer and apply their knowledge. They must learn to teach students who learn in different ways and whose prior knowledge reflects diverse cultural and linguistic traditions and experiences. They must learn to help students acquire basic skills while they also learn to invent and inquire. They must learn to teach language and literacy skills across the curriculum. They must learn to work effectively with parents and colleagues to assemble the resources and motivations needed to help children make progress.

Helping teachers learn to practice in these ways requires both coursework and clinical work that, together, help teachers understand students and how they learn while also developing skills and tools to organize and manage these kinds of rich learning experiences. Behind the scenes, teachers must also be keen diagnosticians and deeply reflective about what they see happening with student learning each day, so that they can respond to the dynamic process of learning for understanding.

Because students are not standardized and teaching is not routine, learning cannot be achieved through a single set of activities that presume uniformity in human experiences and approaches to learning, as scientific managers have hoped since the late nineteenth century. In a world of human diversity and cognitive complexity, teaching that aims at deep learning requires sophisticated judgments about how and what different students are learning, what gaps in their understanding need to be addressed, what experiences will allow them to connect what they know to what they need to know, and what instructional adaptations will be needed to ensure that they can reach common goals.[17]

In fact, the more common the expectations for achievement are across a wide range of students, the more personalized must be the teaching strategies for reaching these goals. If teaching is uniform, assuming a single mode and pace of learning, learners who start at different places and learn in different ways will end with equally diverse levels of achievement. This is currently the case in the United States, where the range in school outcomes is much wider than in many other countries.[18] As John Dewey noted in 1929 in his *Sources of a Science of Education,* the better prepared teachers are, the more their practice becomes differentiated in response to the needs of individual students, rather than routinized:

> Command of scientific methods and systematized subject matter liberates individuals; it enables them to see new problems, devise new procedures, and in general makes for diversification rather than for set uniformity. . . . This knowledge and understanding render (the teacher's) practice more intelligent, more flexible, and better adapted to deal effectively with concrete phenomena of practice. . . . Seeing more relations, he sees more possibilities, more opportunities. His ability to judge being enriched, he has a wider range of alternatives to select from in dealing with individual situations.[19]

If teachers are to figure out how to help learners who begin and proceed differently ultimately reach similarly challenging outcomes, they will need to be able to engage in thoughtful experimentation, insightful interpretation of complex events, and knowledge-rich reflection, combined with a wide repertoire of strategies that allows them to continuously adjust their teaching based on student outcomes. This means that teachers must become "adaptive experts" who can not only use routines that help them work with greater efficiency, but also use their knowledge to innovate where routines are not enough—to figure out what the problems are when students are not learning and to adapt materials, teaching strategies, or supports accordingly.[20] Adaptive experts also know how to continually expand their expertise, knowledge, and competencies as needed to meet new challenges. Preparing teachers who can learn *from* teaching, as well as learn *for* teaching, is one of the key challenges for teacher education today.[21]

What Experiences and Processes Prepare Teachers for Deeper Learning?

As we have discussed here, the ideas that Dewey advanced a hundred years ago—and which many researchers and progressive educators have been working on since—have emerged continually in multiple theoretical frameworks that describe teaching, learning, and teacher preparation, culminating in the current calls for deeper learning for a twenty-first-century education for all students. We call on these and other related frameworks in the chapters that follow to illuminate the work of the programs we studied. Building on knowledge from the learning sciences, we define teaching for deeper learning as having the following five dimensions, which also create goals for teaching:

1. *Learning that is developmentally grounded and personalized.* Learning experiences build on prior knowledge and experience, and account for learners' active construction of new knowledge. Learning connects to who students are as well as to what they already know, attending to both cognitive and socioemotional realms, and school tasks are designed to be scaffolded according to students' needs, intrinsically interesting based on their experiences, and appropriate to their level of development.

2. *Learning that is contextualized.* Learning experiences recognize that people develop as they use the tools and symbols of their cultural contexts to make sense of the world and their experiences in it. Learning builds on students' personal, cultural, and linguistic knowledge, and is embedded in meaningful contexts and applications. Learning is connected to students' experiences and is based on a deep understanding of these contexts for development as well as ongoing communication and connection with parents, caregivers, communities, and the world beyond school.

3. *Learning that is applied and transferred.* Learning experiences enable students to apply and transfer content knowledge to novel and complex problems, with abstract and theoretical ideas tightly connected to real-world problems and settings through challenging, authentic activities that promote mastery learning and critical thinking. Clear standards and performance feedback, including the use of both formative and summative performance-based assessments, promote complex cognitive development.

4. *Learning that occurs in productive communities of practice.* Learning is an active, interactive, constructive, and iterative process. Well-designed and well-tended social interactions allow students to support or scaffold one another's learning, combining their different knowledge and experiences into the collective knowledge and experience of the learning community, and helping students to move from peripheral to core participation in subject-matter learning connected to real-world activities. School and classroom communities are built on an ethic of caring, offering supports for social/emotional development, trusting relationships, and restorative practices to create suitable environments for student learning.

5. *Learning that is equitable and oriented to social justice.* Learning experiences are designed to meet diverse students' needs, to reach all students, and to teach them well. All students have access to rich, supportive curriculum experiences that acknowledge and incorporate their social locations and "status" in the larger society, and that are constructed with an awareness of race, class, gender, and other social characteristics that shape student experiences. Teachers consider students' unique identities as strengths and resources; they link social justice values to principles of learning and development by working explicitly to ensure that all students are supported, taking a critical stance, and avoiding deficit thinking.

These features of deeper learning experiences echo Dewey's approach to pedagogy and that of the progressive educators over the past century. Because of his view of students as active, social beings who bring their own purposes to learning, Dewey devised an approach to schooling that provided engaging experiences for students, leading to deep content knowledge, understanding, and an ongoing disposition toward openness to new learning, all consistent with what he saw as preparation for a full life in a democratic society. Dewey's picture of engaged learning also included teachers, who would develop curricula and manage new types of schools, working together across classrooms and disciplines to produce powerful and meaningful learning.

Like the other key features that define teacher preparation's alignment with deeper learning, the prioritization of equity in access to deeper learning is not new. In addition to being embedded in the concepts and practices advocated by Dewey and progressive educators over the past century, there is also a long tradition of support for deeper learning experiences in the Black community. Historian James Anderson has documented that teachers in post–Civil War African American schools incorporated the culture and experiences of their students into their curriculum and their instruction. They used pedagogy that encouraged students to question what they read and to engage in critical thinking and problem solving. They allowed students to work in small groups.[22] These early African American schools were using what scholars now term culturally responsive teaching and a multicultural curriculum, as well as other instructional practices that are culturally congruent for African American students.[23]

Moreover, early in the twentieth century, W. E. B. DuBois and his colleagues in the NAACP argued for a liberal arts curriculum for African American students. Since that time, civil rights groups have battled against persistent efforts to emphasize lower-level, skills-based curriculum in schools serving student of color.[24] More recently, these ideas have taken the form of culturally relevant pedagogy, which Geneva Gay has described as the multidimensional, empowering, and transformative use of "cultural knowledge, prior experiences, frame of reference, and performance styles of ethnically diverse students to make learning more relevant to and effective for them. . . . It teaches to and through strengths of the students. It is culturally validating and affirming."[25] These ideas are also evidenced in the efforts to ground instruction in schools serving Latinx students and other students of color in the rich "funds of knowledge" and cultural practices that students bring into classrooms.[26]

However, today's school and classroom practices are mostly incompatible with the conditions under which students can achieve the ambitious twenty-first-century outcomes through deeper learning. The reality is that most schools and teaching practices remain organized along industrial, rational, top-down lines first laid out by scientific managers at the beginning of the twentieth century.[27] Dedicated to management, measurement, and efficiency, these reformers promulgated the practices of what Tyack and Cuban have called the "basic grammar of schooling," a system heavily influenced by behavioral theories of learning.[28] From this perspective, the teacher's job is to transmit knowledge in small chunks, provide constant rewards or reinforcement, monitor (test) whether chunks of knowledge have been learned, and reteach whatever was missed. Passive, rote-oriented learning focused on basic skills and memorization of disconnected facts has been and remains dominant practice today. Tradition and standardization trump new ideas and diversity. Even today, in the wake of both the cognitive revolution and the recognition of sociocultural influences on learning, schooling continues to follow industrial-era models. Indeed, in an era of mass, high-stakes assessments, top-down control, and the simplistic learning associated with test preparation, it seems that the theories and practices of the early 1900s are alive and well in the early 2000s.

Additionally, to the extent that deeper learning experiences are found in some elementary and secondary schools, they are largely restricted to the most advantaged students within and across communities. Despite increasing awareness of the critical need for such learning, instruction for lower-income children and students of color has been more focused on developing "basic skills"—in part because of the pressures that have accompanied test-based accountability policies.[29] Yet "deeper learning," as the Alliance for Excellent Education put it, "will do little for our economy and democracy unless it is accessible to every student."[30]

To remedy this unevenness, and to meet the challenge of providing deeper learning for all students, these practices must be extended to schools that reflect the growing diversity, and increasing needs, of the US public school population. In public schools today, students of color are in the majority,[31] more than half come from low-income families,[32] almost 10 percent are English language learners,[33] and over 13 percent receive services under the federal Individuals with Disabilities Education Act (IDEA).[34] Accordingly, equity must be prioritized and a social justice orientation adopted to implement deeper learning practices at scale and for all students.

THIS STUDY AND THIS BOOK

In the ensuing chapters, we describe how seven programs are creating and evolving ways to prepare future teachers for twenty-first-century student learning. We examine these programs through the lens of contemporary learning sciences, and we focus on the ways that their values and practices align with the five dimensions of deeper learning, as well as the ways they create the opportunities and experiences such learning requires.

In our research, we asked both how teacher candidates learn to provide these kinds of opportunities and experiences for children, and how the programs offer these kinds of opportunities for the candidates themselves. We also sought to understand the implications of the work of these programs for the creation of policy and practice that can expand and support efforts at preparing teachers for deeper learning and equity.

The programs, spread across the country from New York to California and from Milwaukee to southern Texas, are in public and private institutions of higher education, operate at the undergraduate and graduate levels, and range in size from small to very large. They include recently launched innovative alternatives as well as long-standing models of teacher education that reflect a century's worth of progressive practice. These are the sites of the seven programs:

- Alverno College, Milwaukee, WI
- Bank Street College of Education, New York, NY
- High Tech High's Intern Program, San Diego, CA
- Montclair State University, Montclair, NJ
- San Francisco's Teacher Residency, in collaboration with the University of San Francisco and Stanford University in San Francisco, CA
- Trinity University, San Antonio, TX
- University of Colorado, Denver, CO

To identify these sites, our research team started by asking experts in the field of teacher preparation, as well as those who have experience working with new teachers, to nominate teacher preparation programs aligned with the principles of deeper learning we have articulated. The team then carried out an iterative process of background research on nominated programs to narrow down possible sites, looking at evidence about the program's outcomes as well as its practices. The final step was to consider geographic and program diversity. We wanted a sample of cases that included a cross-section of program types and locations so that teacher educators and policy makers could find multiple routes of access into this work.

We examined these programs through interviews with participants, observations of their practices in courses and schools, surveys of graduates, and document review. (See appendix A for a summary of the methodology.) In the rest of the book, we describe the themes that emerged from these intensive studies, along with the practices we discovered that support candidates in learning to teach for deeper learning. One of the key insights from this work is how the pedagogies candidates experience in their own courses and clinical work themselves model deeper learning strategies, and how teacher educators engage in their own forms of inquiry and deeper learning to create such programs.

Chapters 2 through 4 describe the challenges all of the programs face and the basic features they have created to meet these challenges. Chapter 2 discusses the dilemmas of preparing teachers for deeper learning, describes each of the programs in brief, and identifies some of the key commonalities we discovered across the programs. Chapters 3 and 4 identify the core curricula and key practices we found across programs that support teacher candidates' learning of deeper learning pedagogy.

Chapters 5 through 9 dig into the details of how these programs are aligned with each of the five dimensions of teaching deeper learning: learning that is developmentally grounded and personalized (chapter 5); learning that is contextualized (chapter 6); learning that is applied and transferred (chapter 7); learning in productive communities of practice (chapter 8); and learning that is equitable and oriented to social justice (chapter 9). They show how the teacher candidates teach for deeper learning and describe how they learned to teach that way.

The final two chapters turn to the broader concerns of institutional structures and practices, and the types of policies that would be needed to support such teacher preparation at scale. In chapter 10, we describe the institutional supports the programs have created to enable these kinds of highly focused, clinically intense programs, including their values, leadership, allocation of resources, and partnerships with K–12 schools and districts. In chapter 11, we offer a summary and conclusions about the critical features of program design, as well as the policy levers and supports needed for scaling this kind of preparation so that it is available to all teachers entering our schools.

To launch our account of these remarkable programs, we offer this description of one teacher education course embedded in the San Francisco Teacher Residency program, a partnership of the San Francisco Unified School District, the United Educators of San Francisco, Stanford University, and the University of San Francisco. The program, which prepares residents for urban classrooms in the city's highest-need schools, is focused on deeper learning for all children, enabled by candidates' commitment to equity and social justice and the sophisticated skills they learn to enact that commitment.

Deeper Learning in Action:
Collaboration and Interdisciplinary, Inquiry-Based Learning

As the University of San Francisco Curriculum & Instruction (C&I) class begins late on this Tuesday afternoon, there's an air of anticipation among the twelve students in the room—all of them teacher candidates in the San Francisco Teacher Residency program. Today is a special day: it's one of two classes all year in which the math and science C&I courses are combined for a class session focused on interdisciplinary learning.

The lesson is designed to engage the math and science students in a hands-on interdisciplinary activity in which the teacher candidates work together on an example of a math/science inquiry-based task: in this case, figuring out what affects the period of a pendulum. The instructor, Laura Hodder, introduces the lesson by very simply stating, "I want you to figure out how this works," after which she shows a short video of pendulum waves. The room falls silent as the teacher candidates focus on the graceful movements of weights on strings moving through various patterns in a circle, a sort of dance. As Laura engages the students in a brief discussion of potential explanations for the pendulum wave, they are intrigued and want to figure this out.

Laura, the science instructor, and Nathan, the math instructor, explicitly model for their students how to set up strong collaboration practices for their students. They review the norms for this activity—reminding students that they should ask each other questions and that everyone must participate—and then explain that each group's goal for today is to figure out what variables affect the swinging of a pendulum. Students are divided into three groups of four, with two math and two science candidates in each group. Two-thirds of the class are teachers of color, and three-quarters are women. Each member of the group is assigned a role card, which describes the responsibilities for the role: facilitator, resource specialist, measurement expert, data recorder.

This strategy for organizing group work is also taught in the Stanford Teacher Education Program—the other university partner—as part of a course on complex instruction, a research-based approach to collaborative learning developed, piloted, studied, and widely disseminated by Elizabeth Cohen and Rachel Lotan.[35]

The students spend the next hour or so developing and testing their hypotheses. In Group 1, a student suggests a hypothesis: "As the string gets longer, everything gets slower." Others follow. After the group decides on which hypothesis to test, the students decide how to measure the variable. One student says that they should "use the timer to measure the time it takes for a washer to go from one side and back." A math teacher candidate says that they should measure the swinging of the washer as many times as possible so that the measure is more accurate. A science candidate responds that "gravity is constant and air friction is small," and therefore she doesn't anticipate that the swinging pendulum will slow down with additional swings.

(continues)

Nathan and Laura circulate around the classroom, observing and asking questions of the groups. In Group 2, the students hypothesize that as mass increases, the period between the swings will decrease. Even though Laura knows that this group's hypothesis is incorrect, she shows no signs of doubt to the students and has them proceed to test their hypothesis.

Group 3 is testing their hypothesis that as mass increases, the period between the swings will decrease. They decide to place the pencil with the washer and string between two tables to reduce any friction that might be caused by the rubbing of the table. One student holds a protractor to ensure that they measure from the same angle for each of the group's observations; another student times each swing; a third student watches the string and tells the timer when to start and stop timing, and a fourth student creates a table and records each of the observations. All the students are engaged and collaboratively solving how to most accurately test their hypothesis.

Group 2, which is testing their hypothesis of whether mass contributes to the period, is done collecting its observations and begins to graph the data. The group discusses what should go on each axis and the scale. Laura asks the group, "What did you find?" One student responds that they found that "as mass increases, the time increases, and the period decreases." Laura asks, "So I'm curious if you believe your data." The students say they do. Laura follows with, "What if I told you that you discovered a new law of physics?" The students laugh when they realize that Laura is pointing out that their data are flawed. Laura refocuses the group and says, "My question is, do you believe in your data, or do you believe there are other variables that you have not accounted for that suggest that you have not discovered a new law of physics?" The students begin discussing the variables that they did not account for. For example, one math candidate says, "The angle could have been off because of human error, but that is why we averaged multiple observations to help factor for human error." The group decides to retest their hypothesis, and brainstorm ways to make their measurements more accurate.

After the activity, Laura leads the students in a debrief in which she explains, "This is your opportunity to think about the lesson not only as students, but as teachers." To aid in more structured reflection, each group is given a worksheet that asks questions about how this lesson's content, as well as disciplinary practices and pedagogy, is divided between math and science. As groups reflect, they identify the different content applied in this lesson, such as units for math, scientific method for science, hypothesis. Students continue and begin to realize that much of the content overlaps. One group starts writing down the middle of the sheet (on the line dividing math and science), clearly understanding the overlap, or commonality, between the two disciplines. For example, one group discusses that equations model relationships (which may be more "science-y"), but they are also fundamental to math. After class, Laura shares that one of the major goals of this lesson is to break down the stereotypes that each of the disciplines has about the other—so that, for example, science students can see that "math can be messy."

The final hour of the two-and-a-half-hour class is focused on teacher collaboration. Nathan and Laura provide an example of a math and science lesson that they collaboratively created to teach the Fibonacci sequence and the golden ratio, and then ask students to partner with a member of the other discipline to develop their own lesson together. The math/science teacher pairs engage in rich and challenging brainstorming sessions. A science teacher pulls out the Next Generation Science Standards for her seventh-grade science students, and the math teacher takes a look and shares how the math standards might overlap. One math/science pair, who had recently interviewed together at a middle school to teach math and science as a team, shared with their tablemates the interdisciplinary lesson they had developed for their demonstration lesson: an experiment to determine the area of human skin by wrapping a student in paper.

Another math/science pair developed a lesson on functions from both a mathematic and a scientific perspective, using an inquiry-based approach, in which students analyze factors influencing the number of fish in a pond. The lesson would require students to analyze how the number of fish might go up or down depending on a number of variables, such as the time of year and whether it was fishing season, and to recognize trends and make predictions.

The brainstorm session forces the math and science teacher candidates to grapple with the challenges of interdisciplinary lessons. One student notes that it is challenging to ensure that they are not just creating a "strong math lesson with weak science content" (such as only using the scientific process) or a "strong science lesson with weak math content." But the activity also succeeds in breaking down barriers between the two cohorts of teachers and enables them to identify the similarities between the disciplines. A conversation between a math teacher and a science teacher in response to the question "Why do we teach math/ science?" captures some of their learning:

> **Math teacher:** To make sense of problems in the real world.
>
> **Science teacher:** I feel like I could say the same thing about science. What about math makes it so important to learn?
>
> **Math teacher:** So that students can reason abstractly, and quantitatively . . . that's one of the reasons we teach math. Math builds problem-solving skills, such as what steps do you use to solve a problem, practicing logic . . . these are life skills.
>
> **Science teacher:** In science, we are trying to answer questions, make sense of things. We see a lot of similarities with math . . . taking an approach and being able to apply it to a lot of other circumstances in life . . . being able to look at all the things you observed and be able to see patterns from that, leading to higher-level thinking. I think that science helps to make sense of the real world around you. Something really important about science is learning how to use the scientific method, so if I can't figure out the answer to a problem, I have an approach that if something happened, I could try to re-create it and figure out what caused the problem, or at least eliminate things that didn't cause the problem.
>
> **Math teacher:** Math does a similar thing: we propose questions, and we hypothesize.

The class plunged teachers into the type of intellectually challenging, inquiry-based science lesson they will eventually construct for their own students, and—through example—showed them how to scaffold learning and deepen the inquiry using productive questions, evidence-based collaborative learning models, and opportunities for reflection. And with these inquiries and reflections, teaching careers for reflective, inquiring teachers are launched. The remainder of this book explores how such teachers learn to do what they do.

CHAPTER 2

SEVEN
EXEMPLARS

[Trinity candidates] are my most effective teachers. [This is reflected in] the quality of their instruction in terms of their precision around planning, their ability to execute those plans, their ability to work with students who weren't making the progress they expected, the way that they plan for more complex thinking in the classroom, [their] ability to take on different challenges outside of their classroom instruction."

———San Antonio principal

As I look for teachers, I most immediately look for Alverno applicants. Integrating new teachers into the staff from Alverno is so much easier, because of their high ability to be self-reflective, their personally wide experiences with performance assessment at the college level, and their ability to apply critical research bases to their classroom experiences. They are highly collegial, unafraid to seek out all they need to know from mentors and staff around them. I'll take ten more teachers like the two I've had this year.

—Milwaukee principal[1]

All of the [SFTR] residents we've trained, if we had an opening, we . . . hired them. That's not always true of other student teachers we've had. [The San Francisco Teacher Residency program] does a good job of recruiting strong folks; they do a great job with preparation, and they do a lot to support them. They have a real practice-based lens. We have four residents teaching here this year. I had fellow principals approach me at the principals' meeting last week. I was getting swarmed at the end of the meeting because they wanted to hire them all!

—San Francisco principal

[Montclair State University] graduates are very sensitive to the needs of diverse learners and students of diverse backgrounds. I have seen them to be very well prepared for that sort of challenge in a classroom. They quite honestly embrace it. . . . They are very motivated about creating a classroom culture that is positive and a classroom community that extends to parents as well.

—Two Newark, New Jersey, principals

Fifteen of the twenty-eight teachers on my staff are CU Denver alums. . . . They have the desire to be an urban teacher: a strong work ethic, passionate about wanting to learn, a need to get better every day, and an open mind about practice, not assuming they have answers right away. They are open to nontraditional, nonstandardized ways of teaching; they look at individuals . . . Members of this school community learn as much from the [CU Denver] teacher candidates as the candidates learn from us.

—Denver principal of a CUD partner school

High Tech High interns work hands-on with students in a context of deep inquiry. This allows them to establish progressive methods to support the academic and social-emotional needs of children while being immersed in the language and practice that best supports students.

—San Diego principal

I think they are the best trained teachers in progressive education that I can find. Our school has emphasis in supporting the individual and also helping him relate to a community. The Bank Street philosophy and methodology is closely connected with ours. Socialization of children always seems to be related to the balance between the cognitive and the affective, as well as between the individual and the group.

—Director of New York City elementary school

These accolades for teachers prepared in the programs we studied stand in sharp contrast to the negative discourse that has been cultivated about teacher education for the last two decades. To listen to the chorus of critics, one might think that teacher preparation is an inevitably weak intervention—regularly unable to help teachers learn to cope, much less to engage in the sophisticated practices required to support deep understanding for very diverse learners in the contexts of today's highly challenged schools.

Yet virtually all the graduates of these programs consistently report that they feel prepared for this demanding work, and the vast majority feel "well" or "very well" prepared with the content and curricular knowledge, instructional strategies, tools, and dispositions that will allow them to enable the full range of their students to achieve twenty-first-century learning goals. (See appendix C for survey data.) We do not make the argument that these programs are always better than others across the country. Indeed, we are aware of many other programs that are similarly designed and have equally strong reputations. And with efforts to improve teacher education, other data suggest that candidates in a number of states feel well prepared for contemporary classrooms.[2]

Instead, we make the argument that it is possible to create programs in very different contexts that prepare teachers to support deeper learning for diverse students, and that this cross-section of large and small, public and private, undergraduate and graduate models in states across the country provides useful examples of how this can be done. Three of these are private colleges long committed to the preparation of teachers for progressive urban teaching (Alverno College in Milwaukee, Wisconsin; Bank Street

College in New York City; and Trinity University in San Antonio, Texas). Two others (Montclair State University and the University of Colorado at Denver) are large state universities offering multiple pathways into teaching that prepare hundreds of teachers annually. These two, plus another university–school partnership supported by Stanford University and the University of San Francisco (the San Francisco Teacher Residency program), offer innovative teacher residency programs that coconstruct and embed preparation within urban districts, supporting candidates financially and educationally in exchange for several years of service in these districts' schools. The last is an alternative internship/apprenticeship pathway developed by a charter school network (High Tech High) that prepares candidates within the project-based learning environment the network schools have developed, and extends this support to other district-run schools that share their philosophy.

In this chapter we briefly discuss some of the everpresent dilemmas of preparing teachers. We also describe the seven programs and their philosophies, designs, student populations, and overall strategies. In later chapters we describe common approaches to organizing content and practices that help the programs address both the perennial dilemmas and the additional challenge of preparing teachers to teach for deeper learning.

The programs we describe here have track records of developing teachers who are strongly committed to all students' learning—and to ensuring, especially, that students who struggle to learn can succeed. The programs also develop teachers who can *act* on their commitments, who are knowledgeable about learning and teaching, and who have strong practical skills—teachers who can manage, with grace and purpose, the thousands of interactions that occur in a classroom each day; who know how to teach ambitious subject matter to students who learn in different ways; who can integrate solid teaching of basic skills with support for student invention and inquiry; who can teach language and literacy skills in every grade and across the curriculum; who can work effectively with parents and colleagues to assemble the resources needed to help children make progress; and who defy the persistent social perception that students in poverty and students of color can't be expected to learn deeply.[3]

CHALLENGES OF LEARNING TO TEACH FOR DEEPER LEARNING

Learning to teach—as in learning to practice any profession—is no simple matter. In fact, there are some special—and perennial—challenges in learning to teach.[4] Three, in particular, stand out. First, learning to teach requires that new teachers come to think about (and understand) teaching in ways quite different from their own experience as students—the problem that Dan Lortie termed "the apprenticeship of observation."[5] Second, learning to teach also requires new teachers to not only learn to "think like a teacher" but also to "*act* like a teacher"—what Mary Kennedy has termed "the problem of enactment."[6] Teachers need not only to learn, but learn to *do*. Finally, learning to teach requires that new teachers be able to act purposefully to achieve multiple goals within a complex and busy classroom. They must learn to deal with the cluttered, constantly nonroutine nature of teaching—what we call "the problem of complexity."

The Problem of "the Apprenticeship of Observation"

One of the most significant challenges that teachers face in learning to teach is that they enter teaching having already had years of experience in schools. Although this prior experience of schools and teaching can be an important source of learning and motivation, as the sociologist Dan Lortie argued, such an "apprenticeship" has important limits: students see only the surface of teaching, and only from the perspective of a single student absorbed with many other concerns. Thus teaching may look easier than it is, and the underlying plans, intentions, and outcomes for the full range of students are invisible.

Such experiences often lead to the widespread idea that "anyone can teach" and to assumptions that all that is required are a few technical routines. Prospective teachers often start with a view that good teaching is just the enthusiastic transmission of information, rather than a careful analysis of how to represent subject matter and connect it to students' experiences so that it can be understood, and an ongoing assessment of student learning to continually plan and adapt learning experiences with appropriate supports.

Furthermore, many teachers enter teaching with conceptions of *learning* as being the simple and rather mechanistic receiving of information.[7] This is a particularly difficult challenge for those who aim to help teachers enable deeper learning for diverse students. For many candidates, this kind of teaching requires new understandings about students, learning, and subject matter that are very different from what they themselves experienced in school. As a CU Denver graduate put it, "[In my teacher education program], we learned strategies I hadn't learned as a kid."

A High Tech High School administrator described the experience for novice teachers as "leaving behind their own educational experience and disrupting their thinking about what it means to be a teacher." She continued: "Even for folks who come here with a passion for doing something different, most of them have, as a learner, only experienced very traditional learning environments. So it's really easy, then, to just fall back into what feels comfortable."

Teachers must also come to understand how the constructs of race and class, and the history of schooling and society, impact students' opportunities and experiences in and out of school. Particularly for those who come from positions of privilege, these realities may have been invisible as they went through school. Not only must teachers learn how to come to know their students in order to design instruction that is engaging and developmentally appropriate, but they must also bring to bear, in a critical fashion, a wider understanding of social contexts so as to actively work to provide more equitable educational opportunities for their students.

Programs that successfully surmount the effects of the apprenticeship of observation seek to surface their candidates' initial beliefs about teaching in order to confront misconceptions. They use structured discussions and guided observations of classrooms as means for candidates to share their initial views about teaching so these can be addressed. Faculty model and engage candidates in the teaching and learning strategies they want them to experience and reproduce in their own classrooms. These instructional strategies provide opportunities for candidates to analyze and develop a vision of teaching that can lead to more effective pedagogies.

The Problem of Enactment

Helping teachers learn to teach effectively requires that they learn to put what they know into action—the problem of *enactment*.[8] Teachers must be able to *do* a wide variety of things, many of them simultaneously. Meeting this challenge requires much more than simply knowing one's subject matter or discussing ideas about teaching. The issues teachers face regarding enactment are similar to those encountered in other professional fields, but are even more challenging. For example, teachers do many more things at once, with many more clients assembled at one time, than do most other professionals. Developing an authoritative classroom presence; good radar for watching what many different students are doing and feeling at each moment; and skills for explaining, questioning, discussing, giving feedback, constructing tasks, facilitating work, and managing the classroom— all at once—is not simple.

Preservice teachers must learn to weigh difficult dilemmas and to make decisions on the fly; to plan well and to alter plans for unforeseen circumstances; to respond to children; and to be knowledgeable about the material they are teaching. While some might describe this kind of learning as being able to "apply" knowledge to practice, separating theory from practice creates a false dichotomy. Indeed, Schön argued that in some professions—he includes teaching as a prime example—theory is embedded in and inseparable from the practice.[9] Yet learning how to think and act in these kinds of professional ways is very difficult, particularly if the knowledge is embedded in the practice itself.

There are actually multiple challenges embedded in the "problem of enactment." First, from relying on the apprenticeship of observation, candidates already have ideas about what activities like assessment, group work, or lectures look like in the classroom. Though using the same language as teacher educators, they may have entirely different notions of what these concepts mean and how to implement them. They need to both closely observe teachers in action and try out strategies with well-informed, specific feedback. Since the capacity to enact ideas must be developed *in* practice, it is critical that student teaching begin early and be well supervised. Studies find that candidates are better able to connect theoretical learning to practice when practicum experiences precede or are conducted alongside coursework. They are also more comfortable and confident in learning to teach, and more able to enact what they are learning in ways that are effective for students.[10]

Experience alone does not accomplish these goals. Seeing practices modeled and analyzing how, when, and why they work is key. Teachers who learn to teach without guidance often learn merely to cope rather than to promote learning for all their students, and they can acquire bad habits that are hard to unlearn. Researchers have found that the process of learning to enact new skills is best supported by skilled coaching in peer support groups that allow teachers to discuss strategies and dilemmas as they develop, strengthen, and refine teaching skills together. Teachers hone their skills when they can learn approaches, try them out, and reflect on their practice with feedback from peers and more expert practitioners.

The Problem of Complexity

A third and final challenge in learning to teach is that teaching is an incredibly complex and demanding task. Maggie Lampert observes that the "problems in teaching are many":

> One reason teaching is a complex practice is that many of the problems a teacher must address to get students to learn occur simultaneously, not one after another. Because of this simultaneity, several

different problems must be addressed in a single action. And a teacher's actions are not taken independently; there are inter-actions with students, individually and as a group. A teacher acts in different social arrangements in the same time frame. A teacher also acts in different time frames and at different levels of ideas with individuals, groups and the class to make each lesson coherent, to link one lesson to another, and to cover a curriculum over the course of a year. Problems exist across social, temporal, and intellectual domains, and often the actions that need to be taken to solve problems are different in different domains.[11]

This complexity has several sources. First, *teaching is never routine*. Students' situations, learning needs, challenges, questions, and dilemmas constantly change. Second, *teaching has multiple goals* that often must be addressed simultaneously. At the same time a teacher is teaching content, she is simultaneously teaching social and intellectual development, helping students work in groups, and paying attention to the child who needs some extra support in a different way from the child who wants to be the center of attention. Third, *teaching must address very different learning needs* for different students, who vary in their strengths, areas of challenge, and abilities, as well as their sociocultural backgrounds. Finally, *teaching requires multiple kinds of knowledge to be brought together in an integrated way*—for instance, teachers must integrate their knowledge of child development, of subject matter and pedagogy, of social-emotional learning, of group interactions, of students' different cultures and backgrounds, and of their particular students' interests, needs, and strengths in a way that advances learning for each of their students.

This complexity is magnified when teaching for deeper learning, because practice cannot be standardized. Teaching for deeper learning in ways that are student centered and culturally responsive relies heavily on the classroom and community context in designing instruction. The identities, interests, experiences, prior knowledge, and developmental levels of students, as well as the teacher's own knowledge and identity, figure into the creation of learning experiences. Student agency poses another challenge. If students are to learn to guide and shape their own learning, they must coconstruct aspects of the learning process, which makes teachers' judgments even more complex.

Student voice and agency can spur students' effort and engagement, and they are needed to develop students' ability to learn independently. But at the same time, the teacher must ensure that curriculum goals are being met, necessary scaffolds are put in place, resources are available, and students' energy is well directed. A teacher teaching the same content to multiple classes of students will thus do so in different ways for each class— and even to some extent for each student—and will modify plans each day in response to the learning that occurred or snafus that were encountered the day before.

Some teacher education approaches do not adequately respond to these challenges. For example, telling teachers in general ways about strategies that might be used in the classroom, without examples and models, does not typically lead to deep understanding or enactment. Developing routines can be helpful and can free up teachers' attention for other aspects of their work; however, offering only routines does not help teachers develop the diagnostic and instructional skills for dealing with students who require different approaches or additional supports if they are to learn successfully. Because teachers have multiple goals, students are many and diverse, and teaching requires that many different areas of knowledge be integrated, teachers need to learn to analyze what is going on in the classroom and to make sound decisions about curriculum, instruction, assessment, and classroom management in light of the particular students they teach.

THE DESIGN OF PROGRAMS PREPARING TEACHERS FOR DEEPER LEARNING

In the recent past, traditional teacher preparation often has been criticized for offering theory with little connection to tools for practice, providing fragmented coursework, and lacking a clear, shared conception of teaching among faculty. Programs that are largely a collection of unrelated courses and that have no common vision of teaching and learning have been found to be feeble agents for affecting practice among new teachers.[12] This can also be the case in some alternative routes that give short shrift to important elements of teacher education, omitting key courses dealing with child development and learning, and keeping coursework separate from unguided practice, which provides little meaningful support to beginning candidates.

Beginning in the late 1980s with the efforts of the Holmes Group of Education Deans and others, teacher education reforms began to produce program designs representing more integrated, coherent programs that emphasize a consistent vision of good teaching. These programs—which included postbaccalaureate models as well as traditional undergraduate programs—created stronger links among subject matter and pedagogical courses and connected clinical experiences to formal coursework, in part by interweaving student teaching with coursework and by infusing classroom practices into the curriculum. The programs teach teachers to do more than simply implement particular techniques; they help teachers learn to think pedagogically, reason through dilemmas, investigate problems, and analyze student learning to develop appropriate curriculum for diverse learners. Studies have found that such programs have a greater impact on the initial conceptions, practices, and effectiveness of new teachers than others that are less coherent and less intent on connecting theory and practice.[13]

The programs we studied are among those that have dramatically rethought how preparation is conducted—not only in blending theory and practice, but in doing so around a vision of teaching that supports empowering learning for all students, connected to a social justice mission. In the following sections, we briefly describe how each of these programs approaches the challenges of learning to teach for deeper learning.

Alverno College

Alverno College is a small, private, Catholic college located in Milwaukee, Wisconsin. The college sponsors undergraduate programs for women as well as graduate and teacher licensure programs that enroll both men and women. Although Alverno is a Catholic college, its students represent a diversity of religious and spiritual backgrounds. As of the fall of 2016, Alverno enrolled approximately 350 and 245 full-time undergraduate and graduate students, respectively, plus more than 1,500 part-time undergraduate and graduate students.[14] The School of Education included 76 undergraduates, nearly half of whom were students of color, plus 85 graduate students.

Alverno is well known for its long history of using an "ability-based" curriculum, which requires teacher candidates to demonstrate a set of concrete abilities as evidence of their learning. Ability-based teaching shifts the evaluation of learning to the application of knowledge and skills. This is important because students' success outside of school depends on how well they can apply their knowledge to novel situations. Alverno supports the development of these abilities by providing teacher candidates with the preparation experiences that mirror the ideal learning environments for their students, including project-based activities. This relatively straightforward concept—teach the teacher as you would have them instruct their pupils—helps candidates experience engaging and interactive lessons so they can better understand how to create similar experiences for their students.

Alverno's mission as a liberal arts women's college shifted to a focus on deeper learning in the early 1970s when Sister Joel Read (then president) challenged the faculty to concentrate on their students' learning rather than on their own teaching. She stated: "While the media focus on educational reform and decry the failure of school systems, the real issue is seeing to it that each learner achieves all she or he is capable of achieving. Alverno believes that means organizing the entire institution to facilitate student learning. The students' achievement is the only goal that matters."[15]

This challenge to the faculty contributed to the development of college-level curriculum that focused on real-world connections and applicability, a key hallmark of deeper learning.

As Alverno faculty and staff took up Sister Joel Read's challenge to focus on student learning rather than faculty teaching, they developed the eight core abilities, which line the college's wall as a constant reminder to students: communication, analysis, problem solving, valuing in decision-making, social interaction, developing a global perspective, effective citizenship, and aesthetic engagement. Throughout the college, students' learning and the faculty's instructional objectives are framed around the eight abilities. While the abilities remain constant, the curriculum for how students demonstrate them varies across the disciplines. Alverno's School of Education has not only refined the eight abilities to meet the current demands of preparing teacher candidates, but also developed four additional abilities:

- *Conceptualization:* Integrating disciplinary knowledge with educational frameworks and an understanding of human development to plan and implement learning
- *Diagnosis:* Using frameworks when observing behavior to foster learning
- *Coordination:* Managing resources effectively to support learning
- *Integrative interaction:* Demonstrating professional responsibility in the learning environment

The abilities establish the expectation for Alverno's teacher candidates to cultivate the same skills, practices, and mind-sets in themselves that they will work to reinforce in their own students. Moreover, the focus on abilities, as opposed to grades, within the School of Education and throughout Alverno, models for teacher candidates the type of teaching and assessment they should engage in with their students: mastering a specific skill or subject that will have utility outside of the classroom. The abilities reflect clear standards that candidates should work toward mastering. Candidates provide evidence of mastery through performance assessments in which they demonstrate the critical skills. They are supported in this pursuit through constant feedback and multiple opportunities to improve upon their work. In turn, candidates build knowledge about how individuals learn best, and they also deepen their understanding of the iterative learning practices that lead to the development of deep content knowledge.

One hundred percent of surveyed Alverno teacher candidates in the last semester of their program reported feeling well or very well prepared for teaching. Moreover, 100 percent of these candidates reported feeling well or very well prepared to identify and address special learning needs with appropriate teaching strategies; understand how factors in the students' environment outside of school might influence their life and learning; develop curriculum that helps students learn content deeply, so they can apply it in new situations; use a variety of assessments; and set norms for building a productive classroom community.

Bank Street College

Bank Street College is known for having cultivated progressive, child-centered teaching practices for more than a hundred years. Bank Street was founded as the Bureau of Educational Experiments (BEE) by Lucy Sprague Mitchell in 1916. The progressive movement was in full force at this time and sought "to effect societal change toward greater equity and democratic participation."[16] In 1930, the BEE began preparing teachers by establishing the Cooperative School for Student Teachers—a partnership with eight experimental schools to develop a one-year program for liberal arts graduates seeking to be teachers. The focus of the intensive course of study was on producing "teachers dedicated to stimulating the development of the whole child" by applying scientific methods, flexibility, and creativity.[17] In 1950, the BEE changed its name to the Bank Street College of Education and was authorized to offer teaching credential and master's degree programs in a range of areas and specializations.[18] Bank Street's work with progressive schools set the foundation for its role in New York City, and throughout the nation, as a partner for schools and organizations looking to expand progressive, student-centered approaches.

Mitchell's credo, which guided the endeavor, asked, What potentialities in human beings—children, teachers, and ourselves—do we want to develop?

- A zest for living that comes from taking in the world with all five senses alert
- Lively intellectual curiosities that turn the world into an exciting laboratory and keep one ever a learner

- Flexibility when confronted with change and the ability to relinquish patterns that no longer fit the present
- The courage to work, unafraid and efficiently, in a world of new needs, new problems, and new ideas
- Gentleness combined with justice in passing judgments on other human beings
- Sensitivity, not only to the external formal rights of the "other fellow," but to him or her as another human being seeking a good life through his or her own standards
- A striving to live democratically, in and out of schools, as the best way to advance our concept of democracy.[19]

These goals for children guide Bank Street's "Principles Underlying the Teaching of Teachers":

- Education is a vehicle for creating and promoting social justice and encouraging participation in democratic processes.
- The teacher has a deep knowledge of subject matter areas and is actively engaged in learning through formal study, direct observation, and participation.
- Understanding children's learning and development in the context of family, community, and culture is needed for teaching.
- The teacher continues to grow as a person and as a professional.
- Teaching requires a philosophy of education—a view of learning and the learner, knowledge and knowing—which informs all elements of teaching.[20]

Bank Street provides an example of how a large institution can engage in preparation for this kind of learning for both teachers and students. The Graduate School now offers thirty-six degree programs that enrolled more than seven hundred individuals in 2014–15.[21] With many hundreds of candidates in master's degree programs at any given time—and clinical placement relationships with more than seventy-five schools and early childhood settings in New York City—Bank Street's work is an extraordinary example of how preparing for deeper learning can be conducted in a highly personalized manner at scale.

Our study focused on Bank Street's Childhood General Education program, which enrolled forty-five candidates during the 2014–15 school year, of whom one-third were candidates of color and one-third were male. True to the college's history, the program maintains many relationships with schools throughout the New York area. In addition to the college's own School for Children, a progressive K–8 school located in the same building as the college, Bank Street partner schools have included Midtown West, PS 87, Central Park East II Elementary, River East Elementary, Brooklyn New School, Muscota New School, Manhattan New School, and Community Roots Charter School, among many others.[22] Generally, Bank Street provides professional development support to its partner schools, which tend to have large proportions of teachers and leaders who are graduates of Bank Street. In addition, because many of the partner schools champion progressive learning, they provide rich training grounds for Bank Street teacher candidates to experience and practice student-centered teaching.

Since its founding, Bank Street has aspired for all children to "develop a scientific attitude of eager, alert observation; a constant questioning of old procedures in the light of new observations; and a use of the world as well as books and source material."[23] While this quote is from Lucy Sprague Mitchell in 1931, it reflects the elements of what we refer to as deeper learning. To support the development of these deeper learning competencies in children, Bank Street believes that all teachers must

- understand how children develop and learn in the context of their families and communities;
- actively experiment, learn, and reflect; and
- have deep knowledge of content.

Therefore, Bank Street provides teacher candidates with highly personalized, developmentally grounded, challenging learning opportunities in real-world settings combined with time and social support for critical self-reflection, and for learning in a community of peers, coaches, and mentors.

To do this, Bank Street has created what might be thought of as a "living laboratory" for deeper learning, where the faculty adopt student-centered pedagogies focused on critical thinking, inquiry, and reflection with their candidates on the belief that the candidates will then be able to transfer these approaches to their students. The Childhood General Education program is shaped by a focus on child and adult development, experiential learning, and equity and social justice. This focus involves building on candidates' experiences; using inquiry to observe and record experience; critically analyzing the experience using rich tools developed in a variety of disciplines; and, finally, reflecting on experiences to develop insights that candidates can apply in future, different contexts. These same pedagogies are what Bank Street candidates carry into their work with children in classrooms where they offer a rich set of collaborative, well-supported experiences for students who are carefully observed and assessed to foster their growth and development.

Bank Street teachers are known for their deep knowledge of children, their highly personalized approach, and their strong outreach to families and connections to communities. Bank Street teachers are highly regarded by principals, with 90 percent of employers who responded to a recent survey noting that Bank Street graduates are well or very well prepared as teachers.[24] Moreover, on our Learning Policy Institute (LPI) survey of Bank Street candidates who were completing the program, over 95 percent report feeling "well" or "very well"prepared to do the following: use instructional strategies that promote active student learning, understand how factors in students' environment outside of school may influence their life and learning, plan instruction based on how children develop, engage students in cooperative group work as well as independent learning, relate classroom learning to the real world, choose teaching strategies for different instructional purposes and needs, develop students' questioning and discussion skills, and develop curriculum that helps students learn content deeply so they can apply it in new situations.

CU Denver

The University of Colorado at Denver (known as CU Denver) is also a large teacher preparation program, serving approximately 750 teacher candidates in five distinct, but interrelated, pathways that accommodate diverse students. These pathways vary in their structure, pace, and timing of preparation to attract and support teacher candidates from a wide range of backgrounds and experiences. However, the faculty strongly consider the various pathways to constitute one program and have organized them around common standards and experiences. They all embody CU Denver's commitment to developing in teacher candidates the knowledge, skills, and dispositions that deeper learning and social justice teaching require, as well as the wherewithal to change the structures and practices that make such teaching so challenging in schools located in communities of poverty.

In 2015–16 the five distinct pathways served (1) 350 traditional undergraduate students; (2) forty-three first-generation undergraduates who participated in an innovative residency (NxtGEN) that employed them as paraprofessionals while they were taking classes, as one way to provide much-needed financial and other supports to navigate college and licensure; (3) fifty graduate students training as residents for employment in the Denver Public Schools (Denver Student Teaching Residency); (4) fifty full-time preservice graduate students training in professional development schools; and (5) more than two hundred uncertified bachelor's degree holders, including many Teach for America (TFA) corps members, who were employed as teachers in area school districts and charter schools and who pursued licensure through alternative routes (Aspire to Teach).

The large number of alternative-route candidates is the result of a state education policy context that encourages free-market strategies for teacher education and schooling. This context further complicates the task of preparing teachers to provide historically underserved students equitable access to deeper learning. The CU Denver faculty and their school partners have responded in extraordinarily creative ways to this difficult environment, including creating new pathways into teaching for nontraditional teacher candidates that preserve their commitment to high-quality teacher preparation.

For all pathways, in both courses and clinical placements, teacher candidates' learning is guided by a common set of essential questions and anchor experiences, and their knowledge and skills are demonstrated through common performance assessments. These program elements enable teacher candidates to form strong and supportive teaching-learning relationships with university faculty, teachers and leaders in their placement sites, and their peers—all of which are key to their becoming well-prepared professionals.

Four essential questions serve as a frame for teacher candidates as they move through the program, and for instructors as they design their courses:

- *Essential question 1*: What do I *know and believe* about myself, my students, their families, and their communities within the larger social context?
- *Essential question 2*: How do I *act* on these beliefs to create inclusive and responsive *learning opportunities and transform inequities?*
- *Essential question 3*: How do I *enact principles of social justice and equity, inclusiveness, cultural and linguistic responsiveness, learning theory, and discipline-specific pedagogy within my pedagogical practices to plan, revise, and ad*just curriculum, instruction, and assessment to ensure success and growth for all my students, always acting as a critical urban educator to advocate for my students?
- *Essential question 4*: How do I *reflect* upon principles of social justice and equity, inclusiveness, cultural and linguistic responsiveness, learning theory, and discipline-specific pedagogy within my pedagogical practices in order to further plan, revise, and adjust curriculum, instruction, and assessment to ensure success and growth for all of my students, always acting as a critical urban educator to advocate for my students?

Candidates experience a curriculum focused on deepening their subject-matter knowledge, on instructional practices that reflect the science of learning, and on social and racial justice for students attending urban schools in high-poverty neighborhoods. University coursework engages the teacher candidates in the deeper learning pedagogy that they are being taught to use. Intensive and well-articulated clinical placements in professional development schools (PDS) in neighborhoods of concentrated poverty provide apprenticeships with teachers who themselves teach for deeper learning.

This PDS strategy began in the early 1990s when CU Denver was one of the earliest members of the National Network for Educational Renewal, a group of university teacher education programs that were dedicated to the simultaneous renewal of schools and the institutions that prepare teachers. The PDSs were intended to engage the faculty of the school together with university partners in an ongoing process of improving the education provided to the preK–12 students attending the schools and, at the same time, provide high-quality clinical settings in which future teachers could learn to teach and become part of a professional community. The PDSs became and continue to be core partners in CU Denver's teacher preparation program as they focus increasingly on deeper learning and social justice. We discuss this partnership strategy more fully in chapter 10.

A major goal of all the CU Denver pathways is to have every graduate ready to teach in urban schools with linguistically, racially, and socioeconomically diverse populations. Accordingly, CU Denver aligns its program to a set of deeply held and shared values that include basing instruction on what we know about learning and on the centrality of language, culture, and identity. In addition, deep knowledge of, and relationships with, communities and families inform deeper learning experiences that are rigorous and relevant. These merge in the program's conceptual framework, depicted in figure 2.1, which shows the various dimensions of teaching and learning that must be considered in such contexts and their connections to one another. This framework guides the candidates as they develop their teaching practice as well as experience being learners themselves. When teacher candidates conceptualize and plan for student learning, they place K–12 students at the center of the framework. When faculty are focused on candidates' learning, the teacher candidates are themselves in the center.

As a result of this approach, 96 percent of CUD candidates reported on our LPI survey that they feel "well" or "very well" prepared to teach students from diverse racial, ethnic, and linguistic backgrounds, and more than 80 percent report being "well" or "very well" prepared to teach students

FIGURE 2.1 **CU Denver conceptual framework**

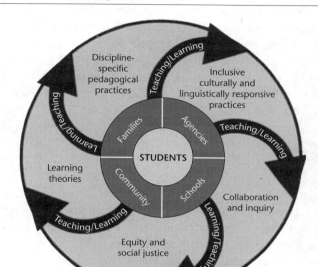

from a multicultural vantage point, to teach in ways that support English learners, to understand how factors in students' environment outside of school may influence their life and learning, and to teach in ways that support students' social, emotional, physical, and cognitive development.

Employers give CU Denver alums high marks as well. A 2015 survey of employers administered by a faculty member found that more than 90 percent judged CU Denver alums to be "very well" or "well" prepared to teach their content areas, to use technology and assessments to support learning, and to establish classrooms with respectful relationships and a focus on learning. More than 80 percent of employers found alums to be "well" or "very well" prepared to support critical thinking and to deepen students' understanding of concepts, to use performance-based assessments, and to support social, emotional, and cognitive development—that is, to enable deeper learning.[25]

High Tech High

High Tech High School (HTH), launched in September 2000, offers a project-based learning environment infused with technology that aims to provide students with deep, engaging, and relevant learning experiences aligned with four key design principles: equity, personalization, authentic work, and collaborative design. The HTH model is designed to integrate technical and academic education, prepare students for future education, and create a sense of community engagement and responsibility. HTH has grown from one high school to a network of thirteen charter elementary, middle, and high schools in the San Diego area. It offers a teacher education program, accredited by the California Commission on Teacher Credentialing, that prepares educators to teach in the HTH network as well as in seventeen other schools that partner with the program.

Established to train educators who embrace High Tech High's design principles and the project-based learning (PBL) approach, the two-year, school-embedded teacher preparation program consists of three separate tracks: a single-subject track for grades 6–12, a multiple-subjects track for self-contained elementary classrooms and some middle school subjects, and the education specialist track for teachers working with students who have mild to moderate disabilities. The program operates alongside the High Tech High Graduate School of Education (GSE), established in 2006. The HTH GSE includes two MEd degree programs, one focused on teacher leadership and the other on school leadership, and is adding a teacher residency program.

High Tech High's internship teacher preparation program is accredited to prepare California K–12 teachers through intensive fieldwork, mentorship, and project-based coursework aligned to state standards. In California, regulations governing intern pathways into teaching require that candidates complete an approved program of teacher education coursework and supervised clinical work that allows them to meet the same competencies as those who are prepared in traditional preservice routes. This includes receiving intensive mentoring and supervision while learning to teach and passing all the licensure tests and a state-approved teacher performance assessment.

Unlike programs that admit and train candidates who are then hired by schools, the High Tech High program admission process begins with the HTH schools' hiring process. Candidates go through the same intensive interview process as any teacher hired by HTH. Depending on their qualifications, candidates may be admitted either as intern teachers responsible for their own classrooms or—if they lack prior teaching experience—as apprentices, who will work side by side with veteran teachers until they are ready to take on their own class.

Interns and apprentices assume full or partial teaching or coteaching duties while participating in the program and take courses in the evenings. These courses are most often taught by experienced, veteran teachers and administrators of HTH schools. Because so many instructors come from the ranks of HTH educators, HTH program faculty model the type of instruction that interns will be expected to use in their K–12 classrooms, using the same design principles and methods used in HTH schools. The expectation is that intern teachers will use HTH's principles in the classroom while simultaneously experiencing them in their teacher training—a feature that makes for strong alignment between preparation and practice.

For example, contextualization of learning in real-world work, student engagement, and personalization are important practices that intern teachers are learning to provide to their students, just as their preparation program provides these opportunities to them. Similarly, comparable structures exist between HTH's K–12 schools and the intern program, as illustrated in "High Tech High: Matching Program to Principles."

Coursework and clinical work are tightly linked and reinforce one another. In their courses, candidates learn about development and learning, teaching methods, assessment strategies, and supports for student learning in ways that take theory and "Put It to Practice." Known within the program as PITP, Put It to Practice is a common course assignment structure where interns learn about a new concept or practice in a course, apply it in their own classrooms, and then come back to the course to reflect on that application.

Being fully embedded in the work of their schools means that HTH intern teachers receive mentoring from a close advisor for two years and have many opportunities to get to know their students and to engage with the work of their schools. They participate in family conferences, Individualized Education Plan (IEP) meetings, collaborative planning with faculty, and other activities outside their own classrooms. Some of these activities, such as Family Collaborative Nights, student advising, and home visits are features of the HTH network. All of these experiences connect interns to the students and families that the schools serve, helping to build on their coursework and develop their knowledge of community.

Not surprisingly, given the many connections between coursework and fieldwork, 100 percent of HTH candidates report experiencing collaborative learning and group work frequently in both their courses and their clinical work, and 90 percent or more also say that they *often* have opportunities to engage in assessments of their knowledge that require them to demonstrate

High Tech High: Matching Program to Principles	
Design principle	**Attributes of the school/intern program**
Equity: High Tech High schools are intentionally diverse and integrated, enrolling students through a zip code–based lottery aimed at creating schools that are reflective of the communities they serve.	• Student population is diverse; program aims for increasing intern diversity. • A variety of teaching approaches are used to accommodate diverse learners. • Technical and academic learning are integrated across the curriculum.
Personalization: High Tech High schools foster student engagement by knowing students well, tapping into students' experiences and interests, and building a strong sense of community.	• Small learning community structure allows teachers to know students well. • Advisory program for all students includes individual advisors (mentors) for candidates • Projects reflect students' interest and passions. • Integrated support services are available for students with special academic and/or social and emotional needs.
Authentic Work: All students engage in community-based learning, collaborating with adults on meaningful work that extends beyond the walls.	• Students connect their studies to the world through fieldwork, internships, and consultation with outside experts. • Projects integrate hands and minds and incorporate inquiry across multiple disciplines. • Students have one-on-one relationships with adults in field placements.
Collaborative Design: High Tech High teachers collaborate to design curriculum and projects, lead professional development, and participate in hiring, while seeking student experience and voice in each of these areas.	• Teaching staff includes experienced master teachers, recent university graduates, and professionals from the world of work. • Curriculum is designed by teachers in collaboration with students, and reflects both teacher and student interests. • Teachers meet in teams for at least one hour daily for planning and staff development.

Source: Adapted from High Tech High, "About High Tech High," https://www.hightechhigh.org/about-us/.

and apply their learning and to revise their work in response to feedback. At least 90 percent report often experiencing culturally responsive practices that draw on students' experiences and/or community knowledge in both their coursework and their clinical placements. Since the program is based on HTH's design principles, it is also unsurprising, though still remarkable, that 90 percent or more feel well prepared to design effective project-based instruction; develop curriculum that builds on students' experiences, interests, and abilities and helps students learn content deeply so they can apply it in new situations; create interdisciplinary curriculum; teach students from diverse ethnic, linguistic, and cultural backgrounds; and teach in ways that support English learners as well as students with special education needs. Also in line with the design principles, 100 percent feel well prepared to relate classroom learning to the real world.

Montclair State University

Like CU Denver, Montclair State University (MSU) provides an extraordinary example of a large, diverse program that prepares teachers for deeper learning at scale while including a variety of pathways into the profession. MSU produces a large share of New Jersey's teachers: between 2010 and 2012, 1,418 certified educators completed the program, and 657 of them (46 percent) were employed in New Jersey public schools the following school year.[26] (Many graduates also go to nearby New York or Pennsylvania, or return to their state of residence after completing their program at MSU.)

Located just across the George Washington Bridge from New York City, Montclair State University was established as the New Jersey State Normal School at Montclair in 1908. The institution became a state college in 1958, gained university status in 1994, and received Carnegie designation as a Research Doctoral Institution in 2016. Through all these changes, teacher preparation has remained a central focus. In the 1990s, the college initiated the Montclair State University Network for Educational Renewal (MSUNER), a partnership between Montclair State and thirty-one member school districts. As was the case at CU Denver, the Montclair partnership is part of the National Network for Educational Renewal, which ushered in many of the practices, policies, and structures that enable the extraordinary work it undertakes. The university has long had a special commitment to nearby Newark Public Schools, the largest school district in New Jersey.

To meet the various needs of those wanting to enter the profession, the Teacher Education Program includes multiple pathways into teaching, including undergraduate, graduate, and postbaccalaureate programs, two residency programs, and dual teaching/special education certification pathways, one focusing on inclusive STEM education. Although the program structures differ and the pathways draw from disparate candidate pools, all are intentionally housed within and linked through the Center of Pedagogy and the National Network for Educational Renewal, which share a common vision. All pathways feature serious clinical practice in a partner school, a focus on inquiry, an emphasis on child and adolescent development, and attention to social justice and teaching for equity in urban settings.

Montclair State's programs are united by a common vision, known as the Portrait of a Teacher, which embodies all the deeper learning competencies and demonstrates the university's commitment to preparing educators for a multicultural and democratic society. The six statements that compose the Portrait define this vision. Teachers should:

1. Have expert knowledge of subject-area content and relevant pedagogy
2. Understand learning and development as complex processes that take place across the lifespan
3. Apply knowledge of learners, disciplinary content, pedagogy, and assessment to teach effectively
4. Create curriculum, instruction, materials, and assessments that are universally designed and accessible to support the intellectual, social, and personal development of all students
5. Embrace leadership roles to create collaborative partnerships with school colleagues, families, and agencies in the community to support students' learning and well-being
6. Demonstrate dispositions critical to the teaching profession

The Portrait is used to guide the admission of candidates as well as their assessment throughout the program. By the last semester, teacher candidates are assessed on all components of the Portrait. The Portrait is also employed in the evaluation of cooperating teachers and supervisors, and integrated into Montclair's Standards for Initial Teacher Programs. The Portrait is a key element of the conceptual framework that guides the work of the Center of Pedagogy, which integrates programmatic standards, curriculum, and assessments for all the pathways. (See figure 2.2.)

It is these unified conceptual and organizational structures that allow Montclair to run a large and varied program with multiple pathways into teaching while maintaining common values and goals. This alignment is further bolstered by the use of common standards that embody the features of deeper learning, learner-centered teaching, and social justice. These standards place special emphasis on democratic classroom learning communities; culturally responsive pedagogy joined with content pedagogical knowledge; an understanding of children's social, emotional, and cognitive development in family and community contexts; responsiveness to all of students' needs, identities, and interests in planning instruction; instructional practice that promotes critical thinking and problem solving; and professionalism guiding reflection, collaboration, and continuous improve-

FIGURE 2.2 **Montclair State University, Teacher Education Program, Conceptual Framework**

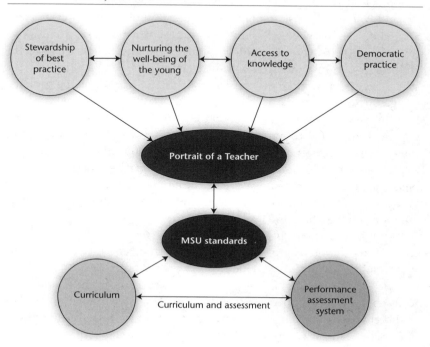

Source: Montclair State University College of Education and Human Services, Teacher Education Program, "Conceptual Framework," ttps://www.montclair.edu/media/montclairedu/cehs/images/ncate/CFW_Diagram_2_25_2014.jpg.

ment. With these emphases, the program is well positioned to prepare today's diverse learners for the demands of twenty-first-century society.

The program's commitment to integrating theory and practice can be seen in all the pathways. For example, the four-year undergraduate program includes clinical work connected to many courses and a full year of clinical practice, placing teacher candidates purposely with other teacher candidates at the same site to promote collaboration in a cohort model whenever possible. The postbaccalaureate and MAT pathways address the same topics in preprofessional and content methods courses while providing a two-semester progression of clinical practice in schools. A dual-certification pathway allows candidates to earn a BA in their major teaching area and then enter the

MAT program; they graduate with a master's degree and subject-area certification as well as Teacher of Students with Disabilities certification.

In 2009, in response to high rates of attrition of new teachers in Newark Public Schools, MSU, the district, and the teacher's union collaboratively created the Newark Montclair Urban Teaching Residency program, with the goal of improving retention for new teachers and mentor teachers as well. Residents work in the classrooms of master teachers while completing graduate coursework, provided on-site by MSU, for twelve to fifteen months, depending on the credential they are completing. In exchange for making a three-year commitment to teach in Newark Public Schools, they they receive a stipend between $26,000 and $30,000, and a tuition waiver that covers two-thirds of their fees at Montclair State. Residents who complete the program successfully receive hiring preference by Newark Public Schools as well as induction support, mentoring, and professional development during their first three years of teaching.

Montclair State has been widely recognized for its exceptional work in teacher preparation by program candidates, alumni, employers, and professional colleagues. In surveys conducted by the program from 2011 to 2015, completed by more than 2,200 alumni, more than 90 percent felt prepared to teach, and over 80 percent reported they felt "well" or "exceptionally well prepared." For example, nine out of ten felt well prepared to create a purposeful learning environment, to engage in culturally responsive teaching, and to support critical thinking and problem solving. The LPI survey of 2016 candidates revealed an even higher level of satisfaction. When asked how well their program prepared them for teaching overall, 99 percent of respondents reported that the program had prepared them to teach, and 89 percent felt "well" or "very well" prepared.

Since 2011, seven MSU graduates have received the New Jersey Distinguished Student Teacher Award.[27] Montclair State's Center of Pedagogy received the 2016 National Network for Educational Renewal's Nicholas Michelli Award for Promoting Social Justice; the program also received the Wisniewski Award for Teacher Education from the Society for Professors of Education in 2010, has twice received the Richard W. Clark Award for Exemplary Partner School Work, most recently in 2009, and was identified as one of the ten leading teacher education programs in the nation by the George Lucas Educational Foundation in 2008.

San Francisco Teacher Residency

The San Francisco Teacher Residency (SFTR)—a partnership between the San Francisco Unified School District (SFUSD), the United Educators of San

Francisco, the University of San Francisco (USF), and the Stanford Teacher Education Program (STEP)—is a postbaccalaureate teacher preparation program in which residents work alongside an expert cooperating teacher all year long in a Teaching Academy school while they take courses at either USF or STEP. The program leads to a California teaching credential and a master's degree. Residents are recruited in shortage fields such as mathematics, science, and bilingual education. They receive tuition grants, living stipends, and housing support while they are training, as well as two years of mentoring after they graduate. In exchange, they pledge to teach in high-need San Francisco schools for at least three years.

The content of the program augments the traditional USF and STEP programs, which also feature a full year of student teaching integrated with the same body of coursework, with these financial incentives and the commitment to teach in San Francisco, along with an additional practicum course that is specific to the district context and activities such as grand rounds that engage candidates in targeted learning to prepare them for urban teaching.

SFTR is guided by a vision of what it calls "transformative teaching." This vision places students at the center of learning, training educators who can facilitate engaging learning experiences for their students that are grounded in rigorous academic content and differentiated to meet students' diverse needs. SFTR's vision of transformative teaching outlines four key pillars that guide SFTR's recruitment process, coursework, clinical experiences, supervision and ongoing support, and definitions of success for both individual candidates and the program as a whole:

1. *Leading for equity and social justice*: SFTR seeks to prepare teachers who "position themselves as students of their students and school communities . . . to create sanctuaries of humanization," and who "understand experiences in classrooms, schools, and school community through a systems analysis, and take action as allies, advocates, and leaders to identify and interrupt oppressive forces."

2. *Placing students at the center of the learning*: SFTR's vision statement describes what teachers learn to do: "They design and implement relevant curriculum that starts where students are and builds on students' prior knowledge, interests, experiences, and rich cultural heritages. They use a variety of student-centered and inquiry-based strategies, empowering students to examine their world. They differentiate to support the needs of all students, and create inclusive communities that value different students' skills, knowledge, and perspectives. They

implement assessment *for* learning, using many different forms of data to give them a window into student thinking, and they use what they learn from students to guide their teaching."

3. *Communicating effectively in support of adult and student learning*: This includes deep and respectful family and community engagement, and the development of strong collaborative relationships with colleagues and families.

4. *Creatively managing the complexity of working in San Francisco Public Schools*: SFTR seeks to prepare teachers who are able to "draw from a wide body of resources and ideas to creatively navigate systems on behalf of students and their school community."[28]

SFTR's DNA embodies key elements of teaching for deeper learning: in addition to its vision for teaching, the program's structure itself values teacher learning that is collaborative and contextualized within SFUSD's local context. Within that context, SFTR is fully transparent about its commitment to achieving social justice through transformative teaching. This goal drives program structure and is key to recruiting aspiring teachers who want to follow an equity-focused path into education. As stated in the Program Overview on the SFTR website:

> The San Francisco Teacher Residency (SFTR) . . . offers aspiring educators the opportunity to help transform lives and communities in San Francisco through the teaching profession. Plain and simple: we are on a mission for social justice. SFTR aims to improve academic achievement and social-emotional development for historically underserved students in San Francisco's public schools by recruiting, preparing, and supporting highly effective and equity-centered teachers.[29]

The program's conception of education extends beyond the classroom and into the community and K–12 students' lives. In the clinical placements as well as in coursework, SFTR provides residents with opportunities to develop their "teaching toolbox" so that all their students can acquire the academic content, skills, and mind-sets they need to succeed in the twenty-first century. By working in a set of schools that serve as Teaching Academies, the program also helps to transform the work of veteran teachers and of schools as a whole. And by reaching out to families in many ways, this transformative work extends into communities. At its heart, SFTR's mission is disrupting patterns of inequity in our society and closing achievement gaps within San Francisco Unified School District. Courses, assignments, and modeling allow residents to develop the pedagogical moves and classroom culture–building skills to deliver on this mission.

The program has been so successful at preparing and retaining highly effective teachers that the district has expanded it each year, from fifteen students when it was launched in 2010 to thirty-two in 2015–16 (the year of our study) and forty-three in 2016–17. Between 2010–11 and 2015–16, SFTR prepared 135 aspiring teachers to work in high-needs schools within the district. Overall, 97 percent of SFTR graduates are still teaching, and 87 percent are teaching within SFUSD.[30] This compares to only about 38 percent of other new teachers hired within that time period. One hundred percent of SFUSD principals report that residents are more effective than other beginning teachers they have hired.[31]

SFTR has also helped diversify the teaching force and fill high-needs positions where the district experiences shortages. Of the past three cohorts, 66 percent of residents were teachers of color, and 81 percent of all SFTR math and science graduates were women and/or people of color, groups traditionally underrepresented in STEM. Fully 96 percent of SFTR graduates work in high-needs schools or high-needs subjects such as math, science, and bilingual education.

Among the 2015–16 residents responding to our LPI survey, 93 percent reported that they feel "well" or "very well" prepared to teach. One hundred percent felt prepared to use instructional strategies that promote active learning; to develop curriculum that helps students learn content deeply, so they can apply it in new situations; to help students learn to think critically and solve problems; to teach students from a multicultural vantage point; and to encourage students to see, question, and interpret ideas from diverse perspectives. More than 90 percent felt prepared to relate classroom learning to the real world; to develop curriculum that builds on students' experiences, interests, and abilities; to develop culturally relevant lesson plans; to engage students in cooperative group work as well as independent learning; and to develop students' questioning and discussion skills. In most of these areas, more than 80 percent felt "well" or "very well" prepared. Program graduates agree. In a 2015 survey of alumni, 98 percent agreed with the statement: "My SFTR experience has contributed to my success as a teacher," with 71 percent strongly agreeing.

Trinity University
Over the past three decades, Trinity University—a small private university in San Antonio, Texas—has established itself as one of the nation's premier teacher preparation programs, known for long-standing partnerships with

San Antonio schools, an inquiry-based approach to teaching and learning, and a focus on developing teacher candidates' cultural competence and sense of connection to issues of social justice and equity.[32] Through a year-long, three-semester, school-embedded Master of Arts in Teaching (MAT) program, Trinity aims to develop teachers who view themselves as advocates in promoting equity and opportunity for all students and their families, who continually reflect on and refine their practice, and who actively engage in collaborative learning communities.

Trinity prepares thirty to forty teacher candidates a year, most of whom come through Trinity's undergraduate pathway into the MAT program, having had strong preparatory experiences along the way. For them, the program operates like a five-year preparation. Recently, the program began to accept a few highly qualified postbaccalaureate students from other universities who join these students only for the final year.

Trinity's program is grounded in a set of standards and core beliefs. To the Texas teaching standards, which focus on planning, instruction, learning environment, and professional practices and responsibilities, Trinity has added standards around cultural responsiveness and technology. Its core beliefs (see "Trinity's Core Beliefs About Principled Practice") focus on ethical responsibility and cultural responsiveness, along with knowledge of content and pedagogy, and leadership of self and others. For example, teachers must not only know how to teach content to diverse learners in ways that "allow them to think and act with what they know," they must also "bridge gaps between the culture of the teacher and the culture of the learner," "advocate for students and their learning," and "stand up for children, their families, and the profession . . . promoting democratic values such as equity and opportunity."

While the core beliefs ground Trinity's goals for its candidates, the core features of the program make these sorts of experiences possible. These key interlocking features include coursework that is tightly aligned with clinical practice; a full-year, nearly full-time apprenticeship under the wing of an expert teacher in one of Trinity's professional development schools; a small cohort of teacher candidates; and personalized relationships with faculty and mentor teachers. Faculty work in the professional development schools alongside mentor teachers and novices, and many of the mentor teachers teach courses with faculty.

The beliefs and features shape how teachers develop principled practice. Trinity's commitment to the apprenticeship derives from the conviction that teachers learn to teach by teaching, combining university knowledge about what to teach with craft knowledge and skills developed

Trinity's Core Beliefs About Principled Practice

Knowledge of content and pedagogy

Teachers must:

- Know what to teach as evidenced by strong content knowledge
- Know how to teach it so they can represent that content for diverse learners and anticipate misconceptions
- Help students develop conceptual understandings that allow them to think and act with what they know

Ethical responsibility

Teachers must:

- View teaching as a moral and political act
- Advocate for students and their learning
- Stand up for children, their families, and the profession
- View schools as serving a transformative function
- View themselves as "change agents" in promoting democratic values such as equity and opportunity

Leadership of self and others

Teachers must:

- Be prepared to assume informal and formal leadership roles
- Be effective participants in collaborative work cultures
- Be able to manage themselves, including their time, focus, responsibilities, roles, and emotional responses

Cultural responsiveness

Teachers must:

- Bridge gaps between the culture of the teacher and the culture of the learner
- Learn about self and recognize how one's culture and identity may affect others
- Know oneself in a cultural context and create an environment in which the learners are invited to explore the cultural contexts for who they are and how they respond and relate to one another

Source: Trinity University Department of Education Conceptual Framework, spring 2010.

in real classrooms with real children under the careful guidance and support of master teachers. In addition, teachers must engage in continual inquiry about their practice to be effective. This involves identifying ongoing questions about practice, developing strategies to address those questions, assessing the effectiveness of strategies employed, and modifying practice. Furthermore, teachers need a community of peers to examine questions of practice and assess student learning. The cohort model and placements embedded in professional development schools allow teachers to engage in professional conversation and experience the power of collaborative work.

All these experiences are geared toward preparing educators to teach for deeper learning, to develop an orientation toward and commitment to social justice in their view of the role of schools in society, and to work for equity in how they teach to reach all students.

As a result of these practices, 100 percent of Trinity's student teachers responding to the LPI survey reported feeling prepared to implement varied instruction that integrates critical thinking, inquiry, and problem solving; to respond to the needs of students by being flexible in instructional approach and differentiating instruction (91 percent felt well prepared); to engage and motivate students through learner-centered instruction (85 percent felt well prepared); and to integrate effective modeling, questioning, and self-reflection strategies into instruction (79 percent felt well prepared). Trinity graduates are sought after in San Antonio and beyond, because they are prepared to teach for deeper learning and for equity, and because they have also been trained to be collaborative leaders within schools.

■   ■   ■   ■   ■

Although these seven programs differ in size and organization, they share a deep structure of theories and values, ranging from a curriculum that focuses on children's learning and development in social contexts to strong social justice commitments that shape an overarching vision guiding courses and clinical work. They have all created intensive relationships with schools that go well beyond placing student teachers in random classrooms to joint collective activity that seeks transformation of the processes of education in support of deeper understanding and equity. In the next two chapters, we examine how the content and practices of each of these programs enact the deeper structure that they share.

CHAPTER 3

ORGANIZING THE KNOWLEDGE BASE

Within the Newark Montclair Urban Teacher Residency Program, I feel that I received the education and training needed to be an effective educator. As I enter into my first year of teaching this September, I feel confident in my ability to develop highly engaging lessons for my students, and well prepared to address their diverse social, emotional, physical, and academic needs.

> —Newark Montclair Urban Teacher Residency graduate

I think the MAT program . . . helped me learn how to question my practice, my environment, and my students. Growing up, we all form a notion of what it means to be a teacher, even if it's subconscious, and the Trinity curriculum aided me in deconstructing those preconceived ideas and rethinking the idea of "teacher" and "teaching."

> —Trinity University MAT program graduate

Each of the programs we studied helps candidates develop a clear vision of what it means to become a teacher who teaches for deeper learning, as well as a repertoire of knowledge and skills to enact that vision. In this chapter, we provide an overview of the key content the programs include to underpin candidates' learning. In the next chapter, we describe the key practices they undertake in enacting this curriculum.

We describe the learning opportunities programs create through both coursework and fieldwork in relationship to the framework for teacher education offered by a panel convened by the National Academy of Education.[1] The academy panel synthesized the research on effective teaching and teacher preparation as it responds to what the learning sciences have discovered about how people learn, work that was published in a National Research Council volume by that name.[2] The National Academy framework suggests that the common practices of effective teaching draw on three general areas of knowledge that beginning teachers must acquire in order to be successful with their students (see figure 3.1):

- knowledge of *learners* and how they learn and develop within social contexts,
- an understanding of the *subject matter* and skills to be taught in light of the social purposes of education, and
- an understanding of *teaching* in light of the content and learners to be taught, as informed by assessment and supported by a productive classroom environment.

To address the complexities of teaching, teachers must integrate various kinds of knowledge about teaching, learning, and subject matter so that

FIGURE 3.1   **A framework for understanding teaching and learning**

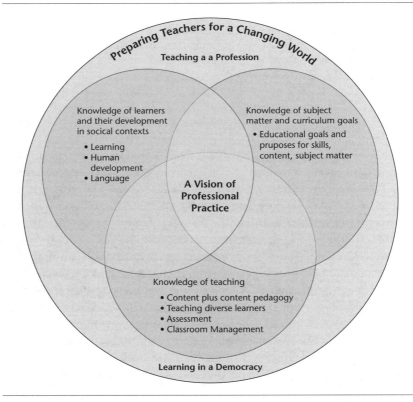

they can be deployed in learner-centered and learning-centered ways that are interdependent. The framework is reminiscent of Dewey's notion, outlined in *The Child and the Curriculum*, that the teacher's role is to mediate the needs and interests of the child and the demands of the curriculum.[3] Teachers must bring the child to the curriculum in ways that are inviting, motivating, and developmentally appropriate, and bring the curriculum to the child in ways that it can be engaged and understood.

These interactions between teachers, learners, and content are framed by two important conditions for practice: first, the fact that teaching is a profession with certain moral as well as technical expectations and, second, the fact that, in the United States, education must serve the purposes of a democracy. This latter condition means that schools assume the purpose of enabling young people to participate fully in political, civic, and economic life in our society. It also means that education—including teaching—is intended to support equitable access to all that society has to offer.

As professionals, teachers make a commitment to learn what they need to know to help individual students succeed. The vision of professional teaching depicted in figure 3.1 reflects a perspective on success—in this case, one that enables the kind of student learning that supports critical thinking and problem solving, social intelligence and compassion, and the capacity to be resourceful and resilient. These goals for education influence what teachers need to know and be able to do and what teacher education is expected to accomplish.

The seven programs we studied helped teachers learn about learners, content, and pedagogy—and about how they can fulfill their moral and ethical responsibilities as professionals serving children in a democracy—through curriculum that reflects the National Academy framework above and emphasizes deeper learning. The following curriculum outline is described in more detail in the sections that follow.

- *Knowledge of learners and their development in social contexts*
  - understanding development and learning
  - families and communities as social contexts for development
  - language and culture as social contexts for development

- *Knowledge of subject matter and curriculum goals*
  - content and content pedagogy
  - literacy across the curriculum
  - curriculum design

- *Knowledge of teaching*
  - assessment of, as, and for learning
  - differentiating and personalizing instruction
  - culturally and linguistically responsive pedagogy
  - classroom management that supports social, emotional, and cognitive learning

In all of the programs, a vision of effective, democratic teaching pervades both coursework and clinical work, allowing candidates to see where they are going in their journey.

In what follows, we describe how programs help develop a vision of teaching that provides a conceptual map on which teachers can hang the many specific things they are learning. We then outline each of the major areas of the curriculum and how they are structured: the *what* of teacher education for deeper learning. In the next chapter, we describe central practices used in these programs: the *how* of preparation for deeper learning.

CONTENT AND PRACTICE INTEGRATED AROUND A VISION OF TEACHING

At the center of the conceptual framework in figure 3.1 is a vision for practice that integrates knowledge about learners, curriculum, and teaching. The development of a vision for teaching relies substantially on the fusion between coursework and clinical work—theory and practice—that enables candidates to develop initial knowledge and skills in a meaningful way. In each case, from the very beginning of the program, candidates are in K–12 classrooms as well as connected courses, and they are seeing and experiencing the practices they are learning about in both settings. This strong coherence is characteristic of effective teacher education programs, and it stands in contrast to the fragmented approach to teacher education that once predominated—when courses were disconnected from each other and from the clinical experience, and when neither was tied to a common vision of teaching.[4]

At Bank Street, for example, a distinctive vision of teaching and learning is supported through this highly integrated process of learning to teach. One of its early intellectual leaders, Barbara Biber, summarized that vision as follows:

We aim for actively involved children acquiring competence and a sense of their own competence. Active investigation, independent pursuit, and learning through discovery are dominant in the learning climate, but we respect and honor the kind of content for which prestructured information or formal instruction may be more efficient and, in fact, satisfying in its own way. The Bank Street teacher uses every opportunity to foster intellectual mastery and to promote cognitive power by creating a pervasive climate of "why and wherefore and wherefrom" kind of thinking. . . . In our philosophy and practice, we feel responsible to nurture equally the intuitive processes, the capacity for feeling and emotion, for reflective as well as goal-directed thinking. . . . The school as a social institution has broad responsibility for the development of the whole person—his affective and social as well as his intellectual development.[5]

This vision of learning and the teaching that supports it is pervasive in Bank Street's courses, hallway discourse, clinical placements, and professional endeavors of all kinds. The School for Children, in the same building as the college, instantiates this approach to teaching, so that candidates can see it in action each time they are in the building. The curriculum goals supporting this vision are achieved through tightly interwoven coursework and clinical work that, together, create the same kinds of experiences for prospective teachers that they are learning to create for their pupils.

Some of the programs focus candidates on explicitly articulating their own vision for their practice. In the San Francisco Teacher Residency, for example, the Vision of Effective Teaching assignment, which is part of the Teaching and Learning course, is the place where residents bring together the ideas about deeper learning from their coursework and integrate them into a picture of their classroom practice, with direct applications to that practice. In their written vision statements, residents show how they hope to translate their philosophical commitments to student-centered learning, teaching for social justice, engaging students and families, and restorative justice into concrete activities in their classrooms this year as residents and next year as teachers of record.

One student used the Vision of Effective Teaching assignment to reflect on her previous experience as a teacher in another country, to articulate a new vision, and to describe how she is implementing this vision in concrete ways:

Since my stint in [a foreign country], both time and experience have allowed me to reflect on my teaching through a critical lens and to revise my current practices. . . . Now, I feel much more equipped to articulate, defend, and practice a vision of teaching that pushes students towards success in a school system set up to disenfranchise those on the margins. My vision of teaching is meant to be a beginning; a framework that can adapt, change, and transform as I continue to grow as an educator. For now, I have identified three main, vital domains in my teaching: I will teach from a place of love and joy; I will implement student-centered learning; and I will approach my teaching through the lens of critical consciousness.

Seeing students as active agents in their own learning, working in tandem with teachers, has become a very important value to me as a teacher. In my current classroom, students fill out an extensive reflection each day, noting what they learned, what they enjoyed, what they would like to see more of, and anything else they would like to share. Through this daily ritual, students are given a voice that can directly inform our teaching practices. The reflections create a partnership in the classroom; students have agency and participate in their own learning process.

This assignment is more than just a paper for a course. Residents told us they find that they use the assignment to structure their practice. One described how she intends to use the steps her mentor and supervisor take to connect to students and their families:

I will learn from my students just as they will learn from me in a community environment that I work hard to cultivate. This I have learned from my collaborating teacher. . . . She engages parents with texts and calls home from the very beginning of the year. She also looks for parent involvement within the classroom. I would like to do those things and go even further. . . . My supervisor described how she sent a survey home (in both Spanish and English) to gather important information. She also sent out weekly emails to inform the parents about what we are currently studying, resources for struggling students, and even resources for those students looking for more to do.

The creation of a vision that can shape teachers' ongoing learning and teaching anchors the schema teachers are developing and makes it possible for them to connect the many things they are learning into a textured and coherent whole.

KNOWLEDGE OF LEARNERS AND
THEIR DEVELOPMENT IN SOCIAL CONTEXTS

All of the programs studied place a deep understanding of how children develop and learn at the heart of the curriculum. These understandings are the foundation on which teachers learn to build their own curriculum that can support learning: designing, sequencing, and pacing activities, diagnosing student learning needs, and teaching social, emotional, and academic skills. This is noteworthy because there are many programs around the country—and some entire states—that do not expect teachers to acquire or need this knowledge base. They have inherited the century-old "factory model" view that teachers merely need some canned techniques for teaching and the ability to follow predetermined curriculum packages or textbooks, rather than the foundational knowledge that will allow them to design classroom environments and activities, and to choose or adapt useful curriculum materials, that support individual children.

When student development is the focus of teaching decisions, teachers plan in light of their students' needs and to support their progression along several developmental pathways—physical, social, emotional, cognitive, linguistic, and psychological. They understand that these dimensions interact with one another and, further, that students will have different developmental needs. While there are strong common aspects of the developmental process, milestones along each of these dimensions do not necessarily occur at the same age for all children nor does development in different arenas occur evenly within the same child. Understanding developmental pathways and progressions is crucial for teaching in ways that are optimal for each child. Furthermore, learning and development affect each other, and both are deeply embedded in cultural contexts. This means that teachers must understand and appreciate the ways children's experiences can differ, and be able to see and build upon cultural experiences if they are to help all students succeed.[6]

Understanding Development and Learning

A developmental perspective is infused in all the coursework of these programs. The High Tech High course How People Learn: Principles of Educational Psychology focuses on cognitive development among school-aged children and includes attention to the adolescent mind. Alverno teacher candidates take Life Span Development and Introduction to Psychology and Human Development early in the program. The very first class they take focuses on human development, learning, and motivational theories.

In the SFTR program, residents doing their coursework at Stanford enroll in an Adolescent Development and Learning class in the fall semester, just as they begin their residencies. This frames the way they come to think about their students. The programs also incorporate issues of inclusion, family contexts, and language learning from a developmental framework that appreciates diversity and supports differentiation to meet individual children's needs with respect for their social contexts.

Bank Street is a strong example of a thoroughly developmental approach. Its coursework emphasizes human development and its variations in ways that support candidates in learning how to teach in a contextualized, developmentally grounded, and personalized way. For example, in Bank Street's Child Development course, candidates "examine the interactions among the cognitive, social, emotional, linguistic, and physical development of children from infancy into adolescence," paying "close attention to children as makers of meaning in the contexts of their development, including family, school, socioeconomic class, and culture."[7] This class aims to equip candidates with an understanding of how to structure learning to meet students' varying developmental needs, while also acknowledging that students come from unique home and community environments that inevitably influence how they engage in learning both within and outside the classroom. In the Social Worlds of Childhood class, candidates dive deeper into how to provide nurturing and meaningful experiences for students who have challenging home environments, characterized by "poverty, changing family structures, substance abuse, community violence, and HIV/AIDS."[8]

Bank Street's Developmental Variations builds on the foundational human development courses by "increasing participants' awareness and understanding of the educational, social, cultural, linguistic and developmental implications of disability from historical, legal, and sociopolitical perspectives," including "understanding how disability is socially constructed at the levels of family, community, school, and the larger society."[9] In Language Acquisition and Learning in a Linguistically Diverse Society, candidates "look at the typical stages of language acquisition" and practice using strategies to help English learners learn the English language.[10] These courses help candidates understand that children develop their cognitive, emotional, social, linguistic, and physical abilities in different stages, paces, and ways and help candidates learn strategies for addressing the range of students' developmental needs.

Students also learn about child development in multiple contexts through two courses. In Family, Child, and Teacher Interaction in Diverse and Inclusive Educational Settings, candidates examine "the implications of working with a multicultural community and differing family structures" as they develop "skills and procedures in parent conferencing" and an "understanding [of] the concerns of parents of children with special needs."[11] The Study of Children in Diverse and Inclusive Educational Settings Through Observation and Recording is another required course where "students become aware of how specific behaviors yield insight into the overall life of the child."[12] As we describe in the next section, the skills developed in this course—and from similar experiences in the other programs—are foundational to teachers' capacities to learn *from* their students in order to teach *to* their students' needs, interests, and experiences.

STUDYING DEVELOPMENT AND LEARNING UP CLOSE. Programs augment in-class learning about development with structured opportunities for candidates to observe learning and development firsthand. Bank Street's Observation and Recording course, or "O&R," as it is fondly called, is constantly identified by students, graduates, and faculty as a trademark of a Bank Street education and a critical means for prospective teachers to learn how to look closely at children, to see them as growing individuals, and to find ways to foster their learning. The course stresses the use of theory and evidence derived from the close observation of children to make informed teaching decisions. The key assignment from this course—a detailed child study—has traveled to many other teacher education programs, including all of those we studied. An instructor of the course described how it seeks to foster rigor in the use of evidence and theory to understand children:

> Observation and Recording . . . is one of the courses specifically designed to help people get evidence from kids. That is one of the ways we help students to be rigorous. They have to see child behaviors in relation to context. They learn about learning styles, about temperament, about special needs, and subjects kids like. They learn about how kids think and how they make friends. The task of serious child study is to help students look for real evidence and to use theories that help them interpret what they see.

Students read texts on the observation and study of children while applying what they learn to their own child study. This document is developed over several months from a number of different assignments, including short weekly written observations of the child at school; a paper that examines the child in the context of his peers or group; an age-level study designed to see the child in light of developmental theory, and observations and interpretations of the child as a learner and a member of a learning community.

Class discussions usually center on these issues and on the evolving nature of children as learners. The course outline describes how the course is designed to sharpen the teacher's knowledge of her personal biases and her skills for seeking evidence:

> Almost everyone "observes" children informally, but what we "see" and remember is influenced by what we are looking for, what we expect to see and what we think about the nature and capabilities of children. Our observations of children are also influenced by our own values and feelings. In this course we will work toward sharpening awareness of our own cultural and personal assumptions when observing children. In this process we will work to develop greater sensitivity to ourselves as observers, to the language we use, and to the data we are choosing to attend to. The aim is to develop a personal style of observing and recording that is precise, vivid and non-judgmental, one that will serve us well in our work with children and families. Class time will be used to present, discuss and practice observational techniques. At times we will use films and videotapes in class in order to have common experiences for observation and discussion.

A Bank Street graduate at Midtown West Elementary School—one of the college's partner schools—described how the course affected not only her practice but, because of the Bank Street influence schoolwide, that of her colleagues as well:

> "O&R" was very important because it showed me how to look at the children in my class and make nonjudgmental assessments of what's going on with them. . . . We do portfolio assessment as a whole school. Individually, teachers have different methods of taking notes on children. Some teachers have separate little notebooks for each kid. A new method that one of the teachers brought in this year is doing it on stickers on a clipboard that you carry around to jot things down. Then you have a book with dividers with each kid's name and at the end, you pull off the stickers and put them next to the kids' names. When we send progress reports, they're all narratives describing what children can do.

Versions of this same assignment appear in other programs, including preparation for secondary school teachers at High Tech High and in the Stanford Teacher Education Program (STEP), which is part of the San Francisco Teacher Residency. High Tech High's course How People Learn looks at the development of morality and identity as well as social-emotional and cognitive development. In addition to helping interns understand children and adolescents, the course also helps them "reflect on and process the interpersonal dynamics between them and their own students that influence relationships, interpretations, and responses to student behaviors and achievements."[13] Developing healthy relationships is critically important to helping teachers personalize learning, including designing relevant and engaging projects.

As part of the process of learning and understanding child development and behavior, interns are required to write a detailed case study that focuses on an individual student in their class. More specifically, the project asks the intern to identify "a student you have some concern about, particularly in regard to your relationship with him/her." The intern is expected to spend time with the student having an open conversation, while also actively listening to the student talk about school, learning, relationships, and more, in an effort to gain further insight into the student's perspective. This insight better allows the intern to personalize instruction and curriculum and to build healthier relationships with students, taking into account their experiences, ideas, and needs. The description of the project includes this guidance: "Teaching is a demanding endeavor, physically, cognitively and emotionally. Teachers don't often have the opportunity to reflect in a highly detailed way about our relationships with students. I encourage you to use this project as an opportunity to contemplate some of the more difficult aspects of teaching."[14]

Requiring interns to critically reflect on and analyze their relationships with students and to seek to understand a student's experience and perspective encourages the interns to reflect on their teaching, at the same time that it challenges them to understand all children, including those who seem hard to reach, and to find meaningful ways to engage them.

Child case studies are also used in many programs to study development for particular kinds of students—for example, English learners, students with disabilities, young learners developing literacy skills—in order to help candidates carefully observe and see how children develop and learn. In all the programs that use child case studies, instructors and candidates noted that this close look at development and learning, which connects research and theory to real children's lives, develops habits of mind—a recognition of the student's experience and perspective—and habits of looking and listening, including the capacity to observe students carefully and tailor responses to their needs, that last throughout their teaching careers.

Families and Communities as Social Contexts for Development

These programs also pay a great deal of attention to children's environments as contexts for development and learning, and they help the candidates learn from families as well as work with them. Being embedded in schools where they can participate in parent meetings and outreach provides candidates with one kind of learning opportunity. Coursework provides other opportunities that are designed to create a different perspective on family interaction than many candidates may have experienced when they themselves were in school. These are intended to overturn the old-style notion that parents come to school only for back-to-school night and an occasional teacher conference where they are told "how their child is doing," and otherwise have little involvement unless their child is "in trouble." Instead, they aim to help teachers create relationships with families and to learn from their knowledge of the child as well as their experiential "funds of knowledge" more generally.[15]

For example, SFTR's Practicum course—one context that entails work with families, includes sessions that involve parents from the district in an exploration of the two-way communication strategy the program hopes candidates will enact. The goal is not only for teachers to provide information to families regarding students, but also for them to learn from students' families in ways that inform teaching and learning.

> During one Practicum session, residents heard directly from families, represented by three SFUSD parents and the coordinator, and former parent member, of the SFUSD Parent Advisory Council, an advisory body to the San Francisco Board of Education—about what they need and want from teachers.[16] The guests participated in a "fishbowl" activity. As one of the residents described it to us: "They actually invited parents in [for a fishbowl]. So the parents were sitting in the inner circle and we were all in the outer circle, listening to things that they need and things that they would want from teachers during the school year. We got to ask them a couple of questions, and I thought that was super helpful."

This activity was followed up by an assignment to do a "positive phone call home." An optional script provided by the instructor offered some scaffolding for the residents:

Hello, I'm _____

I'm calling to let you know how much I'm enjoying working with _____

One thing I really appreciate about your child is _____

Is there anything you want me to know about working with _____?

Looking forward to seeing you at family conferences.

Before making the call, residents discuss their expectations and feelings about the activity. Afterwards, back in class, they debrief on how the process went, including parents' responses and how expectations were reinforced or challenged. Often candidates are extremely anxious about calling a parent and enormously relieved to find out how well-received their call is and how surprised parents often are to hear something good about their child. The experience sometimes transforms the candidate's relationship with the student, who feels reassured and more positive about his or her experience at school.

A resident described some of the practical ideas she drew from the phone call home and the parent fishbowl:

[Make] a positive phone call immediately, so that when something does go wrong later on in the year and you have to make a call, it's not [like] the only contact you've had with these parents is negative . . . [The parents] were saying that monthly or weekly newsletters are really helpful. They were saying having the rules displayed in the classroom is helpful for them, so if they're coming in within the first weeks of school, they said, being able to see what the expectations are for their students is helpful for them. And then, being consistent with expectations. So, the way you lay the groundwork with expectations for the beginning of the year, that should still be what it is throughout the rest of the year.

Some of the partnership schools now require, and many of the graduates in other schools have also adopted, a practice of making positive phone calls home to all of the students' parents or guardians from their classroom or advisory group.

Practicum lessons and activities at SFTR that focus on building relationships with families are often then reinforced in residents' placements, where the yearlong residency allows residents a more hands-on role than what shorter student-teaching placements offer in other programs. For example, an SFTR coach described how a bilingual resident she supervises provides support in translation to the cooperating teacher (CT) and has been a central point of contact for the many Spanish-speaking families in the classroom. A different resident described the responsibility that his CT gave him for working with families, and how this was an important complement to his coursework:

> My CT gave me the opportunity to work with three or four families pretty much independently throughout the whole year. So, I took over communication with those families. I've had the opportunity to make phone calls home, to have meetings before and after school, to send texts back and forth, basically having the same one-on-one conversations. And that has looked really different with different students. With one student who's really struggling with writing right now, Spanish writing particularly, we were writing Spanish opinion writing, and he was writing about how our school should have a skate park. And so I went with his mom and him to a skate park, and created that relationship, and my CT really encouraged that. I feel like I've been really fortunate to be able have those experiences.

Because they work as student teachers (called interns, although they are in the classroom of a veteran teacher) for a full year in their professional development school (PDS) sites, Trinity candidates also get to know their students in a variety of ways. School events provide opportunities for candidates to learn more about their students, their families, and the communities. At both elementary PDS sites, Trinity candidates are encouraged to participate in community outreach events, such as a school's carnival fundraiser or fall back-to-school night. In addition, when elementary candidates start their lead teaching in the spring, they increase their parent communication. They step into the role of facilitating parent-teacher conferences. They also attend RTI and 504 meetings, since they are teaching students with identified special needs for a good portion of the spring quarter. In the classroom, they put together activities that help them know their students, and help the students know one another, as one elementary candidate described: "Once we are able to know them deeply by doing different community-building events and different activities that get the students to work together, we can match what they need with very specific things about the student."

To reflect on the learning gained from their interactions with parents and families and how those relationships contribute to student learning and strengthen the home-school connection, candidates maintain a log that tracks their communication with their students' families. Interns maintain this log across their first and second placements and reflect on the implications for their practice.

Candidates also get to know their students by creating a student interest inventory, which each student completes. The inventory includes student names, where they are from, their interests, and questions about how they learn. The interns can then use the inventory as a basis for community-building activities. As candidates get to know their students, they can further use this knowledge in designing lessons that build on students' experiences.

Culture and Language as Social Contexts for Development

Alongside and integral to understanding development and learning is understanding the critical role of culture and language in shaping them. This knowledge base provides the foundation for a culturally and linguistically responsive and competent practice, which is a major component of each of the programs we studied. (We discuss the applications of this learning to teaching in a later section.)

The importance of this knowledge base is reflected in how centrally programs treat it. For example, High Tech High's Philosophy of Education course—taken at the beginning of the program—serves as a foundation for preparing students to expand their thinking and beliefs about social inequalities and how they manifest in education systems and impact students. The course challenges interns to "examine their own core beliefs relating to education and diverse communities, and how those beliefs affect student achievement in the classroom."[17] This examination is achieved by discussing and analyzing questions such as, Whom should be educated? What subjects should be taught? Can students be treated differently in order to treat them equally?

The first two courses CU Denver undergraduate and graduate students take are Social Foundations and Cultural Diversity in Urban Education and Co-Developing Culturally Responsive Classroom Communities. These courses set the tone for the entire program. Each of the teacher candidates we met spoke about the dramatic impact these two courses had on their ideas about teaching, and many credited those courses with changing their understanding of society at large and the role of the teacher within it.

The first of these courses

> focuses on the role of cultural diversity in the United States school system and what this means for educators oriented toward social justice. The intention of this course is to have teacher candidates engage in exploring the most salient issues surrounding education in the United States, developing an understanding of the complex relationships between schools and the larger society of which they are a part. This course closely examines . . . issues of race, social class, gender, ethnicity, sexual identity, politics, and the dynamics of power and privilege.[18]

The second course

> investigates how people learn and the implications of social and cultural learning for establishing engaging and culturally responsive learning communities. Through this course teacher candidates will better understand their roles in student learning and how their own cultural lenses impact their relationships with students and families, and influence student success in the classroom. Immersing teacher candidates as learners in experiencing a co-constructed culturally and linguistically responsive classroom community driven by the CREDE Standards framework supports them to develop guiding principles for co-constructing culturally responsive classroom communities.[19]

Focused on identity, culture, white privilege, and social inequality, the courses have an eye-opening impact on the mostly young, white, middle-class students who make up a majority of teacher candidates in the conventional undergraduate and graduate pathways. This focus on developing candidates' critical stance to ameliorate inequity connects to one of the two teaching quality standards that CU Denver has added to the state's list. It reads: "Teachers actively advocate for students, families, and schools to support equity and social justice."

One alum, now teaching at an elementary school just outside of Denver in Aurora, Colorado, reflected on these foundational courses, explaining that many of her peers "hadn't even heard of white privilege," and how the content of the courses and corresponding clinical experiences revealed their own naiveté—a point that would have been "an even bigger shocker once they got in schools." Undergoing deep introspective work such as this can understandably be difficult. Another alum remembered that some of her peers "really struggled to learn about the details of their students' realities outside of school," which led us to ask how they managed to avoid seeing students as victims. Another underscored that the strength of CU Denver's social justice–oriented frame serves to facilitate candidates' ability to acknowledge that "[some] kids are facing an insane amount of trauma, and though it's hard to not feel pity, they are incredibly resilient, and our job is to help [these students] stay focused on the assets they possess—and there are plenty."

We spoke to a current teacher candidate earning her licensure in secondary language arts who told us that she was most moved by one of the first-semester courses that prompted candidates to look at the "dispossession" that happens in most high school curricula where there's a premium put on learning about "dead white guys" and promoting "heteronormativity," which sometimes leads students to "not feel confident in themselves or their communities because white academic culture becomes the 'bar' to aspire to as opposed to seeing value in their own cultures." This candidate went on to explain how this transformative experience encouraged her to find ways to bring in diverse narratives and voices reflective of her students into the classroom via the texts she chooses teach. Another respondent on the CU Denver exit survey stated that the best thing about the program was that it "focused on cultural responsiveness as a growing and important field of education."

Trinity candidates also begin to address issues of cultural competence from the very start of their program. In the summer session they undertake a long-term, multistage assignment that has three objectives—self-exploration, experiences with others, and culturally competent change—designed to give interns the opportunity to deeply examine their own identity and how various institutions of influence shape their interaction with others and the world around them. Though they first dig into these challenging topics before the start of the fall semester, candidates revisit these concepts throughout the year. The project includes the development of multiple representations reflecting the beliefs and values that inform interns' worldviews. It also includes a reflection in which candidates aim to recognize their own biases and how these could impact their personal and professional interactions. Interns are encouraged to raise thoughts and questions that come to mind as they carry out these exercises.

Candidates also write a racial autobiography in which they examine how their own identities have been shaped and think through the intersection of personal identity and teaching and the ways that knowledge of self is essential in teaching for equity and deeper learning. Along with the equity orientation of Trinity's work in developing cultural competence, the programs stress throughout how social justice values, in the form of the awareness of the impact of race on schooling systems, are connected to candidates' explorations of their own and their students' identities.

One of Trinity's school-based mentors reinforced the importance of this work for her own awareness. Noting that her student teacher, Lorraine, is "really good about thinking through the equity piece," she added: "We have quite a diverse population of beliefs, religions, family situations. Whenever she makes a plan, she's always very cognizant of, 'Is this going to include everyone? Is this something everyone can participate in?' Lorraine's very culturally sensitive."

Lorraine's mentor and supervisor both attributed Lorraine's cultural sensitivity and her focus on understanding students' backgrounds to her training at Trinity. As a program leader noted, "It's a thread through Trinity. They study their own racial identity as a means to understand kids who are different." Lorraine's mentor also noted how Trinity's focus on cultural competence had challenged her own teaching, showing the value of co-learning that takes place between mentors and candidates. We further discuss the racial autobiography assignment and the programmatic emphasis on the links between racial identity and social justice teaching in chapter 9.

Many of the other programs also launch their work with a frame that shapes awareness of these issues so that they permeate the consciousness of the candidates as they go through the remainder of the program. For precisely this reason, SFTR candidates in both of the associated university programs take a foundational course on equity during their first summer when they are beginning the program: STEP's Educating for Equity and Democracy, and University of San Francisco's Teaching for Diversity and Social Justice. This STEP course serves from the outset to equip candidates with a lens for identifying who has access to deeper learning, and who does not, and to see themselves as having a responsibility to change that dynamic. Peter Williamson, a former USF professor who played a central role in the design of the SFTR/USF course sequence and now leads STEP's secondary program, described a similar rationale for providing the Teaching for Diversity and Social Justice course to USF residents early in the program:

> It sets a framework for their role as teachers of "other people's children" and also brings some new vocabulary for many of them: discussions of race, class, equity, gender identity, the ways students' identities

foster or squelch

play out in the classroom, the way schools are organized to foster or squelch those identities. These [conversations] have to happen early, in part to set the stage for their engagement in many cases with people who are very different from ourselves. How do we be mindful of those relationships and how our identities are shaping those relationships? That needs to happen before working with children at all, so that's why the course comes early at both universities.

KNOWLEDGE OF SUBJECT MATTER AND CURRICULUM GOALS

Lee Shulman, who is generally credited with having first articulated the idea of pedagogical content knowledge, writes that "teaching begins with a teacher's understanding of what is to be learned and how it is to be taught."[20] Shulman further notes that knowledge of subject matter must be even deeper if the task is to connect what is to be learned to the experiences of many kinds of learners. He asserts, "In the face of student diversity, the teacher must have a flexible and multifaceted comprehension [of subject matter], adequate to impart alternative explanations of the same concepts or principles."[21]

Shulman's assertion captures the task that lies ahead of the candidates—having sufficient depth of knowledge in any given content area, or across multiple areas as is the case for candidates working in elementary schools, to be able to design tasks that allow all learners to demonstrate competency and growth. Such depth of knowledge is essential to deeper learning, making it possible for the teacher to make real-world connections, design multiple entry points into learning experiences, prepare students to tackle complex problems, and make adjustments, within authentic and challenging activities, so that all students are engaged.

In addition to flexible understanding of subject matter, Deborah Ball and David Cohen suggest that content knowledge of teachers should incorporate a discipline's major ideas and modes of inquiry, their connections with real-life events, and the pedagogies most suited to teaching these subject-specific approaches to reasoning and performing.[22] To some extent, all teacher education programs begin where the candidate's many years of learning subject matter in high school or higher education leave off, thereby requiring the preparation program to backfill the gaps in learning or reframe the way that subject matter is understood.

Content and Content Pedagogy

Along with differing experiences with previous classroom cultures, teacher candidates also bring with them content knowledge, and this is vital to

(handwritten margin note: Methods)

their teaching. For postbaccalaureate programs like those at Bank Street, High Tech High, and the Montclair Newark and San Francisco Teacher Residencies, candidates bring this subject-matter knowledge with them from their undergraduate studies, often in the form of a major in the content field, but sometimes warranted by passing a subject-matter test, irrespective of major. The job of teacher education is then to teach pedagogy on top of the subject-matter foundation. In the other programs that are undergraduate or five-year models, there are opportunities to connect the teaching of pedagogy to the study of content; programs take advantage of this opportunity to varying degrees.

LEARNING CONTENT IN SUPPORT OF TEACHING. While public policies have generally assumed that a set of defined content courses or a major in a field constitutes sufficient knowledge for teaching, the kind of content knowledge that supports good teaching may, in some cases, be different from that represented by a college major. For example, Liping Ma's research on how teachers in China become expert teachers of elementary mathematics describes how teacher preparation is focused on giving them a richer, more pedagogically oriented understanding of the elementary subject matter they will teach (called "profound understanding of fundamental mathematics"), rather than the kind of upper-level math courses represented in a college major, none of which will ever be the basis of their actual teaching.[23] From the Chinese perspective, "more mathematics" is not a sufficient prescription for content preparation; it is mathematics knowledge related to teaching that counts; that is, pedagogical content knowledge. According to Shulman, pedagogical content knowledge includes

> the most regularly taught topics in one's subject area, the most useful forms of representations of those ideas, the most powerful analogies, illustrations, examples, explanations, and demonstrations—in a word, ways of representing and formulating the subject that make it comprehensible to others. Pedagogical content knowledge also includes an understanding of what makes the learning of specific topics easy or difficult; the conceptions and preconceptions that students of different ages and backgrounds bring with them to the learning of those most frequently taught topics and lessons.[24]

Unlike many programs in the past, which largely ignored the challenges of subject matter by not treating it at all, or by requiring a single generic methods course, all of the programs we studied focus considerable attention on developing this kind of pedagogical content knowledge—and in the process refining and strengthening candidates' flexible and deep understanding of the disciplines they plan to teach. The programs approach content and pedagogy together, ensuring that candidates revisit their understanding of content more deeply with curriculum goals and knowledge of how children learn and develop in mind.

Each content area is a source of deep study, as teachers learn to create learning experiences that enable students to apply and transfer content knowledge to novel and complex problems. For example, as part of its curriculum and inquiry coursework, Bank Street requires candidates to complete:

- one course on science curriculum and methods
- one course on mathematics curriculum and methods
- one course on art curriculum and methods
- a series of two courses on reading and language curriculum and methods
- a series of two courses on geography and social studies curriculum and methods

While these content-specific methods courses emphasize pedagogy and inquiry, they also require candidates to examine students' developmental and social needs in subject-specific contexts. For example, Mathematics for Teachers in Diverse and Inclusive Education Settings explores the mathematics teachers will ultimately teach, seeking the "profound understanding of fundamental mathematics" that Chinese teacher education undertakes. The course uses "theories of development . . . as a basis for designing age-appropriate curriculum" and "explore[s] the range of alternate strategies used by learners to compensate for learning disabilities."[25] These content-specific courses introduce candidates to the theories and pedagogical approaches that will help them create challenging learning experiences to help students engage in critical thinking and project-based activities.

Other subject-matter courses include choices among three different Science for Teachers courses, taught either at the college or at a science center at Harriman State Park about twenty-five miles outside New York City, also cited as useful for their hands-on quality and support for curriculum building. Graduates and current students have described Music and Movement as a course that made them aware of the public nature of teaching and of the need to help children bring their rhythms, histories, and traditions into the classroom. Art Workshop for Teachers and Music and Movement are often cited by graduates as courses where they learned to teach for multiple intelligences and developed a larger teaching and assessment repertoire. Some graduates mentioned that in the art course they had learned to talk to children seriously about their work and about their ideas for representing the world. The recurrence of strategies across courses is often seen as especially powerful. For example, one beginning teacher noted of the many courses she profited from:

> What's nice about Bank Street is that their philosophy is so consistent. And so you really can cull things from each course. For example, in art I really learned how to talk to kids about their work. You don't just give a statement like "I like it," and you don't jump to conclusions about what the child can do, but you comment on what is actually there. And that helped me learn to talk to kids.

Candidates also select from five different two-class series about teaching social studies in early childhood, elementary, or middle school grades. One example of the early childhood social studies classes is Curriculum in Early Childhood Education: Developing Learning Environments and Experiences for Children in Diverse Backgrounds and Abilities, where students use "social studies as the core of an integrated curriculum" to "examine the questions and issues that arise in creating social and learning environments."[26] In the elementary and middle school grades, courses like Social Studies Curriculum Development for Inclusive and Special Education Settings support students in integrating "knowledge from the six disciplines of social studies: history, anthropology, sociology, political science, geography and economics into the design of a constructivist, inquiry-based social studies curriculum."[27] These courses aim to help candidates understand how they can motivate students to learn how to care for themselves and their broader communities, while cultivating students' interests in civically engaging in their communities to advance just, democratic ideals.

CONTENT PEDAGOGY FOR DEEPER LEARNING.   All of the programs squarely confront the challenge of learning to teach for deeper learning—that is, learning to teach content using pedagogies that candidates themselves may not have experienced. Across programs, the teaching methods courses include activities and assignments that help students experience deeper learning strategies as well as understand how these respond to contemporary theories of learning and development and how to apply them to their own classrooms.

> At SFTR, for example, candidates enter the program already possessing a BA and having been selected because they have a strong academic background in the subject(s) they will teach. Beyond this, though, both Stanford and USF offer candidates a yearlong, content-specific curriculum and instruction (C&I) course sequence offering deep content-specific pedagogical training that—in the words of a faculty member who has taught in both programs—"helps anchor [residents'] practice and make sense of theory and practice in action that lasts over the course of the program." Professors and other instructors in these C&I courses are deeply knowledgeable about their discipline as well as how to teach it, having been expert classroom teachers themselves before becoming teacher educators. Across content areas, "all of the C&I courses illustrate inquiry practices—like learning to think like a historian in social studies. It is important that the first experiences candidates have [in their C&I courses] are illustrative of what we want them to do."

Another faculty member described the arc of the yearlong C&I sequence at STEP:[28]

> In each of the content areas, candidates first take up [some basic questions]: Why learn science? Why learn mathematics? What is it about the nature of the learning you get that would be valuable? In this way, they engage with the discipline. Then, by winter, they learn strategies for developing lesson plans and then larger curriculum units. . . . They learn to think about curriculum in the broad sense: How do I help my students get from here to there? We teach them how to map backwards. By spring, when candidates are doing their teacher performance assessment, they have internalized the routine of: How do I plan it? How do I teach it? How do I reflect on student learning?

A common strategy in the content courses is to take up issues of content pedagogy by engaging candidates in the kinds of activities and inquiries they will later do with their students. They use these opportunities to explore thinking and problem solving in the discipline and to acquire a much deeper understanding of how to represent the content so that learners can make connections with their own prior knowledge and experiences.

CU Denver faculty routinely model deeper learning pedagogy in their teacher preparation courses. They also routinely name the strategies they are using, explaining why they are powerful, and suggesting how they can be used in K–12 classrooms. To do this well, faculty often pause at critical junctures to specifically alert candidates to the ways they have organized a lesson, structured questions, or designed groups to accomplish the learning objectives. This explicit transparency in teaching provides rich opportunities for candidates to unpack why and how they might be able to transfer their learning from the university classroom to their K–12 clinical classrooms. In some instances, the university instructors engage teacher candidates in full lessons, from beginning to end, that the candidates could then use in their classrooms the very next day.

This transparent learning process parallels the "experience-reflect-implement-reflect" approach that candidates are expected to use as they learn to teach. When faculty model and name their teaching for deeper learning, candidates have a learning experience, reflect on how it feels to be a learner, visualize their own implementation of the approach as teachers, and then reflect on the effectiveness of that strategy for determining what they need to do next, as a teacher, to ensure student learning takes place. The experience-reflect-implement-reflect approach to building candidates' instructional chops allows candidates to unlock the "black box" of teaching such that they can begin to anticipate how students will experience their approach to content delivery.

Teacher candidates we spoke to universally agreed that the modeling CU Denver faculty engage in is perhaps one of the most useful ways to learn, because the candidates can "feel what it's like to experience a lesson as if they are the students themselves." One alum, now an elementary teacher, explained that upon entry to the program his understanding of basic math properties and content was tenuous: "I thought I always had a growth mind-set about everything, except that I thought I wasn't a mathematical learner. But my methods class made me feel like 'Hey, I can learn this math, and it's open to me.' Ironically, now I primarily teach math!"

Notably, some teacher candidates serve as apprentice researchers in faculty research investigating how K–12 students acquire their content knowledge—a remarkable opportunity to have a deeper learning experience in the subject matter they will be teaching.

Literacy Across the Curriculum

Most of the programs, both secondary and elementary, provide in-depth coverage of literacy, including reading and writing, in addition to the content area(s) the teacher may otherwise teach. At Bank Street, in courses such as The Teaching of Reading, Writing and Language Arts and Teaching Reading and Writing in the Content Areas, students keep reading logs, examine different methodologies, and learn about assessment. A first-year teacher told us how Reading and Writing in the Content Areas included English as a Second Language strategies that help her in her multilingual classroom. She has found she must constantly assess whether children's difficulties arise from not knowing concepts in math or other subject areas or from not comprehending the English language in the texts. Using strategies from the class, she discovered how to better understand student needs by reading through math problems or science directions in the group rather than alone, in order to assess if they need more help in the subject or in understanding the language of the problem or its related instructions.

Similarly, at Trinity, candidates learn about teaching reading and writing across the curriculum with an emphasis on how to teach reading and writing to students at varying age levels with a variety of learning differences. Candidates also learn how to use formal and informal assessment instruments, including collecting and organizing their own information about each individual student's reading and writing, to inform reading instruction and reflect upon their practice. In both courses, candidates learn about guided reading, conditions for learning, differential instruction, and analyzing and interpreting results of assessments for effective and differentiated instruction and intervention, among other things. These courses enable teachers to design engaging deeper learning experiences based on students' diverse levels of knowledge and development, and attuned to their progress through assessment, so as to allow all students to access deep and more rigorous curriculum.

The deeply developmental approach to teaching content, including literacy, was clear in this description by one candidate of the work she did in a class called Teaching Reading to the Middle Grades:

> It was really helpful to think about different strategies that we can use in a reading classroom to help bridge the gap, because reading is one of those things when you get a group of eighth-grade students, some are reading at a tenth-grade level and some are reading at a second-grade level, and you never really know what you're going to get. There's a lot of developmental thinking. I think one of the things that we have been working on in class that helped me particularly . . . [was that] we have been building a developmental timeline of what goes on. All the interns contribute knowledge. We do it in one class--our pedagogy

class. All the interns contribute their knowledge of students and what they've seen in their different observations, and we've come up with this timeline that literally spans sixth grade to twelfth grade, which is a really helpful resource to go back and refresh yourself on where these kids are coming from and where they're headed.

Intensive attention to content pedagogy for literacy instruction also takes place at High Tech High, in part because of the strong literacy skills needed for project-based learning. Thus, a number of the courses are dedicated to focusing on instructional design; setting up and organizing a standards-based reading program; and strategies and practices such as groupings, class arrangements, and individualized reading. One of the methods courses that focuses on beginning reading instruction provides candidates with instruction and experience in developing skills that promote fluent reading (phonemic awareness, phonics, spelling patterns, decoding strategies), comprehension (analysis of text structure, summarizing, questioning and making inferences), and the use of a variety of whole-class, small-group, and individualized instructional approaches.

Curriculum Design

In the history of teaching in the United States, a gigantic arm wrestle has taken place. Are teachers professionals who must bring subject-matter knowledge and knowledge of learning and development to bear in meeting the needs of their students? Or, are teachers bureaucrats who implement learning designs created by others—textbooks, curriculum packages, testing protocols—to be applied in a standardized manner to the students in their classes? The latter view assumes that students are standardized, teaching is routine, and the work of schools is largely context-free, so teachers do not need to know much about learning, development, or curriculum to be successful.

The programs we studied, however, understand that effective teaching is responsive to learners and that the learning process is embedded in the linguistic, cultural, and developmental experiences of students. Furthermore, meeting these needs depends on knowing how to take them into account while undertaking a purposeful journey toward clear curriculum goals that produce deep understanding of subject matter for students. Central to their ability to engage diverse students in this kind of learning is an understanding of curriculum design and skill in developing lessons and units of instruction that can achieve worthwhile learning objectives—something that is missing entirely from some conceptions of learning to teach subject matter.

Interestingly, most of the programs use a common framework for curriculum design—the Understanding by Design (UbD) framework developed by Grant Wiggins and Jay McTighe to support teaching and assessing for understanding.[29] In this framework, the design mind-set starts with the selection of goals and then designs curricula to attain those goals. It requires working backwards from what students should know and be able to do in a particular subject, to help teachers think, first, about curriculum goals; then about rich assessments that represent accomplishment of those goals; then about a process of formative assessments and teaching/learning activities that lead students to an ability to meet those goals.

Trinity provides a good example of how UbD is used to support the school's emphasis on inquiry and knowledge of content, self, and students, all key elements of deeper learning where content knowledge is applied to practical settings and taught for conceptual understanding. Trinity candidates and graduates alike noted the importance of the training they receive in the UbD approach and how it allows them to connect content standards to deeper, more relevant concepts in the real world and to teach students to "synthesize massive amounts of information." Candidates learn to use the essential questions to drive what they want to accomplish in their classes with their students. The UbD approach also forces candidates to consider what it means for students to be "really engaged in content and learning"; this relevancy is built into the UbD template, because candidates have to form essential questions, which are meant to stimulate inquiry and further questions, as the first act of lesson planning.

During the summer, candidates work in teams to design a UbD unit. Elementary candidates have the option of designing one of three different UbD units for use at one of the elementary PDS sites: a two-week UbD unit to establish a classroom learning community that helps a new group of students develop collective identity and establishes safe/supportive conditions for learning; a two-week unit focused on family, based on the kindergarten TEKS (Texas Essential Knowledge and Skills); or a ten-session UbD unit to be used with fourth graders centered on a growth mind-set, a focus at Lamar Elementary, one of the PDS sites. These units, as with other summer assignments, are not intended to be merely theoretical in nature: they introduce candidates to the UbD process and also give them practical experience in looking at district curriculum guidelines and making professional decisions regarding how those guidelines should be addressed so that students will learn the content deeply. The development of the unit and the reflective essay that candidates write regarding what they learned in planning the unit serve as performance assessments for the MAT summer courses.

Secondary candidates also use the UbD approach, working in teams to design an interdisciplinary thematic curriculum unit that can be taught at the secondary level at one of the PDS middle or high school sites. The teams, which are assigned by grade level, start by identifying a theme and "big questions that need to be considered and what students should know and understand 10 years from now." Secondary candidates described their UbD assignment as "one of those big units, where we are learning deeply." Among the units they designed were one on the rumblings of revolution, focusing on how music and art help develop identity during revolutionary war; another combining Chinese, English, history, and music to celebrate East Asian culture during the Chinese New Year; and a third, developed by a ninth-grade team of English, biology, and Spanish teachers, designed to identify and explore what it means to be from from a particular place and how language forms identity. Some of the units were implemented and the strongest ones are included in Trinity's library of UbD units.

Most important, candidates valued the assignment because it allowed them to "dream big." As one secondary candidate reflected, "We need a reminder of the possibility of things we can do and not be grounded by the restrictions set by our standards." Similarly, another noted, "The interdisciplinary project over summer was an example of the way that the MAT program teaches us to think big toward the ideal." They noted also that the assignment "helps us be aware and seek out other content areas as we plan to make learning more meaningful and engaging." In fact, candidates realized that interdisciplinary projects provide students an opportunity to learn and grow through content that is interesting to them, while also allowing candidates to incorporate learning experiences outside their content areas.

Secondary mentors noted that candidates learn to differentiate through the UbD approach; when they design a lesson using UbD, they have to catalog students' interest and determine whether students need specific modifications.

This approach to designing and then teaching curriculum units is used across the programs. Candidates typically then receive feedback on their work, both on paper and in the classroom, and reflect on the evidence of student learning from that unit as part of the refinement of their craft. In most of the programs, candidates must also demonstrate a more modest level of curriculum design capacity as part of a performance assessment before they graduate. (See chapter 11 for further discussion.)

As programs seek to develop curricular thinking on the part of their candidates, they often focus on areas that are difficult to teach and learn. For example, many teachers have difficulty asking higher-order questions in the classroom and end up asking students to simply recite factual answers rather than think deeply and critically about the content they are learning. As a consequence, Alverno requires students to list in their lesson plans all the questions they plan to ask their students. This scripting of questions becomes an opportunity to think and learn about question-asking. It helps candidates realize which questions elicit student responses that demonstrate learning or moments of misunderstanding. Candidates must also clearly articulate in their lesson plan the evidence they will seek to determine whether and what their students learned. A faculty member explained, "We know they won't do this [depth] of planning when the classroom is theirs, but they will do this type of thinking. So, we're really having them practice doing the kind of thinking that they will do when the classroom is theirs."

KNOWLEDGE OF TEACHING

The third dimension identified in the National Academy report as core to what teachers need to know is an understanding of *teaching* in light of the content and learners to be taught, as informed by assessment and supported by a productive classroom environment. Above we described how the programs develop content knowledge and content pedagogical skills. In this section, we describe how these are supported by knowledge of how to reach students, organize instruction, and promote learning. The programs we studied seek to ensure that their candidates acquire this knowledge in ways that build their capacity to teach for deeper learning in diverse classrooms and in communities of concentrated poverty. As described in the sections that follow, particular emphasis is placed on using assessment to support learning; creating classroom learning communities that help students develop social and emotional, as well as cognitive skills; learning to differentiate instruction to accommodate students' needs; and developing culturally and linguistically responsive pedagogies and other equitable practices.

Assessment of, as, and for Learning

Creating a student-centered curricular vision that leads to deeper learning requires also developing both rich and authentic performance tasks that allow students to demonstrate their knowledge and skills and many formative tools to understand what students are thinking and learning along the way. In the programs we studied, candidates are taught to develop performance tasks for their students; they also engage in such tasks themselves, assessed using rubrics that describe the dimensions of performance. Candidates have the chance to discuss what it means to meet levels of performance, as well as how to have the same kinds of conversations with their students.

Students at Montclair State, for example, receive extensive opportunities to learn about the range and scope of student assessments in dedicated courses such as Content Integration and Assessment in Early Childhood Classrooms or Assessment for Learning in the undergraduate pathway, and embedded across courses such as Teaching and Learning I and II in the graduate pathway. The curriculum covers the range of assessments, from formative to summative, including all forms of assessments from project-based assessments and more traditional "test" assessments.

As at several other programs, the emphasis on backwards planning with a focus on "beginning with the end in mind"—what students should know and be able to do at the end of a learning unit—is an important part of the teacher preparation at Montclair State. One faculty member identified *Understanding by Design* as a core text for teaching her students about assessments.[30] Backwards planning helps teacher candidates to understand the ideas of scope and sequence for planning and instruction. Additionally, backwards planning ensures that assessments are meaningful, relevant, and well aligned to the knowledge and skills that teachers want students to learn. This faculty member explained:

> We try to help them match their assessments to their learning goals and student needs. [It's] a massive feedback loop. We do some reading, we discuss a concept, and we ask them to create [an assessment]. Then they share out and workshop it in their classroom and get feedback, revise and resubmit. And they can resubmit as many times as they want.

This deeper learning strategy of reading and analyzing theory, applying the theory to a project, and then utilizing it in field placement with time for reflection and revision is a common form of learning that Montclair State candidates experience in their preparation, and it exemplifies learning that is applied and transferred. It models the learning cycle they are expected to design for their students.

Another faculty member highlighted how she focuses on helping students understand authentic assessments:

> We spend a lot of time thinking about "What does it really mean to have an authentic assessment?" and then they have to design an

authentic assessment, and/or a performance-based assessment—because for some, like in P.E., or music or art, it makes more sense sometimes to think about performance . . . they have to map back each assessment to a learning goal. . . . [T]hey have to say what assessment works for which piece of knowledge, which piece of understanding, which piece of skill. . . . There should be enough assessments, and a variety of assessments, that all of those [aspects of knowledge and understanding] are being assessed; . . .otherwise there's no point in having them.

When students submit their assessments for evaluation, they are pushed to think of ways to revise them, with faculty asking question such as, How do you shift the assessment to be more authentic? The faculty member also explained that the idea is to have students understand that "authentic" falls along a continuum, so they can work to have more authenticity in their assessments. The whole concept of authentic assessments exemplifies learning that is contextualized. Assessments can only be authentic when they are relevant to students' lives and link their experiences to the knowledge and skills being taught by their teacher.

The deep focus on assessment was commented on by current teacher candidates and alumni alike. One graduate laughingly explained in a focus group, "We assessed assessments." He went on to explain the extensive process by which they practiced assessing student learning:

It was a process where you evaluate everything you taught leading up to an assessment; you evaluate what is the purpose behind every single question on the assessment. Then you interview a few students and probe them on their thought process while answering the questions. And then you reflect and revise that assessment for the next time you offer it, if you even choose to offer it.

When asked what types of probing questions they asked students, this same graduate shared, "We . . . ask the kids to be metacognitive: How did it go? Did you find it easy, difficult? Was there any question that felt out of the ordinary? Things like that." In this way, Montclair candidates are learning not only how to assess student learning, but also how to develop students' metacognition and understanding of their own learning process.

An important part of backwards planning and assessing student learning is knowledge of the learner—prior knowledge and skills, knowledge of child or adolescent development, understanding students' backgrounds and experiences and likes and interests—all of these elements allow teachers to backwards map learning from goals that are rigorous and appropriate for their students, and they are a part of the teacher preparation at MSU.

Alverno takes a similar approach, emphasizing authentic, performance-based assessments for candidates, who model the process of assessment for learning that Alverno aims to instill in its teachers. Teacher candidates are assessed in their coursework and fieldwork frequently through performance-based tasks, portfolios, and self-reflections. Candidates are never given a standardized test or a letter grade.

Two current Alverno candidates described how the experiences in their coursework and fieldwork contribute to their ability to assess students. The first noted:

> I think one of the things that helps us to learn how to assess students is that we get assessed in numerous different ways. So we don't, ourselves . . . get assessed with just paper tests. We get assessed through speaking and through observations and through talking with our professors and [through] projects and group projects. I think that, too, just shows the real world, so we want to prepare students for the real world. We're getting graded and assessed that way.

The second replied:

> Right. They're not going to go out in the real world and be like . . . in their job, "Oh, you get an A for the day." No, they're going to get complimented on what they did well and [counseled on] areas that they need to improve on. So I think [of] assessments in the way of not just a letter grade, or percentages, but as positive feedback and what they need to continue to work on.

Faculty not only model the content and form for instruction and assessment, but also the dispositions teachers must adopt to create a high-achieving and supportive learning environment. For example, multiple Alverno graduates explained that the expectation is that candidates earn what would be an A at most other institutions, and that anything less requires candidates to improve their work. This expectation helps teacher candidates develop mastery and internal motivation to learn because it changes the focus from a letter grade to the mastery of a skill that will have real-world implications.

Alverno's approach to assessment illustrates the interconnectedness between the authentic, project-based activities and assessments, and ensuring that candidates are learning and accountable for their learning:

> Assessment for us, in its broadest sense, is evaluation of student learning outcomes on the basis of criteria for the sake of improvement and accountability. When applied to individual student learning, it means a process integral to learning that involves observation, analysis/interpretation, and judgment of each student's performance on the basis of explicit, public criteria, with resulting feedback to the student.[31]

Teacher candidates learn about assessing critical thinking and problem-solving skills through Alverno's articulation of the goals and means of assessment and through candidates' participation in this type of assessment as students in Alverno courses and fieldwork.

Alverno's holistic approach to assessment appears to contribute to graduates' knowledge and effectiveness at evaluating student learning. In our survey of candidates graduating from the program, 100 percent reported that Alverno prepared them very well to "use a variety of assessments, including observations, papers, portfolios, or performance tasks to determine strengths and needs to inform instruction."[32] As one candidate noted:

> We've learned about so many different types of assessments, like performance-based assessments, written assessments, worksheets that students do, things like that. And then you get to go out and try those assessments in the classroom and see what the students take to. And then you have this whole back pocket full of assessment techniques and you have to go deeper and analyze why your assessment worked, the data you collected from it, and how it can help you to teach what the students are ready to learn next.

This candidate understands that assessment is not simply the gathering of data about student learning, but the use of the information to inform subsequent teaching.

Similarly, Bank Street teacher candidates are assessed in several ways—formally and informally, formatively and summatively. Primary assessment tools include collaborative projects, course assignments connecting to field experiences, papers and reflective essays, artistic projects, conversations with instructors, and authentic performance assessments. Similarly, Bank Street encourages its graduates to rely on a plethora of assessment tools, particularly those that are authentic and contextually embedded, in working to support their own students.

There is particular emphasis on getting teachers to think carefully about what they are trying to assess and how they can use the information to improve instruction. As one candidate noted:

> There's a vehicle for assessment and the material you're assessing, making sure that you understand the difference between those when you're giving an assessment. And if you're trying to figure out whether [students] know multiplication facts, you're going to assess that differently as opposed to if you're trying to see how many they can get done in five minutes. . . . It's not about right and wrong answers, but instead can [students] provide the right answers for the right reasons and can I understand [their] thinking.

This prospective teacher highlighted three important points. First, she has learned about the necessity of articulating clear instructional goals and using those goals to inform the form and substance of her assessment. Second, she wants her students to value the learning process more than the outcome. This is a hallmark of deeper learning because developing strategies for solving problems will support students in addressing future challenges, whereas focusing on the correct answer to one discrete multiplication problem may not have as much future utility. Finally, she designs assessments to inform her own understanding of students' thinking, which allows her to better plan her teaching in support of their learning.

Using assessments to more deeply understand student thinking is a goal of all the programs—including the identification of misconceptions and preconceptions so they can be addressed by teaching. Learning to look and listen closely to students is also part of assessment. As an elementary mentor for Trinity explained, her candidates assess students in small groups, practicing both preassessment and formative assessment, before proceeding to whole-group assessments. Formative assessments as young as kindergarten may include interviewing students, listening to and observing them carefully, recording information and questions about their performance, and asking them to draw what they are thinking.

Another elementary mentor talked about how to develop the skills and reflective dispositions for formative assessment:

At the end of the day, in that time when we're reflecting, in the beginning I would talk of my observational assessment of my lesson and then as she [the teacher candidate] would teach, it was, "What did you notice? Who got it? Who didn't?" I would do it and then she would do it. Through that I watched her grow so much in seeing little things because in the beginning it was up to me to see and know, and then as I passed the torch, she had to adjust her own lessons based on the ongoing assessment of the kids and how they were doing.

At Trinity, candidates also practice a form of goal-based, reflective assessment they can carry into their classrooms by completing two self-assessments. They assess their performance against the program's six standards, noting how they've grown and where they want to continue to develop. They also complete a dispositional assessment that addresses six criteria for professional work in educational settings. After reflecting on the self-assessment and feedback from peers and faculty, candidates write a written reflection in which they prioritize three goals they have for growth—one academic goal, one professional goal, and one goal addressing collegial growth. They develop a visual to remind them of their vision and goal and share the visual with their mentor and with the members of the cohort, helping them experience the power of structured reflection and self-assessment they will bring to their own students as well.

Differentiating and Personalizing Instruction

As candidates learn to plan and assess curriculum around the demands of the content and their knowledge of learning, they also learn to plan and implement personalized approaches that meet the distinctive needs of students. The programs emphasize helping candidates learn how to differentiate their teaching in response to students' differences. Trinity's strong programmatic focus on differentiation, for example, pervades every aspect of candidates' experience. As one candidate explained:

There's a focus on differentiated instruction both in our classes at Trinity and in what's required when we're writing our first lesson plans, whether it's identifying differentiated instruction for kids who have a 504 and IEP, or other kids who might benefit from differentiated instruction. It's also the nature of the campuses we're at. We're at PDS campuses, so that puts us in situations where we're able to get support on campus for that type of instruction and group-based instruction, campuses that actually work with their teachers to train them for that type of instruction. It wasn't like we were just learning this at Trinity, but we are also at campuses that are supportive of that type of instruction.

Differentiation is at the core of lesson planning for deeper learning. Thinking about each individual child and his or her special learning needs makes for the personalization that supports deeper learning, while drawing on learners' own funds of knowledge to facilitate the construction of new knowledge. One of the mentors noted that differentiation is an important means to achieve a more equitable classroom:

> Planning for differentiation—that's a big piece. When we do lay out our scope and sequence, I think that's a big piece of laying groundwork before you can take it to the next level. So planning for differentiation around the needs of the kids, and that comes through preassessment, and formative assessment, all the way around. . . . And then not only planning for differentiation, but also planning for that need to build background knowledge. In this environment, our assumptions aren't always in line with what kids actually bring to the table as far as background knowledge is concerned. We talk a lot about that.

At Alverno, in addition to courses on child development, faculty develop candidates' capacity to meet diverse students' needs through both coursework and assessments. The Adaptive Teacher Performance Assessment in the undergraduate course Exceptional Learner requires candidates to identify one learner from their fieldwork and answer the question, "Who is the learner?" Teacher candidates identify a learner's strengths, weaknesses, and characteristics that should be considered in each lesson for the learner. Next, candidates review a lesson and the elements of the lesson that the instructor needs to adjust for the learner to be successful, but also challenged by the lesson. After that, candidates teach the lesson, with the learner in the classroom. The final phase of the assignment is to have the candidates reflect on their lessons.

The experience of focusing on an individual learner helps candidates learn how to structure educational opportunities for an individual student. This can then be transferred to how to structure opportunities for entire classes that are likely to include diverse students with a range of knowledge, skills, and social abilities. As one Alverno student explained about her experiences in the program:

With every lesson we do, we're always figuring out accommodations we can create to differentiate our instruction because we know we have diverse learners. And learning how to help our students that might be English language learners, help our students who are struggling, help our students who are gifted and talented . . . they make us think of those things with a lot of questioning . . . Our teachers have helped us with that and [with] figuring out where I can take my lesson, or how I can modify it for them.

Teacher candidates also learn how to prepare for and convene an Individualized Education Plan (IEP). One way they do this is through a mock IEP meeting where their classmates each have roles (e.g., parent, teacher, administrator, attorney) to reflect the political, educational, and personal elements of an IEP meeting. In our survey of students who were in the last semester of Alverno's undergraduate and graduate preparation program in the spring of 2016, 100 percent said that they felt well prepared to identify and address special learning needs with appropriate teaching strategies and understood how factors in students' environment outside of school may influence their life and learning.

Like instructors at the other programs, Montclair faculty feel it is not enough to simply know students and where they come from, although this is an important step in understanding their lives, experiences, and assets. This knowledge of students must be translated into planning, instruction, and assessment. A Newark Montclair candidate now leading her class during student teaching noted that differentiation was a key part of her program that supported her success: "The dual degree/dual certification program in special education has really trained us well in relating things to how we differentiate our materials for our students. I know that, [as I am] putting it into practice now that I'm in Newark. If I didn't have those skills I would really struggle to meet the needs of my students."

Differentiating does not mean watering down instruction or avoiding approaches that require critical thinking and sophisticated analysis and discussion. It does mean both thoughtful scaffolding for activities, and opportunities to practice and revise in order to improve.

Culturally and Linguistically Responsive Pedagogy

In all of the programs, we heard about the importance of designing curriculum, teaching specific instructional approaches, modeling practices, and assessing learning in ways that take into account the diverse experiences of students. (See chapter 4 for a more extensive discussion of modeling as a strategy in these programs and chapter 9 for an elaboration of teaching across differences as an equity strategy.)

For example, in the USF Learning and Teaching course, part of the San Francisco Teacher Residency program, residents are challenged to make learning relevant to students by knowing what they bring to classrooms in terms of background and culture, and then designing curriculum that flows from that. In one activity, residents watched *Precious Knowledge,* a documentary film describing the controversy over the Ethnic Studies program at Tucson High School in Arizona, in particular the Raza Studies part of the program, focused on Mexican American culture and heritage. "Precious knowledge" refers to knowledge and love of self. After viewing the documentary, the class did a Skype call with Curtis Acosta, a former teacher from Arizona who has been involved in teaching the Ethnic Studies program, pushing back on the passage of HB 2281 (Arizona's law banning ethnic studies classes), and expanding the teaching of ethnic studies to other states and districts. Residents had the opportunity to hear, from a firsthand source, what had happened in Arizona since the documentary, and to ask Mr. Acosta for advice on bringing "precious knowledge" into their schools in San Francisco.

A resident described watching the video and speaking with Mr. Acosta as being among one of the most "powerful" lessons in the Teaching and Learning class. Through this lesson, residents learned about the importance of designing curriculum that is relevant to their students' lives in order to more deeply engage students and promote greater academic success. It was highly relevant to SFUSD's particular context, as recent research on a pilot ethnic studies program in the district highlighted the success of these courses for improving students' academic achievement and attendance, and the district has now expanded these courses to all of its high schools.[33] But the lesson also modeled for residents deeper learning practices—sharing this content through direct interaction with a firsthand source from the film.

High Tech High's summer session before placements begin also includes topics such as equity, cultural diversity, and English learners. Interns are expected to "acquire and become familiar with strategies and best practices to develop differentiated lessons and instructional sequences that are appropriate for individuals with diverse strengths and in a variety of educational environments."[34] Assignments include designing lessons or activities that will promote equity in classroom learning. High Tech High candidates also take a required six-week online course, Foundations of English Language Development, before they can become a teacher of record for English language learners.

All of the programs included courses to enable teachers to work effectively with new English learners. For example, as in several other programs, the University of San Francisco's Education of Bilingual Children course, which is part of SFTR, helps candidates learn in part by putting them in the role of English learners. One SFTR resident described how teacher candidates learned from the instructor's modeling:

> She [the instructor] gave us all, based on our ability to communicate, a CELDT [California English Language Development Test] score, and organized us strategically in the room based on our CELDT scores. I was around a bunch of CELDT 1–2s, presuming the CELDT score was for Spanish, and so she did a literacy lesson around a book in Spanish, probably a first-grade book, and it was basically about how bilingualism is great, you can communicate a lot of different things. But she just modeled a book walk and modeled how to use peer relationships, how to leverage them, and how to normalize those types of interactions in a really authentic way.

Another resident added:

> Throughout the course, she also did other activities such as the Dictogloss. There were all these strategies and activities, direct models that you could participate in. [Dictogloss] is when you read aloud a text and write down everything that you heard from the text, listen to it three times, and reconstruct the text with a partner or with more people.

In the Dictogloss activity, residents learn by doing a language-teaching technique drawn from the work of Pauline Gibbons. As the course proceeds, it moves generally from more abstract and theoretical topics to more concrete methods to put into practice. After talking about language development, the activity gives residents the opportunity to see this strategy at work by experiencing it themselves. In doing so, residents experience the power of collaboration and group work. As the course instructor describes the activity:

> From the perspective of language development that I believe in, language is socially constructed. We should be developing our language with one another. This is an activity where I take a piece of text and read it out loud to them and they just have to listen, and I read it again to them and they have to listen again, and then I read it a third time

and while they're listening they have to write down as much as they can. They aren't going for exact wording, they're supposed to be writing it down for ideas, the main ideas of the text. After that, they meet with an individual and the two of them have to try and reconstruct the text. And after the two of them have reconstructed the text, they go and meet with another pair and the four of them reconstruct the text—so there are all these levels of collaboration that have to happen and, at the end, they have a reconstructed text. And then we have these texts on the wall that we can then look at and analyze as a group. My philosophy about everything we do in the class is I want them to experience it, and we reflect on it as learners and then we reflect on it as teachers teaching this particular population of students. So, we look at all of the activities on two levels.

Another such assignment that is a part of this class and the parallel STEP course is the inquiry about an English learner project, a demanding assignment that counts for a large share of the course grade. The instructor described the value of this assignment:

> The residents do a focal student assignment where they identify an English language learner in their classroom, and they do a series of assignments focused on this one student. I describe it to them as an inverted triangle: they're going to start big with big ideas around context and background and the school, and then over the course of the whole assignment they're going to narrow it down and eventually get to specific instructions for the language needs of the specific student. In that class, in the beginning it doesn't necessarily feel particularly impactful, but in the end, I virtually always hear that it's very helpful to look very closely at one student and their language. I have them collect language samples on that student and have them do an analysis of their language.

Data collection includes field notes, interviews, pictures, maps, and recordings. Residents describe the focal student, his or her school, the classroom environment and experience, and written and oral language samples. They must also modify a lesson to include scaffolds to address the focal student's language development needs, and link their own language use and their work with English learners. Similar to the STEP Adolescent Development project focusing on a single student, this assignment enables residents to develop a deep understanding of a single student—including the child's community context and linguistic development—which in turn enables the resident to appropriately differentiate and scaffold learning experiences to meet the student's needs. In this way, the course provides deeper learning opportunities for the teacher candidates, allowing them to go deep in linking theory with their observations of students as well as their actual teaching.

The strategies that residents learn for working with English learners transfer to other parts of their practice as well, as one resident described to us: "In that class I felt like a lot of the EL strategies she teaches us to use with EL students are also super helpful just in general with elementary students, in how to make things really explicit and make it so that they are all understanding and are able to develop those ideas."

Beyond developing culturally and linguistically supportive practices within their classrooms, the programs we studied seek to enable their candidates to become proactive change agents in achieving a more equitable and socially just context within their schools and communities—and enabling their students to develop agency in recognizing and confronting issues of inequality themselves. Equitable and socially just learning necessitates that teachers understand how race, class, and other social identifiers shape their students and their experiences. In addition, teachers must consider students' unique identities as strengths and resources, and then develop supportive learning opportunities that acknowledge and incorporate the variety of students' traditions and experiences. In this way, teachers link social justice values to principles of learning and development by working explicitly to ensure that all students are supported. We return to this element of the programs in chapter 9.

We noted earlier that several programs initiate this conversation at the beginning of their programs, to create a pervasive awareness and attentiveness to these issues. After the first courses on cultural responsiveness at CU Denver, the rest of the program—the pedagogy courses, the subject-matter methods courses, and the clinical placements—aim to give candidates skills to build on their students' personal and cultural assets as well as to combat the harms brought by inequality and exclusion in their students' lives. All of the four essential questions CU Denver uses to create coherence across its five pathways (see chapter 2) take up the issues of how to create inclusive, responsive learning opportunities and advocate for children in the cause of social justice and equity.

These questions are brought to bear on all of the candidates' experiences in becoming an urban educator. For example, some teacher candidates experience lockdowns and/or violence quite close to where they are placed for their field experiences. CU Denver uses such instances as teachable moments to help students learn to see beyond their own fear and begin to grapple with broader societal inequities and manifestations of inequality that inevitably bleed into the classrooms where they will be teaching. These stories from the field become a springboard for learning to apply the theories and asset-based frameworks that they've learned about in their coursework. The critical perspectives taught in the beginning of the program are a thread interwoven throughout, where issues of equity, social justice, and culturally relevant teaching are a part of preparation. Rather than falling into common patterns of seeing urban teaching as remediating student deficiencies, the program emphasizes that the appropriate teaching response is to employ school and classroom strategies that advance culturally responsive deeper learning.

Classroom Management That Supports Social, Emotional, and Cognitive Learning

As important as the teaching of content is the design of a classroom environment in which subject matter can be well taught. In these developmentally grounded programs, classroom management is approached as constructing a community of learners, rather than merely arranging desks, assigning tasks, and setting rules with consequences. Productive classrooms are organized around the promotion of student responsibility and agency through developing common norms, enabling collaboration, and teaching social and emotional skills, habits, and mind-sets. This work is grounded in teachers building relationships with their students as well as among them, so students learn to respect and work well with each other.

All of the programs are explicit in giving candidates concrete tools for constructing a community-of-learners classroom—often drawing on the yearlong student teaching or internship as an important source of ideas in developing norms and routines. At Trinity, for example, as candidates study developmentally grounded classroom management, they create a "classroom management playbook." This detailed worksheet is divided into sections according to classroom activity (e.g., "learning names," "beginning class," "managing the classroom and classroom materials"), with specific strategies listed under each activity section. In their full-year clinical placement, they use this sheet to record all the classroom management practices and procedures that they observe mentors and other teachers implement, and that they learn about at professional development sessions and conferences, through readings, and through conversations with other teachers. Aside from creating opportunities for observation and discussion of management practices, this detailed and practical assignment also gives interns a way to take this collaborative experience with them after the program: it is structured so that, at the end of their course of study, candidates have essentially created a plan for classroom management practices they will be implementing the following year in their own classrooms.

Organizing Classrooms as Learning Communities

All of the programs help candidates learn how to create collaborative classrooms in which children have many sources for learning—including from their peers—and in which there is a strong sense of common membership and shared responsibility. In many cases, candidates are taught how to help students collaborate in constructing classroom norms through a classroom constitution that is posted on the wall. They are also taught how to socialize students to their roles as community members.

One key pedagogical strategy for which these programs prepare candidates is productive group work. Collaborative learning is an important classroom tool that can be used to provide students with learning assistance from peers within their zone of proximal development, opportunities to articulate their ideas—which can strengthen their learning—and chances to strengthen metacognitive skills. Self-regulated learners are skilled at collaborating with others and seeking out help from teachers, peers, or more expert others; in short, this skill is both exhibited and developed through social processes that teachers can foster.[35]

Hundreds of studies have documented the value of well-designed cooperative small-group learning.[36] Effective group work supports learning as it provides opportunities to share original insights, resolve differing perspectives through argument, explain one's thinking about a phenomenon, provide critique, observe the strategies of others, and listen to a range of explanations.[37] However, group work is a tool that is poorly used in many classrooms. Well-managed collaborative learning requires the ability to create group-worthy tasks in which all must engage for the work to be successfully accomplished, support for students to learn to work together, and sophisticated questioning and scaffolding skills on the part of teachers.

All of these programs introduce their students to well-developed methods for such learning in classrooms. Several draw on the well-researched Complex Instruction model—an approach that uses cooperative group work to teach at a high academic level by assigning carefully constructed, interdependent group tasks.[38] Teachers learn how to teach their students to undertake different roles that support the collaboration (e.g., materials manager, timekeeper, task minder, and others). To support productive collaboration, the teacher orchestrates tasks, relationships, and supports, and actively works to disrupt status hierarchies that might develop based on students' personalities, developed abilities, language backgrounds, or other factors. Teachers equalize interactions between high- and low-status students by structuring tasks and prompts to help them recognize and use their multiple abilities, as students draw on different competencies to accomplish a group task. Teachers can also "assign competence" to a student by recognizing the student's intellectual contributions to the group task through a public statement, conferring a positive evaluation on the students' effort and boosting participation of low-status students without restraining the participation of high-status students.

At Stanford, where Complex Instruction was developed and initially researched, this work is the focus of an entire course: Teaching and Learning in Heterogeneous Classrooms. We saw the use of these or similar strategies throughout the programs we studied, and in the classrooms of candidates and graduates we visited. Voicing a common perspective, a CU Denver candidate described the classroom management instruction they received as "relationship-based, . . . not just academic, but behavioral, emotional, and social," and aiming to address the needs of the whole child in developmentally appropriate ways.

The programs help candidates both develop empathy and respect for their students and provide them with a concrete set of tools for creating supportive classroom environments that teach social and emotional skills. For example, one Alverno faculty member described how she pushes candidates to become aware of their students' social and emotional needs by having them look at the lives of a middle schooler: "Every assignment was based upon the cognitive, social, emotional, physical, and moral domains of a middle school child. One of the things they had to do was write their own autobiography of when they were middle schoolers and how that felt."

These kinds of reflections help candidates think about how their students will likely respond to the classroom environments they develop. In Trinity's summer session, candidates learn about helping students develop social-emotional skills. As one graduate noted, "[Students] need those emotional and social skills to have the mind-set to do that deeper learning." Because of the close relationship with the professional development school in which practices are developed, candidates can continue this work in their placements. Across programs, as candidates work in their clinical sites, the environments they experience shape candidates' practice. Because these sites are so carefully selected, candidates have the opportunity to experience and study how productive learning communities are created.

Restorative Practices

Several programs explicitly teach candidates how to establish restorative practices in their schools and classrooms. Trinity starts with individual cases so that candidates can see what a powerful effect a restorative approach can have. In their Diverse Learners class, Trinity candidates read Ross W. Greene's *Lost at School: Why Our Kids with Behavioral Challenges Are Falling Through the Cracks and How We Can Help Them*.[39] They use the book to talk about plans they could implement with students who exhibit challenging behavior. One candidate described one of the ideas in the book in this way: "[The book]addresses the fact that these students want to learn, they are eager to please, and taking that step back—they might be lacking some social skills or how to communicate with peers, and so when they have these challenging behaviors, just have a conversation with them . . . have them open up to you and express their feelings."

The candidates implement the strategies in the fall, choosing one student whom they notice is exhibiting challenging behavior, asking, "How can I help you? What plan can we have?" Thus, the candidate noted, "Instead of being reactive, we wanted to be proactive: implement a plan, assess, is it working?" Another candidate observed that the practices learned were effective because they allowed her students to tell her how they were feeling and helped her understand the students and empathize with them. She told us, "As teachers, we see what happens and not why." Still another added that the book stressed the benefits of having students come up with solutions to their behavior, getting them to reflect on their behavior and to take more responsibility for their actions.

SFTR teaches about restorative practices and trauma-informed teaching in the practicum class. These two sets of instructional strategies are particularly applicable to the SFUSD context, which has adopted restorative practices as a districtwide initiative for schools and afterschool programs. The approach has been well received by SFTR residents. On the 2016 LPI survey, 90 percent of residents reported feeling "well" or "very well" prepared to build a productive classroom community, and 86 percent of SFTR graduates "agreed" or "strongly agreed" that SFTR helped them to develop a supportive and inclusive classroom community. Three-quarters of residents also felt "well" or "very well" prepared to develop a classroom environment that promotes social/emotional development and individual and group responsibility. Their students agreed. On surveys of more than 1,700 SFTR graduates' students in fall of 2014 and spring of 2015, using the YouthTruth Student Survey instrument, the students were especially confident in SFTR teachers' ability to engage students and develop personal relationships and to create a positive classroom culture, as well as to employ academic rigor, high expectations, and strong instructional methods.[40]

■   ■   ■   ■   ■

These seven programs are very deliberate in constructing a coherent curriculum of studies that will enable their candidates to teach diverse students for deeper learning. This curriculum includes deep knowledge of ***learners*** and the social contexts that shape their development and learning; deep and flexible understanding of ***content and content pedagogy***—including the key concepts and modes of inquiry in the disciplines—and how to represent content and design curriculum in ways that allow others to learn effectively; and a wide repertoire of ***teaching strategies*** that allow them to assess learning in order to guide ever more effective teaching, differentiate and personalize instruction, teach in culturally and linguistically responsive ways, and create productive learning communities. This knowledge base is made useful by the many ways these programs put it into practice in every aspect of their work. We turn to these practices in the next chapter.

CHAPTER 4

PRACTICING WHAT THEY TEACH

[To] anyone who is new to teaching, great teaching seems magical and seamless. And it's my and my colleagues' job to get [students] to see into the practices for their intentionality.

—Alverno professor

If the curriculum represents the "what" of teacher education, the practices used to accomplish curriculum goals represent the "how." In this chapter we describe key practices the seven programs engage in that allow them to achieve their goals. These practices distinguish them from traditional teacher education programs in two ways. First, they intentionally make teacher preparation itself a deeper learning experience for candidates. Second, the deeper learning practices that candidates experience in the program are those that the programs expect them to use as teachers in their own classrooms. The key practices include:

- mission-aligned processes for *recruiting and selecting* candidates
- *integration* of coursework and clinical work
- *modeling* of deeper learning pedagogies
- *applying* knowledge in practice
- engaging in *inquiry* and *action research*
- *collaboration* in productive learning communities
- *feedback* that supports *reflection* on teaching
- *authentic assessments* of progress
- well-designed *clinical apprenticeships*, developed in partner schools

Along the way, each of the instructional practices includes scaffolding—that is, providing and adapting the support given to teacher candidates by more capable others as they move from being novices to more expert practitioners of teaching for deeper learning.

MISSION-ALIGNED PROCESSES FOR RECRUITING AND SELECTING CANDIDATES

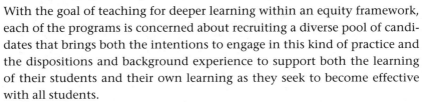

With the goal of teaching for deeper learning within an equity framework, each of the programs is concerned about recruiting a diverse pool of candidates that brings both the intentions to engage in this kind of practice and the dispositions and background experience to support both the learning of their students and their own learning as they seek to become effective with all students.

Thus, while most programs have expectations about the prior academic accomplishments of their recruits—expressed in grade point averages (a 3.0 GPA is a common expectation) and, sometimes, test scores on admissions tests and state basic skills and/or subject-matter tests—these requirements are supplemented with other evidence that speaks to these foundational attitudes and experiences: prior experience with children, essays about educational goals and views, and interviews are common. The nature and extent of content knowledge is also a concern in many programs, going well beyond a subject-matter test or titular major.

Some programs require professional as well as academic recommendations. The strategies are somewhat different at the undergraduate and graduate levels. In graduate-level internships or residencies, employers are more involved. And all the programs assess candidates along the way, with the goal of ensuring that anyone who graduates from the program has met a rigorous set of standards.

Assessment of Abilities and Dispositions

There are a variety of methods to probe candidates' views and abilities—including their ability to collaborate. At both CU Denver and Trinity, for example, once applications are received, applicants are invited to participate in small-group in-person interviews with program faculty and staff. During this group interview, prospective students participate in highly interactive discussions designed to assess candidate dispositions, such as critical thinking, oral communication, and interaction skills. CU Denver adds interactive activities to further assess each applicant's skills and dispositions.

Trinity's strong commitment to content knowledge brings faculty from the content departments into the selection process on a presidentially appointed university-wide committee—the Council on Teacher Education—that looks at each candidate's full profile, including specific content knowledge developed within the major as well as what professors know of the candidate's dispositions toward teaching from the interview process and, in the case of Trinity undergraduates, their time at Trinity. These representatives advise the education faculty, candidate by candidate, on any deficiencies or concerns in their preparation, academic performance, and dispositional readiness for teaching.

For the MAT program, candidates must submit, in addition to grades, test scores, transcripts, essays, and references, a writing sample completed during the interview process and an electronic portfolio documenting their work with children and any education-related coursework. This portfolio is presented to program faculty in an individual interview where the candidate can answer questions about his or her experiences and views.

At Bank Street, the process is also highly personalized. The formal application process usually follows a series of events aimed at informing candidates about the progressive mission of the school: information sessions, catalog review, telephone inquiries, and open houses scheduled several times a year. At open houses, interested students meet with advisors and directors from the different programs; ask questions about programs, courses, and certification; discuss the nature of field placements; and tour the Bank Street School for Children. The process is personalized from the start, as advisors follow up with applicants to try to both determine their commitment to rigorous preparation for student-centered practice and, where there's a fit, begin figuring out how to support them in their process of learning to teach.

The formal process augments an extensive written application form that seeks to understand the candidate as a potential teacher with a personal interview with the program director or one of the advisors. The interview refers back to answers provided in the application form essays that provide opportunities for examining attitudes about children, families, and learning. Sometimes candidates who appear to have a superficial or romanticized vision of teaching are advised to find opportunities to visit schools, do some volunteer work, or take a course and return for a second interview later. This intensive process operates to recruit candidates as well as to support a mutual selection process. Candidates noted:

> The application was so detailed that I trusted I would be taken seriously as an individual.
>
> They were really interested in who I was and why I wanted to teach. I felt that I had the opportunity to really find out what the profession was about and how I could be part of it.[1]

Selecting Teachers for Social Justice

In the residency and internship programs, candidates are on a direct pathway to employment, and both recruitment and selection play an even greater role than in traditional programs.

The San Francisco Teacher Residency (SFTR) program prominently displays its values on a website home page that calls for applicants who want to "Learn to Teach for Social Justice." The careful and intentional recruitment of candidates is an essential piece of SFTR's work—not only because the program is committed to finding candidates who are willing to take on SFTR's mission, but also because they are looking for educators who will stay teaching in the San Francisco Unified School District (SFUSD), where many of the city's diverse students live in high-poverty neighborhoods.

Recruiting materials clearly communicate to prospective applicants that the program is focused on serving high-need schools and closing the achievement gap. The website prominently features the four qualities that the program is looking for:

- passion for social justice
- desire to improve equity and access for San Francisco's children
- interest in teaching as a profession
- commitment to teaching in a high-needs school in San Francisco[2]

Recruits are admitted to one of the partnering universities through a collaborative process. The program has an explicit goal to recruit racially, ethnically, and linguistically diverse candidates. SFTR adds to the applicant pool for the bilingual authorization at the University of San Francisco (USF) by intentionally recruiting native speakers from the USF undergraduate dual degree (BA plus credential) program, and, to assess the language proficiency of all candidates for the bilingual authorization, requires that prospective candidates interview in Spanish. In meeting its recruiting goals for educator diversity, SFTR has been largely successful. Two-thirds of the 2016–17 cohort are people of color, and more than half speak a second language in addition to English.

Recruiting candidates according to these guidelines is meant to serve SFUSD's needs as well as SFTR's other goals. A high school principal from one of SFTR's teaching academies—a school that serves predominantly low-income students and students of color—explained how SFTR's candidates are different from those in other teacher preparation programs he has worked with, and what this difference means for finding and retaining teachers for the district:

If you have a teacher who is not particularly interested in working in a diverse urban school, and they want to work in a suburban school, and they have a retired teacher as their supervisor who taught their whole career in a suburban school, then that person's not going to be someone who would want to work here, and someone we're not going to be willing to hire. [SFTR] is taking a different approach. They are finding candidates who want to work in the type of environment that we're in and they're training them with folks who know what they're doing in these types of environments, too. I think that makes a big difference.

The recruitment messages attract candidates. As one graduate explained:

The aspect that most interested me about SFTR was the focus on developing teachers to work in public schools mostly serving students from historically underserved communities. I was very intentional about working with a specific student population and I felt that SFTR would provide me with adequate training that highlighted a culturally responsive pedagogy and a set of values that resonated with my experience and background.

Additional draws for candidates are the affordability of the program and the intensive level of mentoring and support during the residency year and after. One summed up this appeal as "equity focus, reduced tuition, guaranteed job with SFUSD"—an example of how teachers choosing districts such as SFUSD take these issues into account. Others mentioned the stipends, guaranteed mentoring, and intensive supervision as reasons to apply. The program therefore can be selective: only 30 percent of applicants are ultimately chosen after review of qualifications, examination of essays, and intensive interviews.

Newark Montclair Urban Teacher Residency is equally selective. In 2016, 31 percent of applicants were accepted. As is true with SFTR, candidates are attracted by the explicit focus on becoming a highly expert teacher who can teach for social justice. As one candidate noted, before applying, she had worked as a teacher's aide in a self-contained special education classroom in Newark Public Schools with an exceptional teacher. Her self-stated goal was: "How do I become an amazing teacher [like this]?" After reading about the Newark Montclair residency program, she was clear: "This is where I belong."

In addition to academic review, all of Montclair's many pathways assess candidates on the dispositions of cultural competency and capacity for social justice teaching through a program statement essay, impromptu writing sample, and admissions interview using the Portrait of a Teacher as a guide. While the undergraduate programs accept most applications (70 to 80 percent), throughout the program candidates are assessed on every element of the Portrait of a Teacher (described in chapter 2) and must meet key academic and clinical benchmarks to progress, thus creating selectivity based on teaching skills and dispositions along the way.

High Tech High's intern program requires that candidates be employed at least half time as an apprentice or a teacher of record. Thus, participants are selected through a rigorous process that is shaped by their dual status as employees and students. HTH is hiring educators for their schools, with the expectation that the intern teachers will likely remain at the school upon completing the internship.

Applicants first apply for a position at one of High Tech's thirteen schools or at a partner school, answering question prompts aimed at revealing candidates' orientations toward teaching. Those selected to continue beyond the online application—about 10 percent of those who apply—are invited for the second step, a twenty-minute interview with school directors (principals) and teachers, which can be in person or online. The school directors then meet to determine which applicants—about half of those interviewed—will be invited to the third step of the application process, a unique full-day event called "the Bonanza."

During the Bonanza, the prospective teachers engage in a variety of activities designed to assess how they interact with students, how they collaborate with adults, and how they view issues of equity in education. The day begins at 8:00 a.m. with breakfast, where prospective intern teachers first interact with HTH staff and students, the latter bringing along examples of their project work to discuss. The rest of the day is taken up with a variety of activities, including speed-interviews with directors and staff, discussion of teaching dilemmas, collaborative project planning and discussion, teaching of a sample lesson or debriefing of a lesson video [for elementary candidates], a discussion of an article on equity, and written responses to equity issue cases. Although prospective program participants' fitness as potential teachers is examined, assessing their interest in equity-centered pedagogy is a priority of the process.

The Bonanza is an essential component of the hiring process. At the conclusion of the Bonanza, teachers, students, and administrators all gather to debrief and discuss the candidates. The process entails an open, positive dialogue among staff. During this time, HTH staff advocate for candidates who they believe are passionate about equity, inclusion of student voice, and collaboration, among other things, and defend their position based on experience and supporting materials. Only the candidates staff choose to advocate for are discussed, thereby limiting discussion about individual shortcomings, and keeping the discussion positive in nature. The school directors make the final decision on whom should be hired and, therefore, who will enroll in the intern program.

By assessing potential teachers' interactions with students, and observing their teaching styles as well as their views on equity in education, the process seeks to choose candidates who can work within the collaborative, personalized, and authentic HTH framework, who have the potential to support all students in their learning, and who view educational equity in a way that is consistent with HTH's mission and goals.

Selection by Demonstrated Capacity and Commitment Over Time

Alverno takes a unique approach to admissions to its teacher preparation program. As one Alverno professor noted, "Our philosophy is that we are selective throughout the program and on the way out, but not selective on the way in." Because Alverno College uses narrative grading and competency-based progression rather than letter grades, there is no GPA requirement.

Undergraduates interested in entering the School of Education declare a career pathway in teaching to their academic advisor. After that, the program continuously reviews candidates' eligibility and performance as they move forward in the teacher education program to assess whether they are making sufficient progress. Candidates are typically admitted to the School of Education during their junior year. Nearly half of undergraduate candidates are students of color, many from low-income backgrounds, who are first in their families to attend college and committed to teaching in the Milwaukee neighborhoods they grew up in.

A committee of education faculty reviews all students who register for further coursework in the School of Education to determine whether they should move forward in the program. The committee looks for candidate competencies in their knowledge, dispositions, and performances across ten standards. For example, candidates must be "aware that students' learning is influenced by individual experiences, talents, and prior learning"; must believe "that all children can learn at high levels"; and must seek "to understand families, cultures, and communities and [use] this information in planning a lesson."[3] Ultimately, candidates must also pass all three Praxis Core assessments, as required by Wisconsin, and complete the basic skills requirements set forth by the college.

After the candidates' first semester-long field placement, they complete the "I Have What It Takes" assessment. The goal of this assessment is to help candidates determine whether "they are on a path that is a good fit for them and their current dispositions." This field placement exposes candidates to "exemplars of effective teaching so they can reflect on what they observe and begin to make connections to themselves as future teachers." This gives candidates the time, space, and structure to reflect about what it takes to be a high-quality teacher and the extent to which they feel suited for the profession. One instructor commented, "There are things that people believe about kids that better be true of you if you keep going down this road [such as that all students can learn]. That is a really important conversation you need to have with yourself [before you enter the profession]."

Another instructor explained, "We definitely want people to evaluate early on whether or not the challenges of teaching are ones that they embrace, or ones that discourage them." One or two candidates are counseled out of the program each year through the "I Have What It Takes" assessment. As we describe in the assessment section later in this chapter, there are ongoing performance assessments of the Alverno abilities and specific teaching competencies that are also benchmarks for graduating from the program. About three-quarters of those who begin the undergraduate teaching program ultimately complete it.

Alverno teacher candidates develop into lifelong learners because the college instills a growth mind-set: a conviction that intelligence and ability can be developed over time and a commitment to create a strong educational environment to support that growth. Alverno's admissions policy reflects this mind-set: the college is open about who is admitted, because of the college's belief that people can learn and grow, but selective about who graduates. The faculty believes that "everyone has the potential to do great things," and they model the type of professional dispositions and beliefs that teachers must embody for their students.

An Alverno alum explained how the Alverno faculty's growth mind-set influenced her classroom. She described how she "builds up and motivates" her students, which was what her Alverno teachers did for her. "Even when it was really hard [at Alverno], no one wanted to see anyone walk away from the program. [The faculty] did whatever it took, including meeting outside of the classroom, on the weekends." This translates into a commitment to ongoing learning. Both Alverno graduates and their principals rate Alverno graduates as particularly well prepared to "seek opportunities to grow professionally."[4] And a superintendent of a nearby school district noted that one hallmark of Alverno graduates is their willingness to learn:

"Alverno undergrads never think they are there. They are continuous learners. They don't say, 'Okay, I've graduated and now I'm done learning.'"

INTEGRATION OF COURSEWORK AND CLINICAL WORK

As we noted in chapter 3, each of the programs integrates coursework with fieldwork to support the deeper learning of candidates. The coursework is designed around research-based teaching and learning theories that are then explored and applied in fieldwork experiences. This integration enables candidates to understand the practical relevance of theory and how to theorize practice so that their actions are grounded and principled.

This coupling of coursework and field experiences is intentional across the programs. It is part of the fundamental rationale and design for programs like High Tech High's internship and the San Francisco, Montclair, and CU Denver teacher residency programs. It can also be seen in the university-based preservice programs. For example, in both the undergraduate and graduate course sequence at Montclair, coursework and clinical connections are carefully mapped out together from the very beginning of the program. (See appendix B for a summary of each program's curriculum design.)

Undergraduates at CU Denver experience linked coursework and fieldwork throughout the first three years, starting with their first courses in the program. CU Denver leaders have built structures and practices to operationalize their goal of having candidates move seamlessly from a place of understanding in their coursework to an action-oriented approach during the clinical experiences and as they enter teaching. These experiences include course-related field assignments in communities as well as in schools.

Their first three courses nurture an inquiry stance toward communities, schools, and young people, in addition to introducing core foundational theoretical and philosophical underpinnings of education. Corresponding field experiences ask undergraduate students to choose a question or a topic that "makes them wonder," then spend time observing and applying the learning from the coursework. For example, they might look at the community through the lens of Bronfenbrenner's ecological theory, collect data, and then reflect on the experience through the theory and the theory through the experience.[5] Their work is assessed as they present "poster sessions" on their projects to their peers. The continuity of the inquiry focus across the first three courses, the selection and rumination around a question of their own choosing, and the project-based structure of the assessment make this learning experience deeper and more meaningful for candidates. This structure is intended to translate to candidates' design of learning experiences for their future students, and similar links are made for teacher candidates in the other pathways.

Some of CU Denver's core courses focus specifically on the integration of coursework and field experiences. For example, the syllabus for Internship and Collaborative Learning Community describes this integration as its central goal:

> Teacher candidates engage in systematic observation of, participation in, design of, and reflection on curricular, instructional, and management practices across the full range of educational programs within a school. Additionally, teacher candidates participate in the activities of a school community (the school, its classrooms and the community in which the school exists).[6]

In like fashion, candidates' first experience in Alverno's undergraduate and graduate preparation programs immerses them in the theories they need to craft developmentally appropriate lessons using pedagogical approaches that help students construct their own knowledge. In both programs, candidates begin their teacher preparation with two classes. The first class focuses on human development, learning, and motivational theories. Candidates address learning diversity by studying and practicing a variety of instructional strategies through assignments that require candidates to design unit and lesson plans. In the second class, candidates spend twenty hours in a classroom observing and reflecting on their cooperative teachers' practice. Candidates are also encouraged to assist mentor teachers with group work, class discussions, and one-on-one work with students.[7] Because candidates take the two classes simultaneously, they weave the theory from the first class into their field placement in the second class. Subsequent Alverno courses build on the integrated theory and fieldwork from the first semester and field placement, ensuring a tight connection between theory and practice. Students continue taking courses that complement their fieldwork, including a course and field placement in either literacy learning or in the candidate's content area. In literacy, "The priority is to provide students who are simultaneously taking a methods course in early literacy and gaining experience in classrooms where effective balanced literacy teaching/learning occurs so they can reflect on what they observe and can practice literacy that reflects best practices."[8]

The next semester-long course and field placement in the sequence builds on candidates' prior experiences by providing candidates "with opportunities to develop developmentally appropriate teaching and assessment practices, with an emphasis on the effective use of questions as an instructional strategy."[9] Graduates participate in three integrated course and field experiences before their student teaching. Undergraduates participate in a fourth experience, where students are given "autonomy to plan and execute creative and innovative lessons."[10] In this way, teacher candidates are scaffolded into their roles as primary instructor during student teaching.

The comments of a principal of a local professional development school (PDS) that works with Trinity University in San Antonio reflected the views of many employers and candidates we talked to across all of the program sites:

> The program very quickly gets you into classrooms. They believe there's a marriage between theory and practice—you have to tell that story and have a balance along the way. It's pretty equally balanced throughout the program. As you're learning about things in books and discussing them in class, you're also visiting classrooms and seeing them in action. Pretty quickly you're in front of kids, teaching lessons—whether it's a small group or large group. That's a really clear difference between their program and most programs that teachers are exposed to. It's a really thoughtfully put together program.

Trinity alumni shared a similar sentiment. One told us:

> I feel like the extra time we get to spend actually teaching and practicing what we learn in our Trinity coursework is so beneficial. I am able to relate what we read and talked about to what I am doing in the classroom. I am able to see results and reflect on my teaching in an actual classroom context.

We will return to the design of these clinical experiences at the end of this chapter. Next, however, we describe a core set of instructional practices that the programs use consistently in both courses and clinical work. These include modeling deeper learning pedagogies, helping candidates apply what they are learning, using inquiry and action research, supporting collaboration, providing ongoing feedback and support for reflection, and assessing candidates with authentic strategies that simultaneously support their development and evaluate their progress.

MODELING OF DEEPER LEARNING PEDAGOGIES

Candidates in these programs have extraordinary opportunities to learn to teach for deeper learning by seeing and participating in precisely that kind of learning themselves. Modeling of practices is an ever-present aspect of preparation in all of these programs—as much from university faculty as from mentors in the schools. We heard repeatedly about the power of faculty modeling of deeper learning pedagogies in our interviews, and we witnessed both teacher education faculty and cooperating teachers model these pedagogies in teacher preparation courses and in residents' clinical placements. We saw faculty name the strategies they were using, explain why they are powerful, and suggest how they could be used in K–12 classrooms. This explicit transparency provides rich opportunities for candidates to see how they can transfer their learning from the university classroom to their school sites.

Modeling Within Coursework

The modeling of deeper learning pedagogies begins with how faculty treat their students. As we noted earlier, faculty model knowledge of students for teacher candidates by knowing the candidates themselves well and personalizing their learning. As one Alverno alum observed,

> I can look back to any of my professors in my experience here and they will probably still remember me by name and know where my interests and passions lie. And say, "Oh hey, I heard about this opportunity and it would be perfect for you." And it wouldn't be arbitrary because they would mean it. Having those mentors and role models instilled that in me as a teacher—wanting to get to know my students and their strengths in the same way.

A particularly powerful learning environment exists at Alverno, where candidates experience deeper learning pedagogies not only in their coursework within the School of Education, but throughout the undergraduate college. Thus, teacher candidates observe and experience a variety of student-centered, inquiry-based instructional approaches from across the college and consider how they might adopt or refine them for their own instructional practice.

In our Learning Policy Institute (LPI) survey of graduates, 100 percent of Alverno candidates reported that they often experienced project-based instruction within their own coursework. As one Alverno instructor explained, "Narrative feedback, self-assessment, all of those, our students experience in all of their classes, not just their education classes. [Alverno] is situated within a total experiential learning environment and has been since the early seventies."

Faculty in the School of Education help candidates develop an understanding of deeper learning by explaining their instructional decisions so that teacher candidates can better understand the reasons for their instructor's actions, along with the depth of thinking and consideration required to construct a meaningful lesson. The director of undergraduate teacher education at Alverno explained:

> When we do our instruction here, we break it down for them. We'll say, "We do this because . . . This is why you would do this." So they are experiencing [deeper learning] but also understanding *the why* behind it. After they feel like they have the why behind it, then they definitely want to go and make that happen in the classroom—getting kids to be engaged, hands-on.

In making their pedagogical moves explicit, instructors are doing two things: helping candidates to understand the theory and complexity behind practice and also modeling how to engage in metacognitive reflection. This immersive learning models the type of deeper learning instruction Alverno wants its candidates to provide their students—something they become quite confident in doing. As one Alverno graduate remarked:

> My principal says, "If you don't know what to do, swing by [the Alverno graduate's] classroom." Because you're not going to walk into my classroom and see me standing in front of a classroom and lecturing to my students. You're going to see me going around and facilitating. My kids are at stations, they're moving, they're collaborating, they're constructing.

As the faculty model practices, teacher candidates learn what it is like to be a student, which helps them reflect on the kinds of relationships and instruction they prefer and motivates them to provide those opportunities to their own students. A Bank Street student reflected: "As an educator, I want to be learning myself. So, for the children, I model how I learn best, which is inquiry-based with support." Another noted: "Discussions helped me realize how important it is as a student that I value the breakup of the class structure, that I was able to organize my own curriculum and lessons that way, because I don't like sitting and listening to the teacher for twenty-five minutes." He added, "Bank Street faculty 100 percent use the same pedagogical strategies that they are trying to instill in Bank Street students."

Similarly, one Montclair State alum said simply, "They taught us in the way they wanted us to teach." At Montclair, much like the other programs we studied, 94 percent or more of candidate respondents on the LPI survey reported having experienced the type of learning in their MSU coursework they were expected to demonstrate in their own teaching, including practices that are generally rare, such as project-based learning, performance-based assessments and presentations of student work, culturally responsive practices, differentiation of instruction, research and investigation, and opportunities to revise work in response to feedback.

With project-based learning being the primary pedagogy at High Tech High, the program starts to model this approach from the very beginning. The week-long intensive New Teacher Odyssey in the summer session begins with "Project Slices," accelerated group projects that are designed and facilitated by HTH teachers and administrators as introductions to project-based learning. An HTH school director described this introductory experience this way:

> Basically, it's a project done in its entirety, in an accelerated fashion, in two days. . . . So the teachers take off the teacher hats, and put on the learner hats. And then we'll stop, and say, "Okay, put on the teacher hat. Why did we just do what we did?" And it's focused on being student-centered, using inquiry, using protocols to facilitate group interactions, starting with the learning experience as the content. All of that is modeled.

Starting off with a project is part of HTH's deliberate effort to integrate its pedagogical principles into preparation. The HTH project-based model does not necessarily come naturally to interns because it looks different from the usual methods of schooling. According to one alum, the project experience changed her ideas of how learning could work:

> For me, I was really worried about this whole concept of project-based learning, especially in math class. I wondered, How are we going to teach kids how to factor quadratics through a project? In a very traditional [setting], you lecture, write on the board, then the kids go home and have homework. Then the next day you lecture, they have homework, they go home and do it and the cycle continues. But in my first

week, I learned that we don't do that. We make it [the lesson] more meaningful through giving the students explorations, as opposed to notes that just tell them what they need to know. The explorations are all based on questions that they can answer with their knowledge from past years and it leads them to what we want them to know that's new. So instead of giving them a formula, we lead them through the thinking behind the formula, and in the end they've got it.

The remaining time in the Odyssey experience builds upon the Project Slices. Faculty use facilitated group discussions to provide interns with an understanding of how teaching and learning are experienced from all perspectives by analyzing instructional and learning activities as they occur. One intern described a classroom assignment on diverse learners' experiences:

We had a day where we focused on every type of learner. . . .We picked one lesson and then we laid out how we would support every learner for that lesson. That was really helpful for me and really pushed me. Even in our Teaching Reading and Writing [class], we thought about doing a read-aloud . . . I was thinking, if I'm reading a book aloud, how am I supporting all students? When I'm doing a close reading, how am I supporting students?

This modeling occurs across all the programs. For example, a Trinity elementary mentor noted that her reading instructor, Dr. Pat Norman,

would always model a protocol while we were talking about a reading we had to do. We still had the content of graduate work, but were also shown this valuable way to get learners to speak to each other rather than just listening to the teacher or professor. We always sat in a circle. Everything was very discussion based.

As Dr. Norman herself describes the process:

For example, showing gradual release, when we teach them how to do guided reading, we show them what guided reading is first and give them lots of examples of what it looks like. Then we plan in a group, with one of us leading, so we have shared practice. Then they have a chance to do some guided reading work on their own independently or in a small group.

In SFTR, responsiveness to student input and feedback is modeled as the instructors have residents fill out student evaluations after every session. The results from these evaluations are then used to start the next class and to engage in ongoing reflective practice. After discussing the evaluation from the last class, the instructor also models other practices such as doing a "warm-up" for the class, or teaching mini-lessons on selected topics. SFTR's clinical director described this approach from her own experience:

> We talk about split vision: the idea that in teacher education we're always in this unique position of doing the thing that we're teaching. As teachers of teachers, we're constantly modeling things, like turn and talk; every aspect of teacher identity is up for grabs to examine the teacher-student relationship. There's always an opportunity to hold under the microscope the teacher-student dynamic: How does this feel for you? How might you do this for your students?

Assignments can also model how to construct and scaffold project-based learning and assessment. A STEP instructor explained:

> There's a lot of doing in the class what you want to teach your kids to do. In Adolescent Development, we have a highly scaffolded case study: interviews, case studies, a log every week. When [the teacher candidates] pull those together, it becomes a case study that is then peer reviewed using a rubric, and they then revise it. In this project, they go through a whole project-based learning sequence by themselves. They are always shocked by how much they've written when it's done. But they're writing it three to four pages at a time every week. At the end of the project, we play back for them what they just did, so they can see how the project was structured and scaffolded. This is also true when they are in C&I writing units. Everything is applied. You're doing it yourself: assessments are authentic and based on actual performances that teachers need to learn and do.

Making the implicit explicit is a critical part of effective modeling. Quite often, teacher candidates do not have the knowledge or experience to understand the intentionality that appears "natural" or seamless in an expert classroom. By making teaching decisions explicit and holding them up for discussion, students can understand the complexity found in teaching for deeper learning. As a faculty member at CU Denver noted:

We're always modeling . . . and through the years [we] have realized that we have to be more transparent, we have to do the meta-narrative. So, after a session, we may say, "So did you notice that we used these strategies? What do you think our pedagogical beliefs are that are having us use these strategies? What do they represent? Why are these strategies useful? When would you use them?" We found that we have to be incredibly transparent.

One method instructors use in making the implicit explicit is to pause during instruction and engage candidates in metacognitive reflection. They ask candidates questions such as, "What kind of theory are we using?" and "Why would you use that right now?" with the aim of opening up the decision-making process around selecting and using particular theoretical stances and the teaching methods associated with them. As one instructor put it, "This gives students deeper conceptualizations. They understand why they are doing things, not just how to do things."

Modeling in Clinical Work

Of course, the clinical component of teacher education has always been intended to provide models of practice. However, it is not always designed to provide good models that are well explained and connected to what candidates are learning in their courses. These programs select and train supervisors and cooperating/mentor teachers so that they can provide strong and effective modeling. At Montclair, when asked what she felt her primary goal was as a mentor teacher, one elementary teacher responded, "Being a good model. If I can model . . . how a good classroom flows and she can see that and she can carry that into her class . . . that is what I hope she gets from [me]."

Field supervisors see part of their responsibility as modeling for mentor teachers how to help teacher candidates learn and grow. One MSU supervisor and former dean explained:

> I want to model for [cooperating teachers] the way I help student teachers to unpack their reflection on the lesson. I always start with asking them to restate what their goal was for the lesson. Instead of saying, "How do you think it went?," which I think is not a terribly helpful thing to ask, I say, "Well, how did you do at meeting your goal?"

In this way, the supervisor is building the capacity of the mentor teacher to ask good reflective questions of her student teacher. This helps to build cohesion across the coursework and field experiences and, in the words of one supervisor, helps to ensure that mentor teachers "understand the same goals and understandings of the purposes of teaching and learning" as the faculty instructors at Montclair State. This supervisor put it simply: "I want the cooperating teachers to see what it is we are focusing on and thinking about from Montclair State. We are all in the same program. They are our partners, our critically important teacher education partners."

Thus, not only are teacher candidates being exposed to the modeling of content and processes, they also have professionals in their clinical spheres—a mentor teacher and university supervisor—modeling positive, collegial partnership across stakeholders. This type of collaboration is necessary to fully engage communities in deeper learning pedagogy in a broader, more systemic way.

Bank Street accomplishes similar goals as faculty advisors work closely with the cooperating classroom teachers. A teacher candidate, advisor, and cooperating teacher have three-way meetings to learn how to best support each other in helping the teacher candidate grow. The frequency of contact between advisors, cooperating teachers, and teacher candidates helps to develop trusting and collaborative relationships among one another in a way that supports the growth of teacher candidates and helps advisors develop the capacity of cooperating teachers to become strong models.

One cooperating teacher at the Bank Street School for Children, George, reflected on what he had learned from this process on behalf of the candidate he was working with: "I have been communicating with [Alexandra's advisor] all year. We've had a few shared meetings. He's in the classroom a lot observing, he knows me, he knows her, he knows our relationship." George went on to emphasize their shared goal: that supervised fieldwork is "really explaining decision making. I think that's the biggest thing. It's like a surgical residency—it would be like an intern watching a surgeon operate, 'Oh, I'm removing the spleen, what do you notice about the spleen?' So, it's really explaining things, interacting."

This insight, developed in the context of George's relationship with the university advisor, results from the university's effort to support cooperating teachers who can model and explain their pedagogical rationales to the student teachers.

APPLYING KNOWLEDGE IN PRACTICE

The integration of coursework and clinical work we saw in all these programs provides authentic opportunities for candidates to practice what they learn. This approach supports the type of self-assessment and meta-cognition the teacher candidates will ultimately encourage their students to explore so that they can become self-directed learners.

High Tech High names this in a common weekly course assignment called "Put It to Practice" (PITP). For example, during an introductory methods class session focused on assessment, instructors model (and candidates practice) a variety of ways to formatively check for student understanding. During the class, students also discuss grading scales and the negative effect of a zero on a student's grade. The PITP assignment for the following week is to:

- Try three different ways of checking for understanding and submit a reflection on how they worked.
- Make a video that shows you checking for understanding and bring it to class to share with your video protocol group.
- Retool your grading scale or consider how you might not use grades at all, eliminating the emotional and mathematical effect of issuing students zeros for missing work.

The essence of PITP is that interns learn about a new concept or practice during one of the courses or from faculty, including their mentor, and they are expected to try the practice in their class the next day or soon thereafter. PITP is highly valued. As an alumnus noted:

> Everything that we did in class the night before, I could literally do the next day in my classroom. We had homework that was called Put It to Practice. So I thought this was great; I can do this in my classroom—then I realized that, oh yeah, they're purposefully doing this so that we can practice this and reflect on it and then talk about it in the next class.

We also saw evidence of PITP in action during an observation of a second-grade classroom. The teacher, Lydia, was a first-year intern who had started out as an apprentice teacher in a kindergarten classroom and had just recently assumed the role of lead teacher in a first-grade classroom. We were able to watch as she utilized classroom management strategies she had learned in her coursework. One precocious little boy was proving to be a challenge for Lydia and several of his classmates. Lydia responded with positive behavioral tactics, a gentle touch on the back to calm him, and a reminder to use his journal to write down thoughts he wants to share so that he can remember them later during sharing time. As she used these techniques, she laughingly told us, "I'm putting it into practice!"

Because all the programs interweave coursework with clinical work, they create linked learning opportunities in class assignments and in the clinical setting. One of the ways that candidates learn from their efforts to put concepts into practice is through structured opportunities to plan, implement, and reflect on what they are doing and its outcomes.

Trinity's pedagogy portfolio, for example, helps candidates plan instruction that makes use of a variety of teaching strategies, and creates opportunities for candidates to apply these strategies in collaboration with their mentors. Student teachers develop a chart that provides an overview of each of the teaching strategies from the course text, *The Strategic Teacher: Selecting the Right Research-Based Strategy for Every Lesson.*[11] Candidates develop at least one lesson plan for each family of strategies: mastery, understanding, self-expressive, and interpersonal. They also include differentiation notes for each lesson. Interns share their portfolios with mentors and they discuss the strategies, when they could be used, and things to think through before using them; then they put them into action at appropriate times, with coaching. In the field, mentors also encourage candidates to examine which strategies they have not tried by the end of their first of two clinical placements, and then try them in their second placement, further expanding the tools that Trinity candidates will bring to their own classrooms.

ENGAGING IN INQUIRY AND ACTION RESEARCH

Putting teaching ideas into practice in educative ways can be supported by inquiry strategies that guide reflection. Inquiry and research as a means to analyze practice closely are substantial aspects of these programs' approaches. In chapter 3 we discussed the extensive use of child case studies in the teaching of child development. This kind of research into the learning of a child, based on careful observations and interviews linked to the research base on development, helps teacher candidates understand the applications of research as well as the tools for research. For example, Alexandra, a current Bank Street student, noted the importance of these case methods joined to her work as a student teacher: "I'm taking Observation & Recording right now, so I have to pick a student in the class . . . and I'm doing an age-level study. I have twenty-five pages of all the developmental and personality traits of nine- and ten-year-olds. And it's been really interesting to see that match up with what we're doing [in the classroom]."

Candidates are required to shadow their student to various classes and are encouraged to attend a social event (e.g., a game or extracurricular activity) or eat lunch in the cafeteria with the student, so as to see the child in different contexts. This helps them understand that students have multiple identities and strengths, and these change with contexts. Candidates apply theory to help them understand their case study and learn how their observations can inform planning for teaching.

Across the programs, candidates also conduct action research on topics about which they are puzzled, learning how to find answers to the main problems of practice they will encounter in their careers. The box "Action Research in Action" provides an illustration of the kinds of research topics teachers were taking up in the Newark Montclair residency program.

The programs we studied use action research and case methods in many contexts; for example, to examine how children learn language, how children learn differently, and how schools and communities are organized (or not well organized) to support children and families—and with what consequences. As shown in the Montclair vignette, the action research projects allow teacher candidates to ask burning questions, collect evidence to answer them, discuss the process and their observations, respond to feedback, revise, and improve not only their research projects, but more importantly, their teaching practice.

In addition to what candidates can learn about children and teaching by conducting their own inquiries, inquiry is another source of modeling for candidates, since it is one of the approaches candidates are expected to use with their own students as they pursue deeper learning. As an Alverno graduate noted, candidates learn how to adopt an inquiry approach by observing faculty model inquiry-based activities in coursework and fieldwork:

> Alverno taught us to construct our knowledge on our own. And we are asking our students to do that. I don't think that anyone ever came right out to me and said, "This is the way you need to teach; this is deeper learning." We talked about backwards design. Here is the end, and there is a means to an end, and it's up to you as the teacher to decide what the means are to that end. If your way of doing that is worksheets, fine. But let's look at this now. How are you doing with your students as far as worksheets go? Are you getting the results you want?

An emphasis on inquiry contributes to the development of multiple deeper learning competencies for teachers and students. First, it gives candidates and students agency over their learning, leading to a deeper level of

Action Research in Action

The Teaching for Learning II (student teaching) seminar within the MAT program is held at East Side High School in Newark, New Jersey. All of the teacher candidates are set to graduate next month and you can feel the anticipation in the room. As the teacher candidates file in for the class, Emily Klein, associate professor, comes in and moves the desks into groups where students can caucus together.

After a few moments for candidates to debrief one another on their student teaching experiences, Emily transitions the class to working on their action research projects—a practice-focused research project they complete in their site placements. She asks the class to break up into content areas (mathematics, English, social studies, science, and "specials") and to collaborate with each other to consider how to address their students' needs and improve instruction through their research findings. These are some of the questions Emily poses to teacher candidates to consider during the small-group work:

- How did your content area influence your action research projects? What do you notice about the role of content in the projects?
- What kinds of challenges did you encounter?
- How did you manage them?
- What are the next steps for how you use action research in your future work as a teacher?

Emily slowly makes her way around the room and listens to each group share out about their projects. She jumps in now and again to ask a critical question or push some thinking, but generally allows the teacher candidates to guide their own work. One candidate describes how he learned to implement a student checklist from his methods course into his classroom with his cooperative teacher as a result of his action research project. He then shares a student example, explaining how he used the checklist when grading the final draft of the student work, and admitting the challenges he experienced in using a rubric for evaluation.

Within the English content group, one teacher candidate mentions the use of authentic assessment in the classroom, through the use of a class president speech, autobiography, and advertisements using the concepts of ethos, pathos, and logos. All these assignments required her students to create products that were used outside of the classroom with outside audiences.

Within the same content group, a teacher candidate mentions that students' use of slang in writing is widespread within his classroom and has been difficult to curb in written assignments. Another candidate challenged his framing of the issue, suggesting, "It's not slang that is the problem, it's learning how to write formally, which is the responsibility of teachers [to teach]."

As teacher candidates continue to share with each other in their groups, Emily stops the class briefly and reminds them, "Your action research projects are about making [teaching inquiry] coherent and narrative, and being able to read the data and apply it to your classroom. Your work as a teacher will never be a controlled experiment."

engagement. Second, an inquiry approach gives candidates experience asking the types of questions they will need to ask when they encounter novel teaching challenges, diverse student populations, and different school and community contexts. Inquiry supports candidates' ability to transfer or apply their learning to novel contexts. One explained, "I don't tell [my students] the answer because then I am doing the learning, and I tell them that all the time: 'You have to do your own thinking.' The school is very inquiry-based. As an Alverno person I was drawn to come here and knew I could integrate what I had done at Alverno."

The programs and candidates can bring an inquiry approach to their cooperating teachers (CTs) and mentors as well. A San Francisco coach described how residents often plant new teaching practices into cooperating teachers' classrooms through projects and inquiry-based activities, which CTs greatly value. She gave these recent examples:

One of my candidates has been pushing for integrating the use of technology and the use of assessment in Google Classroom into her classroom, and has introduced all of that to her cooperating teacher. So now their students will write these reflections, and they can analyze the data on Google Classroom and say, "Okay, where are we going to go to next?" based all on this project where they've been investigating outbreaks through the Centers for Disease Control's epidemiological work. Students are arguing: What disease could this be? What if we have to put a quarantine on? What's going on here? She [the resident] brought a lot of those pieces in, and she's brought in all these language supports, and the CT says, "These are great, we're going to use these."

Earlier this year, two of our biology candidates created a group inquiry-based project where students were trying to understand how the drought was affecting salmon in California, and they did this by examining clues from the salmon's Twitter account. They had thirty clues, and all the students were trying to piece together what do these photos and what do these graphs and what do these quotes mean from the perspective of the mama salmon and from the perspective of the person that goes to the park and all these different Twitter accounts. And they created this group task of deep inquiry where they solve this mystery.

During the 2015–16 school year, the series of workshops SFTR sponsored for CTs was structured around inquiry-based instruction, modeling this deeper learning teaching practice for CTs by using questions chosen by the CTs themselves. SFTR's director of clinical education described SFTR's rationale for why they decided to restructure the professional development provided to CTs and the impact of this change on their teaching practices:

> For people to buy into inquiry as a practice—because it's so messy and sloppy and unpredictable . . . there's a leap people have to take. We wanted to give people an experience to do it. We believe that ultimately teachers have everything they need, and if they have the time and they know the questions to ask and they know how to find the answers . . . if we can center on that and value it and communicate and promote the idea that this is not about the top-down mandates, it's not about the things that you're going to be told to do—that feels transformative. The opportunity for them to take an inquiry approach or stance with their residents and their own students feels much higher. And in fact, [after the inquiry-based PD], teachers said, "I took risks that I've never taken before." We were also giving them tools around posing a good question that they could then use with their students, so they were getting some tangible things in terms of process and tools.

Through this inquiry-driven professional development model, CTs took up questions related to their own teaching as varied as "How can I make the most of my conferring time to improve students' writing skills?" to "How can I challenge students who are getting it and support those who aren't, without creating status issues within a group?" Some CTs also identified questions related to coaching a resident, such as "How can I help my resident look critically at the system without being negative or dishonest? How do I help her develop the resilience it takes to do this work?"

A supervisor observed:

> Yesterday, I had a conversation with a CT and a resident, and the CT was talking about how much her practice has been challenged and changed due to two things: the inquiry work with the CT professional development and conversations I've been having with the resident. It helps her to reflect on her own practice and think, "Oh, that's something that I can work on," and really push herself to improve her own practice as well as [that of] her own students.

In reviewing the feedback that CTs provided after the sessions, SFTR's director of clinical education noted, "Many [CTs] talked about the degree to which the PD felt healing, it felt collaborative in a way they had never experienced. It felt like their expertise was being engaged, and they were truly learning from each other."

COLLABORATION IN PRODUCTIVE LEARNING COMMUNITIES

The conviction that both teaching and learning to teach are collaborative permeates all aspects of these programs. Learning to teach takes place in professional communities in which teachers observe one another, share practices, develop plans together, and solve problems collectively. The vision of a single teacher closing the door to operate in isolation in an egg-crate classroom is impossible to sustain in these settings. They place a strong emphasis on authentic relationships among adults, and between adults and young people, as the foundation of deeper learning. As with other practices, what teachers are learning to enact with their own students is what they are experiencing as teacher candidates.

For example, the principal of one of San Francisco's teaching academies described how the collaboration that takes place between residents, their CTs, and other teachers at the school plants a culture of collaborative inquiry:

> Residents are modeling for their cooperating teachers how to do a more hands-on, inquiry-based lesson for a similar concept that they had taught in a different fashion. We have our science team of three, and now we have a group of six people that are all thinking and talking about these things in various combinations. With biology we have the two teachers and the two residents, so now there's four of them thinking and talking about biology. And the residents are bringing with them these ideas that they're talking about in their university C&I courses, that they're talking about in their practicum. And so it's more than them just giving a particular lesson; I think what's more important is that dialogue and conversation [are] pushing the teachers to think about and talk about it a lot more. I think the impact may be even deeper than that . . . I know it is.

Even as these professional communities are built in many of the school sites, they are also built into the university courses through use of a cohort model, which ensures that a group of candidates goes through all of the courses together as a community of learners. This is a crucial component across pathways in the teacher education programs. Cohorts not only act as a source of support for candidates learning to teach; they also give them the opportunity to place themselves into student roles, learn how to manage challenges that arise in collaborative work, and practice giving and receiving feedback. Through cohort-based support and collaboration, teacher candidates learn how to implement facets of deeper learning in their own classrooms.

The cohort model is used in all the teacher education programs at Montclair, from the undergraduate and graduate pathways to the residency programs, though it looks different in these varied contexts. Within the undergraduate and MAT programs, the teacher education program intentionally places multiple candidates at school sites for their fieldwork and student teaching experiences whenever possible. MAT candidates' placements are made as part of a cohort-based, yearlong clinical course. In this program, student teaching seminar courses are held at school sites where the majority of teacher candidates are completing clinical placements, which not only is convenient for the teacher candidates, but also creates deeper connections between MSU and district schools.

The Newark Montclair Urban Teacher Residency forms cohorts of up to fifteen candidates. MSU faculty, along with resident mentors, offer feedback, model exemplary teaching practices and strategies, and foster authentic relationships with residents. The residents themselves provide feedback on their peers' teaching videos and support one another as they carry out their action research projects. Support for these cohorts extends beyond the residency into the three-year induction period, with mentor check-ins and faculty observations helping candidates to not only complete the program, but to remain in teaching afterward. The importance of the cohort was constantly echoed from the current residents and alums. As one alum stated, "I learned collaboration from my peers in the cohort model. [I] also learned how to build a learning community in my classroom."

Thus cohorts not only serve as an organizational structure to support the learning of teacher candidates; they can also model the importance of building authentic relationships with students and help candidates develop learning communities within their own classrooms. One alumnus summed up the impact of cohort learning in this way:

> Learning in the cohort model [with just thirteen total candidates was huge]. That was one thing I never really experienced before, learning so much from my peers. I think that is the same strategy [I use] in my classroom, having them learn from each other, and then us learning, teachers learning from the students, as well.

Many teacher candidates describe the cohorts at their sites as true communities, central to their learning and development. One CU Denver candidate reflected on the value of being with peers who were also learning to teach, seeing herself as moving from the periphery into the core of teaching as part of a community of learners:

> Taking part in [a PDS internship] gave me the opportunity to collaborate with other teacher candidates who were at different parts of their internships and was a valuable experience for me. It was nice to see the growth that I would potentially make throughout my internships. The interns who were ahead of me were a great support system and gave me a great deal of advice in regard to assignments and other experiences. As I moved into my final internship, it was also a time for me to take a leadership role and provide that same advice to the new interns.

A second candidate reflected on the value of learning about data and assessment through participating in this activity, a clear indicator of a deeper learning experience in which one does real work supported by more expert professionals:

> I was able to participate in data teams, which was really helpful in knowing what student data looks like, how to navigate student work, collaborative learning, and using rubrics to assess students and drive instruction. This type of collaboration is something I haven't seen before and I think it was vital to my understanding of assessment.

A third candidate emphasized the value of having an opportunity to reflect on learning to teach—clearly different from a focus on learning to mimic good practices observed in others: "What was most meaningful to me was the opportunity to form a community of colleagues that offered a space for us to reflect upon our experiences."

These views were widely repeated across programs. There were also many comments about the value of the coteaching apprenticeship framework that most programs established for their candidates—one in which candidates genuinely share responsibility for the class, even as they experience graduated responsibility over the course of the semester or year until they are ready to take the lead in the classroom for lessons and units of study. As a Montclair graduate noted, "What is compelling about Montclair's approach to coteaching is that it introduces teacher candidates to teaching as a collaborative profession from the very beginning."

FEEDBACK THAT SUPPORTS REFLECTION ON TEACHING

Both coursework and fieldwork are characterized by instructional conversations that provide candidates with ongoing feedback and support for structured reflection on teaching. All of the programs aim to teach candidates how to become "reflective practitioners," in the words of Donald Schön.[12] Reflection is associated with every activity. Candidates learn to pause and consider what they are doing or have just done and to what effect. Often, they collect data or receive perspectives from others to aid in that reflective process. The same is true for cooperating teachers, supervisors, and faculty alike. Reflection encourages members of each teaching community to monitor how they are progressing, identify how they can improve, and learn to shape future choices and actions. Reflection allows individuals to direct their own learning by providing a structure for diagnosing where they are and identifying the supports needed to continuously learn—a skill needed in the dynamic twenty-first century.

A common practice in all of the programs is to build reflections into coursework assignments. An example of an assignment from the High Tech Methods course shows how "Putting It into Practice" is meant to shape candidates' own reflective mind-sets.

This assignment presents a goal and a challenge for the first day of class, emphasizes that engagement with students in a supportive classroom environment is an ongoing process, and models the sorts of questions that a teacher might ask about the first day. It begins the year by providing very specific scaffolding for the reflection process, which will become routine by year's end. Attention is given not only to issues of procedure and student participation, and to the teachers' objectives and intended achievements, but also to the teachers' hopes and fears. Reflecting on their own emotions is essential to preparing teachers to identify the emotions and needs of their students and to respond appropriately. Getting to know students, communicating classroom norms, and preparing to create a supportive environment all contribute to constructing the sort of classroom community in which deeper learning can occur.

This assignment also illustrates how the methods course explicitly focuses on inclusion of student voice in the feedback and reflection process, another facet of High Tech High's instructional philosophy and a key aspect of deeper learning. As the course syllabus states, "We believe that school-aged students should be involved in the process of helping teachers improve their practice. We will be experimenting with some ways to include young people's' voices in our class." High Tech High candidates learn how

Put It into Practice:
The first day of school

Goal: Use the first day of class to begin developing a strong classroom community and positive relationships with students.

Challenge: This is the first opportunity for you to connect with your students and begin to develop a positive classroom culture. Think about all of the emotions that you are feeling around the first week of school. How might your students be feeling about coming to a new school or returning after the summer? How can you use the first day to get to know your students better and help them learn more about other students in their class? How can they begin to get to know you and understand your goals for the class? How can you find out what they are excited or nervous about in regard to your class? How can you engage them in the work of your discipline in a way that gets them excited to come back for more? These are questions that cannot all be answered on just the first day of school, as it takes time to create a supportive and collaborative environment in the classroom. However, the first day sets the tone for the rest of the year and is an awesome opportunity to start connecting with your students.

Reflection: Write a one-page reflection after implementing the lesson in your class that addresses some of the following questions: What did you do the first day of class? What were your goals for the lesson? What went well? What would you improve if you had the chance to do it over again? How did you get to know your students and provide opportunities for them to get to know each other? How did students learn about supports and services? What are the expectations of the classroom teacher and the student who has special needs? What did students learn about classroom expectations and norms? Were students able to contribute? Why or why not? Did you have the opportunity to begin developing any routines that students can expect? How does this lesson fit into the larger context of what you hope to accomplish during the first week (or first few weeks) of school? What do you think will be your greatest struggle in fostering a supportive learning environment for students? What are your fears? What support can we help provide through this course?

to receive feedback and input from their students regularly and how to co-construct projects and other learning activities with the young people in their classes.

CU Denver uses the Teaching/Learning Inquiry Cycle (TLIC), drawn in part from the framework developed by the Teacher Education by Design (TEDD) project of the University of Washington's College of Education.[13] The tool helps both university and school-based faculty frame teaching as a cycle of (1) planning, (2) teaching, (3) monitoring and adjusting, and

(4) reflection and development of next steps. The cycle, as conceptualized by CU Denver, is depicted in figure 4.1 and includes four steps that site supervisors, site professors, and clinical teachers routinely use to guide teacher candidates' actual teaching experiences.

A second tool used throughout the program reinforces the Teaching/ Learning Inquiry Cycle (TLIC) in diverse classrooms. It is a classroom observation protocol called the Quality Responsive Classroom (QRC). The QRC process begins with having candidates identify a teaching goal around which they will focus their cycle of inquiry. They then engage in a four-step QRC process: (1) questioning/wondering, (2) action steps, (3) collection of data/evidence, and (4) reflection. The tool allows observers to collect data about students, the teacher, and the classroom learning community that help the teacher candidates reflect systematically on the extent to which their instruction is enabling deeper learning in culturally and linguistically diverse classrooms. The QRC and TLIC, used in conjunction with one another, then give candidates tools that help them "drive their own professional learning in an intentional way that can improve their professional practice in order to better meet the needs of their students."[14]

Programs also provide candidates with feedback and reflection through the supervision of clinical work. All the programs carefully structure supervisory relationships to provide routines and feedback that aid in this process. As programs plant ongoing opportunities for teacher candidates

FIGURE 4.1   **Teaching/Learning Inquiry Cycle**

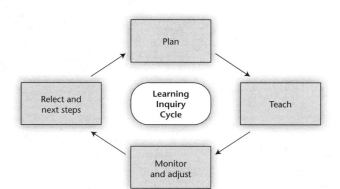

Source: CU Denver, Urban Community Teacher Education Program, "Windows of Development Key,"
http://www.ucdenver.edu/academics/colleges/SchoolOfEducation/CurrentStudents/Resources/program
_docs/Teaching-Learning%20Inquiry%20Cycle%20_TLIC_%20Assessment%GEN_SPEDx.pdf.

to inquire, observe, and reflect on their experiences, they create habits of mind that translate to reflection in the classroom after they have graduated. Doing so, graduates refine their teaching practices, and to help their schools and communities improve to better meet students' needs. One Bank Street candidate emphasized that the abundance of reflection in the college's courses "definitely helped me move into fieldwork, because every day I would think about my day, what worked, what didn't work, how can I touch this student, this one didn't really participate and why. It's all about the questioning and asking a lot of them."

Another shared how the reflection that she experienced translated to her teaching:

> [Reflection is] what we are asking children to do. Even four-year-olds. "Do you think that was a good choice?" That's a reflection. Think about what we learned today. Learn from the person sitting next to you. We're the students here. And then we're going to the classroom and being teachers, so we need to learn what it feels like to be a student, and that's what makes you a good teacher. . . . They make you understand what it is to be a student and if you know that secret, you can teach.

Frequently, this process is supported by videotapes of teaching that allow more considered feedback, study, and reflection. For example, at High Tech High schools, the multitiered system used to evaluate interns' teaching practices includes:

- video recording multiple days of the intern's teaching
- posting and sharing the recorded lessons with the intern for his/her review
- having the intern's students complete the YouthTruth survey, an instrument designed to assess student perceptions of their classroom experiences[15]
- a reflection created by the intern of his/her teaching practice, using information from the videos and survey
- a discussion between the intern and the school director (principal), who acts as the intern's formal supervisor, supported by subject-matter mentors who also work with candidates

We interviewed Robert, a school director who has been with High Tech High for nine years as a teacher, director, and graduate student, and who also teaches in the intern program. During the interview, Robert described how, during his discussion with the intern, they watch one of the recordings, selected by the intern, and discuss the results from the YouthTruth survey. He noted that he uses prompts such as "What did you notice?" "What strikes you?" and "What questions do you have?" to start a dialogue about the intern's practice.

At the conclusion of the meeting, the intern identifies four themes that emerge as strengths, two themes that surface as areas of growth, and any questions he or she has for the students. This information is shared with the students and discussed. There is then one additional discussion between the intern and the school director about what the intern has learned from the process.

The support interns receive from the school director is augmented by their assigned mentor—a veteran teacher in the same building who is teaching in a similar area and grade level. The interns observe their mentors as models for exemplary practice and meet with them weekly. Mentor teachers are expected to observe interns formally four times per school year and provide substantive opportunities for the intern to reflect on his or her practice. Interns produce a written reflection every year that addresses the areas of relationships, reflective practice, and authentic work, which gives them another opportunity to reflect on their practice and to receive and respond to feedback.

In most of these programs, instructional conversations occur when program faculty actively engage at field sites. For example, many Alverno faculty and teacher candidates explained to us how faculty look for candidates' use of the project-based, student-centered strategies discussed in courses when they visit the candidates on-site. Faculty give candidates specific feedback on their performance in their field placement to help them refine their practice, using the same rubric the cooperating teacher and candidate use. A student teacher explained:

> My faculty supervisor knows me as a student and he is able to push me . . . He knows how to tailor his feedback so that I have something to work on. . . . Over the course of the semester [my faculty supervisor] fills out the same rubric; it's for me to fill out as a self-assessment, and it is the same one my cooperating teacher fills out. It is important that I'm getting feedback on the exact same criteria so that I can see different perspectives on how I can improve. . . . I think this is a much more robust way to look at someone going into this profession, because you

can give me an A on your observation, but what does your A mean? So, this [rubric] is very clear.

One of the Bank Street advisors noted that "coursework doesn't mean much if you're not using it in an active way," a statement with which all of the programs would agree. Coursework provides teacher candidates with the theories, frameworks, and vocabulary that they can use to analyze and bring meaning to their fieldwork experiences. The coursework models the student-centered deeper learning practices that teacher candidates develop in their fieldwork, and then receive feedback and reflect on in conference group.

This principle is seen in other programs as well. For instance, at Alverno, the ability-based assessment system is based on candidates' ability to learn from clear, specific feedback. Faculty both give feedback and model how to receive feedback as a means to improve. One instructor explained that the faculty are "constantly talking, reviewing, revising, adapting to what meets our learners' needs." Faculty reflect with each other and seek feedback from candidates. The instructor described how she shares with her students "that I changed this lesson completely in response to what students have said." The instructor does this so that her students understand the necessity for educators to continuously elicit feedback from their students in order to improve their instruction. This is a powerful lesson coming from a faculty member with over thirty years of experience teaching at the college.

Not only do faculty model specific feedback, but they also teach their students how to give and receive quality, actionable feedback, in both coursework and fieldwork. One example is through observation and analysis of videotaped candidate lessons, as illustrated in the box "Learning by Giving and Receiving Feedback."

In this vignette, the candidates are directing their own learning and reflection. The Alverno instructor provided the necessary structures to give the candidates agency over their learning through her clear expectations for the assignment, for giving feedback, and for self-reflection. The instructor's experiential lesson models the types of preparation and tools required to support learning opportunities driven by students. The lesson also helps candidates ask the types of questions that will help them continue to improve throughout their career. Candidates' experiences providing feedback during their preparation at Alverno support their ability both to continually self-assess and to provide feedback to their students to help them grow.

Learning by Giving and Receiving Feedback

It is the last day of class in ED 225, Literacy in Early Childhood. In this course, candidates learn about emergent literacy, oral language, reading, writing, and literature. This course is the second of four field experiences for Alverno undergraduate students. It is an opportunity for candidates to observe and practice literacy teaching in an elementary school setting.

Candidates practice making sound decisions, teaching literacy learning strategies, selecting appropriate materials, and designing developmentally appropriate learning activities and assessments.

Before the class begins, six students are gathered around the back of the room, sharing a potluck feast of Oreos, pepperoni pizza, cheesecake brownies, hummus and pita chips, pastries, and caffeine. They are about to celebrate their progress in teaching literacy, but first they will each share a fifteen-minute video of themselves teaching a literacy lesson in their field placement. Candidates observe themselves and each other, and then give each other specific feedback based on the theories and pedagogies they learned in this class and in prior Alverno coursework and field experiences. As the syllabus describes, the goal of this activity is to "share and reflect on video-clips to build a deeper understanding of effective literacy lessons in relation to student learning and theory."

The instructor has prepared a variety of materials to support the teacher candidates during this class. She has printed PowerPoint slides for her students that include helpful notes, such as

Key Questions for Teaching and Learning: (1) What do we want our students to know and be able to do? (2) How do we know the effect of our program on student learning? (3) What can we do to facilitate learning?

The instructor's notes also outline a helpful approach to scaffolding:

Teacher	Student
I do . . .	You watch
I do . . .	You help
I help . . .	You do
I watch . . .	You do

The instructor provides many tools to support the candidates' learning during the video activity:

- A self-assessment framework.
- Criteria for evaluating candidates' fieldwork lessons, which are informed by the Wisconsin teaching standards and Alverno's educational standards.
- A rubric for evaluating candidates' self-assessments. For example, when considering a candidate's effectiveness at "observing the entire teaching performance" during a lesson, a *beginning* or *emerging* rating would be "Identifies the strengths and weaknesses and provides accurate observations as evidence for strengths and weaknesses"; whereas an *advanced* or *distinctive* rating would be

"Applies disciplinary concepts and frameworks to observations, showing creative judgment in their individual or combined use."
- Prompts or "thinking frames" for the candidates to help them give each other feedback that connects to theories about teaching and learning, such as "I noticed the student(s) when you (the teacher). _____ This reflects _____ theory because _____."

After the instructor begins class with a brief overview of the goals for the day, the six students split into groups of three, in separate classrooms. They spend fifteen minutes observing one candidate's videotaped lesson and another fifteen minutes giving the candidate feedback on her lesson. This feedback includes "Glows" (i.e., the effective teaching strategies that the candidate adopted in the video), "Evidence of Student Learning," and "Grows" (suggestions for changes). As the candidates review each other's videos, they notice tools and resources that the mentor teachers use in their classrooms. For example, in one video, a teacher illustrates a classroom management technique for getting students' attention—saying "one, two, three" and having the students clap. Through the videos, teacher candidates can observe multiple classrooms and multiple approaches to teaching literacy and organizing a classroom.

During one video, a candidate presents a vocabulary lesson that she provided in her first-grade field placement. As the video plays, the candidate presenting the video acknowledges that the reading she selected for the lesson "is too complicated" because "the sentences are too long" for first graders. The candidates provide each other feedback and note observations through the video clips. The instructor takes notes during the candidates' videos and discussions. She rarely joins the candidates' conversation and does so only to ask a clarifying question.

AUTHENTIC ASSESSMENTS OF PROGRESS

The contexts for feedback and reflection in coursework and clinical work are many and varied and constitute a range of formative assessments from faculty, instructors, supervisors, peers, and candidates themselves. The value of this constant iterative process is that it is rooted in a range of authentic assessments of candidates' practice. These include regular supervisory evaluations of practice in candidates' clinical placements; formal benchmark assessments at the university that evaluate progress on specific skills and may determine continuation in the program; and culminating assessments that often determine graduation and even licensure.

Supervisory Evaluations

Formal observations of candidates in their placement classrooms are common at regular junctions, bracketing many informal observations with feedback from supervisors and mentors in between. SFTR's approach is similar to that used in other programs. In addition to regular visits and feedback from supervisors, three formal quarterly evaluations across the academic year are used both to track individual progress over time and to look for trends across the resident group to see where there may be a disproportionate number of people struggling in a given area. Fieldwork assessments—based on observations of residents' teaching practice—are aligned to the California Standards for the Teaching Profession (CSTP), which are used both by SFTR and the SFUSD teacher evaluation system. The cooperating teacher, the resident, and the coach all independently fill out the evaluation, rating the candidate against the CSTP standards with cited evidence, before they meet to discuss and reflect on next steps.

These formal quarterly observations are a key lever in facilitating deeper learning for residents about how to engage their own students in deeper learning. They assess whether residents have incorporated teaching strategies to "use knowledge of students to engage them in learning," "connect learning to students' prior knowledge, backgrounds, life experiences and interests," "connect subject matter to meaningful, real life contexts," and "promote critical thinking through inquiry, problem solving and reflection."

In addition to these quarterly formal assessments, SFTR supervisors visit residents' classrooms weekly. For these more informal observations, supervisors collect observation data to support residents in, for example, examining patterns of participation in their classroom or studying what effect their classroom language may have on targeted students and on how the classroom community functions. In their many debriefing conversations with their residents over the course of the residency year, supervisors play a variety of mentoring roles, depending on the context that day: *instructive*, in which the mentor offers suggestions and solutions, such as pointing out ways to differentiate instruction; *collaborative*, in which the mentor and the resident coconstruct materials and solutions, such as codeveloping a lesson or curriculum unit; and *facilitative*, in which the mentor acts as a facilitator of the resident's thinking and problem solving, and the resident self-assesses and self-prescribes.

Benchmark Assessments

A number of programs have organized formal benchmark assessments to track progress throughout the program and to ascertain that critical skills are being mastered. Alverno's ability-based curriculum calls for frequent benchmark assessments, linked to statements of outcomes and explicit criteria that are very specific about what is being assessed.[16] To support students in becoming self-directed learners, Alverno also emphasizes self-assessment, which requires a self-aware student to judge "what she has achieved in her performance, how she achieved it, why she did what she did, and what she might yet do to improve."[17] The standards and assessment instruments for each ability are established to create an agreement between the teacher candidate and the evaluator on what the candidate should be learning, thereby holding both parties responsible for fulfilling the relative implied conditions to achieve the learning objective. Next, assessors, including the student, judge the student's performance, give feedback, and then evaluate the performance and learning process.

The assessment process is collaborative. One Alverno professor explained how "assessment" comes from the Latin word *assessus*, meaning "sitting beside." She explained how during assessment at Alverno, "[teacher candidates] have the criteria, I have the criteria, we are having a conversation. This takes root into a person and contributes to transformational learning. You can't master deep content knowledge unless you are aware of the knowledge."

Throughout candidates' coursework and fieldwork, they complete a series of performance assessments. For example, after candidates' first field placement, they complete a portfolio and interview assessment. This assessment requires candidates to connect evidence of their teaching practice to two Interstate Teacher Assessment and Support Consortium standards and two Alverno education abilities. This assessment lays the groundwork for narrative evidence-based writing.

Before students advance to student teaching, they complete another portfolio and interview assessment. For this assessment, candidates prepare evidence of their readiness to student teach from their prior coursework and field experiences. Candidates must demonstrate that they have developed the dispositions and mind-sets teachers need to help all students develop deeper learning competencies. As part of the assessment, candidates meet with K–12 practitioners (e.g., principals and teachers) to discuss the portfolio and challenges of teaching. This interview assessment serves as a gateway into student teaching. If students do not successfully complete their interview they are counseled out of teaching and into a more appropriate course of study at Alverno.

After frequently experiencing this type of ability-based performance assessment and reflection approach, teacher candidates are well situated to apply it in their classrooms when they become teachers. Fully 100 percent of surveyed candidates report that Alverno prepared them very well to "use a variety of assessments, including observations, papers, portfolios, or performance tasks to determine strengths and needs to inform instruction."

CU Denver's benchmark assessments—called Program-Level Assessments (PLAs)—occur at three points in time and help create coherence across the multiple teacher education pathways. These formal performance assessments, which are guided by the essential questions (see chapter 2) and anchor experiences (see appendix B), look much like an oral defense. Candidates' actual teaching performance is assessed through a process called residency internship-based assessments.

PROGRAM-LEVEL ASSESSMENTS. In the PLAs, candidates present their own growth and development related to the four essential questions, drawing on specific evidence from anchor experiences, coursework, and clinical experiences. The PLAs are conducted in small groups with faculty, K–12 partners, and peer evaluation. In addition to presenting before an audience of their peers and faculty members, candidates also submit written self-reflections that are then scored according to a rubric. The PLAs occur at the following times:

- End of semester 1—Focus on Essential Questions 1 and 2 and AnchorExperiences 1 and 2
- End of semester 2—Focus on Essential Questions 1–4 and Anchor Experiences 2–5
- End of program—Focus on Essential Questions 1–4 and all six Anchor Experiences

Candidates are guided in their classes to prepare PLAs, using their course-based research and student teaching experience as evidence. As they present their ideas prior to the formal assessment, they gain peer feedback and access the knowledge their peers are gaining from the program as well. By pulling together material from coursework, clinical experiences, and their own reflections on their learning, the candidates can apply and reflect on what they have learned. The PLAs inform improvement strategies for the program itself as well as for the candidates. The CU Denver program gathers formative data from these common program assessments, and faculty use these data to both inform their work with candidates so they will meet the Colorado teaching standards and to guide broader program revisions.

RESIDENCY INTERNSHIP–BASED ASSESSMENTS.   In addition to the PLAs, assessment of a teacher candidate's actual teaching practice occurs throughout the residency-based internships that stretch across the program. Residency internship performance is guided and evaluated through a well-developed Residency Internship Assessment Body of Evidence that uses multiple evaluation and coaching tools to support and assess the development of complex urban teaching practices across the sequence of all clinical placements. These tools are used by teacher candidates as a means of self-assessment as well as by site professors, site coordinators, and clinical teachers. In addition, as at High Tech High, a Student Perception Feedback tool is used to involve K–12 student voice in the overall body of evidence.

Culminating Assessments

All of the programs have some set of culminating assessments that reflect the candidates' ability to integrate theory and practice and to put teaching principles into action. High Tech High participants are required to maintain a digital portfolio of their PITP assignments, final project or signature assignments, and notes received from their mentor, including observations. This portfolio becomes a tool that provides a clear and accessible way for candidates to reflect on their practice and observe their progress. By modeling reflective teaching, the digital portfolios scaffold learning about teaching while also helping the intern teachers think about how to provide such experiences for their own students. By combining applied coursework with notes and observations, and putting into place a cycle of practice and reflection, these portfolios give interns the chance to apply their learning to the complex problems of teaching, to receive feedback, and to revise and reapply their ideas accordingly.

This requirement also serves to introduce the intern teachers to digital portfolios, knowledge they need because those teaching at one of High Tech High's schools are expected to maintain a separate digital portfolio as a communications tool and resource for students and families. At the elementary level, the portfolio is primarily intended to communicate with parents about what is going on in the class, including information such as available resources and ways to volunteer. At the secondary level, the portfolio serves as a platform for teachers and students to engage around course expectations and assignments.

Trinity candidates complete a portfolio based on the Texas Teacher Evaluation and Support System (T-TESS) rubric, which is used in teacher evaluations statewide.[18] Candidates have midyear and end-of-year conferences with their clinical faculty advisor and mentor teacher, the first led by clinical faculty, the second led by the candidate. Candidates must show evidence of their practice, in part by meeting proficiency on the T-TESS, and must invite their faculty member and mentor to provide feedback. Candidates are also required to discuss how their perspectives and biases affect their instruction and how they have worked to address them.

Trinity's teaching employment portfolio highlights learning and accomplishments from the MAT program and preparation for future employment. Required components of the portfolio include a resume, an internship description, an account of professional development, and a description of their program curriculum. Candidates also include evidence from their teaching practice, including examples of family communication, classroom learning, community development, contributions to the schools and profession, and technology proficiency. They also add other items such as certifications, letters of reference, evaluations, degrees, and academic transcripts. In addition, the exit portfolio includes assessments completed during the exit conferences at their field placements, assessed via the Trinity University T-TESS Professional Teaching Standards rubric. To illustrate their readiness to enter the profession, candidates are required to incorporate an "authentic and important artifact for audiences beyond the MAT program," including potential employers, future colleagues, and department faculty.

Bank Street candidates' culminating project is the Integrative Master's Project (IMP), which is an opportunity for students to apply their theoretical knowledge to their work as educators. Teacher candidates can select from a variety of options for their IMP, including a portfolio that includes reflective essays and artifacts from their graduate work, an essay or research project directed by a faculty mentor, or a collaborative inquiry project where one to six students meet with a faculty advisor to define and complete a small-scale site-based research study.

In addition to these internally developed assessments, in recent years, performance assessments for licensure have begun to spread across the country. These stand in stark contrast to the multiple-choice tests that have predominated in the teacher licensure space, none of which have been found to be strong predictors of teaching effectiveness, both in their design and in their relationship to teacher effectiveness.[19] While many universities have used portfolios for decades, more structured performance assessments of teaching for large-scale use were first developed by the National Board for Professional Teaching Standards in the early 1990s for evaluating accomplished teaching of veteran teachers.

In 1998, California passed a law requiring teacher performance assessments as a condition of licensure for beginning teachers. The state developed a version called the CalTPA, in collaboration with the Educational Testing Service (ETS), and a group of universities (organized by Stanford University and including all the University of California campuses and a number of California State University campuses, plus Mills College), designed the Performance Assessment for California Teachers (PACT), which was accepted by the state as an alternative.[20] Used by thirty-two California programs, the PACT was picked up by other programs in other states and eventually evolved into a nationwide assessment, the edTPA, now used for licensure or accreditation in eighteen states and by local programs across forty states.[21] The initial CalTPA, now being replaced by a new design that is more deeply grounded in classroom practice, was designed by ETS and is now marketed by ETS in other states as the Praxis Performance Assessment for Teachers (PPAT).

These performance assessments call on teachers to demonstrate that they can plan instruction, modify it to meet students' special needs, teach a planned lesson within a curriculum unit (with a videotaped artifact and commentary explaining the teaching decisions), analyze student learning, and reflect on what else is needed to ensure student learning. As candidates complete planning, instruction, and assessment tasks, as well as reflections on the lesson and student learning from it, they must also provide evidence that their decisions are based on knowledge of the teaching context. They must focus on and analyze the work of individual students in assessing the lesson and describe how the lesson met the needs of English learners.

Six of the seven programs we studied are in states that have recently begun to require the use of one of these assessments, and several of the programs had faculty involved in designing the PACT or the EdTPA. High Tech High and SFTR have used the PACT.[22] Alverno, Bank Street, and Montclair use the edTPA. CU Denver has developed a homegrown performance assessment that draws upon features of the edTPA, which they studied closely, and the Teacher Work Sampling Methodology they had previously used, contextualizing the final version in the teaching tools and student assessments that are used locally. Trinity uses the PPAT.

We heard accounts of the impact of these assessments at several of the programs we studied. For example, at Trinity, the PPAT assessment reinforces the program's focus on differentiation and analysis of individual students' needs. As in the PACT and the edTPA, candidates pick focal students for instructional and assessment tasks that have different learning needs. Candidates may, for example, pick a special education student or an English language learner. They design accommodations for those students in their lesson plans, look at data about them, evaluate how they scored on assessments, examine samples of their work, and then analyze the effectiveness of their strategies. One elementary candidate described this process: "Every part of PPAT was collecting and analyzing data on an individual student basis and classroom basis and how lessons would be impacted." Candidates said that the process provided them with "good practice in differentiation" and allowed them to reflect on their practice and the changes they would need to make to their lesson if they needed to reteach a concept or skill.

By posing tasks that capture the essence of student-centered teaching, these assessments help support candidate learning. Equally important, the assessments shape program design in noticeable ways, guiding, deepening, and connecting coursework and clinical work—an important lever we discuss more fully in chapter 11, where we examine teaching policy.

WELL-DESIGNED CLINICAL APPRENTICESHIPS

Of all the ways that these programs support learning to teach for deeper learning, perhaps the most important is how they structure clinical work. Many schools of education send candidates into short student teaching placements unconnected to their coursework and, too often, into classrooms that fail to illustrate high-quality teaching. In contrast, these seven programs all work to structure extended clinical placements so that candidates become apprentices to accomplished teachers in classrooms that instantiate the practices described in their tightly connected coursework. In these apprenticeships, they can watch excellent modeling of instruction and learn how to emulate it step by step, with explanations about decision-making that support their own developing abilities to make complex judgments about practice.

All of the programs take a careful and deliberate approach when selecting cooperating teachers and all seek to work with partnership schools to create communities of practice focused on deeper learning and equity. Program faculty also engage as members of those school-based learning communities.

Extended, Carefully Selected, and Well-Supported Placements

In various ways, each of the programs assures that candidates have the equivalent of at least a full academic year of supervised clinical experience as part of their training program. In the case of the residency programs and MAT programs, candidates are in school under the wing of an expert cooperating or mentor teacher from the start of school to the last day of the district's school year. Undergraduate programs have clinical placements of various lengths throughout several years and then at least a full semester of full-time student teaching when they can take on coteaching responsibilities. The five-year Trinity model adds a full-year apprenticeship to significant undergraduate clinical experience. The High Tech High apprenticeship or internship offers two years of supervised practice either in the classroom with another teacher (for apprentices) or independently (for interns who have taught previously) with close mentoring.

Graduates of all the programs described the power of extended, closely supervised clinical experience. As an SFTR graduate reflected:

> I think the people that started SFTR . . . knew as new teachers exactly where we'd end up and made sure that we had that whole experience. I think being with the [cooperating teacher] before the students come is huge—understanding how you get your classroom ready and how you get it all started is another big part. Then being there until the end [of the school year] and just having that CT there every day and having other residents at our location to talk about bigger school issues. . . . It was a good setup.

A Trinity alumnus shared a similar sentiment:

> The internship is the best part. Oftentimes I've heard my colleagues write off formal teacher prep programs as all theory with no real transferrable knowledge. The MAT program definitely takes care of that. I always tell people that it was like having your first year of teaching with a safety net in the background. You get all of the experiences of a first-year teacher, but with an experienced teacher to help guide you in the most difficult times and assist you in reflecting on what works and what doesn't.

The value of a full-year student teaching or residency experience, the cohort experience, and apprenticeships with supportive and knowledgeable faculty and mentors were repeatedly highlighted in candidates' responses to open-ended questions on the end-of-year and program exit surveys. CU Denver students praised the intensity of the full-year placement: "Being at the same school for a whole school year, and the experiences I gained in the classroom" was a key part of the program for one respondent, while another reported, "I was able to spend a year in the classroom figuring out

what [the] heck it is I am supposed to be doing and the best way to do it."
A third cited "the ample opportunities in the classroom" as a key program
feature, adding, "Being able to put learning into practice is huge!"

University Supervisors: A Linchpin for Supports

All of the programs provide intensive support from university supervisors,
who generally meet with the candidates in small groups weekly and visit
them regularly on-site in their schools. At Bank Street this small-group meeting is referred to as "conference group" and it provides a place for teacher
candidates to discuss the issues they are facing as educators in their field
placements. The Childhood General Education program director explained:

> [The conference group] is a core component of the supervised field-
> work experience where . . . a small group [of candidates] meets to-
> gether and . . . the topics emerge from the needs of the students. It's
> a confidential group. It gives them a place where they can talk about
> issues . . . it's a place where they start to question the things they are
> adopting as their own belief system.

The conference group—sometimes called a supervisory group in other
programs—is an opportunity for teacher candidates to gain perspective and
reflective insight into their practice as educators. It is also an opportunity
for teacher candidates to apply the material from their coursework to their
practice.[23] As Bank Street president Shael Suransky explained, it "enables
students to integrate the study of theory with practice and develop a strong
professional identity as teachers."

All the programs agree with one of the Bank Street advisors who noted
that "coursework doesn't mean much if you're not using it in an active
way." Coursework provides teacher candidates with the theories, frameworks, and vocabulary to analyze and bring meaning to their fieldwork experiences—and this process occurs within their conference or supervisory
group. The coursework also models the student-centered, project-based
teaching and learning that teacher candidates experiment with in their
fieldwork, and then reflect on in conference group.

Supervisors/advisors typically also work closely with the school-based
mentors/cooperating teachers. Supervisors are the bridge between the program and the school site: they discuss candidates' experiences, help them
connect theory to practice, support ongoing problem solving, and communicate regularly with the school-based mentor through emails and phone
calls, on top of their in-person interactions. In these programs, supervisors

usually have from four to eight candidates to support—a smaller number than in many other institutions. In many programs, supervisors are former teachers who have been recruited to this work at the university, perhaps in retirement or when teachers go on to doctoral work. At Alverno, Bank Street, and Trinity, faculty also often serve as advisors or supervisors to candidates in their clinical settings, which strengthens the relationship further as they are seeing and supporting candidates in both their school and university classrooms.

Close relationships between university faculty and placement sites also allow schools to improve the quality of the placement itself. Across programs, we heard many mentor teachers explain how their own practice had improved as a function of the work with the student teacher and supervisor. One elementary mentor at Trinity noted, for example, "I hope to be a mentor next year. It increases my practice tenfold." An Alverno instructor and alum explained how one candidate in a physics placement had a mentor teacher who engaged in traditional, teacher-centered instruction, and did not model deeper learning practices and dispositions or allow the student teacher to engage in student-centered instruction. Due to the limited number of physics teachers willing to be mentor teachers, the Alverno instructor and the student teacher had to find a way to make this placement a productive experience for the candidate. To do this, the instructor explained to the mentor teacher that Alverno candidates are required to implement certain practices in their placements—in this case, implement more labs and more interactive small-group activities. The instructor also worked with the candidate and mentor to modify the mentor teacher's curriculum so that she could practice engaging students in active, collaborative lessons.

SFTR changed its supervisory model recently, moving to a full-time coach model from one in which, in the words of SFTR's director of clinical education, "there was a conglomeration of folks who were supervising and a lot of them were in an adjunct, hourly capacity." This conglomeration of hourly supervisors is common in many teacher education programs—an approach that makes it hard to build a coherent process. The director explained what prompted this structural shift:

> It was really clear that it was challenging to help build staff community, to make them feel like they were part of something. It was hard to ask people to do things that weren't part of their job responsibility, and so things felt pretty disjointed because they were really going to clock in for an hour every Friday and then do eighty minutes a week for each person—anything else wasn't totally fair to ask them or we

needed to pay them extra. So the move toward these lead supervisors grew out the recognition that [the previous approach] didn't really seem like the best model.

SFTR's coaches support both current residents and first- and second-year graduates of the program who are full-time teachers receiving mentoring. One SFTR coach, who had served as an SFTR cooperating teacher for six years prior to becoming a coach, described the more intensive supervision that SFTR provides its residents, as compared to other programs:

> [When I was a cooperating teacher,] I worked through another credentialing program and also SFTR. I feel that, when I had that student teacher through the other program, she was not as well prepared. I did the best I could at being her mentor teacher, but I didn't have, honestly and realistically, the time to coach her to the extent that she needed.
>
> Through my work with SFTR, I see that there's such great value to the coaching that's happening by someone who comes in from the outside on a regular basis. I think that that's the consistent difference that says that they're better prepared to work with SFUSD students, because they've been better coached. [When I was a cooperating teacher] in other credential programs, I'd see a supervisor once a term, and I'd be left a business card on my desk saying, "Call me if you have any questions." Whereas [with SFTR], I always had a supervisor coming into my classroom, and I knew that my practice as a mentor was also being helped and supported because somebody was coming in and willing to work with the resident and do professional development, which is the most powerful difference.

One SFTR graduate reaffirmed the strength of this approach in a survey comment: "Part of the reason I was attracted to this program was the opportunity that I would receive from my supervisor and teachers. . . . This program, hands-down, is much better than a regular teacher prep program because the supervisor provides feedback on lessons I give at my placement."

In addition to supporting residents and first- and second-year SFTR graduates, coaches often end up providing support to the CTs themselves. As one coach noted:

> What I find is that the longer I work with a teacher, the more in tune I become with their practice, [so] they can start reaching out for other

kinds of support. This year, two of my cooperating teachers are former residents. I coached them as residents and one of them I coached through one year of the [induction] program. Now she's a cooperating teacher, [and] I'm coaching her as a mentor. For those teachers, we have well-established patterns of talking about practice. When I go to see them, they're very ready to talk about their practice and receive feedback.

In all the programs we studied, this set of relationships that supervisors create—coupled with their expert knowledge of teaching—builds possibilities for improving practice in ways that extend beyond the novice teachers themselves.

School-Based Mentors: Experts, Partners, and Learners

These programs are very focused on finding school-based cooperating teachers or mentors who can model deeper learning practices and are eager to develop their abilities to do so further. In fact, Alverno recently changed the title of "cooperating" teachers to "mentor" teachers to convey that they are looking for teachers who do more than just cooperate. They want to place teacher candidates with teachers who invest their time and energy in helping candidates improve. We use the terms "cooperating teacher" and "mentor" interchangeably in this section because the programs use different terms to designate the same function.

FINDING MENTORS. When selecting mentor teachers, Alverno's list of desired qualities is very much like that of the other programs.

- Teachers who model the types of deeper learning pedagogies and dispositions that the college aims to instill in its candidates
- Teachers who can explain their instructional choices
- Teachers who are strong in assessment—who know how to utilize a variety of assessments and then use the results of those assessments to adjust instruction accordingly
- Teachers who are strong in classroom management
- Teachers who understand their student population, meaning they know their students and their backgrounds
- Teachers who feel confident in their classroom, so that they will be comfortable turning their classroom over to the candidate
- Teachers who do not think "they are the best and the greatest" or want to "turn their student teacher into a 'mini-me'"

In addition to these qualities, Trinity faculty particularly emphasize that the mentor teacher is willing to learn, to collaborate and welcome a partner in the classroom, and to let the teacher candidate eventually fly. Mentors must be curious and willing to learn, in keeping with Trinity's emphasis on inquiry. A program leader noted:

> [The] mentor's openness to learning is what we hope they possess. We want them to have a commitment to continued growth, including an interest in learning about the program and the practice of mentoring. We think that being a good teacher is necessary but not sufficient to being a good mentor. So, are they willing to come to mentoring training and develop their practice? And, are they going to make space for a novice to learn and grow with and from them, as well as find their own voice in the process?

A High Tech High leader added, "We also are looking for mentors who are reflective in their own practice and strong practitioners of project-based learning, [and who are] also using structures within that PBL that do support equity within their classroom."

SFTR adds to these qualities that cooperating teachers see themselves as teacher educators who are committed to deepening their own skills and that of new teachers:

> Cooperating Teachers (CTs) for SFTR are committed educators working in San Francisco classrooms and are interested in training the next generation of teachers. CTs have successfully established productive and caring learning communities, possess strong classroom management skills, and deliver differentiated, student-centered instruction in San Francisco neighborhoods that have been traditionally underserved. CTs see themselves as teacher educators, are reflective, are comfortable making their practice public, and are committed to deepening their own skills as teachers and mentors.[24]

Like other programs, SFTR prizes in CTs the willingness to learn and reflect on practice that is so essential to deeper learning. As a long-time supervisor noted: "The most important quality of a CT is the disposition to be open to trying new things, to be open to questioning their practice, to being a learner. No one has every teaching tool in their backpack."

To select mentors, these programs go beyond what many do—which is ask the principal whether there is any teacher who will accept a student teacher. Faculty or clinical directors are in schools observing classrooms, working with a variety of teachers, and inviting promising mentors who exhibit these characteristics to consider accepting a student teacher. Most have developed long-term relationships with a group of mentors and partnership schools where these practices are cultivated. Most include a substantial number of their own alumni, who understand the programs' approaches and have developed deeper learning teaching practices. SFTR's director of clinical education describes a process like that of other programs:

> I like to meet each and every person and sit in their classroom and just talk to them about how they became a teacher, what their mentorship experience was like. So through that interview-like experience, I feel like I gain a lot. Obviously, the other piece is being in their classroom. I think that if you asked me this question ten years ago, I would have said that "you need to be doing reform math curricula" and "you need to have balanced literacy." I think that I don't prize those things as heavily as I once did, which isn't to say that there aren't curricular approaches that I have a stake in, but I think that the culture of the classroom, the way that learning is talked about or engaged in, the way that children or adolescents are treated . . . feels like a really great indicator, the amount of student work and quality of student work that I see.

When the Newark Montclair Urban Teacher Residency started, potential mentors were required to submit a letter of interest, analyze a video of someone teaching, and demonstrate how they would provide feedback and advice.[25] Understanding the framework a teacher brings to supporting educator development is critically important for selecting successful mentors.

Compensation for cooperating or mentor teachers varies across programs. With few cash resources, Alverno and Bank Street pay small stipends but provide free credits to take graduate coursework at the college. The opportunity to take these courses and to work closely with faculty to support a new teacher proves a strong incentive to many professionally driven teachers. At High Tech High and in the teacher residency programs, cooperating teachers/mentors receive a stipend on the order of $2,000 to $2,500 per year. These incentives acknowledge the extent of the commitment being made and help support the recruitment of talented teachers to this role.

In San Francisco, the district, rather than the programs, willingly pays the CT stipends, because, according to a district official, serving as a CT with the San Francisco Teacher Residency pays off in terms of both professional growth and increased job satisfaction:

> We look for [cooperating teachers] . . . who are really excited about
> the opportunity to learn with the residents, learn with the team of
> cooperating teachers, be part of a coaching conversation, who are will-
> ing to open their classroom to interrogation in that way. For the most
> part that's been well received, and definitely very well received by the
> district. I think that they see it as a way of improving the quality of
> teaching more broadly. I think people's engagement with us is a way
> to retain more veteran teachers who would have otherwise considered
> something else, so [the district is] enthusiastic about it.

The process does not end with selecting mentors. Because the relationships between the residents and their CTs are vitally important to residents'
success, SFTR uses an extensive process to ensure a productive match between CTs and residents. SFTR's director of clinical education described this
process in detail:

> I developed a questionnaire/application for every CT, in which they
> talk both about their practice and some basic stuff about years of ex-
> perience, things like that, some details about their classroom, and also
> about what kind of person do you see yourself working well with—
> sort of like a college roommate questionnaire. Residents, once admit-
> ted into the program, get a similar document; we use those pretty
> seriously.

A SFTR graduate agreed that SFTR's CT-resident matching process was a
strength of the program:

> It is evident through the directors and supervisors in the program, in
> how strongly they work together, and also they really try to match up
> the resident with the right CT so that . . .you're able to work together.
> There were a few residents where there was a mismatch, and they re-
> ally try to get in there to deal with it and solve that problem.

SUPPORTING MENTOR DEVELOPMENT.   Whereas many programs provide little or no support for cooperating teachers or mentors, all of these programs
provide training for mentors in a variety of ways. High Tech High mentors

attend three professional development sessions per year. The first of these sessions includes an orientation and the opportunity for mentors to meet their mentees, describe expectations, and set goals for the school year. The second training focuses on "facilitative coaching," described by a program leader as "a coaching model that uses questions to guide the mentee to coming to their own solution to an issue they were having." The final meeting of the year in this two-year training model allows HTH staff to work with mentors to review the school year and prepare for the next, with mentors providing feedback on their needs and ideas for support. The mentor relationship extends over the two-year period.

At Montclair and SFTR, professional development for mentors aims in part to help them develop a coteaching relationship with their residents, with graduated responsibility over the course of the year. SFTR's professional development for CTs occurs during three professional development days for which paid substitutes are provided and optional evening courses are also held. The director notes that the new supervisory structure has allowed the supervisors to build a professional learning community together, which has strengthened their coaching ability: "We have monthly meetings, we talk about coaching for equity, we talk about things that are coming up, and we've been doing our own inquiry—the same process we've been using for CTs."

At Trinity, support for mentors also begins with a joint orientation of candidates and mentors. One of the elementary mentors noted the value of this orientation, which takes place before the school year begins, in providing time for mentors to prep with their candidates before classes start. A secondary mentor reported that the mentors get a "very comprehensive binder" from Trinity that reviews what it means to be in a coaching position and when to fade away, with faculty walking mentors through the process in summer. The preparation process addresses specific issues before they arise in classrooms. For example, mentors noted that during the orientation, they talk to candidates about how they best receive feedback, develop signals for when intervention is needed, and ask whether the candidates prefer written or verbal feedback.

As the school year progresses, Trinity provides ongoing and extensive support and training to mentor teachers. Mentors receive syllabi the candidates are using in their Trinity coursework, so they know where to focus when they see candidates trying those practices in the classroom. Both the elementary and secondary MAT coordinators facilitate mentor study groups for their respective cohorts. Faculty also work with mentors on the "practice of mentoring" and provide training on how to give feedback to candidates. They study the practice of mentoring by examining actual past cases of mentor-candidate interactions as well as the work they are doing with candidates in the moment. An elementary mentor reported that these monthly meetings with the elementary MAT coordinator allow the mentors to "troubleshoot things that have been challenging" as well as to know what is coming next for the candidates. The monthly meetings also provide mentors with an opportunity to collaborate with each other, gathering as a group to check in on how things are going with candidates.

As mentioned previously, mentors also benefit by learning alongside their mentees. In one such example, one candidate told us about a helpful course session where she had learned about new uses of technology. Her mentor then described how the benefits of this session carried over to her own teaching: "That's one of the neat things about being a mentor in this program, because the mentees bring fresh-off-the-block stuff to us. That's phenomenal. She's bringing new technology, so now my lesson is going to be improved because of her. She's learning . . . all this best-teacher stuff and brings that in. That's awesome!"

This informal flow of information from mentee to mentor demonstrates the ways that the tight alignment between coursework and fieldwork, along with the relationships between faculty, teachers, and students, produces benefits in all these programs beyond those that occur in traditional "drop in the student teacher" models.

Partner Schools: Communities of Learning and School Improvement

With the exception of High Tech High, which trains its own candidates in an entirely project-based environment, all the programs have had to figure out how to find site placements for candidates to learn to teach in the deeper learning approach the programs advocate. As the SFTR director of clinical work noted:

> A challenge for me . . . is finding quality placements where candidates can see deeper learning in action. That's one of the dilemmas with growing the residency program. Where do you find good practices where our candidates can observe and do, and if not, where can you find places where teachers can explore what they learned here and start to change practice? That was one of the goals of the residency model—to impact schools.

The answer for all the programs has been the creation of deep partnerships with schools that want to develop schoolwide practices that are increasingly powerful and equitable. In chapter 10, we describe the structures that support these partnerships; our focus here is on the learning communities and collaborative relationships they foster, as well as the practices they enable for teacher candidates, program faculty, and K–12 teachers, schools, and districts.

CU Denver's model of partnership—built on a vision of "simultaneous renewal" where candidates, clinical teachers, site teams, and the broader school faculty engage in ongoing professional learning and jointly commit to improvement of practice in the school as well as the university—is depicted in figure 4.2.

Programs explicitly seek to grow communities of practice within these schools. Placing cohorts of learners at partnership school sites, as each of the programs seeks to do, extends the benefits of collaboration to a set of peers. Some programs, like Trinity and SFTR, attempt to place at least two candidates on a grade level or within a department within a partner school so that they have a colleague directly at hand with whom to plan and share experiences. What is often considered "practice teaching" turns into a deeper learning experience at these partner schools, as candidates experience all aspects of the school as a community of practice in which supervisors and mentors coach and actively engage candidates as well as veteran teachers in an intentional cycle of planning, action, and reflection.

FIGURE 4.2 **Professional development schools' common goal and four initiatives**

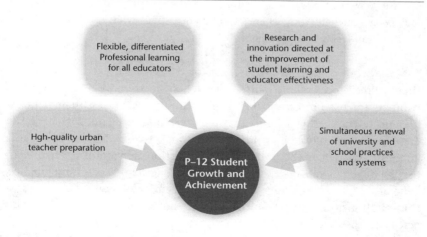

Flexible, differentiated Professional learning for all educators

Research and innovation directed at the improvement of student learning and educator effectiveness

Hgh-quality urban teacher preparation

Simultaneous renewal of university and school practices and systems

P–12 Student Growth and Achievement

Source: CU Denver Program Overview.

For example, the director of clinical education at SFTR described SFTR's approach to candidate placement:

> We are very interested in developing partnerships that go beyond just plopping residents into your schools . . . places where our graduates are now CTs themselves. So, increasingly, we're trying to think about sites as places where we're part of the professional development of that site . . . we're not just mentoring residents, we're mentoring CTs and trying to improve the practice across the board. If there are a couple of strong CTs at a site, we might think about taking on a couple more as mentors who might not have the same mentorship skills or teaching skills yet, but because our folks would be clustered at that site, there are opportunities for cross-fertilization—there would be a benefit in residents being there versus being at what we would call a "lonely placement" with some star teacher by themselves.

The faculty director of STEP's secondary program described what makes a particular teaching academy—El Dorado Elementary School—a "crown jewel":

> We have a large number of graduates there. We have BTSA [Beginning Teacher Support and Assessment, the induction program] mentors that spend quite a bit of time there. We've placed a number of residents there over the years. There have been only two principals since we've worked there, and they've come to view the residency program as part of their work. There's a coherence about what the work is in terms of teacher development.

The work of teacher preparation for deeper learning relies upon authentic, reciprocal relationships with school districts that facilitate rich contexts for teacher candidates to learn and grow during their field experiences. The SFUSD schools that are "teaching academies" for the San Francisco Teacher Residency program are supportive, collaborative working environments where the staff and administration are committed to preparing the next generation of teachers and to strengthening teaching practice, generally. The development of teaching academies allows the program's vision of "transformative teaching" to take root in more and more schools across the district.

One long-standing SFTR teaching academy is June Jordan School for Equity, a small, diverse high school that serves 77 percent low-income students and has the second-highest four-year-college eligibility rate among high schools in San Francisco.[26] Named after June Jordan, a writer and activist, the school has an explicit social justice orientation, a focus on project-based learning, and a graduation requirement where seniors must prepare and defend a portfolio of their work—much like a dissertation defense. A long-time SFTR coach described how the community of practice has evolved and grown over time as she has built relationships with the CTs and other teachers at June Jordan:

> As I develop my relationships with teachers, we tend to start adding things on to [the formal supervisory structures in the program]. So, for example, here at June Jordan School for Equity, I will take a day with the biology department and we will do planning for the day; it will be the residents and the teachers and me, and they'll say, "Oh, have you thought about this?" So, we're really pushing in different ways. I was talking in the parking lot the other day with one of [the cooperating teachers], and they said "Oh, I really want you to come in and work with me on talking less. I want to talk less and shift it to student talking. Can you come and help me do that?" Or I'll get emails, "Oh, I need help with curriculum. This is what I'm thinking about. What kind of ideas do you have?" So, some of those meetings are pretty informal.

The collaborative nature of the partner school experience does not end with the placement process, the professional community, and the mutually beneficial PDS-university relationship. The long-standing and ongoing engagement with partner school sites allows for the development of common philosophies and practices across preservice and in-service teaching.

Thus, as the community of practice expands, so does the influence of teacher preparation for deeper learning in the school and the district as a whole.

In the chapters that follow, we examine how the curriculum and practices of these teacher education programs result in candidates' abilities to teach for deeper learning in developmentally grounded and personalized ways that contextualize and apply learning to real-world problems in productive learning communities that explicitly address issues of equity and social justice.

CHAPTER 5

GROUNDING LEARNING IN DEVELOPMENT

You have a strong sense of child development: You know about the specific age you're working with, what they're cognitively able to manage and understand; emotionally and psychologically, what they are feeling; and how to nurture the skills that they need to handle the challenges they face at that point in their life. There's also a lot of emphasis on the variety of different types of learners. There is not a one-size-fits-all approach to teaching. You have to find ways to differentiate to different kids' skills and strengths and scaffold them when they need extra support and [learn] that different children will need different sorts of assistance in different ways.

—A Bank Street teacher candidate

In this chapter, we begin our deep dive into the five dimensions of deeper learning experiences identified in chapter 1 by focusing on how teaching can support children's development in ways that personalize learning. Teacher candidates in the programs we studied learn how to build learning experiences based on students' prior knowledge and cultural experiences, helping them actively construct new knowledge. They connect learning to who students are as well as what they already know. School tasks are intrinsically interesting based on students' experiences, appropriate to their level of development, and scaffolded according to their needs.

The report of the National Academy of Education Commission, *Preparing Teachers for a Changing World,* outlines the knowledge and skills of a developmentally aware teacher in this way:

> Understanding development requires not only a sense of the "whole child" but also a consideration of the "whole child developing in particular social contexts." A teacher who is developmentally aware will know, for example, how the child's prior knowledge and cultural experiences will inform what the child knows and how he may approach new ideas and tasks . . . This teacher will know that a curriculum which encourages children to learn actively and concretely—by observing, collecting information, describing, counting, manipulating, and using what they have studied—will later support abstract thinking that relies on these concrete understandings.

A developmentally aware teacher . . . will also understand that some students still need to learn skills others have mastered earlier, and will know how to diagnose these needs and target teaching and assistance accordingly. A developmentally aware teacher will know that as students progress in their understanding within a domain, they will be increasingly able to look for patterns, to think abstractly and contingently, and to manage multiple variables in more complicated ways. This teacher will be prepared to help students engage in this progression toward more systematic reasoning and symbolic thinking.[1]

These features of a developmentally aware teacher are exemplified by Ted Pollen, a graduate of Bank Street College, now a cooperating teacher, whom we observed in action at Midtown West in New York City—a Bank Street partner school staffed largely by Bank Street graduates. See the box "Developmentally Grounded Teaching in Action"

This short vignette illustrates how Midtown West School and Ted's class are grounded in a developmental framework that supports strong, trusting relationships; collaboration in the learning process; connections to prior experience; teaching that promotes inquiry interspersed with explicit instruction where appropriate; and support for individualized learning strategies as well as collective learning.

Authentic and engaging tasks with real-world connections like the task Ted chose—measuring and comparing children's heights in two classrooms of different ages—motivate student effort and engagement. Students' work is supported through teacher scaffolding and a wide range of tools that allow for personalized learning and student agency. Other scaffolds—like the charts reminding students of their learning processes and key concepts—support self-regulation and strategic learning while reducing cognitive load, in order to facilitate higher-order thinking and performance skills. These also enable student self-assessment, as well as peer and teacher feedback that is part of an ongoing formative assessment process. Routines for reflection on and revision of work support the development of metacognition and a growth mind-set. Meanwhile, students' identities as competent writers, scientists, and mathematicians are also reinforced as their work dominates the walls of the classroom and is the focus of the learning process.

All students feel they belong in this room, where together they are learning to become responsible community members, critical thinkers, and problem solvers. A range of culturally connected curriculum units and materials fosters that sense of inclusion, while a wide array of school supports reinforces that inclusion by addressing student and family needs in multiple ways while incorporating families as partners in the educational process.

Developmentally Grounded Teaching in Action

In Ted Pollen's fourth-grade classroom at Midtown West school in New York city, a racially diverse group of twenty-seven students is deeply engaged in a mathematics inquiry focused on understanding the concepts of range, mean, median, and mode. Some are seated around tables, while others are in pairs or trios on the rug in the classroom meeting area. While some teachers might introduce the three terms with definitions and rules for calculating them and give students a worksheet of problems to fill out, Ted's class has been conducting a study that provides them with the data they are now analyzing: Earlier in the week, they measured and recorded the height of everyone in their own classroom and all the children in one of the kindergarten classrooms who are their "reading buddies." Each then figured out how to display the data distributions with bar graphs they constructed individually, so as to be able to figure out the range, mean, median, and mode for each class and compare them. Working in teams, they use various tools, such as manipulatives and calculators, as they advise and query one another about what to do.

Ted and his two student teachers move unobtrusively among groups, watching the process and occasionally asking questions to help move students to the next level of understanding. It's clear that he is thinking about students' zones of proximal development as he chooses his questions. Ted says to one group: "Think about your design. What's the best way of displaying the data so you can make an actual comparison?" In another, he asks, "Can someone give me the range for kindergarten? Our range? Are there any outliers?" This led to a realization that there was little overlap between the two groups, but there were a few relatively short fourth graders and one very tall kindergartner. A student said proudly, pointing to that data point: "That's my reading buddy!"

In yet another group Ted observes to one of the boys, "You're having the same problem that she's having," pointing to a tablemate to encourage the two of them to work together. They begin counting and calculating to solve the problem jointly. Ted never gives away the answer, but he assists the problem-solving process with questions that carefully scaffold student understanding. In their groups, students engage in vigorous debates about the answers, explaining their reasoning to one another, re-counting their data, marshaling evidence, and demonstrating their solutions in different ways. Ted does not attempt to adjudicate the disputes or provide the right answer. He allows the groups to work through the problem.

Ted watches over a student with autism who is doing her work with a one-on-one aide. The student sings to herself periodically while she is doing the work but continues to make progress. In the hubbub of the classroom, her singing is not a distraction to the others, as they all focus intently on communicating to find solutions to this highly motivating puzzle. Every single student has made significant progress in developing a deep understanding of these key statistical concepts that often elude much older students.

Around the hardworking groups of children, student work covers the walls: a classroom constitution that was collectively developed and signed by each student and teacher is displayed, along with a "Problem Parking Lot" with stickies listing

(continues)

various problems and questions the class has agreed to return to. Especially prominent are student accounts of their lives as slaves in New Amsterdam and New York: 1621–1680, along with fractions posters illustrating various problems they have tackled and solved, including how they have split submarine sandwiches among various odd numbers of people.

On the back shelves, one set of tubs offers manipulatives for mathematics. Another set of tubs includes books labeled by type, all connected to current topics of study: authors who have been studied by the class each merit a tub, as do African-American biographies, slavery, other biographies, Ted's favorites, and more. Hand-made globes and a time line string with chronological date cards of important events hang from the ceiling. The meeting area in front of a whiteboard is covered with a rug that is a map of the world.

Also on the wall are many posters reminding students about their routines. One summarizes the rules for "Book Club." Another asks, "What is figurative language?" clarifying that it is "when words mean something other than their literal meaning." The poster defines what most would think of as high school terms: simile, metaphor, hyperbole, personification, alliteration, onomatopoeia, idiom, allusion, and oxymoron, offering concrete examples of each.

Other posters developed by students and the teacher include a "Writing workshop conferencing protocol," "Poetry guidelines," "Persuasive essays," "Jobs in a reading conference" (enumerated for both the student and the teacher), and "Elements of a news magazine article." These are often in the students' own words, codifying their learning so they can share it and go back to it as needed. Another poster enumerates, "What we know about maps," while still another describes "Multiplying 2-digit by 1-digit numbers: The traditional algorithm."

Invisible in this moment are the school supports that make this productive hubbub possible: free breakfasts for all children; free transportation for children who live in temporary housing; a Family Center that offers educational workshops, cultural connections, and family support services; extended afterschool time and services; twice annual student-family-teacher conferences; and a set of children's rights that include: "I have a right to be happy and to be treated with compassion in this school." "I have a right to be myself in this school. This means that no one will treat me unfairly." And "I have the right to be safe in this school." Community building and conflict resolution are explicit schoolwide efforts. Although the school is overcrowded, it is welcoming in every respect.

Jarod, a Bank Street student teacher who works with Ted, explained to us how his coursework applied to his fieldwork at Midtown West.[2] Jarod is currently enrolled in Mathematics for Teachers in Diverse and Inclusive Educational Settings, which is teaching him many of the practices he sees modeled in Ted's classroom. Jarod noted that this course has provided him with "easy prompts that you can make yourself do as a student teacher . . . constantly asking [students] why: Why do you think that? Why did you do that? Can you show me how that works? Can someone else repeat what that person just said? Did anyone do something different?"

Jarod described how he has seen Ted, his cooperating teacher, model this type of inquiry in his classroom. Jarod remarked that "as a student teacher, there is a lot of mimicry; you do what you see your head teacher do, and then some of that you just internalize and it becomes part of your practice, and others you start to tweak for your own personality." Because both his Bank Street mathematics course and his cooperating teacher model inquiry-based instruction in mathematics, Jarod is learning how to develop questions that guide students to direct their own mathematics learning, as well as how to draw on Vygotsky's theory and support children's learning within their own different zones of proximal development as they collectively teach and learn.[3] As Jarod learns to scaffold students' inquiry and thinking by asking questions, he is also learning how to interpret the answers he receives from students in terms of their developing thoughts and understandings, so he can figure out what they are ready to do next and what kinds of supports they may need.

As we noted in chapter 3, this fusion between coursework and clinical work—theory and practice—is organized to help teachers develop a vision for teaching as well as to develop knowledge and skills. Bank Street's vision of teaching and learning is supported through a highly integrated process of learning to teach and is ever-present in how the faculty teach, just as it is in the formal curriculum that faculty seek to transmit. This "hidden curriculum" is, as Biber explained, quite deliberate:

> We have assumed for many years that, beyond the structured curriculum that is provided, the students internalize the pervasive qualities of the learning environment we try to create for them, that the qualitative characteristics of their own teaching styles will reflect, later, the qualities of their own personal experience in learning to become teachers.[4]

The belief that teachers must have opportunities to learn in the same ways they will someday be expected to teach develops a strong and distinctive practice, immediately visible the moment one enters a classroom or a school touched by Bank Street training. In the Bank Street School for Children, children are building with blocks, making books, designing architecture and science projects, constructing and visiting museums, arguing mathematics, and collaborating with one another on a kaleidoscope of projects. In college classrooms, prospective teachers can also be seen making picture books for children and curriculum books for teachers;

experimenting with beans, sand, water, and other manipulatives for mathematics and science; constructing museum and community trips for themselves and future students; and collaborating with one another on a variety of projects.

LEARNING TO TEACH CONTENT FROM A DEVELOPMENTAL PERSPECTIVE

Activities such as those described above are frequently part of content-specific methods courses, outlined in chapter 3, that use a developmental frame for learning to teach each subject area, from language arts and mathematics to science, social studies, the arts, and physical education. In addition to a class on child development, Bank Street candidates take a series of courses grounded in a developmental perspective: Developmental Variations; The Study of Children in Diverse and Inclusive Educational Settings Through Observation and Recording; Family, Child, and Teacher Interaction in Diverse and Inclusive Educational Settings; Language Acquisition and Learning in a Linguistically Diverse Society.

The developmental needs of students and the demands of the curriculum for deep understanding are brought together in curriculum planning. For example, the lesson we saw in Ted's classroom was the product of careful planning that took into account how to engender the kind of mathematical reasoning demanded for a robust understanding of central tendency and variation—the fundamental underpinning of mean, median, and mode. The planning also considered students' individual needs and modes of working as the teachers designed the groups students would work in, shaped the questions they posed to individuals, and decided on follow-up learning activities. Ted explains this thinking to his student teachers throughout the year, as they are increasingly able to contribute ideas.

In addition to planning with their cooperating teacher, candidates develop their own skills as they learn to design curriculum throughout their courses, considering how to account for student needs and differentiate to accomplish their curriculum goals. In one course, candidates are expected to create their own curriculum unit based on the local context and their students; they then learn to improve their instruction as they gather information from their observations and analysis during the lessons they test out in their fieldwork placement. Throughout the assignment, candidates receive feedback, review models of curriculum, and make multiple revisions to refine their curriculum. This iterative lesson planning assignment requires teachers to build on the experience of their students based on careful observation and analysis, and then to reflect on the effectiveness of their lesson for individual students in order to improve it for future students.

In this example, Jarod is learning to bring the child to the curriculum and the curriculum to the child, as Dewey described.[5] One part of this work is understanding subject matter and curriculum deeply, so as to engage children in learning the content in developmentally appropriate ways. The other part of this work is understanding children and what they bring to the classroom. Through a series of courses on development and developmentally grounded content pedagogy, Bank Street aims for candidates to learn how to "engage and educate children in active learning"[6] that supports their cognitive development as well as their deep understanding of concepts. Our visit to a Child Development class as shown in the box "Learning to Teach History Through a Developmental Lens" illustrates how candidates learn to apply foundational child development theories to inform effective student learning experiences within content areas. Social studies was the focus of the examples taken up that day.

Learning to Teach History Through a Developmental Lens

On a Thursday evening, a racially diverse group of eighteen Bank Street teacher candidates—about 40 percent of whom are students of color—stroll into an eighth-grade School for Children classroom for one of the graduate school's hallmark courses, Child Development. They find their way to tables where they cluster in groups of three to five.

Even before class begins, the candidates are immersed in a classroom marked by deeper learning activities. Products of the eighth graders' learning are spread across the walls, including evidence of a unit on governance. One poster notes the elements "A Democratic Nation Needs," including People, Currency, Taxes, Elected Officials, Laws, Police, Army, Income Equality, Fairness for All Persons, Freedom, Fair Courts, and Strong Information.

Other posters outline assignments for the eighth-grade students for their civil rights project, including (1) Johann—President Johnson & the passage of Civil Rights Acts, (2) Ruthie—Montgomery Bus Boycott, (3) Cole—Malcolm X, and (4) Raf—The role of women in the movement. This type of project pushes students to consider how race, gender, and privilege have shaped the history of the United States.

Today, the teacher candidates are studying cognitive growth during adolescence. They are learning how to create an environment that supports students at a period marked by significant developmental variation, especially in adolescents' ability to move from concrete to abstract thought. The instructor, Nancy Nager, frames the central question for the session, modeling the type of inquiry-instruction

(continues)

that candidates should apply within their classrooms: "What represents a good enough environment for formal thought to emerge" for adolescents? She begins by grounding the class in candidates' personal experience, with a three-minute written reflection on "what was adolescence like for you?"

As they debrief on the central themes of adolescence, Nancy raises the social process of developing identity, the importance of peers, and the periodic emotional roller coaster that can occasion a need for teacher support. She says of students at this age: "It's their job to push. It's our job to be the wall," reinforcing the notion that the teacher must offer the stability that allows adolescents to explore. She also notes that, without explicit teaching, formal thought—often known as higher-order thinking skills—does not always emerge, so this is a particular mission and challenge for teachers.

Margaret Silver, a seventh-grade teacher at the School for Children, is a guest in the class. She begins by asking the teacher candidates to reflect on their own experience as seventh graders—what it was like socially, emotionally, and academically. After helping teacher candidates empathize with adolescents, Margaret presents two examples of projects from a seventh-grade unit about the encounter between Native Americans and European settlers.

The first activity is aimed at helping her students develop symbolic thinking and perspective-taking, two aspects of formal thought that are challenging to develop, and that are not always explicitly taught. The activity involves pairs of students in analyzing an iconic painting, *American Progress*, that shows an angel hovering over European settlers moving west. The students are then asked to produce their own drawings to illustrate what this image of westward expansion might look like from a perspective other than that of the European settlers, such as that of Native Americans.

The second activity is also aimed at developing perspective-taking, along with analytic skills and empathy. It involves a role play of a special session of Congress set in the 1850s. Each student receives a different historical figure to enact during debates about various issues related to slavery. The artifacts of this activity include the student's notes, their roles, statements they made in the course of the role-play, and a self-evaluation students wrote about the role-play.

After describing the activities, Margaret drops off her students' artifacts from these two projects to groups of four teacher candidates sitting around circular tables. The teacher candidates pore over the projects, asking questions of each other and of Margaret when she is nearby. One teacher candidate, reviewing a student's drawing that illustrates the westward expansion from a Native American perspective, asks, "How do you get the students to think symbolically?"

"That's a really good question," Margaret replies, describing how she scaffolds the activity. She explains that she first gives students speeches by multiple Native Americans that are rich in imagery. Next, she has the students talk in pairs about the images—what they mean, why they are powerful, what are the commonalities in the images across speeches. In explaining her teaching moves, Margaret also describes how the class analyzed the *American Progress* painting together and learned what a parody is as the basis for their consideration of other messages or alternatives. "[The project] needs a lot of steps," she notes. "But the students need a lot of options."

Margaret also explains how she thinks about students' dispositions and needs as she selects partners and roles for them. Choosing pairs of students to work together as abolitionists or as defenders of slavery in the mock Senate role play was essential in the design of that unit. "I want a partnership that works but I also want to stretch them a little bit. I usually don't have them with a close friend," she said.

Similarly, for the role-play, Margaret offers insight about the importance of selecting appropriate roles for students. "Who is going to end up working together as abolitionists, as Southerners; where are there leadership opportunities? Who would it be unfair to have run as chairman because they are socially so insecure that they couldn't weather that?" Depending on what students are ready to learn and how they might be able to take on different roles, she thinks hard about "who plays Lucretia Mott or John Calhoun." Margaret's comments highlight for the teacher candidates the importance of considering the whole student when creating a lesson, including his or her intellectual and social development.

Nancy identifies how the practices being described relate to the concepts of cognitive development, observing, for example, "You helped them move into 'flexible thinking,'" and later, "This is an example of how you scaffold for student learning, how you find that ZPD [zone of proximal development]."

Candidates ask Margaret to comment on the concepts they read about: "How did students take on these perspectives so different from their own?" "Did you notice them thinking about their thinking?"

Margaret describes how she uses self-assessments and written and oral reflections with her students to help make these decisions and to help them see their own growth. As she notes, "There are few gifts better for students than knowing themselves as learners." She underscores the fact that "they tend to underestimate themselves in seventh grade," emphasizing that it is in part the teacher's role to help them see what they can do.

The teacher candidates finish asking Margaret questions, ranging from developing the content of the projects to managing the classroom during the project. After Margaret leaves, the class reflects on the rich, project-based activities they just observed and analyzed. One notes how cool it was for the students to be asked to role-play and do creative work in seventh grade—something that was far from her own experience in school. Another comments on the structure of the project, noting the varying degrees of challenge in the tasks and prompts the teacher could use for different students within the project.

One student comments, "The way that she has prompted them, given them suggestions, not told them the answers, really allows for her students to be challenged. . . . It could be developmentally appropriate for so many different kids."

Building on this rich experience, Nancy ties in another body of learning theory from their readings, noting that Kuhn's view of the evolution of thinking was more differentiated than that of Piaget; for example, that aspects of formal thought—such as propositional thinking, flexible thinking, symbolic thinking—do not all develop together at the same time. She asks them in pairs to think about examples of these kinds of thinking and understanding that they have seen in student work or in other contexts. Armed with their own examples and the ones they just reviewed, the candidates dive into their own process of thinking about thinking together.

Nancy Nager's class illustrates Bank Street's focus on child and adult development and how it contributes to teacher candidates' ability to teach for deeper learning. Specifically, teacher candidates must consider the intellectual, social, and psychological needs of each of their students in order to create safe and nurturing learning environments where teachers can push their students to think critically and deeply. The beginning of Nancy's class provided the candidates with a framework for thinking about adolescents' development. This framework was then used to observe and analyze a seventh-grade teacher's pedagogy and her students' work within a specific content area. Teacher candidates' time at Bank Street is marked by a parallel process—a focus on child development that provides the foundation for their understanding of students and education within each of the areas relevant to teaching: curriculum development, pedagogical strategies in the content areas, and classroom management.

DEVELOPING SOCIAL AND EMOTIONAL CAPACITIES

In addition to teaching content and developing students' cognitive skills, developmentally grounded teachers learn to help students develop the social and emotional skills, habits, and mind-sets they need to be successful in guiding their own efforts in school and life and in engaging with others. This preparation was also prominent in the seven programs we studied, especially where professional development school relationships allowed candidates to train in partner schools where social-emotional learning was valued and taught. In the box "Developing Social-Emotional Skills and Mind-sets" we illustrate how a Trinity University candidate was working on the development of a growth mind-set with her young students in her yearlong student teaching assignment.

Along with teaching students about growth mind-sets, this lesson illustrates student-centered pedagogy, group work, role playing, and giving students the opportunity to associate their life experience with important concepts. This lesson grew out of the work Cassandra had done during the summer when she worked with other candidates in a team to design a ten-session Understanding by Design (UbD) unit to be used with fourth graders focused on growth mind-set.

As we noted in chapter 3, these units, as with other summer assignments, are not merely theoretical in nature: they introduce candidates to the UbD curriculum planning process, and also give candidates practical experience in looking at district curriculum guidelines and making professional decisions regarding how those guidelines should be addressed so

Developing Social-Emotional Skills and Mind-sets

It is afternoon on a rainy day in San Antonio. We are visiting Cassandra, a Trinity candidate who is teaching in a first-grade class at Lamar Elementary, a neighborhood school. In a small room, crowded with tables and chairs, the class typically includes seventeen children—eleven boys and six girls, although today two students are absent. The class is a mix of African American, Latino, and white students. Cassandra's mentor, Monica, notes that the neighborhood is becoming gentrified, and there are more white students now than in the past.

Today's lesson focuses on Lamar's five "constellations" of a growth mind-set: empathy, persistence, resilience, optimism, and flexibility. Cassandra is using everyday scenarios from students' lives to help them learn the concept of growth mind-set. Students are working in small teams to create a skit related to their growth mind-set "constellation" and act it out for their peers. Peers then determine which "constellation" is being presented. The activity is itself a means to develop social-emotional skills, as students must collaborate and learn to observe closely the emotions others are communicating.

Cassandra is sitting in a chair with students sitting on the floor in front of her. She hands out paper strips to groups of students. Each piece of paper has a scenario that aligns with one of the five growth mind-sets. Students are divided into groups of three. Cassandra and Monica help each group read the scenario they have been given and develop a skit. Cassandra walks around helping different groups, while Monica focuses on a small group of three.

After about ten minutes, Cassandra gives students a one-minute warning. She then tells students to go to their desks and sit if they are finished. Students go to their desks and wait. She asks for helpers to pass out paper napkins and markers. Another student passes out sheets covered with plastic protectors on which they can write with the markers. For the few off-task students, she adds, "We are not going to play with markers. If I see you do that, I'll take them. The napkins will be your erasers."

When everyone is settled and has their materials, Cassandra says, "Let's see which group wants to go first." As students eagerly raise their hands, Cassandra picks a group and provides instructions: "If you're acting it out, you may go to the front of the room. Tristan is going to read the story. After they act it out, you're going to write down which of these [constellations] their story represents, based on what they say they should and should not do." The first group of students reads their story out loud. It is a story about not being good at playing soccer during recess. The three students act out the story. Cassandra then asks the students, "What should you not do?" A student says: "Give up!" "What should you do?" Cassandra asks. "Write it down on your board." Students write and then Cassandra adds, "You're going to flash [your board] to the group." The students hold up their papers.

Cassandra reads the papers that students are holding up and says, "I see persistence. Did you all get persistence? Was that right?" The group of students nod yes and sit down. The students use their napkins to erase their plastic protectors.

(continues)

The next group of students reads their story. Cassandra summarizes: "They want to play basketball but there is no basketball, but there are jump ropes. What should you not do?" A student says, "Don't grab the ball." Cassandra then asks, "What should you do?" Another student responds, "You should play jump rope, since so many jump ropes, it's fine." Cassandra then asks, "Which of these is their story?" Some students hold up flexibility, and others hold up resilience.

Cassandra asks a student why she selected resilience. The student responds, but too quietly to hear. Cassandra says, "I could see how it could be resilience," and adds, "The thing they wanted to do, they couldn't, so they were flexible . . . but sometimes more than one word fits."

The process repeats itself with the rest of the groups. One group reads a story and does a skit about empathy in which a student is sad that his dog is sick. Cassandra asks, "What should you not do? Would you laugh? What would you do?" A student responds, "Say, 'Sorry your dog is sick.'" Cassandra acknowledges the student's response and says, "Maybe they could write a get-well card. Which word?" Students hold up empathy.

Another group does a skit on persistence, in which a student is doing an art project, but cutting and folding the paper the wrong way. Some students believe it is an example of resilience. Cassandra acknowledges both answers and then explains the difference between resilience and persistence. The final group reads a story about trying new food in the cafeteria. Cassandra asks, "What should you not do?" A student says, "Throw it on the floor." Cassandra follows up, "What should you do?" Another student responds, "Eat it. It might not be too bad." Students then write optimism on their board.

At this point, the class has gone over all five "constellations," and after a quick summary from Monica, the master teacher, the bell rings.

that students will learn the content deeply. The development of the unit and the reflective essay that candidates write regarding what they learned in planning the unit serve as performance assessments for the MAT summer courses.

Cassandra linked her decision to teach a growth mind-set lesson in her own classroom to the Trinity summer session, Lamar Elementary School's focus, and Trinity's emphasis on applying coursework in clinical experiences:

> So, we started talking about growth mind-set over the summer. And how our own mind-sets can influence our students. Lamar also really embraces growth mind-set, the five constellations, as we've called them. We started introducing these to our students last semester. We've been doing read-alouds all throughout the year. I think it's

really cool that the work I started doing at Trinity with growth mind-sets, readings, and talks really ties in with what I'm doing here.

Cassandra was able to reflect on this lesson in curricular terms, describing how and why she made specific decisions about the groupings of students and the choice and structuring of the task they were asked to undertake:

> I really like having them work in groups and I've tried doing different groupings and seeing which kids work well together as well as the ones who don't usually talk: What group can they be in where they'll feel more comfortable? I've done a lot of observing. Lead teaching was a great way to play around with that and see where they work best. At first, I was thinking of having them make a poster for each [constellation] and saying that we could put the posters in hallways for visitors to see what we are working on. But then I decided that I wanted to make it more relatable to them personally with the little scenarios about their lives because they can say "empathy" or read it in a book, but being able to notice it between each other is something I think they could use a little more practice on. That's why I decided to make the scenarios.

Cassandra also exemplified the sort of reflective teaching that Trinity promotes among its candidates when she described how she thought the class went and how she could change the lesson to better achieve her goals:

> It went well. It was rushed at the end. I would have done a wrap-up—more of a closure. When we went through each of the five, we did "turn and talks" about which ones they could identify easily and which ones they were struggling with. One they needed more work with is optimism. I would have done some reflection with them on that, to see if their answers would have changed.

Cassandra will have opportunities to act on her insights in future lessons, as she has a full-year placement in her master teacher's classroom to put into ongoing action what she is learning. As Trinity interns work in their clinical sites, the collaborative learning that is an essential part of the Trinity-PDS relationship also shapes interns' practice through the integration of Trinity's approach to planning and the work of the professional development schools.

Lorraine, another Trinity candidate placed at Lamar Elementary, also incorporated the five facets of growth mind-sets as much as possible into her daily lessons. Over the extended period of time in her placement, she told us that she had seen students internalizing them. "The other day we were sitting on the carpet and one student was upset that another kindergarten student was sitting in his spot. He said, 'I'm going to be flexible' and moved." She gave another example: "We had a scuffle coming back from music the other day. [A student] said, 'I'm really mad that she called me a crybaby, but I'm going to be optimistic and think that she's going to make a better choice later.'"

PERSONALIZING INSTRUCTION BY UNDERSTANDING AND ATTENDING TO DIVERSE NEEDS

As the teaching candidates highlighted in this chapter illustrate, having considered how students can learn specific content, as well as thinking, reasoning, and social-emotional skills, it is equally important to bring knowledge of individual students to the planning process. All of the programs we studied use a variety of strategies to help candidates learn to think deeply about student needs.

The Child Case Study

One common strategy is the child case study. As we described in chapters 3 and 4, case study assignments are used in multiple classes, and often include the opportunity to develop a lesson that is tailored to the needs of a specific student. Bank Street candidates do both in a literacy class, as do SFTR's candidates' classes for teaching English learners. This approach gives teacher candidates a chance to experiment with the skills and the potential methods that a teacher might deploy to make a lesson more challenging, more accessible, or engaging for a particular student. By focusing deeply on one student, candidates practice their process for differentiating their instruction—something they eventually will do for all students in their classroom.

These experiences help teachers learn to observe students closely, as they study aspects of learning and develop their own courses in order to understand how to teach different students well. A good example of how these skills are developed is Bank Street's Observation and Recording course, described in chapter 3, which helps students "learn to use a variety of observational approaches and recording techniques as basic assessment tools to increase their understanding of and skill in planning for children who are developing normally, as well as children with disabilities and special needs."[7] This course helps teacher candidates differentiate between subjective and objective observations of children and their development, and thus to recognize and better distinguish implicit bias from meaningful, actionable observations. Strengthening observational skills further provides educators with important evidence for building practice tailored to students' observed strengths, interests, and needs.

Much like assignments in other programs' courses on development, a foundational assignment in the Observation and Recording course requires teacher candidates to observe one child throughout the duration of the semester-long course. For the final project, candidates complete a paper that outlines:

- their methods for observing and recording
- a multifaceted description of the child (e.g., age, size, race, disabilities, abilities, family, school history)
- a description of the child's neighborhood, school, and classroom
- a summary of themes the candidate noticed about the child and why these themes are relevant
- an annotated list of the candidate's field notes, broken down by the themes the candidate noticed while observing the child throughout the semester
- an essay that connects the description of the child with the themes, and answers the following questions:
  - How does the child's behavior in each of the themes fit together to make him/her a unique individual and a complex person?
  - How do temperament, background, and any other personal qualities play a role in what you see?
  - What are the child's strengths? Vulnerabilities?
  - Is there any information that might be useful for the child's parents or next year's teacher to have?
- recommendations for ways that teachers could best support the student
- a self-evaluation reflecting on the following questions:
  - Have your ideas and feeling about the child and your relationship with him/her changed during the study?
  - What did you learn about other children in this class, or about the group as a whole, as a result of your study?
  - Did you find anything about a hidden curricular aspect of the classroom (e.g., unplanned influences from the physical

environment, scheduling, school/child interaction, etc.) as a result of your study?

- What particular lessons did this child teach you? Has this process changed the way you teach, think about, or relate to children? How?

Instructors review weekly observations and provide feedback. For example, on early assignments instructors' comments might include questions related to the language the graduate students uses to describe a child, or the clarity of contextual descriptions, and the eternal "Why do you think that?" "How do you know?" and "What is the evidence for this interpretation?" that often fill the margins of observation logs. Later in the semester, the questions are more specific to the child as a learner and call for the use of a variety of recording techniques such as a running record of a child's use of expressive materials; observations of the child's use of language in different contexts; a collection of the student's work; recordings of children's responses to on-demand performance of specific tasks, and children at play or in unstructured interaction with other children. Final requirements ask that students review all documentation, create categories of evidence, triangulate evidence to support their assumptions, make recommendations for teaching or further study, and use theoretical understandings to back up their recommendations.

Evan, a current Bank Street student, noted how this assignment helped her learn "to observe and not be biased right away, and not just assume things" and instead to recognize that "there is a deeper meaning about the child." The combination of teacher candidates' deep understanding of child development and their ability to observe and record children in detail with "diminishing subjectivity" helps them derive actionable insights into children's learning needs. Moreover, the process of observing and recording provides teacher candidates "greater sensitivity to the effect that their emotions and interactions may have on their observations."[8] The insights derived from objective observations are critical for a teacher to be able to identify where a child may be struggling or thriving. It also helps candidates find the activities that are most interesting for a child and how best to help the child advance in his or her learning.

For Bank Street teacher candidates to apply the theoretical child and adult development frameworks and insights from unbiased observation and recording, they must adopt an inquiry mentality. For example, a Bank Street instructor explained how she models questioning to encourage students to get to a deeper understanding of children: "What we do is when someone brings up a question or problem, I tell them don't just go in with solutions. Explore. Ask more. What happened before? What happened after? How did you feel? Explore more before jumping in because you have a better idea. And when you have a better idea, you're better able to think about things."

As the instructor and Bank Street more generally continuously stress, questions are more important than answers, especially when exploring child and adult development to inform teaching and learning. This inquiry approach empowers teachers to adapt their instruction to meet students' needs. For example, the instructor explained how "a few of my students were having problems leading book groups. The kids were acting out. And not one of them blamed the kids. Not one of them." Instead, the teacher candidates asked, 'What did I do, what could I have done, what was going on'—that's the discussion we had."

This kind of case study is also a major assignment in each of the other programs. In the STEP Adolescent Development course taken by SFTR residents, the study includes not only a cumulative assignment (the creation of the case study itself), but also weekly observation logs that residents are required to complete and submit. Candidates are asked to choose a focus student who is puzzling to them: a child who is different from the type of student they were in school or who seems enigmatic in some way and from whom they might learn. Once they have chosen a focus student, they spend the rest of the quarter interviewing and observing that child in and outside of classrooms, as well as meeting and talking with parents or a guardian in a home visit and looking at the student's schoolwork and record.

Part of this process is learning to engage in nonjudgmental observation that does not label students' behaviors, but carefully examines them for clues to what may be going on with the child. These clues then raise questions for the teacher to pursue, rather than immediate decisions about how to treat the student. Another key goal of the assignment is for the teacher to see the world, including teaching, through the students' eyes. A critically important element of the case is for teachers to shadow their student through a full day of school. This often proves a powerful experience as teachers realize how exhausting and stressful high school can be; how some teachers engage students and others do not; how their student may not be spoken to by any adult throughout the entire day, or may have relationships with peers that can provoke anxiety or reassurance. This perspective, many say, changes their approach to teaching and stays within them throughout their careers.

Each week, the class spotlights one of the central components of adolescent development—physical development, cognitive and moral development, social and emotional development, or a different context (including family, peers, school, community)—that ultimately affects student learning and motivation. Teacher candidates synthesize the information they have gathered from their focus student and from the assigned readings into a reflective log that contributes to the case study and is keyed to the weekly topics and readings in the course. The course covers all areas of development, including cognitive, social, emotional, and physical development as well as the development of racial/cultural identity.

In one SFTR Adolescent Development class, teacher candidates used what they had learned in a candidate-led in-class activity where they formed a physical web of their students' developmental assets—the set of skills, experiences, relationships, and behaviors that enable young people to develop into successful and contributing adults, such as adult role models or high expectations. After a presentation on developmental assets led by a group of teacher candidates, everyone stood in a circle and described the developmental assets they had experienced in their lives, tossing strings of yarn to create the visible instantiation of this web. They then created a web of their own students' developmental assets, drawing on their case study work. The latter web was smaller, and the class discussed the role that teachers play in helping to create a robust web of developmental supports for each of their unique students.

A Developmental Frame of Reference

This frame of reference extends across multiple courses in these programs, not just a single class on development or differentiation. A current Alverno teacher candidate noted, for example:

> Everybody comes to the table with something different, and I think Alverno did a great job of hitting that in probably every class I took there, particularly in 611 [Human Learning and Development], studying all those theories and looking at what sorts of things influence students from the outside, what they can control and what's out of their control. And things that influence them inside of school, things they can control and not control, and knowing that everybody is bringing something different to the table.

Understanding what a child brings to the table allows the teacher not only to identify needs, but also to build upon strengths. Asked how she would describe her teacher, a young child diagnosed with behavioral challenges responded about her Alverno student teacher, "My teacher makes me feel calm . . . She treats me like I'm smart." The young child's response reflects how the teacher was able to use developmental and learning theories to identify students' assets and needs, and then apply her pedagogical knowledge to help ensure all students are supported and thrive.

The superintendent of a Wisconsin district described how Alverno-prepared teachers in her district excel at engaging in developmentally appropriate teaching and differentiating instruction in their classrooms to meet the needs of all learners:

> The expectation is that [Alverno teacher candidates] are in classrooms early on and it's not a one-size-fits all kind of thing, like all kids have to learn reading this way. That's not the expectation. . . . It's not just, "You're going to hear a lecture, and then you're going to do a worksheet. And then we're going to be done. And when you come back tomorrow we're going to redo that worksheet and talk a little more, and you're going to get a new worksheet." That's not what we see from Alverno graduates. But you do sometimes see that from other graduates who aren't ready to deal with the level of diversity in our district.

This range of pedagogical strategies is evident in classrooms of Alverno teacher candidates. It is not unusual to see students working collaboratively in small groups, engaged in a project with real-world implications, while the teacher candidate moves from group to group to provide support and push students' learning through pointed questions. To address individual learning needs, the teacher candidates engage in a range of activities, including grouping students based on their interests, allowing students to work on computers or tablets rather than using paper and pencil, and giving students opportunities to show what they were learning through a variety of channels, including presentation, visuals, and writing.

This same range of practices was obvious in Ted's Bank Street partner classroom where Jarod was learning to teach—helping students learn in the ways that were most supportive for them. This included figuring out what to do when students struggled to learn. Jarod noted that "encountering those students for whom your plan does not work forces you to think, 'What do I do now?'" Jarod also described the critical role of his cooperating teacher in helping him learn to differentiate his instruction for students in the context of specific lessons, and the importance of not just reading about differentiation, but having an opportunity to try to teach students with a range of social, emotional, and intellectual strengths and needs: "You can talk about it in the coursework, but I don't think it's until you are in the classroom that you see what that means."

Similarly, an urban teacher resident in Montclair's Newark program, who was working for a full year in the classroom with a veteran teacher, described the value of "learning how to differentiate instruction: how to cater to all of the students' needs in a mindful way where it's not obvious that I'm doing this for this student. [The student] doesn't know [differentiation is happening] because everyone's enjoying it. It's just embedded in there: meeting the learner where they are and working from that place to develop them into everything that they can be."

Like other programs, Montclair carries a strong developmental framework into multiple courses on child and adolescent development that help candidates understand their students more deeply. In addition, Montclair augments these courses with other developmentally grounded courses such as Cultural and Social Contexts of Families and Communities, Working with Diverse Families, Meeting the Needs of English Learners, and Inclusive Classrooms in Middle and Secondary Schools. This approach to examining child development and learning in cultural and family contexts and in ways that attend to students with different language backgrounds or learning needs is common across these programs.

CREATING STRONG LINKS TO FAMILIES AND COMMUNITIES

The ability to meet student learning needs is built on an understanding of what each child brings to the classroom from home as well as what he or she has learned in school. A CU Denver candidate described how important this knowledge base is for her practice: "In this program, we're taught to have an explicit respect for students no matter where they might be for their grade level; everybody comes to an academic classroom setting with experiences and knowledge that ranges . . .. Respecting our students means seeing them as individual people with assets that we can work with . . .. As teachers, we can use that as our ultimate resource for teaching."

One strategy for developing this knowledge is engaging in clinical placements in community contexts other than schools—such as afterschool programs, recreation centers, or social service agencies. A CU Denver alum, now working as an elementary school behavior interventionist, reflected on what she'd learned in such a field experience, which was part of the program's coursework on cultural diversity and understanding students in urban contexts:

> I see our job as special agents who go into the trenches and try and figure out all of the information possible—try and support students and the families, and we can't do that unless we know, and I mean, genuinely *know* the whole child—tapping into the whole family, the community, the culture . . . knowing what it's like to walk home in the neighborhood, what kind of music is blaring in the windows . . .it's only then that you can curate and differentiate your interventions and support.

At High Tech High, the process of learning about students and their lives is facilitated by the fact that, in their work in the schools, they serve as student advisors as well as teachers. Advisors are assigned to a group of fifteen to twenty students who remain together for multiple years: for example, one advisor keeps an advisory group for grades 6–8; another takes the group in grades 9–12. Advisors keep track of how students are doing socially, emotionally, and academically; they are the liaison for other teachers and for the family; and they serve as advocates, guides, and supports for the students. The regular advisory class they lead is a place where students can share their experiences, learn coping strategies, and receive help in everything from homework and projects to college applications. These relationships are beneficial in getting to know students and linking their life beyond school to their experiences in school. As one HTH leader noted, "It's incredibly helpful for making a connection with a family and having empathy or understanding with where the kids are coming from."

These kinds of advising relationships, which create a stronger knowledge base about students and their development in family and community contexts, are also present in partnership schools that work with other programs, including SFTR and Trinity.

Another practice that helps HTH intern teachers further their understanding of the student and families that they serve are home visits and Family Collaborative Nights. Abbreviated as FCN, Family Collaborative Nights are evening events where teachers meet with families to discuss additional supports for students. While teachers in the secondary schools are expected to conduct home visits for all new advisees in the student's first year at HTH, elementary teachers largely rely on the FCN to get to know families better. These activities are in addition to the traditional back-to-school nights and parent-teacher conferences. Home visits from advisors and FCN interns provide a better understanding of who the student is, including any unique challenges, and allow the intern to better design projects that reflect the students and their experiences. In many instances the home visit and FCN serve as families' earliest introduction to HTH and the teacher. One first-year intern teacher described Family Collaborative Night as an opportunity to "hear from parents about their concerns, educate parents on access to books, how to read at home with your child. I think that extra time for parents to come in and connect definitely helps you understand where they're coming from; you can learn about a kid from talking to their parents and hearing about what life is like for them."

Working closely with students and families during home visits and FCNs, serving in advisory roles, and taking courses such as Healthy Environments empowers interns with the tools and knowledge to develop appropriate tasks, experiences, and projects based on student interests, while also recognizing students' prior knowledge and advancing new knowledge, all of which contribute to developing deeper and more engaging learning experiences.

The work of getting to know students and their communities goes beyond the field experience, school events, and coursework, as it is part of the culture of HTH schools. Intern teachers participate in professional development experiences and problem-solving sessions at their schools that engage them in constant collaboration with their colleagues, often focused on supporting students.

During our visit, one school director gave an example of such a professional development effort undertaken by the faculty at the HTH secondary school where he works. The teachers got together with their teaching partners for the next school year and looked at their student rosters, focusing on students who had struggled in school. Each team picked out two students, then set out to learn more about the neighborhoods where they lived by visiting them. "So, they went out into these neighborhoods, these communities," he told us, "with the question of 'How can we use this community as a resource for a project next year, and how might this community serve as an audience for student work?'" These are important goals for HTH teachers, as having an authentic topic and a real audience for project work are two ways that HTH aims to make student work relevant and authentic. He went on to describe how two of the ninth-grade teachers visited one student's neighborhood, a community with many refugees.

> Here's the address where the student lives, and a block away this big apartment with all these people hanging out . . . so they went and talked to the men, just about who they are, and what they aspire to, if they had kids, and were they in school, what they hope for them. And they figured out, wow, they want to do a project next year, documenting their stories. Having kids go out there and document these stories . . . to best meet the needs of kids from these communities that we're serving least well.

THE "HIDDEN CURRICULUM": TEACHER EDUCATION THAT IS PERSONALIZED AND DEVELOPMENTALLY GROUNDED

As is true of all of the principles of learning to teach, faculty in these programs teach and treat the teacher candidates in the same way they want those candidates to teach and treat their students—what Bank Street's Barbara Biber called the "hidden curriculum," which is, in fact, not so hidden. All of the programs take a developmental frame with their adult students, planning for their learning along a trajectory that anticipates the initial perspectives of a novice and supports their growth toward the more sophisticated set of understandings and skills possessed by a well-prepared emerging professional.

This process is enacted through the advising systems the programs construct—the small supervisory groups (usually four to eight candidates) that debrief and problem-solve with each other and their university supervisor weekly. The developmental perspective is also visible in the ways in which faculty attend to candidates' evolution and needs as teachers and as people, and the learning-oriented assessment systems the programs use to support candidate development on explicitly taught knowledge and skills.

For example, Bank Street's approach emphasizes teaching for understanding, respecting and building on learners' interests and experiences, looking at individual learners with care and attentiveness, and creating community. Each of these ideals is as carefully represented in the way teacher education faculty nurture their students as it is in the formal teaching curriculum that faculty seek to transmit. Advisors, who teach courses as well as meet with teacher candidates individually and in groups every week, know them as intimately as the candidates hope someday to know their future students. The faculty model the student-centered instructional practice that they hope to instill in teacher candidates, a practice that also helps faculty learn how to customize their instruction, advising, and relationships to best serve each of their teacher candidates. As one Bank Street instructor explained,

> My main goal when I first meet my students is to establish a relationship with my students and get to know who they are as individuals, and to learn about them, to support them. Not to tell them they are doing it right or wrong . . . There is that parallel process with children—we tell the students the first thing you do is observe kids and recognize and identify their strengths because that's how you work with a child.

Through this "hidden curriculum," the prospective teachers see their own development as being nurtured and their interests and passions as being respected and extended—learning intuitively how to create these same relationships with their students.

Observing expert teachers who illustrate a developmental approach—both in K–12 classrooms and in the teacher education program itself—is a key part of the learning process. For example, Alverno candidates learn how to create "developmentally appropriate learning environments" and to "facilitate positive social interaction, active engagement in learning, and self-motivation" in part by observing exemplary teachers in their field placement and in part by experiencing it in their own classrooms. One principal noted that "understanding the whole child" and "integrating character into the curriculum" were strengths of Alverno-prepared teachers."[9]

Candidates examine their own experiences in a highly supportive, personalized setting as they consider how to create those same kinds of experiences for their students. Alverno's small classes allow faculty to develop rich, caring relationships with their students, which supports their social and emotional development. Faculty learn about each candidate's interests, goals, and family situations, which helps them determine how they can best support each of their students in becoming an effective teacher.

Alverno faculty's modeling of social and emotional values illustrates for candidates how this awareness can support students' growth and give them the foundation students need to be able to engage in deeper content, such as critical thinking and problem solving. For example, many current students and alumni said that using performance assessments to demonstrate mastery and narratives, rather than grades to capture progress, reduces feelings of competition and encourages teamwork throughout the college. This example helps candidates consider how they might create collaborative learning environments within their own classrooms so that students can learn how to positively interact with others.

We have noted that teachers' deep understanding of development and how it occurs in social contexts is a foundation for student-centered teaching. In the next chapter, we describe how teachers learn to draw on their knowledge of students' experiences to contextualize learning so that it creates powerful connections from what students already know to what they want to learn. In addition, we describe how these programs similarly contextualize candidates' learning so that it, too, offers powerful opportunities for deep understanding and development.

CHAPTER 6

CONTEXTUALIZING LEARNING

We're not teaching you how to teach in some utopian bubble. It doesn't exist. We're helping you learn how to teach in real contexts, so that you'll know how to navigate those contexts when you leave us. We make that explicit all the way through, from the very beginning when prospective students say, "I'm interested in this," to the minute when undergrads are admitted into that senior professional year, or for our graduate students during the year they spend with us.

—Rebecca Kantor, Dean, University of Colorado, Denver

The concept of contextualized learning, our second dimension of teaching for deeper learning, has its roots in the learning theories that we discussed briefly in chapter 1. Long after Piaget observed that children interpret the world based on their prior experiences and understandings, cognitive researchers found that people learn most readily when they connect new information to their prior knowledge—that they rely on their preexisting conceptual frameworks or cognitive maps to organize information and recognize the relationships among concepts. Learning tasks are much more difficult when people encounter an unrelated set of facts or a decontextualized introduction to discrete skills.[1]

Sociocultural researchers like Vygotsky, Cole, Tharp, Moll, Nasir, Rogoff, Gutierrez, and others have recognized that prior knowledge and preexisting mental schemes are not only "academic." People also rely on cultural tools, symbols, and ways of knowing as they make sense of the world and their experiences in it. The concept of contextualized learning recognizes that people are always learning—they are observing, thinking, and solving problems by connecting new experiences to their prior knowledge. Children learn a wide range of concepts and skills while they are watching chess games in the park, helping their parents, playing basketball, or ensconced in media or video games.

One challenge of school, then, is to connect this organic learning to the knowledge, skills, and concepts of "school" learning—to contextualize classroom teaching and learning in meaningful opportunities and applications that allow students to connect new knowledge to their prior knowledge and existing schema in ways that deepen their understanding. That means, in addition to building on what students already understand about the subject matter they are expected to learn, teachers can draw on students' personal, cultural, and linguistic knowledge to support their deeper learning.

Scholars have emphasized the importance of the community-home-school connection, delving into students' "funds of knowledge" as a way to connect teaching and learning to the prior knowledge embedded in students' everyday lived experiences.[2] Thus, central to contextualizing learning for students is getting to know and understand students' lives, communities, and families in order to learn how to teach them best. This requires that teachers have a deep understanding of students' cultural contexts as well as ongoing communication and connections with parents, caregivers, community organizations, and the world beyond school.

The seven teacher preparation programs contexualize the learning of teacher candidates as well as teach them how to contextualize learning for the students they will teach. They all seek to connect the new information and skills candidates are expected to learn to their own prior knowledge, experience, and social locations (race, economic status, language backgrounds), and some do so extensively. This situated learning both ensures that candidates themselves have a deeper learning experience and provides a model of contextualized learning that candidates can apply as they learn how to teach.

In this chapter, we begin with examples of teacher candidates contextualizing learning for students. We then describe how the teacher preparation programs contextualize teaching and learning for candidates themselves, preparing them in the schools and communities in which they will enter the profession. Finally, we dive more deeply into the strategies and structures that the programs use to help teacher candidates learn to gather and use knowledge about students in order to contextualize learning in classrooms.

As we delve into this second dimension of teaching for deeper learning, the interconnections among the five dimensions that we identified in our study become clear. The more individual focus of personalized, developmentally grounded learning discussed in chapter 5 is broadened by the social and cultural factors associated with contextualizing learning, discussed here in chapter 6. Because contextualized learning connects abstract concepts to real-world experiences, it is also related to applying learning so that it can be transferred to other contexts, which we discuss in chapter 7.

Among these important contexts are intentional learning communities, discussed in chapter 8. When contextualized learning occurs in productive learning communities, drawing connections between academic concepts and students' cultural knowledge, it also enhances equity, as we detail in chapter 9.

CONTEXTUALIZING LEARNING FOR STUDENTS

One way to contextualize learning in classrooms is to connect curriculum and pedagogy to students' preexisting experiences. At Hinkley High in Aurora, Colorado, for example, a CU Denver teacher candidate and an experienced mentor teacher coteach biology to tenth and eleventh graders in one of the nation's few International Baccalaureate (IB) programs at high schools located in low-income communities of color.[3] Because the IB curriculum allows the students to go deep, rather than skim superficially over many topics, the class spent a full month understanding the basis of evolution, focusing on such essential questions as, What is the theory of evolution by natural selection, and what evidence supports this theory?

The teachers found many ways to help students connect biology to their everyday lives and interests. In one lesson, knowing that her students had much experience with and connection to the topic of skin color, the teacher candidate engaged them in a Socratic seminar about skin color and natural selection—an approach that contextualized the science curriculum. Her science goal was to deepen their understanding of natural selection, using skin color as one of the examples of how evolution has unfolded. She also wanted them to have an engaging text-based conversation, grounded in their watching a video on the biology of skin color and reading an article about an anthrobiologist who delved into the topic because "it's one of these things everybody notices, but nobody wants to talk about."

During the activity, the teacher candidate took notes on student participation and waited for times to step in and provide them with a question. In her planning, she had decided to "start with scientific questions and then ask more personal questions so that all voices can be heard during the discussion." After the conversation, she asked the students to reflect to one another about how the discussion went, whether they were respectful of each other's opinions, and what they might have missed during their conversation, thus also teaching metacognition along with discourse skills.

Another way to contextualize learning is to create contexts that provide new experiences on which to draw, as High Tech High intern Michael did in his environmental science unit described in the box "Creating Contexts

That Allow for Deeper Learning." Instead of having students study science concepts by memorizing facts in a classroom, Michael contextualized the concepts by creating a garden with his high school seniors, thereby developing a shared context in which real-life problem solving could take place. He further connected the work to students' lives in a number of ways and involved the wider community by inviting local chefs to give feedback on students' projects, providing an authentic audience for their work. Michael's project-based approach is strikingly different from the abstract learning of concepts that dominates traditional classrooms, and it provides opportunities for deeper learning that derive from students' experiences.

As Michael's unit illustrates, High Tech High's project-based approach contextualizes instruction in a number of ways. The identities, interests, experiences, prior knowledge, and developmental levels of students, as well as the teacher's own knowledge and identity, figure into the creation of learning experiences. In this case, Michael was contextualizing environmental science by embedding the concepts into the process of planting, harvesting, and creating dishes as a learning community. He brought in community members as an authentic audience to provide feedback to students, and he created a common, real-world context in which all of his students collaboratively experienced the tasks and activities that were then connected to the concepts.

Candidates across the preparation programs contextualize teaching and learning for their students, often through project-based learning like this. At High Tech High, 100 percent of respondents to LPI's survey reported experiencing project-based instruction in both their coursework and their fieldwork. Across all programs, 92 percent of candidates who completed the survey reported experiencing this type of instruction in their coursework, as did 65 percent in their field placements. It is a sign of how rare deeper learning practices are in schools—and how focused these programs are on ensuring that they are modeled in coursework—that candidates were more likely to experience project-based learning in their university courses than in their schools. As hard as these programs worked to find placements for their candidates where they could experience deeper learning pedagogies, a third of respondents did not experience project-based learning in their fieldwork.

On a related item, 95 percent of those surveyed from High Tech High reported that the program trained them to "design effective project-based instruction in which students conduct inquiries and produce ideas, solutions, or products"; Alverno, Bank Street, Montclair State, and Trinity also stood out in terms of emphasizing such practices.

Creating Contexts That Allow for Deeper Learning

It is nearing the end of the spring semester at High Tech High, and Michael, an intern teacher, is teaching a twelfth-grade environmental science class. He has an MA in ecology and has worked in several educational settings, including a nonprofit in Seattle that ran field-based activities in a local park and a farm in California that offered a sustainable agriculture certificate program. Michael shares how he saw a way to combine his passions to create a contextualized, experiential learning project for his students:

> I was just really interested in food and agriculture, and food systems, and how humans connect to the environment, and a big part of that is through food, and that's kind of an easy way to think about your relationship with nature. And it opens up a lot of doors for other subjects. Through having a school garden, we're able to talk about soil, and nutrient cycling, and all these things that I have experience with.

The project his students are working on allows him to explore such ideas with students. On this particular day the class is preparing the final presentation for the project, which has been in the works for some time. The project is rooted in work that Michael began the previous semester, when the environmental science class had retilled a four-thousand-square-foot patch in the HTH garden, all by hand. This was hard work, and not without setbacks. At one point the students had to completely retill the garden. All the fruits and vegetables had been destroyed when someone—who Michael believed was trying to be helpful—sprayed some type of chemical on the garden.

Michael reported that this mishap turned out to have a positive effect, giving students a firsthand opportunity to learn about the use of chemicals on food and how they interact in a garden. This challenge also taught a lesson about persisting through adversity.

This final project, to be presented in the HTH garden, has been designed as an exhibition of food. Michael describes the project:

> We're going to be in our outdoor garden space . . . kind of like a Top Chef–style gala, expo thing, serving bits of food to guests that come. These bites of food represent a concept or a theme that we've studied over the course of the semester in environmental science. So, for example, we have some students doing composting and how to actually do that, and that's represented in this bite of food. And we have another one that's talking about plants that grow well together, or in season, so that's represented in a bite of food. And then they have these accompanying infographic posters that are gonna go with it and kind of educate the consumer about what they're eating, where it's coming from, and whatever messages they want to convey.

A diverse class of twenty students (thirteen boys and seven girls; nine are students of color) is divided into groups and seated around a table. Michael is helping the groups with final presentations of their bite-sized portions, or "tastes," by giving

(continues)

formative feedback. By this time in the project, the students have had two practice cooking rounds with critique and feedback—by a professional chef in the first round and by other HTH teachers in the second. They are trying to decide, as a team, which of the tastes will be a part of the final presentation. To help facilitate this decision for students, Michael projects pictures of the most recent tastes at the front of the room and begins commenting on each, sharing his impressions with the whole class, who listen attentively as he gives this public review of their work. He projects a picture of the first group's taste:

> I thought they did a really cool job with using, like really embracing, all different types of ingredients and putting it together. . . . For those of you who got to taste it, it had this kumquat jam (kumquats are in season), and they came from your grandpa's backyard, and you guys made it together. You guys had this nasturtium pesto, and nasturtiums are all over our garden.

Michael knows his students and lives well enough to connect to the fact the kumquats come from the home of one of the group members, making the connection between home and school. Michael shares his thoughts on the quality and composition of the taste, and he next describes how the taste met the requirements of the assignment and how it conveyed the principle that the group was working on.

> Everything was used . . . microgreens in the greenhouse, and all of the ingredients you used, you really took the things that were in season, that were from that list, and said, "What can we do with these? And how does it fit our message of water conservation and drought and low water?" So I thought that one had an awesome message, and embodied our challenge really well.

He also has some words for them on their presentation, adding, "The downside was I thought the presentation could be a little flashier," but he wraps up on a high note, telling them, "So that [taste] was a standout for me."

For a second group, he also lays out an assessment of the taste based on the same criteria:

> Just the thoughtfulness of taking all those ingredients . . . and doing something new and different. It broke down those elements into compost, and again there was a clear story and a clear message, and the education and the science was communicated really well on the plate!

Finally, he moves on to a third group, commenting on the revision process by which their taste had evolved from their initial efforts:

> This strawberry one . . . from the first time you guys made it to the second time, I thought it was a huge transformation. . . . To go from that to something like this, they took the critique, and they just kicked it into high gear. . . . They used the strawberry to plate the dish, and everything in it is a companion. I thought that, conceptually, artistically, taste-wise, I thought it was a really smart dish overall.

He then sums up his commentary to the whole class, focusing on the growth he witnessed through the revision and refinement process: "I think that I could say

> really wonderful things about everyone's work in here. What you guys did from the first week to this week . . . the transformation from that first go-around to this one was completely mind-blowing."
>
> Students now have an hour and thirty minutes for group time to figure out what they will present on the day of the exhibition, and Michael tells them, "For now, I would like you guys to work in your groups, work on your infographics. I'm going to pop around and check in with people." Before they begin he gives them a preview of what's coming next:
>
>> If you guys know that there's stuff in the garden that needs tending to, we're gonna be out in the garden all day tomorrow. It might be our last really full day out there, maybe next Tuesday as well. But really, by tomorrow, we'll have that idea of these dishes and what we're going to do, and we'll really be able to rally behind and start planning as well.

Other programs tap into their understanding of students' cultural experiences and knowledge to provide meaningful contexts for learning what might otherwise be very abstract concepts. Overall, 92 percent of candidates across programs responded to the LPI survey that they felt prepared to "understand how factors in the students' environment outside of school may influence their life and learning," and 87 percent felt well or very well prepared. Fully 98 percent of respondents across programs reported feeling prepared to "relate classroom learning to the real world." Whichever methods they emphasize, it is evident that all seven programs are moving their candidates toward providing the sort of contextualized experience that is evident in the description of Michael's classroom.

A third strategy for contextualizing learning is to create explicit connections between home, school, and community. This is the central premise of the Art Backpacks Program at Montclair State University, described in the box "Connecting Home, Community, and School Contexts."

The Art Backpacks program helps make teaching and curriculum relevant to students' lives in several ways. First, the instructor connects with students' families via surveys to help shape the projects she develops for the students. Second, part of the assignment utilizes local artists' work (most of whom are artists of color), which connects the curriculum to the broader community and frequently to students' own cultures. Finally, students engage in art creation at home, with their families; thus their home contexts become central to the learning process.

By contextualizing teaching and learning, the Art Backpacks program helps prospective teachers learn about the students and parents at Franklin

Connecting Home, Community, and School Contexts

The Art Backpacks program is a family-school-university partnership focusing on students' learning *in* and *through* visual arts. The program is housed at Benjamin Franklin Elementary School, a dual-language school located in Newark, New Jersey. Franklin School third- and fourth-grade students take home Art Backpacks that are filled with several activities focused on local artists' work that involve them in making art, reading, and writing. Before the students take the Art Backpacks home, parents complete a pre-project survey about their perceptions of art, homework, reading, writing, learning, and schooling, helping to shape which projects go into the backpacks.

At home, students work with their families to complete the activities, creating familial collaborative learning experiences. In one activity, students discuss pictures they drew with their parents, and parents read what students wrote in a community journal. Students conclude the activity by writing thank-you letters to their parents, reflecting on their learning experiences.

The Art Backpacks program serves as a clinical field experience for Montclair undergraduate and graduate students and is open to students who have applied to the Teacher Education Program, as well as those who have not. One of the goals of the course is to help Montclair students learn about the Portrait of a Teacher (described in chapter 2) and understand the demands of teaching more clearly, specifically the demands of teaching in an urban setting.

The instructor, Dorothy Heard, is an MSU faculty member as well as a volunteer guest artist-educator at Franklin School. The Montclair teacher candidates help with the Art Backpacks program by previewing the Art Backpacks activities with the students before they take them home and reviewing the activities once completed and returned to school, working one-on-one with students and in small groups. Teacher candidates are immersed four times over the course of the semester in an art class with the third- and fourth-grade students and have class once a week at Montclair. Dorothy invites local artists of color into the course, connecting Montclair students with community members through art—a shared passion to create bridges across differences.

Within the Art Backpacks program, through articles, assignments, and class discussions, Dorothy creates an environment that introduces prospective teachers to parents and local community members as well as to students, and supports teacher candidates in learning how to contextualize learning and enact an equity-centered pedagogy. Through this work, teachers learn about students, families, and communities while students and parents also learn about and through their home and community contexts.

School, helping them move beyond preconceived notions of students and communities. This supports more equitable teaching. A key component of the Art Backpacks field experience is learning how to create an equitable environment where all students think deeply and metaphorically. Dorothy framed the goals of this project in this way: "It's [a form of] equity that's giving students access to themselves. How do you [as a teacher candidate] help them access who they are?" She continued:

> Thirty years ago, one of the things that I was told repeatedly was that African American students can't think metaphorically or abstractly. I heard teachers say, "Don't even waste your time talking to them about that. They are never going to get it." But that deficit narrative about people of color never did, and still doesn't, fit with the fact that "a brain, is a brain, is a brain." Unless there's something organically wrong, then everyone has the possibility to think metaphorically and abstractly. We owe every student an education that supports their abilities to learn, think, feel, and act through the full range of our intellectual and creative capacities as human beings. It's simply that the education students of color are provided asks them to do rote learning; we ask them to learn this content and pass that test.
>
> At the center of my work with MSU students is sustained engagement in expanding and developing their understandings of what it means to be social justice–minded and culturally responsive. Within this course we talk a great deal about how to help third- and fourth-grade students become more metacognitive, to think about how they're thinking, why they're thinking what they thinking, and to consider and experiment with new or different ways of thinking. This is a particularly important focus on deeper learning as for some of our undergraduate students, this is the first time they've had any classroom experience outside of their own K–12 schooling. And for most, it is their first time in an urban public classroom, surrounded by students of color.

For this effort to succeed, it is critically important to directly contextualize the candidates' learning in the community and with students and parents in ways that extend beyond abstractions in the university classroom or even traditional activities in the schools, where stereotyping is often implicitly enacted and accepted. Dorothy is very intentional about discussing race with her students. This has been a challenge, she admits. "Our undergraduate and graduate students tend to call each other out over LGBTQ offenses, over special education, over women's issues or sexism. They rarely touch on religion and race. They don't go there." Dorothy, however, asks her students to "go there."

She does this by creating an environment where MSU students feel comfortable making statements or asking questions about race. She gets students talking about what expectations they had coming into the school and about their own experiences and how these might have shaped their expectations. She provides resources for them and structures class discussions to help students understand racism and how it shows up in schools and learning spaces. She then, through her teaching and interaction with the third- and fourth-grade students, models equity-centered pedagogy for the Montclair graduate and undergraduates.

CONTEXTUALIZATION OF TEACHER PREPARATION

All seven programs provide contextualized teacher preparation for their teacher candidates as part of their effort to make learning to teach a deeper learning experience. The overarching principles are that people develop knowledge and skills within specific contexts as they use them on a regular basis, and that these tools are more deeply understood and better applied when they have been learned, refined, and tested within the settings in which they will ultimately be used.

The garden unit created by High Tech High intern teacher Michael, described earlier in this chapter, illustrates the application of these principles. It also brings to life the words of Duke University professor Barohny Eun about how best to contextualize learning:

> One of the most effective ways to realize contextualization in instruction is to immerse students in real-life problem-solving situations that require the direct application of knowledge and skills that have been acquired in schools. By engaging in problem-solving situations encountered in the real world, students will also come to understand that knowledge is not acquired for the sake of knowledge per se but to be put to use for real-life purposes.[4]

These words are as true for teacher candidates as they are for elementary and secondary school students. And, notably, each of the programs contextualizes learning for its teacher candidates while teaching them to do so for their own students. This begins with intentionally situating candidates in schools and communities similar to those in which they will eventually get hired, placing them in schools that use the knowledge and tools of deeper learning that the candidates themselves are learning.

The programs use partner schools and the integration of clinical work with coursework to contextualize learning in a variety of ways. Figure 6.1 illustrates, along a continuum, the range of contextualization that prep-

FIGURE 6.1 **Continuum of contextualized teacher preparation**

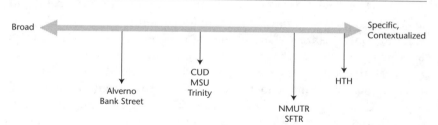

Source: This figure is a modified version of one that Peter Williamson, STEP Secondary Director, Stanford University, developed in 2018.

aration programs can undertake. On the left side of the continuum are programs that are "broad"; that is, they prepare teachers for a variety of possible teaching contexts. Potential characteristics of broader, more general programs include multiple field placements that offer a wide range of experiences, such as the geographic diversity of rural, suburban, and urban placements. Coursework in these programs is designed to be able to accommodate a range of teaching sites, although still ideally maintaining a tight connection between theory and practice.

On the right side of the continuum are programs that are highly specific and contextualized, and that ready teachers for a particular district, or even school. These include programs like High Tech High's, which prepare teachers with particular pedagogies as enacted in specific schools, and teacher residency programs, in which residents learn and practice in the schools and districts where they will get hired as permanent teachers.

One might also place "grow your own" programs on the right of the continuum, as they sometimes develop a pipeline of teachers reaching back to high school, and at times, even into middle grades, helping these young people prepare to be teachers in the very schools where they grew up. Specific programs that support the professional transition from classified staff to classroom teacher might also be included in the category of highly specific contextualized teacher preparation programs, where those teachers train in and return to the same schools in which they had previously worked.

The seven preparation programs in this study fall toward the right of the continuum, with the residency programs—San Francisco Teaching Residency (SFTR), the Newark Montclair Urban Teacher Residency (NMUTR), the CU Denver (CUD) Teaching Residency and its NextGen pathway, and the High Tech High intern program being the most specific and contextualized. The residency programs are intentional and explicit in their strategies to contextualize teacher candidate learning to the school districts in which they are embedded. For these programs, at least at the secondary level, the context for learning to teach over the full year of practice is a classroom, within a school, within a district. (Elementary candidates, even in residencies, typically train for a semester each in a primary and an upper-grades classroom in one or more schools.) Thus, teacher candidates get to know their school, district, and school communities, just as they get to know their students' backgrounds and experience. Figure 6.2 illustrates how the San Francisco Teaching Residency identifies key instructional practices and dispositions that candidates learn and develop through their residency experience.

FIGURE 6.2   **SFTR's contextualized program**

Context as content: Preparing teachers for San Francisco's particular urban schools			
District and school demographics, policy, and practices	**Student and community background**	**Teaching practices and strategies**	**Dispositions or stances**
District data: • Achievement scores • Health and parent satisfaction surveys • School Accountability Report Cards (SARC) *District policies:* • Lau Plan • Inclusion *District organization:* • Human resources • Teachers' union	*San Francisco:* • Neighborhoods • Community resources • Trauma • Immigration and immigrant experiences	*District practices:* • Restorative Justice • Complex Instruction • Lesson Templates • Beginning Teacher Support and Assessment (BTSA) • Balanced Literacy • Common Core Implementation	• Building relationships with students • Collaborative nature of teaching • Communities as assets • Reflective practice • Belief that all students can learn

Source: Peter Williamson, Xornam Apedoe, and Christopher Thomas, "Contextualized Teacher Preparation Through the San Francisco Teacher Residency" (paper presented at the annual meeting of the American Education Research Association in San Francisco, CA, May, 2013).

The clinical director at SFTR describes how, while many courses attend to broad principles as they apply in many different settings, the residents' practicum course takes up the role of placing ideas and practices in context:

> In everything we do we try to focus on context. We're not talking about how it works in teaching or how it works broadly. We're talking about how it works in SF. It starts with learning about the history of schooling in San Francisco, reading texts or videos or things that come directly out of this space. We have a lot of visitors who come to practicum and they're all people who are either coming from the district or coming from the schools. We had a parent panel that was all parents from schools where our residents are working. Everything has some connection back to this geopolitical space.
>
> We're trying to think about the things that the district cares about and we're trying to help residents understand those initiatives. Whether it's the standard on parent and family engagement, or whether it's restorative practice and the way it's getting implemented or how it's happening in the district. [We] also help them understand the practice more broadly: What are the benefits of using restorative practice? [At the same time,] how has it been co-opted as this practice that comes from indigenous peoples and how has it been used as a quick fix? We're trying to complicate social justice teaching and not make it appear as something that's formulaic or easy in any way to understand.

While this level of specificity makes sense for a residency program that is designed to prepare teachers for districts with significant teacher shortages that have pledged to hire the residency candidates, the same degree of specificity is not appropriate for all teacher education programs, since most have to prepare teachers for a wide range of places. At the same time, to learn deeply, candidates must apply their learning in particular contexts, just as medical students do in internships and residencies. Thus, they must come to understand general principles and a range of applications *and* how to work effectively in a given context—and they must learn how to discern the factors that could accompany different ways of applying those principles.

The question that teacher preparation programs must answer is to what extent do they prepare teachers for all contexts, versus preparing them for a specific context, or a specific *type* of context? In all of the programs we studied, students have common coursework that cuts across pathways and placements and that emphasizes general principles as well as explores their instantiation in particular contexts. (This is even true in the High Tech High program, which includes partner schools beyond those in the HTH network.) In addition, the internships and residencies have opportunities to deeply investigate a particular context. The larger programs, CU Denver and Montclair, have the luxury of size to be able to offer a variety of pathways that are contextualized to a range of teaching environments, while both make an explicit commitment to preparing teachers for urban schools in specific pathways.

Several programs (MSU, Trinity, Alverno) hold teacher preparation courses on-site in partner district schools instead of in the traditional college and university buildings. Bank Street's courses are in the same building as the Bank Street School for Children, and university classes are often held in these classrooms, involving interaction with the school's teachers and, sometimes, students. Similarly, High Tech High courses and SFTR practicum courses are often held in participating schools. In the same way that the Art Backpacks program described earlier seeks to blur the lines between home and school, holding university courses in preK–12 classrooms blurs the line between theory and practice. Candidates see the artifacts of learning on the walls and may explore students' and teachers' work up close. Additionally, many of these same programs use the expertise of partner district teachers to teach or coteach what are traditionally thought of as "university" courses. Often these instructors are well known by university faculty because they themselves spend extensive time in partner schools.

The programs also seek to contextualize candidates' learning to teach all students for deeper learning by prioritizing field experiences in schools serving low-income communities of color. The nature of the teaching context matters: not only do the programs want to provide settings in certain kinds of communities, but they also want to ensure that their candidates learn where they will see strong, effective, deeper learning practices enacted in schools with a strong equity focus.

As a consequence, these programs have worked to develop relationships with schools that can provide the *right* kinds of contexts for learning to teach diverse students for deeper learning. SFTR, for example, has identified a set of teaching academies in San Francisco that illuminate deeper learning practices in low-income communities. One that we described earlier is the June Jordan School for Equity, the small, diverse high school that serves 77 percent low-income students and has the second-highest four-year-college eligibility rate among high schools in San Francisco.[5] Another is Mission High School, a large, comprehensive high school where teachers have implemented complex instruction, group work, and performance assessments such as graduation portfolios. The school's deeper learning practices are described in Kristina Rizga's book *Mission High: One School, How Experts Tried to Fail It, and the Students and Teachers Who Made It Triumph.*[6] Buena Vista Horace Mann K–8, a Spanish dual-immersion school serving a diverse student population, is one of SFTR's elementary teaching academies.

CU Denver recently readjusted its group of partnership schools to ensure such placements for their candidates. Schools in more advantaged communities were eased out of the relationship, and those in low-income communities added. The alignment of commitments and approaches to teaching and learning remained a core criterion. For example, one of the newest partnership schools, Hinkley High, is a clear match. Hinkley's principal, Matthew Willis, described the relationship as one in which both the school and the CU Denver program subscribe to a definition of rigor that hinges, not on test scores or numerical markers exclusively, but on students' capacities to understand their own communities with depth, communicate to various constituencies in multiple languages, and act to promote justice in their own lives. Both insist that teachers focus on a combination of academic rigor, relationships, cultural relevance, and a determination to combat institutional racism. The written agreement between the program and the school specifies that learning relationships must be grounded in asset-based perspectives and reciprocal trust.

Contextualized field experiences focused on equity and social justice extend beyond candidates' placements in schools and classrooms. Bank Street's Council of Students (a group of Bank Street graduate students) facilitates dialogue between Bank Street's graduate students and the larger community. The council accomplishes its mission through events and initiatives, such as the Bank Street Anti-Racist Allies, which holds monthly conversations for students and the broader community "to address issues of privilege and prejudice and support community-wide conversations and actions about racial justice."[7]

In the winter of 2016, close to the Dr. Martin Luther King Jr. holiday, the Council of Students hosted a conversation with Bank Street students, graduates, and community members about discussing race in the classroom. The group considered how King's message "also dealt with issues of gendered stereotypes, poverty, and privilege" and how "the danger of saying nothing, of not acknowledging the problem is far more harmful than addressing an issue that may be uncomfortable to talk about."[8] To support Bank Street teacher candidates, and the broader community, in leading conversations about advancing justice with their students, the council shared books and resources to facilitate this important work.[9] These types of intentional interactions with community organizations and communities as a whole are essential to contextualizing learning for their candidates.

Alverno also leverages the diversity of its surroundings in Milwaukee, Wisconsin, by partnering with local organizations to provide experiences that help contextualize learning for candidates and to help them consider how they might advance social justice as educators. For example, one Alverno instructor and an Alverno candidate worked with the local police department to develop a behavior management curriculum for adults in the police force and students in urban schools, with the goal of improving their ability to empathize with each other. Experiences such as this immerse candidates in community contexts, helping them to consider local perspectives, and give candidates experience at developing inclusive, relevant educational practices for their students.

PREPARING TEACHERS TO ACQUIRE AND USE KNOWLEDGE OF STUDENTS TO CONTEXTUALIZE LEARNING

This chapter began with examples of what contextualized learning looks like in the classrooms of teacher candidates. It then went on to describe ways in which the teacher candidates' own learning was contextualized. We turn now to the strategies the programs used to help candidates contextualize their teaching and students' learning through coursework and field experiences. The importance of teachers' knowing students well and using that knowledge to contextualize learning is a common theme that cuts across domains of deeper learning and is discussed throughout this book. In the following sections we describe how the programs help candidates to develop the understandings and skills that are necessary to inform contextualized learning.

Learning About Students and Their Communities

As Michael's lesson at the beginning of this chapter suggests, High Tech High emphasizes to candidates the importance of contextualization as a part of teaching and learning. Two of High Tech High's design principles, personalization and authentic work, require that teachers have deep knowledge of their students and the communities in which they live. Knowing students well positions High Tech High faculty to understand each student's areas of strength as well as those where they need support. Moreover, High Tech High's pedagogy is grounded in the belief that project-based learning should reflect student interest and passion, and that the projects should contribute to the workplace or community through presentations to adult audiences. The authentic nature of HTH projects, their connections to students and communities, and the personalization built into them are all important aspects of teaching for deeper learning that are integrated into HTH's intern program.

The work of getting to know students and their communities goes beyond the field experience, school events, and coursework, as it is part of the culture of HTH schools. Intern teachers participate in professional development experiences and problem-solving sessions at their schools that engage them in constant collaboration with their colleagues, often focused on supporting students. During our visit, one school director gave an example of such a professional development effort undertaken by the faculty at the HTH secondary school where he works. The teachers got together with their teaching partners for the next school year and looked at their student rosters, focusing on students who had struggled in school. Each team picked out two students, then set out to learn more about the neighborhoods where they lived by visiting them. He explained: "So, they went out into these neighborhoods, these communities, with the question of 'How can we use this community as a resource for a project next year, and how might this community serve as an audience for student work?'"

These are important goals for HTH teachers, as having an authentic topic and a real audience for project work are two ways that HTH aims to make student work relevant and authentic. The school director went on to describe how two of the ninth-grade teachers visited one student's neighborhood, a community with many refugees:

> Here's the address where the student lives, and a block away [there's] this big apartment with all these people hanging out. . . . So they went and talked to the men about who they are and what they aspire to, if they had kids and were they in school, what they hope for them. And they figured out, wow, they want to do a project next year, documenting their stories. Having kids go out there and document these stories . . . to best meet the needs of kids from these communities that we're serving least well.

High Tech High intern teachers spend a significant amount of time getting to know the students and families that they serve and the communities in which they reside, and this shows in their responses to the LPI survey, where 100 percent reported they were prepared to "work well with families as partners to better understand students and to support their learning." They are not alone. Alverno, Bank Street, and Trinity matched High Tech High at 100 percent, and across all sites, 93 percent of respondents reported the same.

The preparation programs in this study all help teacher candidates learn about the value of authentic relationships and teach candidates how to get to know and better understand their students. This is done in a variety of ways, including introducing teacher candidates to the use of surveys and case studies of students, community and home visits, and ways to engage with students outside of classrooms and schools.

Many programs have courses that include learning opportunities that challenge teacher candidates' perceptions of students and communities, especially those who are underserved in urban areas. In addition, multiple courses across programs require teacher candidates to spend time in students' communities to get to know students outside of the school environment and to understand students' neighborhoods.

For example, in Montclair State University's MAT program, students are required to complete a field placement at a community organization during their summer session.One Montclair alumni recalls the summer component of their program and how it helped him to better understand students and who they were: "We [were] working in the summer program and it let us really get to see who the children were, who we would be serving, what the area was like. You get a better grasp of things that they were dealing with and becoming part of the community that way."

In MSU's undergraduate course Teaching for Learning I, candidates' first assignment is to develop a case study of a student they work with in their classroom (a common strategy discussed in chapters 3 and 4). There are several goals for the assignment, including getting to know a particular student, his context, and his experiences in differing settings. Candidates are required to shadow their student to various classes and are encouraged to attend a social event (e.g., a game, an extracurricular activity, or even a lunch date in the cafeteria with the student) to see the student in different contexts to understand that students have multiple identities and they change depending on the setting. Candidates also apply theory to help them understand their case study and begin to understand ways in which the knowledge can be used in their planning and instruction. The instructor for Teaching for Learning I shared: "[I]t is like an ethnographic study of one student for them. [T]o be able to adopt a 'funds of knowledge' kind of lens, they have to have time to gather some funds of knowledge. We think that the relationships that they build with their students are essential for them to then be able to promote deeper learning."

Without getting to know students and developing authentic relationships with them, teachers may "miss the mark" by making assumptions about students and their backgrounds, lives, and experiences, resulting in curriculum that falls flat at best, or is offensive or based on stereotypes of groups of students, at worst. As Luis Moll and his colleagues put it, "[C]ulture is a dynamic concept, and not a static grab bag of tamales, quinceaneras, and cinco de mayo celebrations."[10] Too often, approaches to incorporating students' cultures and background experiences become additive to what is considered the "main" curriculum. These additions are often celebratory, or what some researchers have referred as "heroes and holidays," "3-D" (dance, dress, and dining), or "Taco Tuesdays."[11]

> By strictly focusing on a celebratory approach of non-dominant experiences to fill out the regular or prescribed curriculum, the teacher fails to address the real experiences of non-dominant students and instead focuses on the accomplishments of a few heroic characters. This strategy often means that all students may learn to consider the contributions of non-dominant groups as mere side notes rather than as important knowledge in their overall understanding of the world.[12]

The many ways that the preparation programs work with their teacher candidates to go beyond such superficial additives begin with helping them to get deeper in their understandings of their students, families, and communities and then incorporating that complexity into their curriculum and lesson plans.

A "Class Web" learning activity that SFTR residents complete in their practicum class is one example of the type of experiences that teacher candidates encounter to translate knowledge of students to relevant curriculum and pedagogy. It is aimed at helping residents learn more about their students' needs and interests, without essentializing them, so they can meet these needs and, in doing so, provide contextualized learning experiences for them. The assignment addresses not only what residents know about their students, but also how they know it, what they do not know, and how they could learn more, with the idea that residents will develop ideas about how to build a holistic picture of their students and use that picture to construct meaningful curricula.

The activity begins with residents writing the names of their students on sticky notes, jotting three things about each student on the notes, and putting them all together on a large piece of paper, on which they build the Class Webs. The webs consist of this knowledge about individual students along with connections between students. After residents create their webs, they examine them in light of a quote from Chris Emdin's book, *For White Folks Who Teach in the Hood . . . and the Rest of Y' All Too: Reality Pedagogy and Urban Education*:

> Instead of seeing the students as *equal* to their cultural identity, a reality pedagogue sees the students as individuals who are *influenced* by their cultural identity. This means that the teacher does not see his or her classroom as a group of African American, Latino or poor students and therefore does not make assumptions about their interests based on those preconceptions. Instead the teacher begins to form an understanding of the students as unique individuals and then begins to develop approaches to teaching and learning that work for those individuals.[13]

Residents then reexamine their webs, asking whether their information about students is unsubstantiated—that is, based on limited information, predictive information, and/or assumptions. They also ask themselves what they do not know about students, and what is important to know to better serve them. Residents are then asked to consider how they have come to this knowledge, to think about the quality of that knowledge, and to ponder what more they need to know. The activity ends with an action step, as residents share ideas that they are "excited to try this week" to learn more about their students.

Understanding how students view themselves and others also enables teachers to have healthier interactions with their students. Understanding students is critical to achieving deeper learning. Helping intern teachers to develop empathy and awareness of the diverse backgrounds of the students and families with whom they work better positions them to develop authentic relationships. This, in turn, enables them to design instruction and projects that reflect student's interests and backgrounds and are thus more likely to be both relevant and engaging.

LPI's survey provides evidence that this focus on understanding is getting through to teacher candidates, with 96 percent of respondents across programs reporting they felt prepared to "develop curriculum that builds on students' experiences, interests, and abilities." Teaching for deeper learning requires such knowledge on the part of teachers, as well as efforts to link instructional design to students' experiences, needs, and identities. Further, the equity aspect of deeper learning requires that teachers work to reach all students and to make learning accessible and engaging for them. The coursework that imparts these lessons moves teacher candidates toward teaching in equitable ways that truly engage all learners, especially learners whose backgrounds are different from those of most teacher candidates.

Using Knowledge About Students to Contexualize Learning

As noted, it is not enough to simply know where students come from, although this is an important step in understanding their lives, experiences, and assets. Knowing students, their backgrounds, and communities enables teachers to create lessons that are relevant and build on students' prior knowledge and experiences. Faculty across the programs and their mentor teachers facilitate teacher candidates in learning how to use knowledge about students as they create rich, engaging, culturally relevant learning activities. The weight that programs place on the creation of such activities is indicated by the fact that, across all programs, 96 percent of respondents to LPI's survey report that they experienced "culturally responsive practices" (that bring student experiences and/or community knowledge) in their coursework, and 94 percent said the same of their field placements. Examples of these experiences follow.

TAPPING INTO STUDENTS' EXPERIENCE AND PRIOR KNOWLEDGE. In their core coursework on pedagogy and from the modeling of their clinical teachers (CTs) during student teaching , the CU Denver teacher candidates learn that the teacher's job is to create relevant curriculum by tapping into students' own experiences and prior knowledge to create accessible and interesting learning tasks, activities, and projects.

One teacher candidate spoke of her seventh-grade science classroom where students were asked to write a paper on water waste in an agricultural setting. Given her school's context, she realized that this prompt would not mean much to most of her students. She asked her mentor teacher if she could recreate the prompt and instead have students look at water waste at the school itself. Her mentor teacher was enthusiastic about the revision and encouraged the teacher candidate to build out the project even further to include opportunities for students to interview school administrators and district operations personnel and craft a proposal with strategies to conserve water. The teacher candidate explained that the confidence she gained from the CU Denver program allowed her to think outside of the box to craft strategies to bring all the content standards together in ways that lead to more appropriate performance goals and learning objectives to ensure high student engagement. Thus, student interest and real-world application become central as curriculum is developed rather than tacked on at the end as an afterthought.

Another teacher candidate in the same program spoke about doing something similar in a fourth-grade class during a series of lessons on letter writing. Students were given the freedom to write to whomever they wished on a topic they chose. After taking the letters through a writer's workshop process, replete with peer feedback and multiple drafts, the teachers mailed the letters—something many students found "so cool." Yet another teacher candidate spoke of how she and her mentor teacher reworked a unit on *Romeo and Juliet* in an English class to include a discussion of how the rivalry between the Capulets and Montagues could easily be translated to modern-day sects of Muslims. Students in this literature course "couldn't stop talking about it" and felt that the central conflict in the Shakespeare classic "came alive" in a different way given the modern translation. This teacher candidate explained that "if you tap into what [students] are actually interested in, and can relate to, you get much more meaningful learning to happen."

COCREATING LEARNING ACTIVITIES WITH STUDENTS.   As teacher candidates learn from and about their students, developing authentic relationships, they are then positioned to better design contextualized, student-centered learning opportunities. A shift from teacher-centric teaching necessitates learning to cocreate learning experiences with students, incorporating student voice and choice into lessons. As the HTH methods course syllabus states, "We believe that school-aged students should be involved in the process of helping teachers improve their practice. We will be experimenting with some ways to include young people's' voices in our class."

This importance of student voice was echoed by an HTH alum:

> We talk a lot about our design principles, and one of them is "teacher as designer." I really feel like we need to change that to "teachers and students as co-designers" because we really get a lot of student input in the projects . . . one of my colleagues started doing democratic classrooms in his class and the projects just changed because not only were students bought in, but they had a voice in either the assessment or the implementation or the project.

This can be challenging for teacher candidates, particularly since this is not the structure or culture of most classroom environments. Teacher candidates likely bring learning experiences more aligned with teacher-centered practices—which they experienced in their own K–12 schooling. High Tech High leaders Janie Griswold and Rob Riordan note the following in a piece they wrote about the program:

> Our goal is to disrupt traditional notions of authority, classroom practices, and sources of curriculum. Teachers need to get comfortable with sharing authority with students in a variety of ways—from helping shape curriculum to using the bathroom without a pass. Learning the balance of student productivity vs. social time in an interactive project environment also can be uncomfortable for teachers accustomed to a more tightly teacher-controlled classroom. Giving students a voice in what they learn and how they learn it also can be uncomfortable at first. Nevertheless, interns pick up approaches and skills for planning and management that will serve them well in a traditional environment.[14]

In addition to helping intern teachers understand children and adolescents, HTH coursework helps them "reflect on and process the interpersonal dynamics between them and their own students that influence relationships, interpretations, and responses to student behaviors and achievements."[15] Developing healthy relationships is critically important to helping teachers contextualize student-centered learning, including designing relevant and engaging projects.

BRIDGING THE SCHOOL-COMMUNITY DIVIDE. We conclude this chapter with an example of how teacher candidates can contextualize learning for students in a setting where their own development as teachers is contextualized. It illustrates the key principles of how programs can support candidates' efforts to contextualize for deeper learning and how the results of these efforts can have ripple effects of many kinds.

At Jackson Middle School in San Antonio, Trinity faculty have done staff development on the Understanding by Design curriculum framework (UbD) so that all teachers are trained on what the approach looks like. Lamar Elementary, which has been a PDS partner since 2013 and is one of the two elementary PDS sites, has gone even further to engage students in authentic work that matters for the community. The Trinity elementary supervisor and the Lamar principal are working closely to support all Lamar teachers in developing their practices around project-based learning and expeditionary learning, using the same UbD framework in which Trinity interns are trained. The Lamar principal reflected enthusiastically about the effects of this common philosophy on the work of his school, and about future opportunities:

> We want kids to care about their work and believe it matters. We want their work to tell a story, not only about grade level standards but how that learning relates to them and the context of San Antonio. We want kids to be thinkers and dreamers of what can happen. We should be having kids leave here after seven years doing amazing things. If we put the right [opportunities] in front of them and if we plan well up-front, then we can just get out of the way and facilitate [their learning]. We're just on the front edge of that now. It's happening in pockets, but nowhere to the degree that it could.

At Lamar, Trinity alums have also been active in leading change in the community as well as providing deeper learning in classrooms. One kindergarten teacher collaborated with her class to start a schoolwide recycling program. Another developed a project-based unit on voting for her fourth-grade class, after learning about low voter participation rates in the state. They created public service announcements, encouraged family members to register and vote, and even ran a local "Rock the Vote" event. Another Trinity alum collaborated with a fellow teacher to develop a unit on race relations, and they shared this unit with the next generation of Trinity MAT candidates.

This example shows how the collaborative nature of the partner school experience, aimed at contextualing learning for candidates, does not end with the placement process. It builds a professional community and a mutually beneficial PDS-university relationship. The long-standing and ongoing engagement with partner school sites allows for the development of common philosophies and practices as the contexts for learning to teach for deeper learning. It also allows for powerful applications of knowledge and commitments in practice, an aspect of preparation to which we turn in chapter 7.

CHAPTER 7

APPLYING AND TRANSFERRING LEARNING

At Alverno, we contend that acquiring and storing knowledge is not
enough. Unless the student carries knowledge into acts of application,
her learning is incomplete.

—Sister Joel Read[1]

As Sister Joel Read, former president at Alverno College, notes, deeper learning relies on experiences that engage students in applying and transferring content knowledge to complex and novel problems. In our third dimension of teaching for deeper learning, abstract and theoretical ideas are tightly connected to real-world problems and settings through authentic activities that promote and critical thinking and mastery.

In some sense, the whole point of school learning is to be able to transfer what is learned to a wide variety of contexts outside of school.[2] Yet the ability to transfer information or ideas from the classroom to other situations is not a given. Quite often, information learned by rote, without application, does not get carried into other contexts. For example, students may memorize vocabulary words for a quiz, but they may not be able to use the words in their writing. Students may learn mathematical facts, but not know how to apply these concepts when they are confronted with an unstructured problem outside of school. Students may conjugate verbs in a second language, but not remember how to use them correctly in conversation.

Long before learning scientists created terms for it, John Dewey noted the difference between "inert knowledge" that is unavailable for later use and "transferable knowledge" that results from immersion in educative experiences that support deeper engagement and understanding. As he put it:

> Almost everyone has had occasion to look back on his school days and wonder what has become of the knowledge he was supposed to have amassed during his years of schooling, and why it is that the technical skills he acquired have to be learned over again in changed form in order to stand him in good stead. . . . One trouble is that the subject

matter in question was learned in isolation; it was put, as it were, in a water-tight compartment. When the question is asked, then, what has become of it, where has it gone to, the right answer is that it is still there in the special compartment in which it was originally stowed away. If exactly the same conditions recurred as those under which it was acquired, it would also recur and be available. But it was segregated when it was acquired and hence is so disconnected from the rest of experience that it is not available under the actual conditions of life.[3]

Studies of learning in environments where people work have found that, unlike most schools, these settings tend to emphasize learning in practice, collaboration rather than working alone, and the use of tools and technologies to help get things done, rather than exclusively mental work.[4] The implication is that for effective transfer to take place, learning should be organized around the kinds of authentic problems and projects that are more often encountered in nonschool settings. Rather than simply memorizing facts or procedures, learning for understanding—often called active learning—includes grappling with principles and ideas in collaboration with others, exploring the meaning of new ideas, drawing connections to other ideas, and applying learning to real tasks in which the tools of work are used both to determine patterns and to practice new skills.

An old Chinese proverb, sometimes attributed to Confucius, encapsulates this idea: "I hear and I forget; I see and I remember; I do and I understand." Learning scientists have found that the outcomes of active learning for student understanding are significantly better than when students listen to a lecture.[5] Active learning involves students in reading, writing, discussing, solving problems, and applying their learning to other situations.

This mode of learning is ultimately more effective for deeper understanding and transfer because of the *constructive nature of knowledge.* Beginning with the insights of Jean Piaget, psychologists have documented that learners are active explorers of the world around them who attempt to interpret the world based on their existing knowledge, skills, and developmental levels.[6] Experiences that engage them in productive exploration and help them connect what they are observing to what they already know produce more powerful learning. By contrast, being given discrete, unconnected facts outside of a broader context reduces the likelihood that students will be able to remember and apply their knowledge later. Acquiring information that is never applied or put into practice reduces the likelihood of later transfer.

Finally, learning abilities are developed by access to rich experiences that stimulate the brain. Early studies on the effect of the environment on brain development compared the brains of rats raised in "complex environments" containing toys and obstacles with those housed individually or in small cages without toys.[7] Researchers found that rats raised in complex environments performed better on various tasks, liked learning to run mazes, and had 20 to 25 percent more synapses per neuron in the visual cortex. This work and hundreds of studies since suggest that brain development is "experience-dependent."

"Rich environments" that support brain development provide numerous opportunities for social interaction, direct physical contact with the environment, and a changing set of objects for exploration.[8] Similarly, rich classroom environments provide interactions with others in the classroom and community, hands-on experiences with the physical world, and frequent, informative feedback on what students are doing and thinking.

To develop transferable understanding or proficiency, people must put skills to use in an integrated fashion, rather than merely recalling information in disconnected bits. Researchers have found that the more learning is meaningful to the individual, the greater the likelihood of its acquisition, retrieval, and later use. When students work collaboratively to inquire into phenomena and solve problems, their conceptual understanding is enhanced, and their thinking becomes more explicit regarding the processes they are using. A social context where students have opportunities to share ideas, receive guidance from others, and present for an audience can help students learn to become aware of their thinking, test their ideas or hypotheses, use feedback, and learn to offer explanations—all of which deepen understanding and promote transfer.[9]

In the teacher education programs we studied, candidates learn to create meaningful tasks and projects that allow for inquiry and applications of knowledge, guide student learning with skillful scaffolding and supports, and evaluate learning with authentic assessments that reveal the results of those applications and require deeper learning. Student inquiry is not random or unguided, as some novices may imagine of project-based learning. These strategies are most effective when students encounter material in a way that reveals the structure of the domain, illustrates the big ideas and how they are connected, and ensures that careful scaffolding and strategically placed direct instruction are available to provide insight alongside students' explorations.[10]

The seven programs structure the candidate's work toward these important curriculum goals by organizing inquiries around "essential questions" and teaching them to "backward plan" from their desired learning goals—from reflecting these goals in meaningful assessments to developing a sequence of tasks and activities that will achieve these goals. (See chapter 3 for further discussion of this approach to curriculum planning.) In the next sections of this chapter, we illustrate how teacher candidates use these processes to create opportunities for students to apply and transfer learning. This type of immersive "learning by doing" is not only the goal for candidates' eventual classrooms. It is also the approach used by program instructors themselves, so that candidates experience the same kinds of pedagogies they will use to create active, student-centered classrooms. We conclude this chapter with descriptions of how the programs create these opportunities for candidates.

APPLIED LEARNING IN ACTION

In all of the programs, teacher candidates learn and experience teaching strategies that enable learning to be applied and transferred. Indeed, of candidates from all programs who responded to LPI's survey, 98 percent felt prepared to "use instructional strategies to promote active student learning," and 88 percent reported they were well or very well prepared to do so.

As discussed in chapter 3, the programs emphasize an inquiry-based style of pedagogy that stimulates critical thinking and problem solving, coupled with thoughtful differentiation, scaffolding, and culturally relevant pedagogy to ensure access for all students. Responses to the LPI survey demonstrate this shared emphasis, with 97 percent of candidates across programs reporting having been prepared to "help students think critically and solve problems" as well as to "learn content deeply." In both cases, more than 80 percent felt "well" or "very well" prepared. As noted in chapter 6, 92 percent of candidates across programs reported they had been prepared to "design effective project-based instruction in which students conduct inquiries and produce ideas, solutions, or products."

An inquiry approach in the classroom helps teacher candidates learn how to ask questions that lead to deeper understandings in various contexts. Following the advice of Alverno's Sister Joel Read, which launches this chapter, one Alverno teacher candidate described how she supported inquiry-based instruction in the context of a unit about the transfer of electric energy in her fourth-grade field placement. To help her students understand that objects can be insulators or conductors of energy, she brought seven objects on the first day of the sequence of lessons and asked her students to predict which objects would be insulators or conductors. Next, she demonstrated how to test their hypotheses. On the second day, students took control of the learning process and identified objects to test. The teacher candidate explained how she supported this inquiry-based instruction with her questioning:

> I did a lot of questioning and a lot of prompting on day 1 to help support my students' learning. On day 2, I lessened that scaffold, and it was less supported, where the students had to find the materials in their own environment to test, and test on their own predictions that they had created on day 1. But I was there to answer their questions and to walk around to see how they were doing and if they needed help.

This teacher has clearly internalized the inquiry process. Further, she has thought hard about the sequence of learning and how best to lead her students through the inquiry process by providing and later removing scaffolds as academically appropriate.

At Montclair State, as at Alverno, instructors model inquiry-based learning in their classes and then ask candidates to create a unit to demonstrate their understanding of how to implement this type of learning in their own classrooms. Instructors help teacher candidates revise their units to deepen their focus on critical thinking and inquiry. One Montclair instructor explained her goals in this way: "We read our Dewey and . . . most of our theoretical work is inquiry-based. . . . My goal is to model that: So how do we co-negotiate a curriculum? How do [teacher candidates'] questions drive what happens in the curriculum? I model that throughout our work."

Candidates learn to create inquiry-oriented units that include their own students' questions and concerns while helping them to apply what they are learning in multiple ways, as the unit described in the box "Applying Concepts in Multiple Ways" illustrates.

Janine's lesson exemplifies many of the elements of deeper learning for her students. The lesson focuses on applying and transferring knowledge: the initial activity (which builds on the reading of *The Lorax* from the day before) is a multimedia presentation of key elements of conservation. This is followed by a discussion of the concepts of "reduce, reuse, and recycle"; a read-aloud of *Beautiful Oops*; and then a chance for students to experience reducing waste by reusing recycled classroom materials to create their own crafts. The activities are planned to build on one another and then end with an application of the concepts for the kindergartners, which Janine first models to the class.

Applying Concepts in Multiple Ways

"Students, the Earth needs our help! We all need to keep the Earth clean and safe! We all need to put in our fair share to help keep our Earth clean!" Thus begins the lesson for Janine's kindergarten class. It is one in a weeklong series of integrated reading and writing activities leading up to an Earth Day celebration at the end of the week. The dimmed classroom is teeming with a racially diverse group of twenty-twoe students, exercising their choice to sit on the floor, in a chair, or stand for the lesson's launch. "We want to relax your body," Janine, a teacher candidate in MSU's undergraduate pathway, says. She begins a two-minute video on ways to take care of the earth.

When the video concludes, Janine switches on the lights and transitions the class to the mat, where each student claims a large circle on the carpet pattern. She asks for a volunteer to retell Dr. Seuss's *The Lorax*, a story on conservation they had read the day before, which serves the dual purpose of connecting the theme of the video to prior learning and catching up a student who had been absent. Janine greets the flying hands and volunteer chatter with affirmation and gently prompts for key concepts: "Dirty, right?" "Remember that 'p' word . . . ? Pollution, that's right!" she exclaims when the students recall the vocabulary word from the previous day. Reminding students of Earth Day, she introduces a chart displaying the "3 Rs" of conservation that is an orbiting image of the Earth and asks the class to give examples of recycling, reducing, and reusing that they have observed. One small voice breaks the brief pause, and this initial response sets off a chain reaction of shared student experiences. Janine affirms each example by adding it to the chart paper. The student who had been absent the day before raises his hand to tell the class he recycles at home. Janine seizes the opportunity to rope him in, exclaiming, "That's awesome! What are some of the things you recycle?"

She then segues these shared experiences into the day's read-aloud, *Beautiful Oops*, a book about transforming scribbles and spills into crafts. As she narrates, Janine ad-libs connections between the text and class: "Thumbs up—how many of you have ever had a torn piece of paper? Every single one of us." After showing the crafts in the story, she produces an example of her own: a pool flotation noodle and tissue paper fashioned to look like one of the Lorax's Truffula trees. Excitement peaks, and Janine calms the class with a redirection to sit along the edges of the carpet.

This transition marks the beginning of the day's culminating activity: students are challenged to create a craft of their own using recycled materials. Janine dismisses students to their mixed-ability table groups, where they collaborate for the next ten minutes on fashioning various animals, shapes, and figures out of recycled scraps. Janine circles the room, crouching at each table in a hum of excited chatter: "Look at this!" "What part is this?" "What else do you need?" "Very clever!"

This sequence of learning activities is also developmentally appropriate and personalized for this age group. The activities support their learning of more conceptual ideas (reduce, reuse, and recycle) with examples from the short film, their own experiences, a book that illustrates the concepts, and the final concrete task of reusing recycled materials. The whole lesson depends on the learning community engaging in thinking and doing together, illustrating social and collaborative learning. The classroom is designed for group interaction (e.g., the learning rug, tables with group seating) and students build on each other's thoughts and ideas as they share out examples of the three Rs; they work together and share materials to create their crafts and then share out their projects with their peers at the end of the lesson.

Janine contextualizes the lesson by situating the content in the need for students to help the Earth. She invites students to share from their own lives and experiences how they have observed or engaged in reducing, reusing, and recycling. This acknowledges and honors students' experiences and helps to make the curriculum relevant to their lives. Finally, students are allowed to engage in the activity to create a craft of their own choosing. Evidence of Janine's focus on equity is highlighted through the retelling of the story, ensuring the student absent from the class the day before has access to some of the content he missed. Most important, we see a classroom organized to support multiple learning styles: read-aloud, multimedia presentation, teacher questioning, hands-on activities, and independent practice. This variety of learning activities allows for multiple access points for students with varying knowledge and skills, a hallmark of equity pedagogy.

Backwards Planning to Focus Inquiry Learning on Conceptual Understanding

One of the reasons Janine learned to develop such a strong curricular sequence and implement it successfully in her classroom is Montclair's approach to planning, which is used at most of the other programs as well. As we described in chapter 3, *Understanding by Design*, which focuses on backwards design of units from goals expressed as Essential Questions and encapsulated in performance assessments, is a core text in virtually all the programs.[11] Backwards planning, or a focus on what students should know and be able to do at the end of a learning unit, helps teacher candidates to understand the ideas of scope and sequence for planning and instruction. Additionally, backwards planning from applied learning goals ensures that assessments are meaningful, relevant, and well aligned to the knowledge and skills that teachers want students to learn.

In chapters 4 and 5, we provided examples of Trinity candidates who had planned backwards using the Understanding by Design (UbD) framework to develop authentic learning experiences. The strength of Trinity's training in instructional design is evident from candidates' responses to LPI's survey: 100 percent of candidates who completed the survey reported feeling prepared to develop curriculum that helps students learn content deeply, so they can apply it in new situations, and to develop curriculum that builds on students' experiences, interests, and abilities; 94 percent said they felt well or very well prepared.

During the fall semester, all Trinity candidates must design one UbD unit to be taught within the first weeks of their lead teaching during the spring semester. The unit must consist of a curriculum design plan and unit overview using the UbD template, lesson plans, assessments, and student materials for two to three weeks of teaching. During our visit, elementary candidates talked about how they were able to develop a variety of pedagogical strategies in the process of implementing their UbD units, including ways for getting students engaged in constructing knowledge together, for applying knowledge to real-world problems, and for using questioning strategies for group discussions. As one explained:

> We're always encouraged to have developed PBL [project-based learning], particularly UbD, to track our growth. Like how we were taught to think about essential questions and understandings first, and how students not only need to be able to understand what's written on paper, but also apply it to the real world—that's the final step you start with. In doing that, you're forced to make adjustments, modifications, and differentiations based on the students in your class. Our UbD training, and our unit designs more generally, prepared us for PBL because that's just naturally where you'd have to go to hit all the essential questions and understandings.

Another reported:

> Instead of a math discussion being just teacher-student interaction, there is a lot of student-student interaction. So, how can we get students engaged in learning with and from each other and questioning each other's answers and agreeing and disagreeing, where students are almost facilitating the instruction? That way the teacher is able to play the role of monitoring and facilitating but isn't just directly teaching and is letting students explore and figure out concepts on their own.

Through their curriculum planning, candidates internalize the value of deeper-learning-aligned pedagogical strategies that put students at the center of their own learning and teachers in the role of facilitators of that learning. Mentors noted the value of UbD in supporting inquiry-based learning. As an elementary mentor observed, "When they are learning to do UbD, it helps you develop essential questions. Rather than me telling you what a poem is, I'm going to show you some stuff, and at the end you'll tell me it's a poem." Another elementary mentor provided an example of a lesson on punctuation where the teacher either asks students to find punctuation in a text before being told its purpose or gives them a sentence and lets them figure out which punctuation is missing. In aiming to get at essential questions around how punctuation helps the reader make meaning from texts, this lesson focuses students on examining texts for patterns in the punctuation and how punctuation facilitates their understanding, rather than teaching punctuation as a set of rules to memorize. Deeper learning—which also ultimately supports the recall of rules—derives from examining how punctuation supports comprehension.

We observed inquiry-based strategies in action in the class of Helen, a third-grade teacher and mentor at Lamar Elementary and an alum of the Trinity MAT program (see the box "Applying Mathematical Learning in the Grocery Store"). Her lesson taught a number of mathematical skills by engaging students in selecting and weighing fruit at a grocery store and determining costs within a given budget. This applied lesson on measuring weight also incorporated concepts of teamwork and persistence, along with how to behave in a grocery store.

While students were very engaged in applied learning of both the mathematics and the elements of teamwork, Helen noted later that she wished she had remembered to model the use of the scales before they started. This offers an example of how this kind of inquiry-based teaching on real-world topics requires significant planning and preparation, including anticipation of students' responses and questions as well as planning for difficulties that might arise in the course of students' participation in activities.

Finding Multiple Pathways and Scaffolds for Inquiry Learning

Skillful design and management of inquiry-based teaching requires not only careful planning of tasks that are good sites for deep understanding of the concepts being learned, but also thoughtful design of pathways into the material that meets the needs of diverse learners. Learners are building on different kinds of prior knowledge and have distinctive ways of accessing and processing information, often learning through different modalities

Applying Mathematical Learning in the Grocery Store

Perched on her chair with students around her on the floor, Helen begins the lesson with a question: "How do you use measuring in the real world? Today you are going to be measuring at Lucas Grocery Store. The goal is by the end of your visit, I want you to be able to explain how to measure metric weight. We talked about grams and kilograms. There's a couple of things you have to keep in mind." Helen turns on the projector, and reviews the worksheet and instruction for the activity.

The worksheet says, "Welcome to the Lucas Grocery Store! You are ready to shop and create your very own fruit salad. Your fruit salad must have a variety of fruits (eating the rainbow is healthy!), weigh as close to 350 grams as possible, and cost no more than $14. Browse the store first and decide what you'd like to put in your fruit salad." The worksheet includes a list of fruits, their amount, and price. For example, one slice of kiwi costs $1. The worksheet includes a rubric for students to self-assess on their grocery store manners, teamwork, persistence, and ability to measure weight. On the back of the worksheet is a table where students can track their shopping list and record the type and amount of each fruit, its weight, and its price. Once they find their total price, they are to check out at the register with Helen.

After reviewing the instructions, Helen adds, "Things you have to keep in mind: You have to have a variety of fruits. Remember when we went to museum, they said if you ate lots of different color things, your diet is healthy. You want to eat the rainbow. You want to get as close to 350 grams of fruit as possible. How many?" The students respond, "Three hundred fifty." Helen says, "You have to get the price [of the fruit], so the total cost is no more than $14." She then says, "If you can hear me, touch your head, then turn and tell your partner what you are going to get at the grocery store." The students turn and talk, and the room gets loud. To capture the students' attention again, Helen says, "Eyes right here. If you can hear me, touch your nose."

The students quiet down. She then provides additional instructions, saying that they have to score themselves on four things that are on the rubric for the activity: grocery store manners, teamwork, persistence, and measuring skills. She says, "One thing you have to look at is grocery store manners; next thing is teamwork. I'm going to tell you your partners in a second. Persistence. Elise, what does *persistence* mean?" Elise responds by describing how a baby falls down but keeps trying to learn to walk.

The inclusion of persistence in the rubric is intentional as it is one of the five constellations of a growth mind-set that students at Lamar are learning about. Helen adds, "So when you're trying to get 350 grams, and you don't get it, are you going to quit? Your goal is to get as close as you can to 350 grams. This whole lesson is about measuring weight. . . . There are some tools over by Dr. Norman. When I call you and your partner, you're going to get up, get your tool, and pick an area to go to. I'll make sure containers are open. I'll get everybody a bowl. Then we'll get started. The first partnership I have is Kristina and April. Can you get sheets and containers?"

Helen calls out the other pairs and the students spread out. She then stops and asks students to listen while she gives more instructions, finishing with, "I will give bowls to those who are listening." Helen walks around and gives bowls to pairs of students. They are to collect fruit from the back of the room and weigh the fruit using the scales that are at the tables. Several students are in the back of the room putting fruit in their bowls. They have lots of options to choose from, including red and green grapes, mandarin oranges, kiwi, pineapple slices, apple slices, bananas, blackberries, and strawberries. Helen shows students how to use the scales, which are all different. Because there are not enough scales, several pairs must share scales. There is a high level of engagement in the activity.

Helen talks to a small group. She reminds them that they cannot have their scale on a crack or on a book, and asks, "Will it be balanced?" She then walks around, checking on groups of students. After a few minutes of helping students, Helen says, "If you can hear me, put your hands on your head." When the students grew quiet she said, "I noticed something. I noticed that there are a lot of bowls on the balances. Maybe I didn't mention it. You have to have individual fruit weight so putting a bowl on the scale won't help." The students continue weighing their fruit and figuring out how to achieve the multiple goals of the lesson for a varied collection of fruit weighing at least 350 grams for less than $14 while demonstrating perseverance and teamwork.

and requiring different kinds of scaffolds and reinforcements. The need for teachers to be able to carry out these design tasks is emphasized across programs, as the LPI survey shows: 97 percent of all program candidates who responded to the survey reported experiencing "differentiation of instruction to meet different student needs" in their own coursework, and 95 percent in their field placements. Furthermore, 96 percent of surveyed candidates reported feeling prepared to "identify and address special learning needs with appropriate teaching strategies."

In the lesson described in the next box "Applying Science Learning in an Ocean Ecosystem," Jody, a San Francisco Teaching Resident from the Stanford Teacher Education Program, illustrates the use of a wide range of pedagogical and curriculum building skills in working with an inclusion class of high school students—half of them identified for special education—in a high-poverty school. Drawing on what she has learned in her Curriculum and Instruction course about unit planning (also based on UbD), we can see how she supports guided inquiry, checking for understanding and adapting instruction as needed, providing multiple ways to access the course content, and differentiating instruction.

Following the lesson, Jody and Lenore debriefed, reflecting as colleagues on whether their objectives had been achieved, whether they had reached all students, and whether the lesson had engaged the students in

Applying Science Learning in an Ocean Ecosystem

On a sunny March day at June Jordan School for Equity in San Francisco, Jody DeAraujo—a teacher resident in the San Francisco Teacher Residency—teaches a lesson about the effects of pH on an ecosystem to a diverse group of ninth and tenth graders in a block period field biology class. Eight of the sixteen students in the class today are identified for special education services and have individualized education plans.

Jody's lesson centers on teaching the concept of pH through a real-world example of how CO_2 combines with H_2O in the ocean to make the water more acidic, thus lowering the pH value. Class begins with a whole-class warm-up activity. Jody reviews a "range of tolerance" graph that had been discussed in the previous lesson. She asks, "What would happen to the portfolio ecosystem if the pH changed from 7 to 6?" Students share out responses, and she asks, "What would happen if the pH changes? What's actually happening in the real world?" A student responds, "Global warming."

The next part of this fast-paced lesson involves students working in pairs through a set of questions on ocean acidification to understand how and why pH in the ocean is changing. Jody intentionally pairs up the students and provides them with two images—which she reminds them are similar to the graphs they will have on an upcoming quiz. One is a time series graph of CO_2 levels in the North Pacific and the ocean pH between 1958 and 2012, and the other is a picture depicting how atmospheric carbon dioxide and water create carbonic acid. The students get to work in their pairs, spending the next fifteen minutes deciphering the images in front of them and answering the questions on ocean acidification. Jody and her cooperating teacher, Lenore Kenny, circulate around the classroom, supporting pairs who need it and redirecting a couple of distracted students.

Jody then leads the class through a series of short activities designed to deepen students' understanding of ocean acidification and provide different entry points for those still struggling with the concept. First, Jody screens a five-minute video on ocean acidification, after which she questions the class to assess their understanding. Next, students work in pairs to read and annotate two short texts (one on ocean acidification and another on coral reefs), and then complete the response questions. Then, Jody leads the class through a post-reading no-stakes check-in quiz to assess their understanding.

The last thirty minutes of the class are led by Lenore, who works with the students on their Ecosystem Data Collection project, a two-week project they are undertaking. Jody has solo responsibility for a class period she teaches later in the day. However, in this period, she and Lenore operate on a coteaching model: when teaching with Jody, Lenore will often model a lesson, which Jody will then teach on her own the following day during her solo period. The staggered lessons allow Jody to maximize the benefit of Lenore's modeling, reflecting on what she has seen and done, and then adapting it based on her own style.

Lenore asks students to take out their observation sheets for their ecosystem project. Each group of students has a container with two fish (their ecosystem), which they have designed themselves. She asks students to observe the fish and use clues to determine why their fish are or are not still alive. Students are very engaged in observing their fish and figuring out whether and why their fish have died. Lenore says, "I want you to write detailed observations. At this point, there are detailed changes happening. How many people have seen *Law and Order*? They're trying to figure out by looking at clues. Why is it dead?" She then points out that a student named Christian has said something that the rest should all hear. She says, "Sometimes you can add up all the clues and there's not a good reason you can see. Sometimes the fish just dies of something that led to its demise, its death. You have fifteen minutes. You should be writing that whole time."

The students come back together after fifteen minutes. Lenore asks students to read their observations out loud. She calls on one student: "Alan, read me one of your observations. Out loud so everyone can hear."

Alan responds, "I see the fishes are dead and they're floating and their eyes are white."

Lenore probes, "Was there anything in the water around them? Was there another fish chewing on them? Or are they all dead? What did their tails and their fins look like? I want to give people a sense of how thorough I want you to be. Give me another one."

Another student says, "The plants are growing."

"What's your evidence?" Lenore asks.

"They're stuck on the top of the bottle," the student replies. Lenore continues her questioning, and the student answers, describing his methods for gathering evidence. "How much did they grow?"

"Three inches."

"Did you measure it or guess?"

"Yes, I measured them."

"With a ruler? How did you know how much to measure them from the last time?"

The student replies, "Last time, they were two inches."

Lenore asks the student one last question, "From the top of the soil or the bottom of the soil?" then makes a comment to the whole class, which explains the reason for her close questioning: "Is everyone understanding the depth of the observations?" Lenore asks for one more example, "Give me one reason why your fish might have died. The tube that they have is in the water."

She waits a moment, then adds, "One end of the tube is in the water. The other side is where the plants are at. So the fish are swimming in CO_2. There wasn't enough CO_2 going into the top. When Ms. DeAraujo was teaching, you learned we're polluting the air with a lot of CO_2. Maybe some CO_2 is getting from the animal into the water."

Lenore then sends the students back to their ecosystems to do a more thorough analysis, reminding them to measure the plants and to look at the fish fins and gills.

deeper learning. The collaborative relationship between Jody and Lenore is evident. Additionally, it is clear that the resident is both a teacher and a learner in this activity—having the opportunity, like her students, to apply what she is learning in practice rather than only in theory. Jody independently led the first part of the lesson, but then had the opportunity to observe her cooperating teacher modeling inquiry practices—pushing students on their observations of the ecosystem they have built, getting them to be specific and descriptive and to provide evidence for their conclusions.

This final part of the class period is part of a larger two-week-long project involving building an ecosystem, observing and developing hypotheses about what happens in it, and testing those hypotheses. The project provides an opportunity for students to learn academic content—the factors that influence an ecosystem—while building their scientific analysis and writing skills, collaborating with a partner, and persevering through a two-week undertaking. Applying and transferring knowledge is at the core of every step.

Jody had the opportunity to collaborate with her cooperating teacher on the design of this project, observe her cooperating teacher lead this project, and then lead it herself in the "solo" class she teaches each day—having collaborated with Lenore in teaching the same content earlier. Jody also reflected on how her lesson was informed by her Science Curriculum and Instruction course at Stanford. In the activity in which she had students look at the CO_2 ocean acidification graph:

> The questions from that were . . . very much like guided inquiry. That's definitely something I learned a lot from my C&I teacher, Bryan Brown. He's fantastic. The other thing I learned from Bryan is to use "confirmatory reading." You don't want to introduce language to students through a reading. The reading should be the last step. So that's why I had them to do the readings right at the end after we had three lessons on pH and ocean acidification and range of tolerance. I felt like now we can do a reading and really confirm what you know. These words aren't going to be new to you.

The resident added that she uses formative assessments to check for students' understanding of the material and their ability to apply it to other settings. In this class, for example, she did a multiple-choice formative assessment after a series of learning activities. She observed that this choice of assessment was a good one because she learned that some of her students were confused about pH increasing and decreasing. She further explained that, although the graph was new to the students, a lot of the lesson was focused on consolidating prior knowledge. "I wasn't sure how solid an understanding they had of range of tolerance graphs, and if they could read them," she explained, "so I wanted to do it all together."

Jody included the video in her lesson to support multiple access points, something that she and her classmates had talked about in their coursework. She noted that readings are not equally accessible for all students, so she uses a few different sources of information. Likewise, to support equity-centered pedagogy, Jody went around to talk to students, checking on their understanding and scaffolding her language with the aim of meeting them where they are. She noted that some students could read the graph and understand it immediately, while others could not, so she needed to do more one-on-one work with them. In reflecting on the lesson, Jody said:

> There were moments when I was realizing there could have been better differentiation of learning; some people were ready to move on to the next thing, and other people weren't. Overall, I feel like the pace moved from activity to activity, I didn't lose anyone . . . except potentially those two in the back. I think the activities helped them consolidate what they know. Especially the formative assessment at the end, and the warm-up. I did a much better job on warm-up than in the last class period on reading a range of tolerance graph. I was pretty pleased with that. This wasn't a lot of new information, but I felt that they were able to latch on to what they know and make sense of everything in this class period.

Other SFTR residents also participate in such practices as both learners and teachers, with 81 percent reporting they experienced "opportunities for students to research and investigate ideas and events," and "opportunities for students to revise their work in response to feedback" in their fieldwork, and even higher percentages reporting these experiences in their coursework (87 percent and 90 percent, respectively). Additionally, 97 percent reported they experienced "opportunities for students to raise questions, discuss, and debate ideas" in their coursework, and 90 percent said they had experienced such opportunities in their field experiences.

Performance-Based Assessments to Support Applying and Transferring Learning

In each of the inquiry-based lessons we have discussed, the teachers were focused on helping students develop understanding that could be authentically demonstrated in a performance-based assessment associated with the unit of study: the ability to create a work of art out of recycled materials; the ability to select and weigh fruits to meet a size and cost constraint; the ability to create an ecosystem and understand its effects on living beings. The design of this assessment was part of the backward planning in which teachers engaged to develop thoughtful hands-on and minds-on activities to achieve their curriculum goals.

In doing this, the candidates are expected to take knowledge of the learner into account: an important part of backwards planning and assessing student learning is understanding learners' prior knowledge and skills, building on knowledge of child or adolescent development, and knowing students' backgrounds and experiences and their likes and interests, as described in chapters 5 and 6. All of these elements allow teachers to backwards-map learning from goals that are rigorous and appropriate for their students, and are reflected in assessments that are engaging and motivating, as well as good representations of the concepts to be learned.

The candidates we just discussed also used formative assessment practices to determine their moves in the classroom—checking for understanding, listening to and questioning students to understand and guide their thinking, drawing out ideas that could support everyone in the class, and sometimes correcting misconceptions or offering new information that could help students make progress.

This capacity to assess student learning is critical to inquiry-based practice, so that the teacher can ensure that students are moving toward deeper understanding that enables them to apply and transfer knowledge. As we described in chapter 3, candidates in all the programs get significant support in learning how to do this, as candidate responses to LPI's survey demonstrate: 97 percent of candidates across programs reported they had been prepared to "use a variety of assessments, including observations, papers, portfolios, or performance tasks, to determine strengths and needs to inform instruction."

For example, candidates at Montclair State receive extensive opportunities to learn about the range and scope of student assessments in dedicated courses ranging from Content Integration and Assessment in Early Childhood Classrooms or Assessment for Learning in the undergraduate pathway to courses such as Teaching and Learning I and II in the graduate pathway. Teacher candidates' curriculum covers the range of assessments, from formative to summative with understanding of all forms of assessments, including project-based assessments and more traditional tests. As one faculty member noted: "We try to help them match their assessments to their learning goals and student needs. [It's] a massive feedback loop.

We do some reading, we discuss a concept, and we ask them to create [an assessment]. Then they share out and workshop it in their classroom and get feedback, revise, and resubmit. And they can resubmit as many times as they want."

This deeper learning strategy of reading and analyzing theory, applying the theory to a project, and then utilizing it in field placement with time for reflection and revision is a common form of learning that Montclair State candidates experience in their preparation. It models the learning cycle they are expected to design for their students.

Another faculty member highlighted how she focuses on helping students understand authentic assessments:

> [W]e spend a lot of time thinking about "what does it really mean to have an authentic assessment?" And then they have to design an authentic assessment, and/or a performance-based assessment . . . They have to map back each assessment to a learning goal. . . . [T]hey have to say what assessment works for which piece of knowledge, which piece of understanding, which piece of skill. . . . There should be enough assessments, and a variety of assessments, that all of those [goals] are being assessed; otherwise there's no point in having them.

When students submit their assessments for evaluation, they are pushed to think of ways to revise them, as faculty ask questions like, "How do you shift the assessment to be more authentic?" The faculty member also explained that the idea is to have students understand that "authentic" falls along a continuum, so they can work to have more authenticity in their assessments.

The deep focus on assessment was commented on by current teacher candidates and alumni alike. Of the Montclair State candidates who responded to LPI's survey, 99 percent reported that they felt prepared to "use a variety of assessments, including observations, papers, portfolios, or performance tasks, to determine strengths and needs to inform instruction," and 86 percent said they felt well or very well prepared. One alumnus laughingly commented in a focus group, "We assessed assessments." He went on to describe the extensive process by which they practiced assessing student learning:

> It was a process where you evaluate everything you taught leading up to an assessment; you evaluate what is the purpose behind every single question on the assessment. Then you interview a few students and

probe them on their thought process while answering the questions. And then you reflect and revise that assessment for the next time you offer it, if you even choose to offer it.

When asked what types of probing questions they asked students, this same alumnus said, "We . . . ask the kids to be metacognitive: How did it go? Did you find it easy, difficult? Was there any question that felt out of the ordinary? Things like that." In this way, Montclair candidates are learning not only how to assess student learning, but also how to develop students' metacognition and understanding of their own learning process. This can also be seen in the results of LPI's survey, where 96 percent of Montclair candidates reported being prepared to "help students learn how to assess their own learning," and 86 percent reported being well or very well prepared in this assessment practice.

An alumnus who still uses the practices learned at Montclair noted that asking questions like these is at the heart of the program:

> I think a lot of [the program] is centered around the pedagogy of questioning skills. I think that's where I really started my preparation as a teacher and developing the deeper understanding and deeper content knowledge. We started in the summer, and then we had that whole summer to prepare for how to ask those questions with the classes and the teachers, and they chose the right way, then followed by whole mentoring steps. I think that really influenced me.

This process is not only constructivist in nature, but multiple alumni of the program, including the person just quoted, noted how inquiry-based learning helped them deepen their own content knowledge by helping them understand concepts more completely to support student learning: "I gained a deeper understanding and deeper content knowledge . . . by learning to ask those questions."

Similarly, at Trinity University, along with their training in the UbD framework, candidates are introduced to various forms of assessment, including pre- and post-assessments, performance-based assessments, and formative and summative assessments. As with candidates at Montclair State, at Trinity, 100 percent of candidates responding to LPI's survey reported they had used a variety of assessments, and 93 percent of them reported being well or very well prepared to do so. Mentors also work closely with candidates on assessments, often expanding their own repertoires as well. One mentor talked about how her intern pushed her to do preassessments based on what she was learning in the Trinity program, and added that they talked a lot about aligning assessment to lessons, noting the value of backwards design in facilitating this process.

An elementary mentor noted that she talked with her intern about watching for misconceptions when assessing students' preconceptions in a kindergarten class. Elementary interns assess students in small groups, practicing both preassessment and formative assessment, before proceeding to whole-group assessments. The elementary mentor described the complex process of formative assessment in her class: "In Kinder, we do a lot of formative assessment on the fly. Formal assessment is so difficult because they can't write. So it's a lot of interviewing, you draw what you know. That looks very different than what you might learn in a textbook about what assessment should be."

Another elementary mentor talked about how her intern developed formative assessment skills as they worked together on how to engage in the in-the-moment judgments of where students are in their learning and the reflection that informs that judgment:

> At the end of the day, in that time when we're reflecting, in the beginning I would talk of my observational assessment of my lesson, and then as she would teach, it was, "What did you notice? Who got it? Who didn't?" I would do it and then she would do it. Through that I watched her grow so much in seeing little things, because in the beginning it was up to me to see and know, and then as I passed the torch, she had to adjust her own lessons based on the ongoing assessment of the kids and how they are doing.

Both the candidates' metacognition and that of their students are goals of these kinds of assessment practices. We saw in the earlier examples how having students elaborate on their thought processes can help them become aware of their own understandings and misconceptions, provide opportunities for students to assist their peers, and give teachers insights to use in scaffolding and assisting students' learning. That these examples are widespread is confirmed by the LPI survey, in which 100 percent of Trinity candidates reported they had been prepared to "give productive feedback to students to guide their learning," with 90 percent of them reporting they had been well or very well prepared. These results were echoed at the other six programs, where 97 percent of candidates at all programs reported such preparation.

As we saw throughout the example, both mentors and teacher candidates can help their students make their own thinking visible by helping them *articulate* their reasoning and *reflect* on their problem-solving strategies by thinking aloud as they solve problems or by discussing their different solutions to a problem with others. Each of these activities helps to make students'—and teacher candidates'—development of expert processes visible. This allows them to call on these strategies more purposefully when they want to apply their learning in a new situation.

EXPERIENCING APPLIED LEARNING IN TEACHER EDUCATION

As we have noted, the programs also engage prospective teachers in the same kind of applied learning they want candidates to be able to use with their students. What we know about learning, teaching, and transfer is as relevant for preparing new teachers as it is for educating K–12 students. Simply having prospective teachers memorize facts about how to teach is as limiting as simply having students memorize facts about what scientists have discovered. Just as students studying science need to experience the inquiry processes involved in discovering and testing ideas relevant to science, prospective teachers need to experience what it is like to learn in environments that are consistent with the principles of development and learning. In fact, learning in the ways they are expected to teach may be the most powerful form of teacher education. Most people tend to teach in ways that mirror how they were taught. If we want to change the way teachers teach, we need to change what they experience as teaching in their programs of teacher education.

For example, in Bank Street's "deeper learning laboratory," teacher candidates are always learning within immersive experiences themselves. They are also researchers in the laboratory who investigate and analyze the elements and conditions that support the acquisition of deeper learning competencies. In the box "Learning How to Teach Language Through Applied Experience," we see how teacher candidates are learning pedagogical strategies for English learners through an immersive experience in which candidates uncover these pedagogical strategies by experiencing what it might be like to be in a classroom taught in a nonnative language—and by experiencing the teaching strategies that enable them to learn as a second language learner.

Luisa's class illustrates Bank Street's approach to providing experiences that put teacher candidates in the shoes of the learner. Bank Street values this kind of instruction based on the progressive educational belief that individuals learn by doing, "when they are actively engaged with materials, ideas, and people."[12] For teacher candidates, experiential learning means

Learning How to Teach Language Through Applied Experience

At 8:00 p.m. on a Wednesday night, Luisa Costa is in the middle of teaching her course, Language Acquisition and Learning in a Linguistically Diverse Society. Despite the late hour, the room is overflowing with energy from the racially diverse group of twenty-three teacher candidates. One candidate is participating over Skype, with her classmates moving the computer with her face on it to different corners of the room during the engaging class. This is an accommodation Luisa notes that she gladly makes for students to help them balance their personal and professional commitments. Luisa understands her students' individual needs, and adapts her practice to accommodate them, just as she encourages the teacher candidates to do for their students.

It is the second-to-last class of the semester and Luisa is modeling a lesson that embodies effective instruction for all students, especially English learners. Luisa teaches the lesson in Spanish, even though many of her students only speak English. In this lesson, she wants to reinforce the pedagogies, dispositions, and mindsets the class has discussed throughout the semester. This is not the first time that Luisa has modeled a lesson for the teacher candidates using a language other than English. During the semester she has given model lessons in Farsi as well as Spanish. Luisa notes, "I put them in the shoes of the learner. We learn by doing." And by having students sit through a lesson in a nonnative language, "the students have to strategize the way students in their classrooms would strategize."

Luisa begins singing a catchy chant to the teacher candidates, who are sitting in a circle: "*?Cual es tu fru-ta fav-o-rita? Mi fru-ta fav-o-rita es la ba-nana, la ba-nana.*" During the chant, she points to the phrases written in Spanish on the board, and points to the different fruit names written in Spanish next to pictures of the fruit. Luisa goes through the chant a few times, and then welcomes the entire class to join, with all the students following her visual signals as she points to the phrases and pictures of fruit.

Next, Luisa asks for volunteers to respond to the question. Some of the fluent Spanish speakers respond with their favorite fruit. Luisa makes a tally mark next to the image of the person's favorite fruit on the board, *la manzana* (an apple). The class begins to chant the question again, with another teacher candidate volunteering an answer. Next, Luisa explains, in Spanish, that the teacher candidates need to ask each of their classmates for their favorite fruit. To help, Luisa gives each student a paper that lists the Spanish word for different types of fruit next to a picture of the fruit. The sheet also includes the Spanish question and response for those who need the additional assistance. The teacher candidates jump up from the circle and begin excitedly moving around the room, practicing their Spanish by asking each other for their favorite fruit, responding, and tallying the responses. Because this is an abbreviated lesson, Luisa calls the teacher candidates back to the circle after a few minutes. She asks them to share, in Spanish, the number of teacher candidates who listed each type of fruit as their favorite. *La banana* was the most popular fruit. Luisa concludes the class by asking, "*?Cual es le fru-ta fav-o-rita de la clase?*" The teacher candidates cheerfully respond, "*Le fru-ta fav-o-rita de la clase es la ba-nana, la ba-nana!*"

(continues)

After the model lesson, Luisa asks the students to reflect on the lesson and their experience. One teacher candidate comments on the importance of "how you allow access to challenging content, regardless of the language diversity in the classroom, through the visible cues, charts, speaking slowly, repeating yourself or other comments that allow a child who might not have the language or skill to access the critical academic content." Another teacher candidate remarks, "Consistency and routine are useful supports for students—in all stages of language development—to independently navigate tasks at their own pace." Finally, another highlights the need to "meet students where they are and use what they *do* know to inform further learning and inquiry."

Luisa reflects on the lesson after class: "I model the lesson flow, of how to start with the motivation, guided practice, independent practice, which doesn't necessarily mean individual practice; it could be in small groups or partnerships. One of my goals is for them to be able to teach using effective strategies. . . . [The lesson on fruit] is simple, but makes a point about lesson flow, which is the slow release of responsibility from the teacher to the student."

that candidates experience what it feels like to be a student, as well as have opportunities to engage in activities where they can practice leading a classroom using personalized, project-based pedagogies, applying what they've learned in their courses. Consequently, coursework and fieldwork provide active learning opportunities for teacher candidates, with time and support to self-assess and reflect on the meaning and learnings from their experience.

At Bank Street, 100 percent of candidates who responded to LPI's survey reported they felt prepared to "use instructional strategies that promote active learning," "design effective project-based instruction," and "teach students from diverse ethnic, linguistic, and cultural backgrounds."

The same commitment informs the teaching in other programs. For example, at the University of Colorado at Denver, teacher candidates we spoke to universally agreed that the modeling CU Denver teacher education faculty use is perhaps one of the most useful ways to learn, because the candidates can "feel what it's like to experience a lesson as if they are the students themselves." One alum, reflecting on her experience, explained how being in the position of her students in the university setting allowed her to "discover the impact that that type of teaching might have. . . . When I didn't get something right, my professors still made me feel successful and important"—a sentiment that she intentionally replicates in her classroom as students wrestle with acquiring new knowledge and skills.

The vignette "Applying Learning in a Science Inquiry for Teaching Candidates" describes such a lesson in an elementary science methods course. Note both how the activity in which the candidates are engaged enables deeper learning through applying concepts and engaging in instructional conversation, and how the instructor's comments provide the scaffolding that allows the candidates to understand and be ready to apply the pedagogical strategy they are experiencing.

Applying Learning in a Science Inquiry for Teaching Candidates

It is 3:00 p.m. on a Tuesday afternoon and nine female teacher candidates are sitting in groups of three around rectangular tables in the science methods classroom at CU Denver—a setting much like one would expect to see in a K–12 science classroom. Along the back wall of the room is a set of glass-front cabinets filled with a host of assorted science paraphernalia—beakers, batteries, dissection trays, magnifying glasses, stray textbooks—loosely organized and threatening to spill out if not removed with great care.

Sandra, the course instructor, introduces the next activity as something that candidates might use with their students during a lesson on circuits. She first asks students to make a prediction before beginning their investigation and reminds them that students' answers to this question can be a preassessment. The question is: How can a light bulb, a battery, and a wire be connected to light up the bulb? After candidates have answered the question, they are prompted to share their answers with their tablemates and share out to the whole class.

The next segment of this lesson requires candidates to manipulate a battery, a small lightbulb, and a wire to determine all of the different ways to light the bulb. Each candidate takes a role in the group—one person draws on whiteboards, another is responsible for reading off the questions in order, and another is a timekeeper. All are expected to contribute ideas and keep a log of the different ways they have attempted to light up the bulb in their own "investigation journal."

At all three tables, candidates huddle together and begin trying to figure out the circuit; first one student tries, then another. Conversations can be heard around the room:

Candidate 1: So how do we think it will work?
Candidate 2: Let's try this way . . .
Candidate 3: Oh wow! That's so cool! It worked!
Candidate 1: Wait, why didn't that work? It's the same as what we just did.
Candidate 2: No, it's not the same; the copper has to touch both the positive and negative sides of the battery.

As dialogue ensues, Sandra circulates the room to listen in and ask probing questions. She pauses by one group to ask: "So, what's your claim?" After listening

(continues)

to the response, she follows up: "And what's your evidence?" Her series of questions lead the candidates to explain: "Our reasoning is that the lightbulb and battery must form a circle in order for energy to be conducted. Yeah, I think those are the right words." Sandra probes even further while pointing to the configuration students have on their table: "Explain to me why that is considered a full circle."

This type of trial and error, questioning and clarification, continues for over twenty minutes while students simultaneously work their way through the different prompts on their worksheet. At the end of this hands-on activity, the professor pauses and asks students to engage in metacognition.

> **Sandra:** Let's stop for a minute and share our ideas out to the whole class.
>
> **Candidate:** We learned that the wire should touch both ends of the battery—whether using one wire or two.
>
> **Candidate:** We learned that the lightbulb should be between the battery and the wire.
>
> **Candidate:** We realized after trying a couple of times that the wire has to touch the silver and black bottom part of the lightbulb—not just the silver part.
>
> **Sandra:** Our focus today was around writing during an investigation, and you'll notice I was asking you to talk *and* write about your exploration. This process of going back and forth, I'm curious whether you found that helpful or not helpful?
>
> **Candidate:** It was nice for me because I didn't know anything about circuits when we started, so I could talk to my tablemates to figure it out.
>
> **Candidate:** I liked how we could draw or write in the investigation journal. That was helpful especially because we didn't know the exact science behind it yet—in fact, I think this would be something that might be useful for working with ELLs.
>
> **Candidate:** Yeah, I liked the drawing part too because it helped me first articulate something I was learning before I had the vocabulary to express it and it helped me keep track of what we were doing.
>
> **Sandra:** This is all great stuff. One thing to remember with elementary students is that you have to have different options available for them to keep track of their ideas.
>
> **Candidate:** That's so true. You could also encourage kids to use a word bank or *build* a word bank once they've gone through this process and they then learn the actual terms for what they discovered.

This vignette illustrates the kind of lesson candidates experience in a university class as a model for what they would be expected to teach in their clinical placements. Not only does this example show how students could be taught to build a scientific argument, but it also addresses the question of how academic language and literacy development (e.g., copper, conduct, battery, circuit, etc.) can be applied and transferred in an inquiry-based science instruction/exploration.

In this class, candidates also got to see how structuring the learning environment in strategic ways can foster understanding. For instance, researchers have found that experiential learning can be made even more powerful when coupled with a structured examination of the central ideas to be learned. Creating an inquiry experience in which students explore materials or data and then following it with a structured explanation of those ideas through a lecture or guided discussion—as the instructor did in this case—produces stronger learning than either experience or explanation alone.[13] Following this explanation with opportunities for structured reflection solidifies the learning even further.

Exposure to this type of instruction was not limited to this class; 92 percent of CU Denver candidates who completed LPI's survey reported that they had experienced "opportunities for students to research and investigate ideas and events" in their coursework, and 93 percent reported feeling prepared to engage students in active learning. Ninety-five percent felt prepared to "relate classroom learning to the real world," as did 98 percent of the overall group of program respondents.

These powerful experiences for candidates help them learn how to structure their own lessons for deeper learning in ways that support their students in applying what they know and making their understanding vibrant, flexible, and transferable. As they structure their practice around real-world applications, candidates also learn to design collaborative settings in which students engage in these highly motivating inquiries, a process we explore in the next chapter.

CHAPTER 8

LEARNING IN COMMUNITIES OF PRACTICE

Student collaboration is something we always try to do—the students are almost never quiet. . . . They bounce ideas from one another, get feedback. We focus on building relationships, teacher-student and student-student, to create a classroom community where it's a safe space for students to share feelings and ideas. Part of how we achieve this is we start each day with a community circle and pass a talking piece around. This gives students opportunities to make connections with each other and builds that safe space, so they know, "this is what it sounds like, this is what it looks like." It's not abstract.

—Teacher candidate, CU Denver

More than a century ago, John Dewey proposed that learning is an active experience in which children learn as they interact with others to make sense of the world and their experiences in it. In 1896, he wrote in "My Pedagogic Creed":[1]

> I believe that the only true education comes through the stimulation of the child's powers by the demands of the social situation in which he finds himself . . . Through the responses others make to his own activities, he comes to know what those mean in social terms. . . . I believe that the psychological and social sides are organically related, and that education cannot be regarded as a compromise between the two, or a superimposition of one upon the other.

This concept of learning as fundamentally social flew in the face of prevailing notions of teaching and learning as knowledge transmission, accomplished primarily by having the teacher (the "expert") pour knowledge into students, who passively waited like empty vessels to be filled.

In the 1920s, Lev Vygotsky, like Dewey, described social experiences and mental processes as strongly interrelated, emphasizing that learning and problem solving occur *between* a learner and others.[2] He noted that, as people express their thinking, they actually understand concepts more deeply while forming new and more sophisticated ideas. Over the past one hundred years, scientific researchers from across disparate fields—psychology, linguistics, neuroscience, and anthropology—have come to agree. Vygotsky also placed great importance on the teacher's role in organizing activities and social groupings that would keep students stretching productively.

The importance of the teacher in fostering learning as both a social and a cultural process was taken up more recently by psychologist Roland Tharp, after he studied Hawaiian children learning in the context of their families and communities.[3] In the 1990s, Tharp and his colleagues developed a set of pedagogical standards that codified what they had learned in the context of other deeper learning principles:

1. *Joint productive activity*: Learning is facilitated through collaborative activity between teachers and students working together on a shared project.
2. *Language and literacy development*: Teachers provide structured opportunities for students to engage in reading, writing and speaking activities to develop competence in language and literacy across the curriculum.
3. *Contextualization:* Teachers connect new information with what students already know from home, school, and community.
4. *Challenging activities*: Teachers design and enact challenging activities with clear standards and performance feedback to develop complex cognitive development in their students.
5. *Instructional conversation*: Teachers engage students through goal-oriented dialogue and elicit student talk by questioning, listening, and responding to assess and assist in student understanding.

These standards, disseminated by the center Tharp once led—the Center for Research on Education, Diversity, and Excellence (CREDE)—are used to anchor the CU Denver program, functioning as a pedagogical guide for faculty, staff, partners, and teacher candidates. Their underlying principles motivate the approaches in all of the seven programs.

Key among these standards is the concept of "joint productive activity," wherein learning occurs as teachers and students talk and work together. Teachers create settings where diverse learning activities, including dialogues in pairs, as well as small and large groups, make social interactions the foundation of learning. Using language to exchange ideas, prior understandings, and out-of-school experiences, students develop new, more complex knowledge and skills. In such settings, teachers draw on students' diverse backgrounds and experiences so that differences become an asset rather than an obstacle to learning; in the process, classrooms become active, social, and multidimensional.[4]

Today, these ideas lie at the heart of our fourth dimension of teaching for deeper learning—communities of practice. Learning is an active, interactive, constructive, and iterative process. Learning occurs through the interaction of people, problems, ideas, and tools as people get feedback from their actions and about their ideas. It takes place as adults and young people engage together in conversation doing real work. Well-designed and well-tended interactions among groups of students allow them to support one another's learning, combining their different knowledge, abilities, and experiences into deeper knowledge and skills. Scaffolding—assistance from teachers and peers—helps students move from the periphery to core participation in subject-matter learning.

These deeper learning practices require classroom relationships that are built on an ethic of caring and trust, and support social and emotional development to sustain safe and productive learning communities.[5] These kinds of practices take advantage of collaborative group work, a much-studied approach that has been found, over decades of research, to strengthen student learning when it is well designed and implemented.[6] But, as everyone who has ever experienced group collaboration knows, group work is not always productive, as teachers have not always learned strategies for designing tasks and managing student work processes that allow everyone to participate equitably, focus on challenging content, and learn with and from each other. There are many pedagogical puzzles to work out.

Teaching for deeper learning as a social process means considering the role of instructional conversations in the learning process, the design of the learning environment, and the ways in which teachers' and students' interactions can facilitate learning. Each of these areas raises questions teachers can pose as they seek to make their classrooms settings for academically useful social interaction. In considering the role of conversation, a teacher asks, Who is asking the questions? Who leads the discussions? Which voices are heard and how often? How is student-to-student communication facilitated? Consideration of the learning environment prompts the following questions: How authentic and purposeful are the activities? What role do collaboration and community play in accomplishing tasks? What are the mechanisms for feedback and critique? Finally, key questions about teacher and student interactions include: Who is valued as an expert and source of knowledge? How does the teacher's role change as students develop expertise? How does the teacher facilitate this growing expertise? Preparing teachers to answer these questions in ways that facilitate deeper learning through social processes is a major goal of each of the seven teacher education programs.[7]

In each program, we observed teachers design lessons to make learning a joint productive activity with instructional conversations as the guiding strategy. They structured both small- and large-group opportunities for peer interaction in which students combined and constructed their knowledge. Teachers scaffolded students with questions and supports that moved from their current level of competence to demonstrate more advanced skill.

Each of the programs supports its teacher candidates to recognize and build on the social nature of learning in their courses, in their clinical experiences, and in the structure and cultures of the programs themselves. As the vignettes in the previous chapters of this book make clear, learning in productive communities intersects with the other dimensions of deeper learning. It is linked to how learning becomes developmentally grounded and contextualized and how students apply and transfer what they know to a variety of situations in and outside of school. And as we will see in chapter 9, it is very much a part of how learning becomes equitable and oriented toward social justice.

In the remainder of this chapter we provide examples of teacher candidates facilitating learning as a social process in their clinical work at K–12 school sites and then describe the strategies the teacher preparation programs use to help the candidates learn to teach that way.

DEEPER LEARNING THROUGH JOINT PRODUCTIVE ACTIVITY

Sara, a teacher candidate at CU Denver and her mentor Kim, a clinical teacher at Laredo Elementary in Aurora, Colorado, use these standards as they design lessons for the classroom of fifth graders they teach together. Laredo, a CU Denver professional development school, enrolls a diverse group of 513 K–5 students, 61 percent of whom are Hispanic, 19 percent black, 10 percent white, 4 percent Asian, and roughly 1 percent Hawaiian/Pacific Islander and Native American; 4 percent of students identify as two or more races. Nearly half are English language learners; 11 percent have special learning needs; 84 percent qualify for free or reduced-price meals.

In the lesson highlighted here, Sara and Kim engage students in contextualized learning through social interaction—in this case sharing their personal experiences with one another to generate and use sensory details to enrich their writing.

Joint Productive Activity in Action

A crisp wind and intense sun beat down on the carefully manicured lawn that lines the walkway up to Laredo Elementary. Below undulating American and Colorado flags, bold blue letters above the entrance exclaim: "Laredo Lions." At 9:15 a.m. on a Wednesday morning, in a portable classroom at the edge of a grassy courtyard, Kim's class is in full swing.

Nineteen fifth-grade students—all of them Hispanic or African American—are sitting on a carpet at the front of the classroom with an easy view of the screen that displays student work projected from a nearby document camera. Kim is standing and enthusiastically walking students through samples of student work that was turned in the day before. Sara, sitting nearby, is very much a part of the conversation.

The lesson is focused on how to infuse writing with sensory details so that readers can see/hear/feel/taste/smell the events that the student-authors are describing. The assignment asks students to pick any memorable moment in their lives that evoked strong emotion from them. One girl writes about breaking her leg during a soccer match; another writes about her first day in an American school after immigrating from Ethiopia; a third writes about being with her sister during her miscarriage.

Kim: Luis has come so far in his writing—everyone give him a hand! [Students enthusiastically clap.] Yesterday Luis shared with us about going to the Lantern Festival but, Luis, instead of just telling us you went, I want you to be able to *show* everyone. What were the lanterns doing? [Students start to chime in.] Hold on, give him a second. [pause]

Luis: Moving, crackling, flickering.

Kim: Which one do you like best? [pause]

Luis: [shrugs shoulders]

Kim: Okay, try this—close your eyes. Can you imagine it?

Luis: Yes! The lanterns were *flickering*!

Kim: Great—that word is more specific and now we can see it like you saw it!

This process continues for two more student-authors whose writing needs a bit more specificity. Kim ends her mini-lesson with: "We're going to continue to get better, and when I read what you work on today I'll expect to see this level of sensory detail in all of your stories. I want to be able to really visualize what you're describing—I want this from you today, tomorrow, and in ten years!"

At this point Sara launches into the next portion of the lesson wherein small groups of students work together to describe different sensory objects without looking at them first.

Sara: You may notice that there are brown bags on each of your tables. Inside of these bags is a mystery surprise. You know how I love my mysteries! [Students laugh, and some say "yes" and "she does like mysteries!"] The

(continues)

challenge here is that you have to come together as a team to describe what's in the bag and share out with the whole class. I'm going to walk around and listen to your conversations, but I want you to hold everyone in the group accountable, so that means you ask each other questions if you notice someone isn't talking.

Students immediately disperse to tables in groups of four—it's clear that they've done this sort of group work many times before as the transition is swift and precise. Students are immediately talking and on task. Some are sitting at their tables; some are standing; some are wiggling around, gesticulating with their hands, eyes closed, trying to find the most accurate words to describe the sensations associated with the objects. When Sara brings the class back together, the groups share out in a round-robin style.

Sara: Tell us what your sense was and then give us a sentence that describes the item in your bag.

Group 1: This smells like a sunflower after a storm on a Monday morning breeze.

Group 2: The back of the heart is shining bright like a star on a summer day.

Sara: Do you mean night?

Student: No, *day*. Miss, the sun is a star. [smiling]

Group 3: This popcorn is salty, buttery, and crunchy.

Group 4: The cotton balls feel like the inside of a teddy bear after it's been ripped or like the inside of a pillow.

Sara: [addressing one girl in the group who did not speak during the share] Do you want to add anything? [student shakes her head no] Not today? Okay, I'll be looking for it in your writing.

Group 5: The coins hitting each other in an annoying way.

Sara: "Hitting"? What else could you use?

Students: Clanging or chattering.

Sara: I'm not going to take simple words—your writing has to show your ability to go deeper. I won't accept "hitting" when you could use "chattering" or "clanging."

Kim then transitions students to the final portion of the day's activities where students are given time to work on their writing independently, in groups, or in pairs, as needed. When she says "go," two students immediately begin passing out notebooks, and five students move to the front of the room to sit on the carpet to work with Sara. Sara elicits more descriptive language from students by asking detail questions such as, What is an example of that? What else? How could you write that?

Meanwhile, Kim is circulating around the room to check on student progress. She pauses at one point to ask some probing questions of one student, saying, "How terrified were you holding your baby sister in the hospital? . . . Okay, great, add that detail to your paper." At another table Kim, reading over the shoulder of one student, says, "You're on the right track. I want you to keep going." These individual conversations with students about their work continue as the class proceeds.

In one instance, a student is considering adding another layer of detail to describe the sound of her mother weeping.

> **Student [reading from her notebook]:** "She cried with elephant sounds."
> **Sara:** Okay, put down your paper. I want to hear it and I want to see it. Tell me more.

The student tries to explain further the depth of sadness she wants to capture in adding the phrase "elephant sounds" and Sara follows up with, "Read back to me what you have. Okay, you're the author, so you have to decide if adding that detail makes the image better or is distracting." The student nods and then, grasping the pencil tightly between her fingers, bows her head low to the page and continues writing.

In our interview with Sara following the lesson, she was explicit about how her instructional approach reflects the principle—emphasized both in her CU Denver coursework and at Laredo—that learning is fundamentally social:

> We usually start with modeling, so kids can see what we're going to ask them to do—this is how we launch the lessons. We then share student work and focus on getting students talking to each other and sharing out as a way of testing out the "teaching point"—we usually do that piece on the carpet in the space at the front of the class. Then we do small groups where we'll rove around the room. If we see something important, we share it out with the class. At the end of the lesson, we always come back to the carpet to summarize learnings.

Sara also underscored how social interaction, such as that in this lesson, has the additional advantage of "making content relevant" to the students. She explained that she and Kim "always try to have the purpose for what we're doing connected to [students'] lives." Asking students to tell their own stories not only validates students' life experiences, but it also enables them to learn new writing skills by applying those skills to content (i.e., their own lived experiences) in which they are experts.

The teaching practices captured in the vignette, coupled with the teacher candidate's explanation of how she and her mentor craft learning experiences, illustrate perfectly how learning occurs through joint productive activity. Throughout the lesson, the interactions allowed experts and novices to work together (as they do in families and communities) and talk about their work. There was an ebb and flow to the instruction where the teachers offered initial framing, students then worked with teachers as guides, and then embarked either on their own or with a partner to complete a challenging and meaningful task.

Joint activity also means teachers share power with students—they share decisions about the selection of topics as well as responsibilities for how to proceed. The teachers at Laredo recognize and honor student differences and preferences. When we asked Sara why some students were working alone, other in pairs, and still others in small groups, she explained that as teachers they "take into consideration that some kids might want to be more individualistic and want to work alone sometimes—though if they do feel like collaborating, they can, and if they don't want to, they don't have to." Joint productive activity requires dialogue, negotiation, and compromise.

In the following sections, we explore four aspects of joint productive activity that we observed in classrooms across the seven programs: instructional conversation, peer interactions, scaffolding, and classroom communities.

Instructional Conversation

Tharp and his CREDE colleagues used the phrase "instructional conversation" to capture the dynamics in classrooms where teaching and learning occur through student interactions supported by the teacher.

> To truly teach, one must converse; to truly converse is to teach. In the Instructional Conversation, there is a fundamentally different assumption from that of traditional lessons. Teachers who engage in conversation, like parents in their natural teaching, are assuming that the child may have something to say beyond the "known answers" in the head of the adult. They occasionally extract from the child a "correct" answer, but to grasp the communicative intent of the child requires the adult to listen carefully, to make guesses about the meaning of the intended communication (based on the context and on knowledge of the child's interests and experiences), and to adjust their responses to assist the child's efforts—in other words, to engage in conversation.[8]

The idea of teaching as engaging in conversation is not unique to the CREDE researchers. A team at the University of Wisconsin, which spent five years studying hundreds of classrooms, used the term *substantive conversa-*

tion for one of the most powerful strategies they observed for enhancing the intellectual quality of students' schoolwork.[9] They were referring to students' engagement in extended conversational exchanges about subject matter with the teacher and/or their peers that built a shared understanding of ideas. They stressed that these subject-matter conversations went beyond reporting facts, procedures, or definitions; they focused on making distinctions, applying ideas, forming generalizations, and raising questions.

Teaching through conversation is neither scripted nor controlled by the teacher. Rather, participants share ideas through conversations as they work to understand a concept or finish a project. Teachers use skill, artistry, their understanding of students, and their own subject-matter knowledge to guide the conversation, connect it to learning goals, and offer overarching themes and principles. Although such conversations may appear to require little more than students' interest and willingness to participate, they are not self-sustaining. The teacher's role is pivotal. Teachers attend to many factors, including the contributions of individuals, the group's construction of meaning, and what those reveal about students' understandings (and misunderstandings). They also make dozens of decisions—for example, whether and when to go with the conversational flow and when to interject or redirect. Instructional conversation is a strategy that teachers of any grade or subject can employ, but the knowledge, experience, and relationships that teachers bring to the equation will make all the difference in the quality of the learning that occurs.

Instructional conversation is a key element of the lesson we described earlier at Laredo Elementary. In large- and small-group configurations and in one-on-one interactions with students, the two teachers artfully posed questions and engaged students in questioning one another as they generated increasingly vivid sensory details in their writing. Nearby, at Hinkley High School, another CU Denver professional development school, we watched another teacher candidate facilitate instructional conversation in a mathematics class (see the box "An Instructional Conversation in Mathematics").

Following the lesson, Maria and Joan debrief the lesson, talking together as colleagues exploring whether their objectives were achieved and, more specifically, whether the lesson engaged the students in deeper learning. Joan explains, "When students ask me a question, I try to go to the deepest level of understanding that I can. I avoid the easy answer— not wanting students to be told what to do and doing it—and move away from the procedural." Maria observes with satisfaction that the lesson

An Instructional Conversation in Mathematics

On a spring afternoon, Maria Sanchez—a teaching candidate at CU Denver—is coteaching a diverse group of Hinkley High tenth graders with her clinical teacher, Joan Simmons. During their five-week unit on probability, Maria and Joan have been helping students learn to "write and answer questions about the likelihood of an event" and "prove whether two events are independent, using the multiplication rule."

Eight boys and eleven girls sit in preassigned small groups of threes and fours, each with a data set and poster paper. As class begins, they pair up and stand, swinging arms past each other to "wake them up" after lunch, as their teacher puts it. Then, as a preview to the small-group task they will be doing, the teachers pepper the students with questions, using familiar examples of two events that might or might not occur independently—being a girl and wearing sneakers, for instance— and having them generate ideas about how they could know.

After a quick reminder about the roles they will play in their groups, the students go to work to make sense of the data in front of them and create at least five questions that could be asked and answered using that data set. Then, on their poster paper, they write at least two simple probabilities, two conditional probabilities, and a fifth probability of the group's choice. Each group also needs to prove whether the events in their given data sets are independent using the multiplication rule. The two teachers circulate, probing, answering questions with more questions, giving hints—scaffolding the groups' work.

As the students finish their posters, they move casually into the wide and empty hallway outside the classroom and tape their posters to the wall, chattering about their own work and eagerly peering at what other groups have done. They do a "gallery walk," carrying calculators and graphic organizers to assist them as they write and answer questions posed on the posters and explain whether two events being reported on the posters are independent.

After the hallway activity, they return to the classroom and engage in a whole-group conversation about the experience—asking questions, reporting what they have learned, and boasting about what they have accomplished.

reflected their commitment to engaging students in thoughtful instructional conversations:

> [We wanted to] give students some private reasoning time (read this, make sense of it, see what you can do), then partner them up, give them time to talk, have them take on listener roles knowing what to listen for, switch and swap roles, then come together as a table to make sure that everyone's voice is heard. This gives a student who may not have generated such a response access to the mathematical reasoning of their peers, something that doesn't happen very often in a math class.

In many ways, this math class defies commonly held stereotypes about instruction in comprehensive high schools like Hinkley High, located in neighborhoods of concentrated poverty and racial isolation, and the teaching and learning that goes on inside them. Conversational problem posing and solving was the dominant mode of instruction in this International Baccalaureate class, with question-asking, head scratching, hypothesizing, and scribbling ideas on paper as the primary activities. Students applied principles of mathematics and constructed complex knowledge, rather than engaging in rote memorization. The atmosphere was friendly, noisy, and easy, but very much on task.

The two CU Denver clinical experiences we highlight here are typical of what we observed in this and the other programs. Teacher candidates and alumni spoke about learning to create classroom activities where teachers are the guide, but not the "main event," as one teacher candidate explained. In university courses and in the partner K–12 schools, we observed teacher candidates, cooperating teachers, and university professors respond to student questions with more questions to prompt thinking and unpack potential misunderstandings.

Evidence of these practices also emerged in the LPI survey of teacher candidates, where 97 percent of respondents across all sites reported experiencing "opportunities for students to raise questions, discuss, and debate ideas" in their coursework, and 94 percent reported the same of their field placements. Additionally, 98 percent of all candidates reported that they had been prepared to "develop students' questioning and discussion skills" and to "encourage students to see, question, and interpret ideas from diverse perspectives." Candidates experienced "opportunities for students to research and investigate ideas or events," with 93 percent seeing this in their coursework and 90 percent in their field placements. Fully 98 percent of candidates at all programs reported they had been prepared to "engage students in cooperative group work as well as independent learning."

In all, the "heavy lifting" done in the classroom was the job of the student, not the teacher, whose own major effort occurred not in lecturing, but in careful planning for the lesson and intense listening during it, in order to evaluate and continue to scaffold student learning. One teacher candidate characterized the pedagogical approach as a true "focus on student learning, which means we're the guide. . . . We facilitate students working together and we ask critical questions to help them delve deeper." Another teacher candidate explained, "When [students] are talking, they're learning. . . . We have to make sure that the students' voices are heard more than ours." And indeed, across the programs, instructional conversation was a key strategy. Several teacher candidates used the Socratic seminar, a specific technique for engaging students deeply in instructional conversations among teachers and peers about subject-matter content. We provide examples of this technique in the next chapter.

Peer Interaction to Combine, Iterate, and Construct Knowledge

In the lessons we've described so far, teachers used multiple forms of social interaction to create productive learning conditions, including structured peer interaction. The rooms were abuzz with productive peer-to-peer conversations in which students were learning. Peer interaction in small groups expands the number of social learning opportunities for students far beyond what teacher-student interactions alone will permit. Peer interactions enable students to serve as experts as well as novices, asking questions and offering suggestions to help their peers stretch beyond their current levels of understanding and skill.

Giving students the opportunity to exchange ideas and learn from each other reflects Vygotsky's theory that individuals learn as they participate in communities working together. Through carefully structured collaboration in small groups, students participate in a shared practice or a group project that takes up a real-life situation, as in the box "Learning Through Peer Interaction."[10]

Throughout the lesson, Lily makes sure that all students have an opportunity to make valuable contributions to classmates' work and have their work appreciated by others. She explains that there are multiple ways that groups can solve the problem, emphasizing the importance of the problem-solving process, as opposed to the correct answer. Despite (or perhaps because of) all the interactions among students, any one student's strengths and weaknesses need not become fodder for comparison or embarrassment. When working with others, students can safely watch and learn how others become successful. In addition, well-designed tasks for peer interaction offer a variety of paths to success, so they stand a good chance of accommodating students' differences.

Lily told us after the lesson that collaborative teaching and learning is a core strategy she and her mentor teachers use with their shared group of students. Note that, in addition to engaging the students in mathematics learning through peer interaction, Lily also taught her students about the process itself. When she asked them what it means to work in a group, the students' responses revealed their awareness of social behavior, which

Learning Through Peer Interaction

Lily, an Alverno College candidate in her last semester, is student teaching at Walker School in a former suburban factory town outside of Milwaukee, where more than half of the students qualify for free or reduced-price lunch. The innovative, student-centered, technology-rich school features multiage elementary grade classes that span multiple classrooms and incorporate multiple teachers. Walls have been removed from many classrooms to make them open and collaborative. On this day, in Lily's classroom of sixty students and three teachers (Lily and her two mentor teachers), she is engaging twenty fourth graders—each with a computer tablet in hand—in a collaborative mathematics lesson.

Lily supports her students' growth as mathematical thinkers by helping them see how quantitative thinking can solve a real-world technology problem. Because her students frequently use technology, Lily focuses the lesson on a common mathematical question for tablet users. Lily explains to her students, who are seated together cross-legged in a circle, "Mrs. Lily is out of storage on her iPad. She needs to delete 157 MB to upload her newest lesson on problem solving." She makes the problem concrete by using a box with pictures, a lesson-planning book, a DVD, and papers to ensure that students understand what "storage" means when talking about technology. She explains that on her iPad, a picture is 10 MB, an old lesson is 47 MB, a video is 171 MB, and a Google Doc is 5 MB. Her framing also demonstrates the relevance of the lesson to the students' lives.

Lily provides a framework, known as CUBE, to help her students read the instructions actively:

C = circle numbers that are important to a problem
U = underline the question
B = box math words
E = evaluate

Lily has her students work with one another to share and combine their ideas and strategies for solving the iPad storage problem. The students first work in pairs to read the question on their iPad, using the CUBE strategy and their pointer finger to circle, underline, and box words, and then evaluate the question after they are done reading. After a few minutes, Lily calls the class back together: "Students, turn your apples up" [referring to the glowing apples on the back of their iPads]. The students place their tablets on the ground, with the screen facing down so they are not distracted. Lily begins by asking the students what they know about Lily's iPad:

"It's full!" one student exclaims.
Another calls out, "You need to delete 157 MB."

Students continue to share the key numbers, questions, and mathematical concepts in the problem. As the students share, Lily synthesizes their insights by drawing a visual representation of the problem on the board, drawing her iPad, with an

(continues)

arrowing pointing from a drawing of her lesson-planning notebook to the iPad, and then an arrow pointing away from her iPad to all the things she could remove, such as a DVD, a picture, or old lessons. She then divides the class into groups of four, so that students of different skill levels can work on the problem together, combining their knowledge and strategies as they use their iPads to record their solutions on a shared Google Doc.

Before students split into their groups, Lily asks, "What does it mean to work in a group? What is one thing we need to do when we're in a group?"

"Be collaborative," eagerly shares Emma.

Lily inquires, "What does *collaborative* mean?"

Emma explains, "Be quiet and respectful to others."

Dylan, who is sitting next to Emma, adds, "Just what Emma said, but collaborative is also involving everyone and not leaving anyone out."

Lily concludes, "And making sure that everyone has a chance to add their thinking." Lily continues, "You will all be responsible for your own thinking because in a Google Doc, when you share it, I can see who did the adding of information. You are all responsible for the thinking of the group. You have the remainder of the time today to work on this. Tomorrow the goal is that you present your solution to the group, because not everyone is going to solve it the same way."

As students work together, they take charge of the assignment.

helps create a collaborative and caring environment that nurtures student learning. Lily explained:

> For the kids, the communication and collaboration piece is very important to their learning and the college and career readiness standards at this school. So, you notice when I asked about what it means to collaborate, they knew what it means to collaborate in a group. Whether it works out that way or not is something else—they're ten and eleven years old—but they understand what it means, that everyone's got to have some sort of say, and that we've got to be working together for a common goal.

As we explain more below, Lily's careful structuring of peer interaction didn't happen by chance.

Scaffolding

A third strategy we observed teachers use to facilitate learning through social processes is scaffolding. As we noted in chapter 1, Vygotsky, as part of his development of sociocultural learning theory, postulated that the development of higher mental processes is most likely to occur when learners move beyond what they can do and understand independently to what they can do and understand with targeted assistance, or "scaffolding." The space between these two points is what Vygotsky called the *zone of proximal development* (ZPD).[11]

Accordingly, one of the teacher's principal roles is to support, or *scaffold*, students to acquire knowledge and skills that they cannot learn on their own but can learn with targeted assistance. A teacher can provide several kinds of assistance, as can peers: Teachers can provide a model to show a learner how something is done, or they can demonstrate a process or skill both physically and by talking aloud about how an expert thinks. A teacher can also assist by breaking up a task into smaller units or by reorganizing the sequence of a complex task. Both teachers and peers can assist through questioning, explanations, feedback, encouragement, and praise.

Students who have had less experience with an area, a field, or a domain will need more scaffolding than those students who have had more experience with that field or domain. They may need more sequenced supports, more attempts, and more opportunities to revise to develop expertise. Assistance can also be provided by more capable peers, by resources in the classroom, or by the Internet, software, and books. The teacher's role is to make sure that the student has access to a variety of resources appropriate to the student's needs and an understanding of how to use them. Inherent in the notion of scaffolding is the idea that the teacher eventually fades her support as students become more skilled.

In the lesson above, Lily scaffolded students' mathematics learning by relating the problem to a familiar experience, by reviewing skills needed to solve the problem, by providing tools for students to work with, and by offering support while allowing the students to find their own solutions.[12] Lily also artfully used technology as a scaffold. We typically think of technology-assisted learning as an individualized activity. However, used in the context of authentic and active learning communities, these same technologies can help scaffold learners' collective explorations beyond the bounds of their current knowledge. Lily's lesson illustrates her effective use of technology to build on students' ability to collaborate and communicate with one another as they engage in real-world mathematics problem solving. Well used, technology can provide scaffolding for investigation, concept attainment, individual and/or collaborative sense-making, and community building, to name but a few possibilities.

Perhaps the most important form of scaffolding is the well-timed question, which can serve many purposes. Questions can determine when and what a student is ready to learn. They can also press students' thinking further and provide them opportunities to articulate and reflect on their thoughts. Questions can guide the student through a logical thinking process or prompt the learner to think about a problem in a new way, as we saw in the first vignette, where Kim and Sara helped students envision vivid language as they asked the children questions about their ideas and perceptions.

This lesson also illustrated how scaffolding is an iterative process of assessing and assisting with sensitivity to the needs and the readiness of the learner. Apparently, this was not the lesson that Sara, the CU Denver teacher candidate, and Kim, her mentor, had originally planned for the day. But after assessing the work the children had produced the previous day, the teachers decided to dig in more deeply before moving on to the next segment of the unit. They assessed students' current understanding and skills, as reflected in the work they were producing, and decided to engage them in doing more advanced work with the assistance of more capable others, both teachers and peers. Sara described this nimbleness, where their instructional choices are dependent on the performance and needs of the students, as "typical."

These teachers realized that the process of scaffolding is not necessarily a linear one. In fact, it is probably best compared to a spiraling process where the teacher anticipates when the students will be competent enough to work independently but is also prepared to step back in to support students who are not quite ready. Instead of designating a specific time when they will relinquish control to the learners, effective teachers are aware that they are always trying to enable greater independence on the part of students, while being available for needed assistance. Even as they give students more room to direct their own learning, they are mindful of the indicators that will signal when students can continue to move forward in productive ways and when they will need to step in again. The teacher is always ready to provide additional scaffolding if withdrawal of the support was perhaps premature, and she is also ready to step back in when the level of challenge increases.

The following mathematics lesson (see box "Scaffolding Through Questions"), taught by Amy, a Montclair University MAT program graduate now teaching fourth grade in Newark, New Jersey, provides another rich example of scaffolding through questions—this time from students to one another, as they learned to engage in productive instructional conversations in a collaborative learning space. Note that Amy ends the lesson by asking metacognitive questions that scaffold her students as they reflect on their own learning is this social activity.

Scaffolding Through Questions

"I want you to turn to your partner. Tell them something that you know about area and perimeter. Go!" The excited chatter of students sharing their ideas fills the air. It is another busy day at Benjamin Franklin Elementary School (BFES) in Newark, New Jersey. Bright and colorful student artwork adorns the walls along the hallways as well as in Amy's classroom on the second floor. A graduate of Montclair's MAT teacher preparation program, Amy is now in her ninth year of teaching, and an instructional coach. She's been at Benjamin Franklin her entire career.

After the pair/share, students transition into their collaborative groups to work on word problems. The fourth graders are sitting in groups of four. Each student has a laptop open and paper is spread around the group. Amy circulates around the classroom, pauses at one student's desk, and bends down to answer a question about the math problem. Then she stands up and praises the student by telling her she's on the right track and going in the right direction. The student smiles and jumps back into the group discussion with confidence. The name of the class is Math Congress, and groups of students are engaged in solving mathematical word problems that incorporate error analysis. One problem is displayed on the smartboard:

> A student uses square tiles measuring 1 inch on each side to find the area of the rectangle. Her reasoning is shown: "I covered the top and bottom edges of the rectangle with 7 tiles each. I then covered the left and right edges with 3 tiles each. I added up all the tiles I used to get the total area of 20 square inches. 7 plus 7 plus 3 plus 3 equals 20."
>
> Identify the two errors in the student's reasoning and describe how to correctly use the tiles to find the area of rectangle.

The problem synthesizes and applies the concepts the students reviewed the previous day: area and perimeter, multiplication and division of whole numbers, multiplication of fractions and whole numbers, factors and multiples, and strategies for solving word problems. Each student has a defined role to play in answering the problem: data collector, group leader, encourager and timekeeper, and materials manager.

As Amy continues to circulate around the room, she listens in on the conversations and asks where each group is with their problem. There is a digital timer on the smartboard that tells the students how much time they have left to complete the problem. After the timer goes off, the groups submit their work online, so their responses can be displayed on the smartboard.

After the class finishes the math problem, everyone gathers in front around the smartboard, so each group can present, argue, and clarify their answer to their specific word problem. The Green group goes first; one student represents the group and explains the method used to solve their problem. After the presentation, a classmate asks the presenting group, "Why did you choose this strategy? Was there a better way to solve this problem?" To answer the questions, all of the students in the presenting group speak about why they chose the strategy. A student asks the presenting,

(continues)

group, "How did you use the blocks to solve this?" Another student asks "How did you add and subtract to get to the final number?" Then a student from the presenting group walks through each step to solve the problem.

Amy then asks the class to give suggestions for solving the problem using a different method. Hands fly up to offer suggestions, and Amy tosses a stuffed animal to a student (a turn-taking strategy). The student suggests that the group "use a bar model next time to explain their work." Amy asks the class, "What would be a benefit to using a bar model?" After a student answers, Amy repeats and affirms, "To create a picture, which helps visualize word problems."

Amy circles back to the initial pair/share activity to close out this group's word problem: "Before this group presented, you all shared some of what you know about area and perimeter with a partner, yes? Think about some of the ideas you had shared with your partner, and if any of your understandings or misunderstandings were changed by this group's presenting and sharing their thinking with you."

Building Classroom Communities

A fourth aspect of classrooms where learning occurs through joint productive activity is a culture of community—characterized by an ethic of care, trusting relationships, and clear norms of cooperation and sharing. Candidates' learning about structuring their classrooms in this manner came through in LPI's survey, where 96 percent of all respondents across all programs reported being prepared to "set norms for building a productive classroom community." Such classrooms are safe for the self-disclosure and risk-taking that learning in groups requires, and creating such classrooms requires the attention to development and contextualization that we described in previous chapters.

At CU Denver, building classroom relationships that are supportive and nurturing is considered foundational for teaching for deeper learning for every student, and is particularly important for those in urban settings. One teacher candidate expressed his convictions about the centrality of relationships as follows:

> Why would a kid who saw their mom arrested last night [care] about math? You can talk about growth mind-set and grit and that's all nebulous, but when you get down to it, why should a nine-year-old have that intrinsic motivation to say, "I really want to be an astronaut, so I am going to learn my math facts." It's more about the relationships and creating a place where they *want* to be. I don't expect the drive to

come from intrinsic motivation, though for some kids it's there. So, the question is, how do I, as a teacher, reengage kids who don't have "grit"? For me, that's where the relationship comes in.

One CU Denver alum we spoke to referenced the power of relationships for inspiring student motivation and engagement in the classroom. As we discussed in chapter 3 and will elaborate in chapter 9, many of the programs prepare their candidates to use relationship-oriented practices, such as restorative "discipline" practices, to develop a sense of responsibility to the community on the part of each student. Establishing and fostering those relationships *always* matters when it comes to the practice of teaching. However, having strong and trustful relationships becomes *even more* crucial when working with students living in poverty in historically underserved schools and communities. Arguably such relationships can be harder to develop in schools where things like police profiling, violence, and racism are a part of young peoples' day-to-day realities. Of course, even the best relationships can't fix the structural and policy harms that such communities face, but they can help students cope with them and learn despite them. The teacher candidates were well aware of this reality, given the explicit social justice focus of their coursework.

LEARNING TO TEACH FOR DEEPER LEARNING THROUGH SOCIAL PROCESSES

In the first half of this chapter, we've highlighted examples of teaching for deeper learning through social processes. Consider Amy's ability to scaffold her fourth-grade students (and enable them to scaffold each other) in collaborative, inquiry-based learning. She makes the process of students working together and with her to solve complex math problems look natural and easy. How did she learn to do this? Her skillful facilitation did not happen by chance or by dint of her personality alone. Rather, there was much work and intentionality in her pedagogical moves, which she developed through her coursework and fieldwork in Montclair State University's Teacher Education Program. In what follows, we describe three ways the programs support their students in learning about teaching as a joint productive activity and experiencing their own learning in the same way.

Teaching the Theory and Practices of Learning as a Social Process

The teaching of candidates Kim and Maria, featured in two of the earlier vignettes, reflects CU Denver's unrelenting focus on collaboration, relationships, and interaction as central to learning. CU Denver consistently articulates its view that learning is a social process—both in K–12 classrooms and in teacher preparation. Dean Rebecca Kantor pulls no punches when she talks about the centrality of this perspective:

> [In classrooms]: We're not asking you to teach in a way that shoves people into collaboration 110 percent of the time, but ultimately, and especially for second-language learners, which is a huge population that we support, if you aren't creating the opportunity in your classroom for kids to be able to collaborate about 70 to 80 percent of your time, those language learners are not going to grow. You have to. Learning is a social endeavor.

> [In the CUD programs]: Collaborative teacher preparation, at about every level you can think of . . . is threaded through, all the way from the fact that we admit them in a cohort; [from] the fact that, in any one of our classes, there are collaborative learning activities and joint productive activity going on all the time in the coursework; to putting [the teacher candidates] out in smaller teams in the schools, having what we call a collective learning community seminar every week out at their school. That thread is through everything that we do.

As a result, throughout their CU Denver coursework and field experiences, candidates are taught explicitly and experience routinely that learning happens through joint productive activity; this occurs when they have an opportunity to connect new information with what they already know from home, school, and community; and when their instructors engage them—and they learn to engage their students—through goal-oriented dialogue, eliciting student talk by questioning, listening, and responding to assess and assist in student understanding. With the CREDE standards serving as CU Denver's "north star" toward which all the content, pedagogy, and assessment structures and practices are pointed, program faculty, school partners, and candidates are all expected to move away from the unidirectional view that the teacher holds knowledge and transmits it to students.

This clear articulation of learning as a social process is also evident in the curriculum of other programs. For example, Trinity's program is guided by its Core Beliefs on the Development of Principled Practice, which are also a part of the Department of Education's conceptual framework. This set of core beliefs focuses on the importance of apprenticeship, engagement in inquiry, a continuum of practice, and a professional learning community in developing candidates' principled practice and determining the features and functions of the MAT program. Among the principles are several that articulate the social nature of learning and the importance of learning in interactive and supportive communities:

- Teachers develop craft knowledge under the careful guidance and support of master teachers.
- Teachers need a community of peers to examine questions of practice and assess student and practitioner learning.
- Teachers learn to engage in professional conversation and experience the power of collaborative work through the cohort model.

These beliefs, emphasizing the essential elements of learning as a social process, provide guidance on what Trinity's interns should be learning and doing to become the teachers Trinity aims to prepare, and they shape the structure of the one-year MAT program and the collaboration with PDS sites, their faculty, and administrators.

As we noted in chapter 3, a core element of the content of all the programs is knowledge about how children develop and learn. Each includes courses that immerse teacher candidates in theories of learning as a social process and the implications for designing lessons and developing classroom cultures that make learning interactions and relationships central. Course assignments focus on observing children learning in the context of peers and participating in learning communities. Other courses focus on lesson design strategies (e.g., Understanding by Design and Socratic seminars) that structure classroom experiences as joint productive activities. Others support teacher candidates by teaching concepts and skills such as scaffolding by asking higher-order questions that move students toward deeper learning. For example, Alverno requires students to list in their lesson plan all the questions they plan to ask their students.

Programs also teach well-established approaches to productive cooperative small-group learning strategies. At Stanford, where Complex Instruction was developed and initially researched, this work is the focus of an entire course: Teaching and Learning in Heterogeneous Classrooms. We also saw the use of these or similar strategies throughout the programs we studied, and in the classrooms of candidates and graduates we visited.

Building classroom communities is an explicit topic of instruction in these programs. They approach classroom management as constructing a community of learners, rather than as a set of techniques to control student behavior, such as establishing rules with consequences. Teacher candidates learn to develop norms of collaboration, respect, and engagement. At the core are the relationships that teachers build with students so that students are well known, respect and work well with each other, and have a sense of common membership and shared responsibility.

At CU Denver, Anchor Experience 2 (described in appendix B) asks candidates to develop a "Classroom Community Plan in Action" as a response to two of the program's essential questions. Anchor Experience 2 assumes that the foundation of every successful urban community classroom is a safe, engaging, and supportive classroom community—one characterized by meaningful relationships among students and their teachers, where students and teachers know and support one another, both as people and as learners, and where the rich diversity of their backgrounds is not only welcomed and affirmed but is also used as a springboard from which to engage in academic learning. In Anchor Experience 2, teacher candidates develop a comprehensive understanding of the guiding principles that are at the heart of such a classroom community and have multiple opportunities to develop, implement, reflect upon, and refine techniques and approaches to building and sustaining classroom communities.

Teacher candidates also hear clear articulations of learning as a social process in their clinical placements. For example, Matthew Willis, the principal at CU Denver's partner school Hinkley High, is emphatic about deeper learning being collaborative, social, and personalized. Eschewing traditional pedagogy, he insists that "cognitive engagement" requires that lessons be interactive and collaborative. He readily explains what he expects to see in the classroom:

> What you see will contrast with rows, teacher talking, students taking notes, sitting still. This school believes in rigor, relevance, [and] relationships, with relationships being the key to the others. Relationships are what are worked on most; then how to leverage relationships to get depth of knowledge, rigor, and relevance. You will see norms of relational discourse, moving up cognitive levels, and using relationships to do that. Interactive, collaborative, independent work. Relationships is probably the number one value for instruction and classroom management. . . . All students are engaged, especially male students of color.

Willis uses the acronym "RARE" in describing the faculty he wants to hire and develop—teachers who are Relational, Achievers, Reflective, and Equity Focused.

Experiencing Learning as a Social Process

All seven programs created structures, used practices, and nurtured relationships in which the teacher candidates themselves were continuously engaged in social interaction and joint productive activity. One important aspect of Trinity's preparation of candidates to teach for deeper learning, for example, is having faculty model student-centered practices, reflection, collaboration, and guided inquiry. Through this modeling, faculty show these practices in action, scaffolding interns' participation in them. One elementary mentor noted, for example, that the professor teaching her reading methods course "would always model a protocol while we were talking about a reading we had to do. We still had the content of graduate work, but then also [were shown] this valuable way to get learners to speak to each other rather than just listening to the teacher or professor. We always sat in a circle. Everything was very discussion based."

At Montclair, faculty intentionally model collaboration and group work in their courses for teacher candidates, explicitly describing how the learning activity is constructed and why group work makes the most sense for the learning that needs to take place. One Montclair faculty member explained:

> Every week we think about a different cooperative grouping strategy and then we do some metacognition, reflecting on, "What kind of strategies did I use? How might you use these with students? How might they be appropriate or not appropriate?" . . . Some of this reflection happens during class: "Look at what I'm doing right here. Look at how I'm dividing you into groups. What do you notice about how I'm doing this?" And then there is some reflection afterwards: "What are the things I did right or wrong?"

Creating meaningful group work for K–12 students is not just about process; the content of the group work must be "group worthy." One faculty member identifies the importance of having candidates construct meaningful tasks for student groups:

> [It is] really important to me that they understand that group work has to require more than one brain. Many come with superficial ideas about group work; you know, just put kids in a group and that works. . . . So every time I model that, we talk about why this would be in groups and not in pairs and not alone, what were the needs of the task that required this [activity] to look like this.

Additionally, all courses are taught by teams of instructors. It is expected that these teams will help intern teachers unpack their own instructional moves, an important step toward their use of the practices they experience in their own classrooms. Janie Griswold said a bit about how HTH expects interns' instructors to prepare them to see practice from the teacher's perspective:

> One of the things that we expect that partnership or team to do is pause the teaching action and take some time to meta-debrief. What did you just see? You did this group work activity, for example. What worked well for you [in terms of] how it was framed? Or how your actual participation was framed? And then, what do you think the instructor could have done differently or better, or what questions do you have?

SFTR faculty and clinical teachers also explicitly model collaborative practices, showing residents what it means to work with other educators in creating deeper learning opportunities for students. They model classroom structures in which student learning is facilitated through collaboration and group work centered on authentic and complex tasks.

As CU Denver faculty use the six CREDE standards to guide their own teaching, they model and explicate how they are designing lessons and organizing groups to accomplish their learning objectives. This explicit transparency in teaching provides rich opportunities for candidates to unpack why and how they might be able to transfer their learning from the university classroom to their K–12 clinical classrooms.

For example, the class session that the faculty leads to help candidates prepare for the assessment of the Anchor Experience in which they create the Classroom Community Plan in Action itself exemplifies a learning community. Working together in small groups, the teacher candidates pull together material from coursework, clinical experiences, and their own reflections on their learning. They apply what they learned by reflecting on their own teaching and engage in scaffolded instructional conversations with their teachers and peers. (See the box "A Teacher Candidate Learning Community in Action.")

Reinforcing what we saw in this class, a teacher candidate we interviewed explained that building relationships is something that is modeled by the CU Denver professors in how they run their classes. She has learned that at the core of teaching is the responsibility to "build a classroom

A Teacher Candidate Learning Community in Action

On a brisk Tuesday afternoon, twenty-five teacher candidates are seated in groups of four on the sixth floor of CU Denver's concrete and glass midrise building in downtown Denver. Although the room is windowless, the freshly painted lime green walls, purple upholstered rolling chairs, and modular desks with plates of giant chocolate-covered strawberries (graciously provided by Professor Maria Uribe "just because") suggests an upbeat and collaborative learning environment. Uribe is standing at the front of the room with her colleague, Professor John McDermott.

The purpose of today's class is for candidates to practice presenting their program-level assessment in preparation for the "real thing" the following week. To give students a sense of authentic audience, the professors have chosen to combine their classes. The candidates are a mix of graduate and undergraduate students, mostly female (80%) and mostly white (88%). To break the ice, McDermott and Uribe lead the students through a standing "getting to know you" activity that vaguely resembles an assembly line where in pairs, students have short, one-minute conversations, answering questions like "What's one word to describe yourself?" After this brief warm-up, students count off and move into heterogeneously mixed groups of four (by program area, university level) and launch into the work of the day.

John McDermott instructs candidates to reflect as a group about how they will create learning communities in their classrooms. The room erupts into a cacophony of thoughtful conversations. After table groups have a chance to discuss, the professors prompt candidates to share out with the whole group the highlights of their conversations.

One candidate speaks about his desire to create a community in his classroom like that of a football team where learning is collaborative and social:

> I want to nurture the idea of individual responsibility and initiative, so in my classroom I want each student to care about the others, so they can work as a team . . . I've been reflecting on a time in my life where I was part of a very diverse community: a football team. I want my students to be part of a team. That doesn't mean I'm a coach yelling at kids, but I want our team to work together and push each other to get help from one another so that we can have a collectivist classroom. Students with different funds of knowledge can become teachers, so student voice is always at the table and they will feel comfortable knowing that every student has something different to offer the team. So as a teacher, it's my responsibility to find those strengths; not just educational knowledge but other aspects that can help the team grow and learn from one another.

Another teacher candidate says: "At the beginning of the school year we'll have the power to create a safe environment and give students the opportunity to provide feedback and reflect on their own learning in the classroom." In response McDermott reminds her that to achieve this "will require having a conversation with

(continues)

students and intentionally building relationships . . . If you don't do it at the beginning of the year it won't magically happen."

Another candidate builds on these comments, underscoring the importance of
intentional community building in the classroom, saying, "Setting classroom norms
and expectations will make a world of difference . . . We have to teach students how
to work in groups and come back together as a whole group so that they can have
different ways of sharing their voice and getting the attention they need . . . We can
definitely do some of what we did today in my classroom, especially around how to
give feedback in groups."

As this last candidate's comment suggests, her participation in this adult learning
community has allowed her to imagine how to use similar strategies for engaging in
productive peer feedback in her own classroom next year.

community that says: 'This is a place where you come and learn and a place
where everyone is valued.'"

Becoming Members of a Community of Practice

The programs create pathways into teaching—through integrated coursework and fieldwork—that support students as they move, with scaffolding,
from the periphery of teaching into its core. They develop the understandings, knowledge, and skills of teaching, and at the same time took on the
identity of members of the teaching profession.

As learning scientists and anthropologists Jean Lave and Etienne
Wenger have described in other settings, a community of practice is a
group of people who share a craft or a profession and work together to
gain knowledge related to their specific field.[13] By sharing information and
experiences as a group, members learn from each other and develop both
personally and professionally.

As Wenger has described them, communities of practice have several
interrelated components, all of which make learning a social enterprise
that engages participants in joint productive activity that develops shared
norms and collaborative relationships. They develop a sense of belonging
to a group of people who contribute to a collective enterprise. They also
share a repertoire of practices that define their work. Participation in a community that learns and shares practices leads participants to develop their
identity as members of the craft—in this case, they become teachers.

In addition to their explicit teaching and modeling of teaching and
learning as collaborative practices, the seven programs also developed
structures that fostered the candidate's movement into the professional
community of teaching practice. These structures did not just provide

instructional benefits; they also influenced candidates' conceptions of the work of teaching. In the LPI survey, 98 percent of candidates responding across all programs reported that they have been prepared to "collaborate with colleagues to address students' needs and to improve instruction."

Most of the programs use a cohort model to structure teacher preparation in communities of practice from the moment students entered the programs. For example, the cohort model is crucial for structuring deeper learning experiences across the pathways in the large Montclair Teacher Education Program. Cohorts not only act as a source of support for candidates learning to teach; they also give them the opportunity to place themselves in student roles, to learn how to move on when challenges arise in collaborative work, and to practice giving and receiving feedback. Through this cohort-based support and collaboration, teacher candidates learn how to implement this facet of deeper learning in their own classrooms.

Teacher candidates and alumni confirmed how valuable this collaboration was to them in learning to achieve their goals with students. One alumnus recalled: "We are very close in our cohort. We worked a lot in teams, and we were also teamed up with teachers who would come into our classrooms from Montclair to observe our lessons and give us feedback. And then our mentor teachers were within the community."

A faculty member reinforced how the purpose and structure of cohorts support the work of deeper learning: "It goes back to the idea of relationships . . . The smaller we can make the experiences, in terms of class size or in terms of longitudinal relationships with students, the deeper we are able to go. That's just sort of a given."

Cohorts, thus, not only serve as an organizational structure to support the learning of teacher candidates, but also model for them the importance of building authentic relationships with students as well as developing learning communities within their own classrooms.

Collaboration also occurs within more intimate groups inside these cohorts. In most programs, university supervisors or advisors hold both one-on-one meetings with teacher candidates and weekly meetings with their small group of advisees in supervisory or conference groups of four to eight candidates. This meeting provides a place for teacher candidates to discuss the issues they face as educators in their field placements. The smaller cohort group provides a venue for collaborative problem solving and reflection that helps candidates learn to engage in individual and collective inquiry about the improvement of practice.

The development of collaborative, scaffolding relationships for teacher candidates is also supported by the use of coteaching models as a means for learning to teach. As a Montclair faculty member noted about the effort to establish this relationship at the start of the school year:

> They start in September, and we do an afternoon of professional development for [teacher candidates] and their mentor teacher before they even set foot in the classroom together. We talk about coteaching practices [and] different ways to think about coteaching, because we want to move away from the student-teaching model where you sit in the back and observe for a semester and then you jump into the classroom as the full teacher. But that is really about a gradual release of responsibility; there are many ways to coteach that are healthy for the kids and for the new teacher.

At SFTR, residents are placed at schools within the San Francisco Unified School District that the program terms "teaching academies," also known as professional development schools. As is the case at CU Denver, the academies see themselves as collaborators with the university in preparing the next generation of teachers, and they see the process as strengthening their schools' professional communities.

Describing what she looks for in choosing placement sites, SFTR's director of clinical teacher education told us that the principal is key to a successful teaching academy site:

> I think first and foremost we looked for . . . leaders who see having residents in their building as value-add, who see and understand the idea that their teachers will be professionally developed by being in a mentorship role; that their students will be benefited by the constant collaboration between two grown-ups. There is so much power in the coteaching model and in the idea that children have the chance to see adults thinking together and working together.

As described in chapter 4, SFTR's approach to developing strong and stable teaching academies ultimately expands collegial practice across departments within schools and across schools in the district.

CU Denver faculty also rely on the professional development schools to build professional communities that share the commitments, philosophy of teaching, and pedagogical approaches of the program. The two PDSs that we visited in low-income, immigrant neighborhoods of color in Aurora, Colorado, certainly did. At Laredo Elementary, the strong match between the school and the program is reinforced, in part, by the fact that after seven years of partnership, the school's faculty includes many CU Denver alumni. As clinical teachers, these alumni act as mentors and provide models of the dispositions and approaches to teaching that candidates are learning in their courses and from their clinical supervisors.

At Hinkley High, principal Matthew Willis sees the relationship with CU Denver as one that supports the school in achieving its equity goals, rather than seeing the school as doing the university a favor by providing clinical experiences for teacher candidates. He sees a double benefit to being a professional development school. He and his faculty get to train and hire excellent new teachers. In addition, the faculty see considerable benefit from having on-site support and professional development from their university partners, which contributes to the school's own improvement efforts.

The letter that Hinkley sends to teacher candidates who are about to begin their clinical experiences at the school (see the box "Hinkley Professional Development Welcome to CU Denver Interns") makes clear how seriously the school views its responsibility as a professional development school and how much the Hinkley faculty see the CU Denver teacher candidates as like-minded members of the faculty and full participants in their community of practice.

The teacher candidates' "full membership" on the Hinkley faculty is also communicated quite concretely: when beginning their clinical experiences, they are given keys to the building.

Moving from the periphery to the core of communities of practice does not end when candidates from these programs graduate. Several have structures and practices that engage their faculty in learning communities. Trinity, for example, facilitates a monthly critical friends group for alumni. This group, which uses protocols to examine and explore dilemmas of practice, gives graduates the opportunity to reengage with their Trinity professional learning community. The monthly critical friends group acts as an extension of the learning communities Trinity develops during the program, allowing alumni to continue to work together with colleagues to engage in the sort of reflective teaching that Trinity aims to instill in its candidates. As one critical friends group participant put it:

> I know we say it's a profession, but Trinity kind of instills you in . . . it's not just a job. It's this evolving craft, and you have to continue to work at it to get better. And if you're not questioning it, how can

---

Hinkley Professional Development Welcome to CU Denver Interns

We expect all interns to live "the life of a teacher" during internship days. As you take on more responsibility, it is expected that you arrive early or stay late enough to plan with your clinical teacher, make copies, and prepare the classroom for the lesson you are planning. All of our teachers at Hinkley work very closely in PLT [Professional Learning Team] groups with other teachers to plan and implement lessons. Our interns are expected to be an asset to the broader school community to support student success in as many ways as possible.

At Hinkley and at other Aurora district schools, there is a strong emphasis on professional development and coaching for all teachers. The principal, Matthew Willis; assistant principals Brandon Rowland and Suzanne Acheson; and site coordinator Tom Velaquez invest considerable time and resources in teacher development. Interns will fully participate in professional development opportunities (both in and out of the school building) . . .and parent-teacher conferences. We hope this experience prepares our candidates to see the teaching profession as a process of growth and learning, continuing long after the end of UCD enrollment.

On a final and important note, in order to make growth during your internship it is essential that you come to Hinkley with the attitude and initiative of an active learner. We are passionate about providing demanding and rigorous learning opportunities for our Hinkley High School students and protective of the Hinkley community. It is essential that you view yourself as a professional and as an asset to support student learning, while being respectful of the demands and professional expertise of the HSS staff.

---

you be getting any better? Being able to talk openly with people about what you did right, but also about what you did wrong, what you could do better, is something that Trinity makes you a lot more comfortable with than I find other teachers are.

In addition to providing alumni the opportunity to continue the reflective inquiries into teaching that they started as teaching interns, the critical friends group can also ease the transition into full-time teaching after the program. Graduates often end up teaching in schools where faculty may not have the opportunities for collaboration, collegiality, and reflection that they experienced as interns. Being able to return to the Trinity community to reengage can give them the support they need to continue to follow this model of teaching, even when it is difficult to do so. Shari Albright described how graduates can "return to 'the nest,' step above the fray of day-to-day school, and reconnect with the purposes and principles that serve as their drivers in education. It's also a safe place to share their challenges and get new ideas and strategies to take back into their class-rooms and schools."

This feature of the critical friends group was described by one participant in this way:

> I think I would be a different person if I hadn't come to Trinity. I do think that this year changed me and I do think that my thoughts about teaching have changed a little bit since I graduated, but I think I could've gotten really jaded and disillusioned this year, and I'm not. . . . A lot of that has to do with coming back here every month and just being reminded of why I do what I do.

For graduates who choose to participate in it, the critical friends group is an opportunity to continue their connection with Trinity, and to leverage that connection to sustain what they learned in their MAT program as well as continue to develop their practice as educators.

The teacher preparation programs we studied emphasized learning as a social process, carefully structured in classrooms by teachers who make learning a joint productive activity and ensure that instructional conversations and peer interactions are scaffolded in ways that move students toward deeper learning. The impact of this approach is reflected in the confidence teacher candidates expressed on our survey in their preparation to facilitate communities of learning in their own classrooms. We have previously described such survey results across all programs, but a deeper dive into the results for programs featured in vignettes in this chapter is also revealing.

At CU Denver, where we saw candidates using sensory detail to teach writing, engaging in instructional conversations in mathematics, and working together in a scaffolded discussion about creating community in their classrooms, 92 percent of the teacher candidates responding to the LPI survey reported that they were prepared to "set norms for building a productive classroom community." In this same vein, 90 percent reported they were prepared to "encourage students to see, question, and interpret ideas from diverse perspectives," with 92 percent saying the same about learning to "develop students' questioning and discussion skills" and engaging students in "cooperative group work as well as independent learning."

In our vignette from Alverno College, a teacher candidate facilitated her students' working together to solve real-world problems with mathematical thinking. Alverno candidates who responded to LPI's survey reported high levels of confidence in helping students to "think critically and solve problems," with 90 percent feeling well or very well prepared to do so. Alverno College faculty, teacher candidates, and faculty at placement sites all sang the same refrain—that the program's operation itself as a collaborative community provided the necessary foundation for engaging deeply with their coursework and fieldwork, whether as instructors, students, or mentor teachers. Not only did 100 percent of the teacher candidates we surveyed say that they often experienced collaborative learning in their own coursework, but they also all reported they had been prepared to "collaborate with colleagues to address students' needs and to improve instruction." In our survey of current Alverno students, all the surveyed teacher candidates also responded that they felt well prepared to "set norms for building a productive classroom community."

Finally, at Montclair State, where we observed a teacher candidate working with student groups in a fourth-grade classroom to solve math problems, 99 percent of survey respondents said they were prepared to "engage students in cooperative group work as well as independent learning," with the same percentage saying they had experienced "collaborative learning and group work" in their own coursework and were prepared to "develop students' questioning and discussion skills." Candidates also had the opportunity to learn to lay the groundwork for collaborative activity, as 98 percent reported being prepared to "set norms for building a productive classroom community."

These kinds of results are reflected in those for the other programs as well, as we have described in other chapters. In what follows, we show how this work contributes to more equitable opportunities and outcomes for students, and more attention to social justice practices in their schools.

CHAPTER 9

TEACHING FOR EQUITY AND SOCIAL JUSTICE

As a teacher for social justice, I envision a class where I am able to teach to all students' learning styles and levels, cultures and backgrounds. As discussed in . . .class, there is not an achievement gap, but instead an educational debt. We as educators and aspiring teachers owe students an equitable classroom and education.

—San Francisco Teaching Resident

Today's public schools are at the leading edge of a society that must strengthen its democracy and economy by building on its increasing racial, cultural, and linguistic diversity. Today's teachers are pioneers in the nation's ambition to educate all its young people to live, work, engage in, and contribute to an equitable twenty-first century. This ambition—captured in the federal Every Student Succeeds Act as preparing all students for college and career—is a strong driver of the content and practices of the seven programs we studied. If teachers are to achieve this goal, they must be prepared to teach for both deeper learning and equity. They have much to overcome.

Despite countless declarations that education is the civil rights issue of our time, past practices have made little progress in reducing education opportunity and achievement gaps that help perpetuate social inequality. In 2013, the federal Equity and Excellence Commission issued a scathing indictment of US education: "No other developed nation has inequities nearly as deep or systemic; no other developed nation has, despite some efforts to the contrary, so thoroughly stacked the odds against so many of its children. Sadly, what feels so very un-American turns out to be distinctly American."[1] Key reforms in the recent era of educational accountability thus far have only exacerbated existing problems by causing many educators to leave the profession and narrowing educational opportunities for students.[2]

Deeper learning practices, as we've described them in earlier chapters, can contribute to reversing this negative trend. Student-centered, inquiry-based experiences are better able than rote instruction to support the learning and understanding of diverse groups of students, especially those bearing the burdens of increasing poverty and social inequality. There is considerable work to do in this regard. Deeper learning has traditionally been the purview of elite students and schools. Exploring this issue in a provocative essay a few years ago, Harvard education professor Jal Mehta noted that "deeper learning has a race problem," largely because of the ways in which curriculum opportunities are differentially allocated in the United States:[3]

> Deeper learning has historically been the province of the advantaged—those who could afford to send their children to the best private schools and to live in the most desirable school districts. Research on both inequality across schools and tracking within schools has suggested that students in more affluent schools and top tracks are given the kind of problem-solving education that befits the future managerial class, whereas students in lower tracks and higher-poverty schools are given the kind of rule-following tasks that mirror much of factory and other working-class work. To the degree that race mirrors class, these inequalities in access to deeper learning are shortchanging black and Latino students.[4]

Mehta acknowledges that skepticism among many stems, in part, from the widespread myth that students must acquire the "basics" before they can engage in deeper learning, that "inquiry-oriented instruction is fine for students who come with a significant background in 'basic' or 'core' knowledge and skills, but to pursue that approach with students who lack this background is likely to be ineffective and does little to build their basic knowledge and skills."[5]

Mehta suggests that solving this problem requires two actions on the part of educators. One is to argue convincingly that deeper learning is key to providing equitable schooling, in that "joining the culture of power means doing one's own experiments and not just reading about experiments that others have done; such deeper experiences give disadvantaged students the same opportunities to participate in the real world of the disciplines that the most advantaged students have long had."[6] The second is to "diversify their vision of deeper learning" and make deeper learning practices themselves inclusive. This requires recognizing that "in every religious or ethnic community there is some tradition through which people learn deeply" and incorporating those traditions into instruction.[7]

Consonant with Mehta's recommendations, each of the seven teacher preparation programs helps candidates understand the social, historical, and political context of race and inequality in America and how it is reflected in schools and classrooms. Several of the courses emphasize this foundational knowledge, as we've noted in earlier chapters. The programs also frame equity/social justice and deeper learning as mutually reinforcing, and they embed both concepts in the content and practices of coursework and field experiences. For many this includes a focus on having teacher candidates learn to teach for deeper learning in partnership schools serving students living in poverty, those in communities of color, and those with large populations of immigrants and families whose primary language is other than English. By working with educators to strengthen deeper learning in such schools, these programs are able to enact both their commitment to high-quality teaching and learning and their determination to contribute to equity and social justice.

However, the programs do not see this dual focus as appropriate only for teachers preparing to teach students in underserved communities. They also take this approach with teacher candidates who may end up teaching in suburban communities, where inequities are often found inside the school, as a function of tracking systems. Moreover, their concern about equity extends to gender, sexual orientation, religion, and other social identifiers that are subject to marginalization and inequality.

Previous chapters addressing the first four dimensions of deeper learning experiences have described how the programs focus explicitly on helping their teacher candidates create learning opportunities that reflect the growing, research-based understanding of how people learn. In this chapter, we address the final dimension, showing how these programs are also determined to help "right" the pervasive social and educational "wrongs" of inequality and injustice by focusing on learning that is equitable and oriented to social justice. Both the "what" (the content) and the "how" (the structures and practices) of these programs are aimed at giving the young people who are most burdened by inequality and injustice access to outstanding teachers who can afford them learning opportunities often reserved for those in the most advantaged neighborhoods with the most privileged status.

The programs reconcile their explicit attention to the two foci—teaching for deeper learning and teaching for equity and social justice—by recognizing their complementarity. High Tech High's academic dean, Ben Daley, articulated the connection: "We think that constructivist, progressive, project-based learning . . . is inherently an equity argument. . . . That's why we're trying to have high-quality projects that engage all learners. That's why we were doing it, the whole time."

Teaching that reflects a complete understanding of learning requires knowing and accommodating students' developmental needs with personalized, transferable, contextualized, and social opportunities that build on the knowledge students bring with them. As we described in earlier chapters, that prior knowledge is inextricably connected to students' language, culture, and life experiences. This is true for all students, regardless of their family background and social advantages. However, teaching students who are from low-income families and with marginalized identities requires constructing lessons with an awareness of race, class, and other characteristics that shape students' "place" in society and, as a result, their "place" in school. To ensure that such students have access to rich and deep learning they must treat and incorporate students' unique identities as strengths and resources for learning, rather than deficits. They must help students build new knowledge on the knowledge that students bring with them to school.

We begin this chapter by describing how the practices and understandings of teacher candidates and graduates of these programs reflect this intersection of teaching for deeper learning, equity, and social justice. We then turn to how the content and practices of the teacher education programs help prepare them to do this work.

TEACHING AT THE INTERSECTION OF DEEPER LEARNING, EQUITY, AND SOCIAL JUSTICE

The vignette "An Equity-Focused, Equity-Enhancing Socratic Seminar" depicts a contextualized history lesson on South African apartheid taught by Martha, a Trinity teacher candidate, that reflects both teaching for deeper learning and social justice commitments. With equitable teaching uppermost in her mind, Martha uses a pedagogical approach that makes the high-status, intellectual content of AP World History accessible to a racially diverse group of students. This equitable pedagogy provides opportunities and support to all voices in the class.

The lesson focuses on a racial justice topic that is of great interest to the students—apartheid—and that connects with their real-world experiences in segregated and unequal San Antonio. On the previous day, Martha had contextualized the topic, bringing it closer to home by having the school's assistant principal share his experiences growing up in South Africa during apartheid. The main activity—an instructional conversation in a Socratic seminar—engages students in constructing knowledge as a social process.

An Equity-Focused, Equity-Enhancing Socratic Seminar

The Lee High School AP World History freshmen are sitting in two circles, an outer circle with nine students and an inner circle with eleven students. The class is racially diverse; most students are Latino and white, and a few are African American. Martha had asked them to come prepared with written questions about things that they were wondering about apartheid.

Martha begins by reviewing the directions for the Socratic seminar, emphasizing that it is self-directed: "As soon as someone is ready, you can ask a question."

One student says, "I don't think we get it."

Martha explains that only students in the outside circle can ask questions and only students in the inside can answer.

A student in the outer circle raises his hand to go first, and Martha projects the student's cell phone on the overhead. The phone has a picture of a political cartoon on it. The first frame depicts Nelson Mandela when Mandela was first arrested in 1962 and put in jail. The second frame shows Mandela when he is released in 1990, coming out of the jail, taller than in the first frame. The student asks the inner circle to explain the meaning behind the cartoon.

It takes students a few minutes to understand the process, and no one speaks right away. Finally, students in the inner circle begin weighing with responses, such as, "When he was arrested, it made him stronger." The discussion continues for a bit and then students are quiet again.

Martha asks if anyone on the outer circle has a question to ask of the inner circle. She then prompts a specific student to ask a question, and he responds by posing the following question: "Segregation continues to exist in different ways. What kinds of segregation still exist and why?"

Students in the inner circle have numerous responses to this question: "Social class."

"Segregation between rich and poor. The top 1 percent [is wealthy], but the majority of the world is super poor." "To give a real-world example of that, I met this guy. He lives in this huge gated community in a huge house. I have a little tiny house." "Different laws are based on racial groups (like in South Africa)."

"The guest speaker said yesterday that people in Africa were already divided up into tribes. That's still huge today—conflicting views, different languages, stereotypes, regardless of skin color."

A student then asks, "How would the world be if Mandela hadn't stood up and protested against the government?"

Students respond: "Other people have the same mind-set and would have stood up. Without the help of other people, Mandela wouldn't have made impact." "Social pressure." "Suppose that no one else took their place; there would not be as much social pressure, probably things wouldn't have gotten worse."

The student who first asked the question about segregation asks a follow-up question: "Do you think segregation can happen again in the future?"

(continues)

Students respond: "Definitely in other forms." "[People] segregate us to create controversy, to entertain. It kind of works; it separates us, we shouldn't be focusing on that. We're all Americans."

After a few more minutes of discussion, Martha says, "I'm resetting the clock. If you are on the outside, go inside. If inside, go on the outside."

The students switch circles quickly and quietly. Students on the outside continue to ask questions related to apartheid in South Africa and segregation more broadly, with students on the inside reflecting and responding. The students are respectful of each other's ideas, although a small group of students speak up consistently.

Martha does not engage with the students or direct them in their conversation, except to occasionally encourage quieter students to engage, saying, "Okay, you should ask that question you wondered about."

In the last five minutes of class, Martha asks for any final comments. When there are none, she says, "Take a couple of moments, three minutes or so, to finish up writing on the reflection page. Look back, reflect on the seminar process and how you did. . . . Take a moment and do some reflection."

Before they begin working on their reflections, she asks, "What did you think about Socratic seminar? Thumbs up if you liked it, thumbs down if you didn't." On the whole students were very positive and appeared to like the process, even though they found it challenging to come up with responses to the questions.

Students work on their reflections until the bell rings.

Martha also personalizes learning by organizing the seminar around the students' questions and experiences. She welcomes the students' engagement with a cultural artifact (a political cartoon) already familiar to high school students. She positions students in the room (mixing students who differ in skill and confidence), mindful of their differences without compromising access or treating differences as either assets or deficits. She scaffolds the conversation in ways that press all students to participate.

Following the lesson, Martha and her mentor teacher Denise reflect and debrief. Martha observes that the lesson went well overall, noting that some students asked clever questions and engaged in robust discussions about race, which they could relate to their own lives. Martha and Denise also note that the Socratic seminar allowed students who are typically not vocal to participate. Denise observes: "One of the kids that spoke today is a child that sometimes finds it difficult to order in a restaurant. One of the most vocal students you heard today, you would never guess that that person finds it difficult to talk to teachers, to express him or herself." When Ileana, the PDS coordinator at the school site, asks Martha how she had selected students for the inner and outer circles, Martha explains that she had originally planned to let students choose where to sit. But, taking students' differences into account, she realized that choice might not yield a productive mix of participants (more and less confident talkers) in both circles. So, she intervened: "I pulled a couple of strong voices to the outside. I knew some students would sit in the inside, so I pulled them out." She didn't want the confident talkers to dominate the exchange or treat the less confident ones as if they weren't as capable of participating.

Martha is also pleased that her scaffolding encouraged students to engage. "I learned from the first group. I was waiting to see if they would panic because it was too quiet to say something. The second round, I went around and said, 'That's a good question, you should ask that.' That helped because it gave them confidence to know that I thought the question was good enough."

Denise also provides critical feedback, what she called "cool feedback," aimed at improving Martha's future practice:

> I feel that they need more background earlier on, on both [the topic and Socratic method], and maybe scaffolding. If you had mini-Socratic time throughout the year, such as "Okay, our warm-up today is three minutes in and three minutes out," and then move on, keeping track of that, so they have that experience, that would be a helpful tool. I think for the subject matter, maybe another day where they had more of a sense of the facts, the history: What was going on in the United States? At the same time that civil rights issues were being worked out in our country, understanding the dynamic when South Africa plunged itself into an apartheid regime. What was the rest of world doing? Then that spills into World War I, World War II. So [it would be good if] they had more of a bank of knowledge from which to pose their questions. But I am pleased by the level of some of the kids who had that outside thinking or asked big questions.

The conversation makes clear that Martha herself is engaged in deeper learning about how to teach simultaneously for deeper learning and for equity.

That Martha focused on social justice content by teaching about South African apartheid may seem like an obvious choice, given that her course was world history. However, we also saw many teachers infuse topics related to equity and justice in subjects where it would be less expected, such as science and math. The biology lesson described in chapter 6, where the teacher used the topic of skin color to contextualize the more abstract concept of natural selection, is one of many examples.

The focus on social justice topics was not limited to high school teachers. In chapter 5, we described a Bank Street teacher, Ted, teaching mathematics to fourth graders. Revisiting Ted's and teacher candidate Jarod's classroom here, we see that, in addition to engaging their students in developmentally appropriate deeper learning, Ted and Jarod also actively engage them in discussions about inequality, justice, and civic participation.

Ted's class environment reveals many opportunities for students to develop fundamental knowledge and skills as they grapple with social justice issues. The posted time line of American history—which includes dates such as 1929, when the nineteenth amendment was ratified, giving women the right to vote, and 1861, when the Civil War began—serves as a constant reminder to students of America's historical inequities, and the importance of continuing to make history by fighting such inequities. Also displayed are students' own accounts of slavery, written from a slave's perspective (a challenging, complex topic, especially for fourth graders). Such lessons require that both Ted and Jarod understand the scope of students' intellectual, social, and emotional development as they are giving them access to a complex historical topic. They also embed inclusionary messages in everyday classroom routines that help create a culture of belonging. Among the many books on shelves and in labeled tubs around the room are titles featuring characters of many cultural backgrounds, and there is a tub of African American autobiographies. This, too, is an equity move, since so many students of color report low levels of belongingness in their schools and classes. We return to Ted's classroom in the box "Developing Deeper Thinking Through Literature."

Ted's and Jarod's classroom advances social justice and provides for equitable opportunities for students to learn challenging fourth-grade academic content. Ted's singing an African song brings another culture and language into the classroom, which helps to create a culturally open-minded community to nurture students' development of an inclusive orientation. The focus of the book during story time involves issues of free speech, power, and politics. Jarod's thoughtful questions have students consider these issues with their peers, develop their ability to think critically about weighty issues like fairness, and learn to effectively communicate their ideas to others.

Trinity elementary teachers also infused social justice activities into their teaching. As we described in chapter 6, a kindergarten teacher at Lamar Elementary, a professional development school site, engaged her class in launching a schoolwide recycling program. A fourth-grade teacher who was concerned about low voter-participation rates in the state created a

Developing Deeper Thinking Through Literature

As the fourth graders clean up their work and put their folders away after forty-five minutes of mathematics work, Ted quietly sings an African song while he sets up a snack. Students come in groups to receive their crackers and go back to their seats. Ted's singing shifts to English: "In everything we do and everything we say, you and I are making history today." This signals to students that what they do matters and is important. It is also a reminder of the historical references Ted has placed all around the students, with a historical time line hanging literally from a line across the ceiling onto which they clip cards recording events.

After the snack, the students gather around the rug to engage in story time with Jarod, who will read chapter 6 from *The Landry News,* the chapter book they are working their way through. The chapter is about a teacher, Carl Larson, who has risked disciplinary action for distributing a student-written newspaper that includes content to which some board members object. He has been given the choice to re-sign and retire or to undergo a disciplinary proceeding. The reading raises issues of free speech, loyalty to students, and courage to allow the community to address a social issue his students have written about. To keep students thinking, Jarod stops and asks as the plot unfolds, "There's a lot happening here. What *is* happening?" Several students contribute to explaining what happened to the teacher. Jarod then asks: "What's the choice that Mr. Larson has?" Once that is clarified, Ted adds a more complex question: "As you listen, think about this: How is Carl Larson changing?"

After Jarod reaches the end of the chapter, Ted says: "Take a minute and turn and talk: How is Mr. Larson changing?" The students immediately engage with one another about this question. Clearly this is a familiar routine for them, and they are deeply ensconced in conversation. Ted brings their attention back by counting backward—"4, 3, 2, 1"—and saying, "I'm hearing some lovely thoughts. What do you think? How is Mr. Larson changing?" Hands fly up and students give long, de-tailed answers to the question. They begin to have a conversation with each other rather than offering discrete "right answers" for the teacher. Ted encourages them to build on each other's thoughts by asking questions like: "Do you want to add on to that?" "Can someone clarify further?" With this book being read aloud together, there is a level playing field for all students to engage in a deep conversation that calls on them to think analytically and inferentially about the reading.

project-based unit in which students developed public service announce-ments, encouraged voter registration, and created a "Rock the Vote" campaign. A Trinity alum and a colleague together crafted a unit on race relations, which they shared with current Trinity MAT candidates.

Meanwhile, Trinity alums working as teachers at other schools continue to make an impact: one started an antibullying club at his high school, and another, working with a current MAT candidate, established a coffeehouse poetry event focused on race. One teacher wrote an article for the *Texas*

Education Review, reflecting on his teaching at a racially and linguistically diverse campus in the Dallas Independent School District. Another, who is a principal in San Antonio, started a healthy food initiative in her school and in the district. Another has been involved in developing new visions of urban schooling. Working with the university, a Trinity alum and her mentor put together a Women in Science program that brings a hundred female students each year to the Trinity campus to spend a day visiting the labs and working with female science faculty. Activities like these were commonplace both in and out of classrooms across all seven programs.

HOW DO PROGRAMS PREPARE TEACHERS TO TEACH AT THIS INTERSECTION?

This very diverse set of seven teacher preparation programs—public, private, large, small, traditional and alternative, across geographies—shares several characteristics that provide the foundation that supports teacher candidates as they teach at the intersection of deeper learning and equity. Each program is explicit and transparent about its commitment to both social justice and deeper learning values and principles. These commitments underlie the programs' designs, coursework, and fieldwork, including their selection of partnering districts and schools. Each program actively engages candidates in deeper learning about equity and social justice, including self-reflection around their own identity and social location, as well as tools to understand students' identity and social location. These support candidates in developing culturally responsive instructional strategies and nondeficit accommodations for English learners and students with special needs, and taking an activist stance against education inequality and injustice. We provide examples of each in the following sections.

Explicit Commitment to Equity and Deeper Learning

Although the language differs somewhat from program to program, each is loud and clear about its commitment to equity and social justice—shown, for example, in pronouncements of program leaders, mission statements, program descriptions, and ongoing conversations about program improvement.

The San Francisco Teacher Residency program is transparent that its goals are to prepare teachers who seek to promote equitable education in the city of San Francisco and to achieve greater justice in schools through "transformative teaching"—closely aligned with teaching for deeper learning. The language on the program's website couldn't be clearer:

The San Francisco Teacher Residency (SFTR) . . . offers aspiring educators the opportunity to help transform lives and communities in San Francisco through the teaching profession. Plain and simple: we are on a mission for social justice. SFTR aims to improve academic achievement and social-emotional development for historically underserved students in San Francisco's public schools by recruiting, preparing, and supporting highly effective and equity-centered teachers.

These words are far more than rhetoric. The first of four key pillars of "transformative teaching" that guide SFTR's coursework, clinical experiences, supervision and ongoing support, and definitions of success is *leading for equity and social justice*. SFTR seeks to prepare teachers who "position themselves as students of their students and school communities . . . to create sanctuaries of humanization," and who "understand experiences in classrooms, schools, and school community through a systems analysis, and take action as allies, advocates, and leaders to identify and interrupt oppressive forces." In the words of SFTR's executive director,

> As important as anything we do is to prepare people to be successful in culturally diverse communities and in schools that are serving historically marginalized students and high-needs populations. If we're not doing that, . . . or at least if we're not making significant progress in that direction and remaining committed to that front-and-center through all of the work that we're doing—then we don't have any business preparing teachers to teach in San Francisco.

Trinity's program is grounded in a set of "core beliefs" about principled practice that juxtapose deeper learning and equity. Among them, "ethical responsibility" includes fostering awareness of the equity issues that arise in teaching, along with an orientation that encourages candidates to address political and systemic sources of inequity. "Cultural responsiveness" positions candidates to consider the context of instruction, including students' prior knowledge and experiences as well as their community setting.

Similarly, the first of High Tech High's four program design principles is equity. The others—personalization, authentic work, and collaborative design—reflect the programs' vision of equity and deeper learning pedagogy as mutually reinforcing.

CU Denver's program, as we noted in chapters 2 and 3, is driven by four "essential questions" that frame teacher candidates' experiences as they move through the program, and that shape instructors' decisions as they design courses and field experiences. The questions focus teacher candidates' inquiry into their own assumptions and beliefs, and how those intersect with their intentions, actions, and reflections about equitable teaching. Following curriculum scholars Grant Wiggins and Jay McTighe, whose curriculum development guide, *Understanding by Design*, urges planners to start with essential questions that guide student inquiry, CU Denver's questions are "essential" because they are open ended and thought provoking, call for higher-order thinking, point toward transferable ideas, raise additional questions, require support and justification, and recur over time.[8] We repeat these questions here, since they make explicit the program's commitment to integrating deeper learning and social justice.

- *Essential Question 1*: What do I *know and believe* about myself, my students, their families, and their communities within the larger social context?
- *Essential Question 2*: How do I *act* on these beliefs to create inclusive and responsive learning opportunities and transform inequities?
- *Essential Question 3*: How do I *enact* principles of social justice and equity, inclusiveness, cultural and linguistic responsiveness, learning theory, and discipline-specific pedagogy within my pedagogical practices to plan, revise, and adjust curriculum, instruction, and assessment to ensure success and growth for all my students, always acting as a critical urban educator to advocate for my students?
- *Essential Question 4*: How do I *reflect* upon principles of social justice and equity, inclusiveness, cultural and linguistic responsiveness, learning theory, and discipline-specific pedagogy within my pedagogical practices in order to further plan, revise, and adjust curriculum, instruction, and assessment to ensure success and growth for all of my students, always acting as a critical urban educator to advocate for my students?

CU Denver also added a social justice principle to the five CREDE pedagogical standards that guide their planning for teaching and learning. This standard, called Critical Stance, presses teacher candidates to engage their own students in interrogating conventional wisdom and practices, to reflect upon ramifications, and to seek to actively transform inequities through a lens of democracy and civic engagement.

Bank Street's public commitment to social justice can be traced to its century-old progressive underpinnings, as articulated by Barbara Biber, the distinguished mid-twentieth-century Bank Street leader we cited in earlier chapters:

> When John Dewey turned to revolutionizing educational experience as a channel toward reconstructing society, he provided for many of us who were young in those early decades of the century a means of transforming general ideals for social change into the reality of revolutionizing a potent social instrument—the school system. . . . If education was ultimately to effect social change, we had to bring the reality of how the world functions into the classroom curriculum; if we expected children to become awakened to the advantages of a democratic society, we had to provide the experience of living democratically in the social setting of the schoolroom, of being part of a cooperative structure characterized by egalitarian interpersonal relations.[9]

Today that commitment is expressed in the program's intentionality about infusing social justice throughout the program's culture. Cecelia Traugh, Bank Street's dean, shared one example: "One of the things we, the faculty, did was a yearlong inquiry into the conference groups [weekly meetings of faculty with up to seven teacher candidates undergoing their fieldwork]. We focused that around three questions. One was how the conference group and the supervised fieldwork could become sites for social justice learning." Traugh noted that the yearlong process helped to reinforce the inquiry and equity stance of the faculty's work and make social justice a driving thread in her conversations with faculty.

Montclair and Alverno are equally transparent about their commitments. The clear articulation of values and commitments serves as the foundation of all the programs' work. However, as we describe in the following sections, it is the core features of the programs that bring them to life.

Intentional Candidate Recruitment

As part of their elaborate recruitment and selection practices (described in chapter 4), the programs are intentional about making their commitment to social justice and equity a critical criterion for selecting applicants. For example, the heart of High Tech High's candidate selection process—the Bonanza—engages prospective teachers in a variety of activities designed, in part, to assess how they view issues of equity in relation to education. As prospective participants' fitness as teachers is examined, their interest in equity-centered pedagogy and their views on equity in general are priorities of the process.

SFTR's vision of transformative teaching guides its approach to candidate recruitment and selection. Its website calls for applicants who want to "learn to teach for social justice" and articulates the four values they seek in prospective teachers, including "Passion for social justice; desire to improve equity and access for San Francisco's children; and commitment to teaching in a high-needs San Francisco school."[10] From their initial contact with the program, candidates are engaged with SFTR's mission and values.

The programs also have the explicit goal of recruiting racially, ethnically, and linguistically diverse candidates. Most articulated two reasons for this: (1) to take advantage of the educational benefits of diverse students grappling together to learn to teach in diverse schools and classrooms; and (2) to diversify the teaching force in their communities. They use a variety of strategies to accomplish this. For example, SFTR intentionally adds to the applicant pool for the bilingual authorization at USF by recruiting native speakers from the USF undergraduate dual-degree (BA plus credential) program. To assess the language proficiency of all candidates for the bilingual authorization, prospective candidates interview in Spanish. STEP, which also frames its work as "learning to teach for social justice," recruits from the undergraduate theme houses on Stanford's campus: Ujamaa, El Centro, and others. SFTR has been largely successful in meeting its recruiting goals for educator diversity. Two-thirds of the 2016–17 cohort identify as people of color, and more than half speak another language in addition to English. Several are SFUSD graduates themselves.[11]

Alverno is committed to diversifying the teaching force in Milwaukee. Nearly half of undergraduate candidates are candidates of color, many from low-income backgrounds, who are the first in their families to attend college, and they are committed to teaching in the Milwaukee neighborhoods they grew up in. One faculty member noted, "When we start the class, I ask about the students' backgrounds. There are always diverse backgrounds—students whose families struggled, students for whom English isn't their first language." Another explained that many of Alverno's students balance educational and economic demands:

> What's interesting about our students at both the undergrad and grad level is how many other things they are doing while doing school—in terms of how much our students work and how much they are caregiving for adults, their own children, their family's children. They are

so much more similar to community college students than to four-year college students because the vast majority are working over twenty hours a week, and a lot of them are working over thirty hours a week while they are carrying a full-time load.

Like the other programs, Alverno sees having a diverse group of teacher candidates as important for two key reasons beyond contributing to the Milwaukee teaching force. First, it enables the college to live the practices it wants its candidates to adopt—using instructional practices designed to meet the needs of all learners, especially those who are underserved in traditional systems, and scheduling courses flexibly for nontraditional students. Second, Alverno's diverse community also provides candidates the opportunity to communicate and collaborate with people from a variety of backgrounds—critical skills in our globalized society that candidates will need to help their own students develop.

CU Denver, also eager to diversify the teaching force in its city, has responded to the limited racial and cultural diversity among teacher candidates in its traditionally structured "pathways" to certification by developing the NxtGEN programs. The NxtGEN pathway is designed explicitly to attract and support first-generation undergraduates who need financial and other supports to navigate college and licensure. The unique arrangement blends full-time undergraduate coursework with a twenty-hour-per-week paraprofessional position in the Denver Public Schools, providing candidates—most of whom are students of color, low-income students, and immigrants—with the financial wherewithal to pursue a college degree, a dual strategy for supporting candidates and, at the same time, diversifying the teaching force in the Denver area.

Coursework Linking Education and Social Inequality

As we've described in previous chapters, the primary content that programs want teacher candidates to learn centers on children's learning and development; how children's family, community, and social contexts help shape them; and how teaching can support them. We also noted that the programs take seriously the idea that education in the United States also serves the purposes of a democracy. Therefore, schools must both prepare young people to participate fully in political, civic, and economic life, and support their equitable access to these societal spheres. To support teachers' understanding and ability to teach to both purposes, the programs include foundational coursework in which students examine the relationship between schooling and social inequality, particularly that related to the role of race, culture, and language.

Across the programs, courses focus both on historical and social patterns and on the day-to-day routines of today's schools and classrooms that help construct and maintain inequalities. In most cases, these courses are offered early in the programs, because the faculty view this knowledge as providing a lens through which candidates should see their work as teachers. It contributes to teacher candidates' understanding of the context outside their classroom, which shapes their students, their schools, and the communities they serve. It also helps teacher candidates ensure that their instruction is culturally appropriate for their students and that it contributes to our diverse democracy's struggle to be equitable and just.

The High Tech High internship program also immerses its students in this foundational knowledge, in contrast to many alternative programs that focus almost exclusively on techniques for constructing lessons and managing classrooms. High Tech High's Philosophy of Education course, for example, takes a broad look at social trends of the last 150 years.[12] The program's Equity and Diversity: Social and Cultural Foundations course builds on this historical foundation and discusses "contemporary issues in California schools, related to culture, cultural heritage, ethnicity, language, age, religion, socioeconomic status, gender identity/expression, sexual orientation and abilities and disabilities of individuals served."[13] It also emphasizes how to apply appropriate pedagogical practices that provide broad access to the curriculum and create an equitable community within the classroom. Candidates study different perspectives on teaching and learning, examine various theories of education, and identify the inequalities in academic outcomes in American education, as well as consider how teacher and student expectations affect student achievement.

The more traditionally structured programs also use such courses as a window into teaching in schools serving students from marginalized groups. SFTR candidates begin their coursework during the summer, during which they take one of two foundational courses on equity: STEP's Educating for Equity and Democracy, and USF's Teaching for Diversity and Social Justice, which frame all of their later work in the program. Similarly, the first two courses in CU Denver's program have a dramatic impact on many of its mostly white teacher candidates, with many crediting the courses with changing their understanding of society at large. In one, Social Foundations and Cultural Diversity in Urban Education, students examine how schools reflect and often perpetuate inequalities related to race, social class, gender, ethnicity, sexual identity, politics, and the social dynamics of power and privilege. In the second course, Co-Developing Culturally Responsive Classroom Communities, candidates explore how teaching that is grounded in our knowledge of how people learn can result in far more equitable schooling. The pedagogy of this second course gives candidates firsthand experience in a coconstructed culturally and linguistically responsive classroom, and it builds their capacity to create such communities in their own classrooms.

Both CU Denver courses also encourage candidates to develop an activist stance toward reducing inequity. One social studies candidate credited these courses with his own determination to give students a "critical lens" through which to view the world. He regularly asks his students to address the "master narrative" in social studies texts with probing questions like: "Why are we learning about this? Who do you think took these pictures? Why do you think this story is told in this way?" He wants his students to question the curriculum and to thoughtfully interrogate sources of news and information outside of the classroom.

Such foundational knowledge appears in courses in all seven programs.

Field Experiences in Settings Struggling with the Burdens of Inequality

As the vignettes throughout this book illustrate, all seven programs seek to provide field experiences where candidates can learn to engage low-income students and students of color in high-quality deeper learning experiences, and thereby also enact their equity and social justice commitments. At the same time, they want these experiences to be in places where the programs' values and preferred practices are shared by the educators and others who mentor their candidates. In most cases, this has led the programs to develop the deep partnership relationships with schools that we've described throughout the book, where program and school faculty and staff work and learn together to infuse their social justice values into practice.

Deeper Learning About Identity and Social Location

The programs also prioritize knowledge about the critical role of one's own race, culture, and language in shaping development and learning. This is a core element of the content they want teacher candidates to acquire as a foundation for culturally and linguistically responsive and competent practice. But, in addition to having candidates read about these connections, the programs engage the candidates in personalized and contextualized deeper learning activities that bring these concepts home in terms of their own and their students' identities and status. These activities cut across coursework, fieldwork, and the relationships candidates build in the programs, and they are yielding results; in LPI's survey of teacher candidates, 97 percent of respondents across programs reported feeling prepared to "teach students from a multicultural vantage point."

Trinity's racial autobiography assignment draws on Singleton and Linton's 2006 book *Courageous Conversations About Race: A Field Guide for Achieving Equity in Schools.*[14] It is intended to help candidates develop a fuller understanding of their personal racial identity development by writing a paper about how their feelings toward, understanding of, and engagement with race have evolved through the program and over their lives. The goal of this assignment is to help candidates better understand not just themselves, but also the students with whom they are working. As described in the guidelines for the assignment, "Trinity's MAT program is founded on the belief that you can't teach well unless you know your content and your students well. We cannot know our students well unless we know ourselves well."

Candidates share all or part of the racial autobiography at the end of the program, having their own "courageous conversation" and exploring their identities in the company of their cohort. They are assessed both on the quality of the writing and the quality of the autobiography itself, with emphasis on the experiences described, the analysis of the significance of those experiences, and how the candidate came to understand them during the work. Graduates and candidates alike commented on the value of the racial autobiography assignment. An elementary candidate told us, "We've had a lot of courageous conversations about privilege, what your appearance means to other people."

During the summer prior to their field placements, Trinity candidates also begin a long-term multistage project with three objectives—self-exploration, experiences with others, and culturally competent change—designed to give candidates the opportunity to examine deeply their own identities and how various institutions of influence shape their interactions with others and with the world around them. Though they first dig into these challenging topics before the start of the fall semester, candidates revisit these concepts throughout the year.

The project includes the development of a graphic organizer reflecting the beliefs and values that inform candidates' worldviews, and the creation of an aesthetic representation meant to synthesize and express the ideas presented in the graphic organizer. Students then create a digital presentation of the aesthetic representation, and write a reflection aiming to recognize how their own biases may impact their personal and professional interactions when they enter their clinical placement. In the reflection, candidates must identify cultural features they possess that will help them relate to their students and help students relate to them, identity or cultural features they possess that students might not be able to relate to, and cultural features of students they may not easily be able to relate to. These experiences are no doubt reflected in Trinity candidates' responses to the LPI survey question about teaching from a multicultural vantage point, as 100 percent of Trinity respondents reported being prepared in this area, including 80 percent who reported being well or very well prepared.

Candidates are encouraged to raise thoughts and questions that come to mind as they carry out these exercises. These conversations are called "courageous" for good reason. As one faculty member reflected on this process, she demonstrated both the depth of her work and her own efforts around pedagogies of racial identity development through ongoing reflection and inquiry into her teaching practice:

> I'm a white middle-class teacher too. Better understanding my own whiteness, and my white racial privilege, and how that positions me to be a white ally or to continue to perpetuate the racial stereotypes and superiority that we have is a big part of what we're trying to do. By better understanding your own racial identity development and building racial competence, and writing a racial biography, sharing them in class, reading other ones in class, and thinking about the ways that race has impacted every aspect of our lives, then they are in a better position to think about how race impacts every aspect of classroom and school life.

Along with the orientation of Trinity's work on developing cultural competence, this faculty member's comment shows how social justice values, in the form of the awareness of the impact of race on schooling systems, are connected to the candidates' explorations of their own and their students' identities.

The modeling of respectful dialogue is something that Trinity faculty, mentors, and candidates do for their students. As one faculty member noted:

> We have a Muslim student. Some of Jewish origins. We were able to teach factually, respectfully, [and] share an understanding that will help with world history, and understanding current events. A common theme is being a better global history student by understanding the

person you're talking to, so you don't say, "That's ridiculous." Being sensitive, appreciative, interested, nonjudgmental. . . . We have modeled all of that in recent weeks.

CU Denver makes such learning central through the four "essential questions," discussed earlier, that frame candidates' experiences in all aspects of the programs. The first question (What do I know and believe about myself, my students, their families, and their communities within the larger social context?) is meant to help candidates situate themselves within various social contexts along different dimensions of identity, including race, class, gender, ability, language, sexual orientation, immigration status, culture, national origin, religion, age, and appearance. Through coursework and reflection, they are expected to recognize contemporary and historical distributions of power and privilege within social contexts and connect their own identities to themes in the scholarly literature. In their field experiences, they are expected to identify the multiple ways the identity of a teacher may impact teaching and learning, and to apply those understandings to their teaching. Their responses to the LPI survey question on teaching from a multicultural vantage point are similar to those from Trinity's candidates, with 93 percent of CU Denver candidates reporting being prepared to support students in these ways, and 80 percent reporting being well or very well prepared.

Alverno candidates also reflect on their diverse identities as part of their coursework. They are asked to share how they were raised in their family, school, and community, and then consider how they will apply their experiences to teaching. Fostering candidates' awareness of their own background, as well as the diversity of their peers, helps candidates realize the wealth of experiences within a classroom and view diversity as an asset in a classroom. Indeed, 100 percent of Alverno graduates responding to the LPI survey reported they were prepared for multicultural teaching. One Alverno-prepared teacher described how the reflection emphasized during her preparation made her realize how she can learn from her students' diverse experiences:

> My best teaching moments were . . . because I had knowledge of where I was, who I was, my strengths, my weaknesses. . . . I had to position myself in the classroom where I, too, was a learner. . . . All it is is getting to know a kid and really trying to find what you have in common. And you positioning yourself on that same continuum with the student—"I'm learning from you; you're learning from me."

As one example of how this identity work gets embedded in coursework, Montclair faculty member Monica Taylor engages her Teaching for Learning I class in a "Theater of the Oppressed" activity to provide teacher candidates with an opportunity to reflect on experiences in the field through a critical lens, using their bodies as well as their minds to examine the impact of their own identities in classrooms.

Theater of the Oppressed for Critical Reflection

The seats are arranged in a circle to represent a democratic classroom, which is a technique that Monica Taylor, the instructor, prefers. Monica begins the class with a quick check-in with the eleven teacher candidates: How are the placements going? Are there any issues or concerns? Are you beginning to take on the role of teacher? What does that feel like?

After the quick check-in, Monica states that students may be at a point in their teacher education (it is mid-April) where emotionally they need to better understand their students.

Monica asks the teacher candidates to define "place" for their students and to think about how it's pivotal to be aware of one's "place" as both teacher and student in order to engage students and support their learning. She hones in on the importance of knowing where you are, where you stand as a teacher, and your social role in the class, which will help them understand how students' environment may impact their learning.

All the teacher candidates are engaged in the lesson and looking at Monica, who stands in the center of the circle. To help the teacher candidates embody teaching experiences in urban classrooms, Monica introduces the "Theater of the Oppressed," using it as a tool for critical reflection within their fieldwork sites.

Monica asks for a volunteer to demonstrate how the class activity works. A young man raises his hand and steps into the circle with her. The man starts moving and Monica starts to follow him. Every movement he makes, Monica imitates, which ultimately produces a mirror image of what he is doing. They are face to face. Monica stops following his every move and asks him, "How does it feel to see your movements reflected in someone else?" He responds, "It was different to see my reaction reflected in someone else, but ultimately pushed me to be more reflective of all my movements."

After this person's reflection, Monica invites another candidate into the circle to join the two of them. As the activity progresses, more teacher candidates join, imitating her movements. As the activity progresses, Monica identifies new people to originate the movements, eventually asking the teacher candidates how they feel leading and following. One teacher candidate says that she felt "a tremendous responsibility leading and knowing people were following my movements and how powerful it was to see the embodiment of my physical actions in other people and the consequence of those actions."

(continues)

> The teacher candidates noted it was difficult as more and more people were added. One candidate said she felt "frustrated with the leader not taking into consideration the movements of everyone." With this comment, Monica poses a question to the class, "How do you think this activity translates into the classroom?" A teacher candidate responds, "I can see how students may feel misunderstood or frustrated if teachers do not take into consideration the influence of their life circumstances on their classwork." The conversation continues with teacher candidates reflecting deeply about how their "movements" in the classroom will affect their students. After the reflection, students break up and return to their seats within the circle.

During a debrief of the class, Monica shared why she chose that activity for the teacher candidates. She noticed that some candidates in the MAT program were feeling overwhelmed by the different narratives of their students because the student narratives were so different from their own. The goal, ultimately, she shared, was for teacher candidates to be able to respond to students in more dynamic and equitable ways. This goal seems to have been reflected across the program, as 96 percent of Montclair candidates responding to the LPI survey noted their preparation in teaching from a multicultural vantage point, one aspect of the narratives of these candidates' students.

These identity-based deeper learning activities focus on the impact of the candidates' prospective students' identity and social location, as well as their own. For example, Bank Street views the first step toward achieving equity as considering the individual child or adult and his or her context in a nonjudgmental fashion. Only with this understanding can teachers begin to create fairness and equity in their classrooms. Dean Cecelia Traugh described the observation and recording assignment, mentioned earlier, from this perspective:

> You take an inquiry stance toward your work and toward kids. And it's an opportunity to look closely at a child and really try to see what's there, rather than what you think is there. And that is a mind-set that is so critically important if you are going to be working with anybody, but particularly anybody who is at all different from you. If you don't do that, then all you bring are your stereotypes. They may be generous stereotypes [or] they may be hideous stereotypes. But that is all that you'll have to bring, unless you can really stop, look closely, pay attention, and then be able to put some of that observation into language, into description.

SFTR, like several of the programs, engages residents in learning first-hand, from San Francisco students themselves, about the impact of students' identity and social status. The following vignette describes one such experience with young immigrants—including undocumented immigrants—in SFUSD.

Learning from Students About Their Realities

It's 1:00 p.m. on a Friday afternoon in late April. SFTR candidates have come from schools all over the city for their weekly three-hour practicum seminar, which is held at San Francisco's African-American Cultural Center in the heart of San Francisco's Western Addition neighborhood, a historically black neighborhood once a national center for jazz. Today, the thirty-two residents are joined by ten eleventh-grade students from June Jordan School for Equity (JJSE), a small high school in San Francisco Unified School District and an SFTR teaching academy. The topic is "Supporting Undocumented Students" and today, the traditional roles are flipped: rather than residents teaching the students, the students are teaching the residents.

The students are all enrolled in the Peer Resources class at JJSE, a class devoted to building youth leadership skills. All are students of color. Earlier in the spring, they delivered this same lesson to the staff at their school as part of the school's professional development for its faculty. The session was so well received by staff that an SFTR coach heard about it and invited the students to present at the SFTR practicum. Here to support the students are their Peer Resources teacher; the Peer Resources executive director; and the principal of June Jordan School for Equity.

Roni (all student names are pseudonyms), one of the JJSE students, begins the lesson by leading the residents and the other students through a five-minute meditation. The residents are encouraged to leave their worries from the first part of the school day behind, and to clear their minds to be able to be fully present for this seminar. The room has visibly relaxed and participants are fully focused when Roni brings everyone's attention back to the group after five minutes.

Wendy, one of the JJSE students, then begins the lesson by projecting the JJSE mission statement on the wall. Engaging the "class" of residents in the lesson, she asks a resident to read the mission statement and give a brief summary. Wendy then shares why she believes the school is not living up to its mission statement—which is preparing students for college as well as to be leaders prepared to work for a more equitable world—and frames the importance of the lesson today: "We don't even know all of our students who are undocumented. They don't even have social security numbers. How can we get them to college if we don't even know them? And by the time they're seniors and they're going through the application process, and we find out they're undocumented, it might be too late to fight for DACA and AB 540."

The JJSE students model active and engaging pedagogy for the residents. For example, Javier leads the residents through a "forced choice" activity in which the residents have to stand up and walk to the "Yes" or "No" side of the room depending

(continues)

on their answers to a series of questions. After each question, Javier calls on residents to explain their answers and engages them in a discussion. The first question is "Do you think undocumented students are willing to share their stories?" About half of the residents move to the "Yes" side of the room, the other half to the "No" side. As the discussion unfolds, one resident who answered yes says: "It's our job as teachers to know our students' stories as we build a relationship with them." Another student who answered no disagreed: "My students don't really talk about that kind of thing—it's the parents who have approached me." As the discussion unfolds, it becomes clear that residents' experiences talking to their students about their immigration status vary depending on whether they are in an elementary or high school setting.

Next, Joselin shares data from an action research survey the Peer Resources class conducted at their school. The students found that about 10 percent of the JJSE student population is undocumented, a number that came as a complete surprise to many JJSE staff and surprises the SFTR residents today. After sharing their data, Joselin engages the residents in a discussion, asking, "Have you encountered undocumented students at your school, and if so, how have you responded?" One resident shared his concerns that in his third-grade classroom, a couple of students had revealed their undocumented status as part of a classroom community circle. He worried whether his students' willingness to disclose that information so publicly at such a young age could cause them problems later on. Eliza, a JJSE student, mentioned the importance of strong communication with parents, as high school students may not reveal their immigration status because their parents have told them not to.

Maria, another JJSE student, asks the residents to explain what they will do differently as a result of this seminar today, providing an explicit link for residents between their coursework and their teaching practice. One resident in a middle school placement offers these thoughts:

> I always sort of thought they had a right for that [immigration status] to be private if they want it to be . . . But now, from the data and what you guys are saying, my thinking is shifting. Maybe there's some way I can show the class as a whole that I'm an ally so that students have all the information they need to come talk to me. Maybe I could put up posters that show my students that. Maybe I can tell the class as a whole, or some other way to make my door more open to my students to come talk to me.

Another elementary resident describes how this data makes her want to reach out and understand resources to which she can direct her undocumented students and their families. It also reinforced for her the importance of building community. She had had two students come to talk to her about their immigration status, and she wants to keep this communication open. Other residents note that they now want to ask their administrators about the school's protocol for supporting undocumented students. A resident in a first-grade class explains, "I'm taking away the importance of safety in our community. I want the parents of my students to feel safe in the community of our classroom."

Another resident says, "I think it's important that we know we're coming from a place of privilege. I don't have to worry about getting pulled over. If I want to get on a plane and fly to Mexico, I can do that." At that, Wendy, the student who had opened the lesson and earlier shared her personal story as the child of two undocumented parents and an undocumented older brother, responds with tears flowing down her face: "I'm the youngest. My parents tell me that once I go to college, they're going to leave the US because they're undocumented, and go back to their country . . . that is really hard for me. Once I go to college, I'm not going to have my parents there. Talking about privilege, take that into consideration, because not everyone can have their family and be with them."

Many eyes in the room are wet, and the room erupts in the sound of fingers snapping in support for Wendy.

The students end their presentation with some facts about DACA (Deferred Action for Childhood Arrivals), President Obama's executive order immigration reform that provided a work permit and protection from deportation to eligible youth. Yasmine, another JJSE student, anchors this content in her personal story of how she missed the DACA qualification deadline because she arrived in the US three months too late, and what this means for her college opportunities.

The nearly two-hour presentation ends with the JJSE students leading a closing circle and providing an opportunity for reflection. One resident shares how "this PD was way more engaging and powerful than other PDs I go to." Another resident encourages the high school students to connect with undocumented college students at USF who are organizing around similar issues. Lourdes, a JJSE student, gives the residents positive feedback, explaining that she appreciates that they were not defensive, as some of the faculty at their school had been during a similar training.

In this example, the high school students, the residents, and the course instructors are all engaged in deeper learning for equity and social justice. By the end of this practicum session, the residents walk away with a more complete understanding of the number of undocumented students served in SFUSD schools, the needs of these students, and what they can do as educators to support this marginalized group. In our survey of SFTR residents, 100 percent of them reported being prepared to "teach students from a multicultural vantage point," a result reflective of sessions such as this. Perhaps more important is the fact that the residents learn from high school students directly, providing an honest and emotional connection to the content that undoubtedly will help it to stick—and making a powerful point about how important it is to learn from students themselves about their lives.

In addition, the lesson models for the residents the leadership roles that young people can take on when appropriately supported, and the knowledge and skills that students can build when engaged in this type of project-based learning. This lesson was the product of a yearlong action research study and campaign at JJSE by students in the Peer Resources elective, a class focused on leadership development and social change that allows students to choose the issues on which they will act. For the JJSE students, the act of teaching this seminar to the residents was a form of performance-based assessment in and of itself. This lesson exemplifies the ways in which SFTR is providing deeper learning to residents, both in the coursework and in the modeling they see at their clinical placements.

Similarly, during a session of High Tech High's Healthy Environments course (captured in the vignette "Reflecting on the Implications of Status and Privilege"), we saw the faculty instructor push the interns' thinking on identity development. The course explores the attitudes, biases, and assumptions that teachers bring with them to class, as well as how student identities are shaped and influenced by their experiences both in and out of school.

Following the class, the instructor provides more context about the lesson and equity-centered pedagogy. The dialogue between the two bees was intended to highlight the importance of perspective and identity; while one bee perceives her life as laudable and praiseworthy, the other one detests the sunrise because it represents another day of dreaded work. The instructor notes that "the way we interact with kids and families oftentimes comes from a very privileged, white, cultural perspective . . . we really need to think about it when we communicate." He explains that it is important for interns to understand identity and perception, particularly when working with young, diverse learners who come from backgrounds different from those of the interns themselves.

The pervasiveness of the equity focus at HTH appears to pay off: fully 100 percent of High Tech High intern teachers responding to LPI's survey reported being prepared to teach from a multicultural perspective, and 96 percent reported being well or very well prepared.

Equitable Teaching Across Differences

The programs also include coursework that encourages teacher candidates to treat differences among students as traits and assets requiring recognition and responsiveness, not as deficiencies. A theme that runs through all the programs is that pedagogies that engage students in deeper learning can provide rich learning opportunities for diverse classrooms of students. This theme was manifest in the cross-program results of the LPI survey, where 98 percent of respondents across all seven programs reported being prepared to "teach students from diverse ethic, linguistic, and cultural backgrounds," with 87 percent saying they were well or very well prepared.

Reflecting on the Implications of Status and Privilege

As class begins, two interns read aloud a poem entitled "Honeybees," describing a typical day from the perspective of two bees:

BEING A BEE	BEING A BEE
Is a pain	Is a joy
I'm a worker	I'm a queen
I'LL GLADLY EXPLAIN	I'LL GLADLY EXPLAIN
	Upon rising, I'm fed by my royal attendants
I'm up at dawn, guarding the hive's narrow entrance	
	I'm bathed
then I take out the hive's morning trash	
	then I'm groomed
then I put in an hour making wax, without two minutes' time to sit and relax.	
	The rest of my day is quite simply set forth:
Then I might collect nectar from the field three miles north or perhaps I'm on larva detail	
	I lay eggs, by the hundred
Feeding the grubs in their cells, wishing that I were still helpless and pale	
	I'm loved, and I'm lauded, I'm outranked by none
Then I pack combs with pollen— not my idea of fun	
	When I've done enough laying
Then, weary, I strive	
	I retire
To patch up any cracks in the hive,	
	For the rest of the day.
Then I build some new cells, slaving away at enlarging this Hell, dreading the sign of another sunrise, wondering why we don't all unionize.	
TRULY, A BEE'S IS THE WORST OF ALL LIVES.	TRULY, A BEE'S IS THE BEST OF ALL LIVES.[15]

(continues)

At the end of the reading, the instructor asks the class what they think the poem is about and one student responds with a loud and resounding, "It's about class!"

This leads to a discussion about income inequality and how it manifests in our environments, ranging from food, to transportation, to applying for college. One intern, who is visibly passionate about the topic, states that some of her students feel as though they are being "sold a false promise" at High Tech. She goes on to explain that students are promised an education at HTH that will prepare them for college. However, their family income limits their choices and, in some instances, can preclude their attending college at all.

Another intern chimes in about food choices or lack of healthy options that students can regularly bring to school, while another adds that she is aware of students who take multiple buses and travel long distances to arrive at school each day, albeit late.

The instructor then asks why they think he asked them to read the poem. A few interns respond in chorus, "To understand what it is like to be poor." The instructor adds, "We have both bees in our classroom."

In small groups of four, the interns reflect and discuss how society, peers, family, and school impact students, including their attitudes, beliefs, and self-perceptions. The instructor challenges the interns to draw upon lessons from their practice to think about how perspective and identity impact students and the interns and regularly reminds the students to "put it to practice" in their schools and classrooms.

ACCOMMODATING DIFFERENCES IN DIVERSE CLASSROOMS. Montclair candidates are taught that differentiating instruction is a teaching strategy for equity. As one faculty member put it: "One of the tenets of social justice teaching is rigorous learning. So, caring about your students . . . means you are going to demand a lot of them and that you have really high expectations. And that doesn't mean you are not going to differentiate or take into consideration their needs."

In envisioning the practical applications of a similar set of commitments, an SFTR resident wrote in her Vision of Effective Teaching assignment the words that opened this chapter, expressing her view of equitable teaching as providing instruction that is effective in engaging diverse students in learning: "As a teacher for social justice, I envision a class where I am able to teach to all students' learning styles and levels, cultures and backgrounds. As discussed in [instructor's] class, there is not an achievement gap, but instead an educational debt. We as educators and aspiring teachers owe students an equitable classroom and education."

Another described the range of approaches she would use to engage all students, including interactive, hands-on approaches, reader's workshop, and circle/meditation time.

One High Tech High administrator described its program as an "equity project" that believes "all students are best served if they are in schools together, in classes together, and in groups together, working with kids who don't look like them." In the High Tech High schools that the intern teachers are being prepared for, students are selected through a lottery process, by zip code, with the intention that they will be representative of the diversity of the local community. Once enrolled, students are not tracked by academic level. Janie Griswold, the High Tech High director of new teacher development, when asked about "hallmarks" of the program, started with equity:

> What we're striving for is a program where our teacher candidates are prepared to step into diverse classrooms and use equitable practices to meet the needs of all the learners in their classrooms: socioeconomically, racially, learning-profile-wise, kids with IEPs, kids with not. . . . A huge focus of ours is trying to teach structures and mind-sets that honor student voice—honor all student voice—and honor meeting all kids where they're at.

HTH interns are expected, as program materials note, to "acquire and become familiar with strategies and best practices to develop differentiated lessons and instructional sequences that are appropriate for individuals with diverse strengths and in a variety of educational environments." Intern teachers complete specific assignments that require them to design lessons or activities that will promote equity in diverse classrooms. These skills, the program argues, prepare teachers to make rich and engaging curriculum available to all students. High Tech High's LPI survey results on the question of teaching a diverse group of students reflected this, with 100 percent of respondents reporting being prepared to do so, and 95 percent reporting being well or very well prepared.

These seven programs address the diversity of students in complex ways, attending not only to diversity in culture and community, but also to linguistic diversity and the broad array of learning needs that students bring to classrooms. Ninety-two percent of candidates in these programs reported high levels of preparation to "teach in ways that support English learners," and 96 percent reported being prepared to "identify and address special learning needs with appropriate teaching strategies."

High Tech High's six-week online Foundations of English Language Development course introduces candidates at the very beginning of their program to strategies for addressing a range of English language fluency and proficiency levels in a single classroom. A first-year apprentice teacher gave us a positive appraisal of this course:

> The first thing that was helpful before the year even started was the online course that had to do with EL learners. It was a lot of scenario building and [what to do] if you have a student from this background that doesn't speak a lot of English. What are you going to do to plan your lesson to involve that child? Right off the bat that made me think about the kids who may not be able to read perfectly or write super well. I have to build in access points for these students. That has been a common theme throughout this entire year.

Overall, 100 percent of High Tech High intern teachers reported being prepared to "teach in ways that support English learners," with 90 percent answering that they had been well or very well prepared.

The USF Education of Bilingual Children course also gives SFTR residents the opportunity to think about teaching for social justice from a linguistic perspective, as the professor who teaches the course, Sarah Capitelli—a Stanford School of Education graduate who also worked in STEP—explained to us:

> For me personally, what I feel is most impactful is that these programs have this very strong social justice orientation. Often that conversation starts with race. And I think it can be challenging for students to see how issues of social justice play out, not only around issues of race, but around issues of language. They have all taken the teaching for social justice class before taking my class. And I often feel that students who come to my class feel like, "Okay, we did the social justice work, let's get to the teaching now. We've talked about it, now let's get to the teaching." I feel like the journal is often a place where I get to push back on those notions. One way I do that is simply in the way that candidates talk about students in the journal—the words they use to describe the students that they might not necessarily do out loud or I might not be able to address in a class, but I can address in their writing.

Sarah also gives residents a chance to experience school as language learners do by teaching a lesson in Spanish. She describes the process:

> When I teach a lesson in Spanish, that is particularly meaningful—even when I have Spanish speakers in the room. The students who don't have any experience at all talk about the fear they have about being called on;

that they're going to have to participate, the anxiety they have around that. They are also struck by the things that I do that actually enable them to understand me. I read a very simple text and then we do some comprehension, we do some prediction; then I level them by groups and we do some small-group work. We do a bunch of different meaningful things.

In this way, the professor models for the residents the power of experiential learning, as well as how to scaffold instruction so that English learners have access to the core content of the curriculum alongside diverse peers. Through this modeling and other program experience, 94 percent of SFTR respondents to the LPI survey reported being prepared to "teach in ways that support English learners."

The same percentage of SFTR respondents also reported being prepared to "identify and address special learning needs with appropriate teaching strategies," a result likely due in part to the Education of Exceptional Children course, taken as part of the USF program the summer before teaching begins. Residents learn about differing student learning needs and ways of meeting those needs in the classroom. Describing this class, one resident told us, "That class was really helpful in exploring the different learning styles of different students and it really helped us to think about adaptations, or possible accommodations." She also shared how an assignment in this course was applied to teaching:

> In the Ed of Exceptional Children course, the professor had been teaching special education for a very long time. So, what we ended up doing was that . . . we were each assigned a different disorder or different learning disability, and then we basically had to just uncover all the things about this disability—what does that mean in the classroom, what does it mean if you're in an integrated class versus if the student's not in an integrated class, all the different things that you can do for their teaching. And we were able to kind of learn from each other what it would look like in the classroom.

Here too, this key assignment impacted residents because it was experiential and collaborative, allowing residents to develop a deep understanding of how one commonly identified type of learning difference (often called a learning disability) could be accommodated in a diverse classroom.

In similar fashion, Bank Street's course, The Study of Normal and Exceptional Children Through Observation and Recording, also focuses on teaching students equitably in the context of diverse classrooms. As we described in chapter 3, candidates learn to observe and record children's behavior and functioning in school settings to deepen their understanding of children's development. They focus on children with both typical and nontypical development, understanding they represent the normal diversity of children in all classrooms.

Bank Street also offers courses that provide foundational knowledge of how children's differences shape how (not whether) they learn and what strategies ensure that children with atypical development have equitable access to the core curriculum. For example, its Language Acquisition and Learning in a Linguistically Diverse Society course aims to deepen candidates' understanding of language development in monolingual and multilingual children and the political, educational, social, and emotional aspects surrounding the stratification of languages and dialects. Notably, the course focuses on how to both fully integrate the many students in English monolingual classrooms who are emergent bilinguals learning English as a second language and also support the language development of those who are learning English as their native language.

In LPI's survey, 100 percent of Bank Street teacher candidates reported that they were prepared to "teach students from diverse ethnic, racial, linguistic, and cultural backgrounds," to "teach from a multicultural perspective," and to "identify and address special learning needs with appropriate teaching strategies." In an earlier study of New York teachers, Bank Street teachers who graduated between 2000 and 2012 were twice as likely as other New York teachers in their first three years to report being well prepared to teach students from diverse ethnic, linguistic, and cultural backgrounds, and while most Bank Street teachers reported being well prepared to teach English learners, fewer than 1 in 4 New York novices from other programs felt well prepared to do so.[16]

Alverno prepares candidates to accommodate students with special learning needs and Wisconsin's small, but growing, proportion of English learners with universal design for learning. The goal is to have candidates understand the diverse strengths and needs of these learners as well as acquire strategies for meeting their needs and building on their strengths.

Multiple Alverno students and faculty conveyed the emphasis placed on learning to differentiate their lessons for each learner in the classroom, including English learners, gifted and talented learners, and struggling students. In a course focused specifically on instructional strategies for English learners, the instructor teaches in Spanish at times to help candidates experience what it is like to be a second language learner. As she does, she also demonstrates pedagogical approaches that can help them and their future students to understand the lesson across language differences.

Another Alverno faculty member shared that, during observations of teacher candidates, she asks the candidate's students how they would describe this teacher to someone new to their classroom or to share something special about the teacher. One young child diagnosed with behavioral problems responded, "My teacher makes me feel calm." When the professor inquired how the teacher candidate did that, the child said, "She treats me like I'm smart." The child's response reflects Alverno's commitment to helping teacher candidates identify each student's unique needs through learning and developmental theories, and then to apply their knowledge about pedagogical instruction to determine the best method for ensuring that all students can grow and thrive.

A current Alverno candidate described how she felt well prepared to teach diverse learners:

> Everybody comes to the table with something different. I think Alverno did a great job of hitting that in probably every class I took there . . .studying all those theories and looking at what sorts of things influence students, from the outside, what they can control . . .and what's out of their control. And things that influence them inside of school, things they can control and not control, and knowing that everybody is bringing something different to the table.

Of Alverno candidates responding to LPI's survey, 100 percent reported being either well or very well prepared to "teach in ways that support English learners," while 90 percent reported being prepared to "identify and address special learning needs with appropriate teaching strategies."

Ninety-eight percent of Montclair candidates also reported being prepared to "identify and address special learning needs with appropriate teaching strategies." As one example of the range of strategies they learn to maintain a focus on deeper learning while also promoting equitable outcomes, a Montclair teacher candidate shared how he and his cooperating teacher utilized Socratic seminars in an inclusive classroom with a substantial number of students identified for special education. He referenced the scaffolding needed to prepare students for the activity. Part of that scaffolding occurred as revision—students recorded their first attempt at a seminar, viewed the recording, and were challenged, "Okay guys, how would you improve on this?" Whereas some teachers would conclude that an imperfect first attempt meant the students couldn't handle this rigorous approach to instruction, these teachers understood how to support improvement so that students could experience and ultimately master these deeper learning skills. As Dewey put it, they bring the child to the curriculum while bringing the curriculum to the child.

CULTURALLY RELEVANT CLASSROOM MANAGEMENT. In addition to developing candidates' ability to adapt classroom pedagogy to students with diverse language and learning assets and needs, the programs also teach culturally responsive practices, which, as one Bank Street teacher candidate explained, is "a pedagogical practice which equips teachers and children with empathy, deep understanding, and an exceptionally profound engagement with those of differing backgrounds."[17] Bank Street's Center on Culture, Race & Equity provides workshops for candidates, as well as the broader community, to learn how to address unconscious cultural biases and practices to become more inclusive teachers. Through this work, the center "addresses race and equity on three levels—personal, professional, and institutional."[18]

Bank Street instructor Luisa Costa describes the role of teachers as advocates for their students. One way in which they advocate is by "recognizing the linguistic and cultural resources" that students bring to the classroom. "My goal is to allow our candidates to serve all students. There is a notion of democratic access, having access to learning and to ideas." This can mean "acknowledging the languages that are present in the classroom even though [the teacher candidate] might not speak that language" by having "some kind of print, either magazines or newspapers, or just some visual representation of the child's language so that they feel they are a part of that community."

Costa also notes that it is a teacher's responsibility to "bring parents into the classroom" by having them tell stories (which works for all parents, including illiterate parents), as well as having parents read to their children. Costa's instruction models for teacher candidates the role that teachers have in honoring and respecting the diverse strengths and experiences that each of their students brings to the classroom. There is no "one" correct language, mentality, or way to learn. Instead, by using the classroom to reflect the rich heritage that students come from, teachers learn to use their classrooms as models of just societies that celebrate diversity and that provide opportunities for all individuals to contribute and learn. As we have seen in several programs, when teacher candidates are learning pedagogical strategies for English learners, an immersive experience helps candidates uncover these pedagogical strategies by experiencing what it is like to be in a classroom taught in a nonnative language.

A culturally responsive frame of reference has also caused many of the programs to integrate restorative practices in their approaches to classroom management and discipline. Although a restorative approach to classroom management is an appropriate deeper learning strategy in any setting, in schools with concentrations of low-income students of color, it also has explicit equity and social justice goals that counter the harsh and often discriminatory use of traditional punitive school discipline practices, which have contributed to the "school to prison" pipeline for many young people.[19]

In San Francisco, restorative practices have become a districtwide initiative, used both in schools and in the SFUSD ExCEL (Expanded Collaboratives for Excellence in Learning) After School Program.[20] SFTR residents learn these practices in their practicum course. In keeping with the practicum habit of bringing in community and district experts, the lesson on restorative practices begins with a session with an SFUSD district coordinator for the ExCEL After School Program and a restorative practice coach who provides residents with the restorative practices framework, including this statement on the fundamentals, from Cheryl Graves, of the Community Justice for Youth Institute:

> What's fundamental about restorative justice [practices] is a shift away from thinking about laws being broken, who broke the law, and how we punish the people who broke the laws. There's a shift to: there was harm caused, or there's disagreement or dispute, there's conflict, and how do we repair the harm, address the conflict, meet the needs, so that relationships and community can be repaired and restored. It's a different orientation. It is a shift.

Residents then engage with the restorative practices framework, thinking about a particular classroom incident and considering the following questions, which are consistent with the framework: What happened, and what were you thinking at the time of the incident? What have you thought about since? Who has been affected by what happened, and how? What about this has been the hardest for you? What do you think needs to be done to make things as right as possible?

Some of the lessons described in this chapter also illustrate the exchange of ideas that occurs among SFTR's partners, and the ways that the partnership strengthens teacher preparation across programs. For example, the positive phone call home activity originally came from a STEP course and has been integrated into the SFTR practicum. On the other hand, STEP has borrowed from some of the specificity of SFTR's lessons on trauma-informed practices and built these lessons into its practicum for the entire STEP cohort.

One student described her integration of restorative discipline in both her classroom and, ideally, into her students' lives:

> Discipline should not come from our needs of control but rather the needs of the students, and that is where work with restorative practices comes in. Restorative practices are tools to help students express and convey their feelings assertively and effectively. My hope is that the students will be able to use these tools to successfully solve problems for themselves. As I enter my own classroom, I believe teaching and enforcing restorative practices is imperative, because these practices are tools that students can take with them in every aspect of life. They can use them with siblings, friends, and even parents, and as they get older the skills still are relevant. Restorative practices help the students to think about their wants and needs along with the wants and needs of others.

What stands out about these seven programs is their conviction that deeper learning and equity are not only compatible, but mutually reinforcing. This stance underlies the programs' designs, coursework, and fieldwork, including their selection of partnering districts and schools. Each program is guided by a clear vision of teaching and learning that integrates the two. Each includes foundational knowledge about the intersection of race, culture, and other social identifiers with the nation's history and current structures of marginalization and educational inequality. Each engages candidates in deeper learning about equity and social justice through self-reflection around their own identity and social location, understanding students' identity and social location, developing culturally responsive instructional strategies and nondeficit accommodations for English learners and students with special needs, and taking an activist stance against education inequality and injustice.

Teacher candidates noted they appreciate that these equity issues are front and center. As one SFTR resident said: "SFTR provided me an opportunity to complete my credentialing program with like-minded peers who were able to engage in critical conversation around social justice and promoting our students' needs."

CHAPTER 10

CREATING
SUPPORTIVE STRUCTURES

[The College of Education and Human Services] is the heart of this university.

—President, Montclair State University

It's a strong partnership . . .. We co-plan our staff development, we work on budget . . .. It has raised the bar of what we hope to accomplish. It's changed the conversation from test scores to practice and growth in teaching and learning. I hope that I would do the same things without Trinity support, but I don't know.

—Principal, Trinity Professional Development School

As we've shown, the teacher preparation programs we studied seek to instill deeper-learning-aligned values, knowledge, and practices in their teacher candidates. All are determined that their graduates will create classroom learning experiences that reflect the increasing scientific knowledge on how people learn, and that they will make those deeper learning experiences available to *all* students. They are also intensely committed to preparing teachers who will provide deeper learning opportunities to underserved students who, historically, have had little access to such learning in their schools. They all seek to practice what they preach, and they are impressively successful in doing so.

For all of their agreement about purpose and practices, these programs are quite different from one another organizationally. They vary greatly in size, ranging from about thirty candidates per MAT cohort at Trinity University to well over a thousand program completers per year at Montclair State University. They follow a diverse set of program models, from traditional undergraduate and graduate preparation programs, to teacher residencies, to alternative routes featuring apprenticeships and internships; this variation occurs between institutions and, in some cases, within them. The programs are scattered across the nation, in urban and rural settings, and are sited in both private and public colleges and universities. One of them started as an organization to study children's learning and development; another is unaffiliated with a traditional institution of higher education.

These organizational differences offer both encouragement and challenges to teacher educators looking to implement deeper-learning-aligned preparation. On the one hand, it is clear that teacher preparation for deeper learning can be implemented in many types of programs. Teacher educators seeking to emulate the practices of programs described here are likely to find some connection to their own settings and work. On the other hand, the very differences that create points of access for many teacher educators may, in fact, mask what matters most. It may be difficult to identify what we called in chapter 1 the "deep structure" of these programs—commonalities across their different features and operations that define and underpin the programs' core. These elements are what provide the most fundamental lessons for implementing teacher preparation programs for deeper learning.

To bring out the significant commonalities among these programs that matter for their success, we must look beyond superficial features such as size, model, and type of institution. Instead, it is more revealing to focus on how these programs define their missions and values around deeper learning and equity, how their program structures instantiate and support those missions and values, and how leaders sustain those structures by prioritizing the mission and directing resources to structures in ways that support these priorities. With this focus, we discuss here four key components of organizational structure and institutional support that play a pivotal role in providing candidates with learning experiences that prepare them to teach for deeper learning and equity:

1. *Well-established values*: Each program designs and articulates a set of core program values that are squarely and unambiguously focused on deeper learning and equity. These values are instantiated through a closely aligned program culture, structures, and practices.

2. *Leadership that prioritizes teacher preparation*: Institutional leaders provide direction and guidance, as well as ongoing support that make teacher preparation a high priority that is well tended in their institutions.

3. *Dedicated resources*: The values and leadership priorities that guide programs are made real and concrete by investments of both time and money. Those investments support the intensive relationships among candidates, faculty, and mentors that sustain collaboration and mutual support, which models and teaches deeper learning practices. These investments in structures and people enable processes of planning, inquiry, reflection, and iteration toward achieving program goals.

4. *Partnerships with K–12 systems and schools*: Relationship building, which is key to aligning and integrating coursework and fieldwork, is not limited to the interpersonal interactions, but is augmented and strengthened by the creation and maintenance of strong partnerships between teacher preparation programs and K–12 schools and districts, opening up opportunities and spaces for shared and mutually beneficial work. This proves key to ensuring that candidates can see and engage in pedagogies focused on deeper learning and equity—and participate in educative communities of practice—without which the accomplishments of the programs would be impossible.

These four components provide the institutional context for the practices that have been described throughout this book. The values, commitments, structures, and relationships that have been put into place at each of these programs make their work possible and are an important part of the overall picture of teacher preparation for deeper learning. Aligning a program with deeper learning and equity is a matter of the deliberate choices made by faculty and administrators, and maintaining this alignment requires ongoing attention and commitment. Programs wishing to follow this path must consider not only what sort of structures such a program requires, but also the behind-the-scenes work that brings these structures to life.

WELL-ESTABLISHED AND INSTANTIATED VALUES

Each of these programs starts with a set of clearly articulated and publicly shared values and expectations for candidates about the nature of learning, the implications for teachers and their practice, and the connections between education, equity, and social justice. These are not just words on a page. They shape program practices, culture, structures, and processes.

First, they are evident in the program's practices—guiding the substance of coursework, modeled by program faculty in their teaching, and expressed through candidate assessments, field supervision, the structures of field placements, and even relationships with partner schools. Second, these values—which express what candidates are expected to learn and be able to do as teachers—bring direction and coherence to candidates' experiences from admission to completion. Third, the values provide guidance for the administration of programs—everything from the alignment of programmatic structures to the selection of instructors and mentor teachers. Overall, program values, missions, and frameworks are living documents, and programs make intentional efforts to instantiate them in their structures, practices, and commitments.

To frame their values and standards for candidates, the programs start with clear, shared conceptions of teaching, learning, and practice that are consistent with promoting deeper learning and equity. Each program articulates these values in a variety of ways, including in vision statements, program principles, and conceptual frameworks. As described in chapter 2, these articulations are not cookie-cutter statements, but rather, they are tailored to the program's history and context:

- Alverno's college-wide set of desired "abilities," plus the four additional abilities added by the School of Education
- Bank Street's progressive, child-centered values, going back over a hundred years, and its "Principles Underlying the Teaching of Teachers."
- CU Denver's essential questions that frame teacher candidate experiences, the program's conceptual framework, and the CREDE standards of pedagogy
- High Tech High's four design principles
- Montclair State's "Portrait of a Teacher" and conceptual framework
- San Francisco Teacher Residency's vision of "transformative teaching"
- Trinity University's "core beliefs" about principled practice and its development

At Alverno, the college-wide eight core abilities along with the four abilities from the School of Education guide a variety of performance assessments measuring candidates' progress toward mastery of each ability. Coursework and fieldwork are explicitly designed to enable candidates to develop these abilities, which are focused on their becoming diagnostic, thoughtful, and ethical teachers who are well prepared to design curriculum, coordinate learning experiences, and communicate effectively. Faculty evaluate candidates' performance through in-person observations, videos of candidates' teaching, and reviews of classroom artifacts such as candidates' lesson plans and student work. These performance assessments include clear criteria for candidates' achievement of the Alverno abilities, giving them a key role in shaping program practice and learning outcomes.

Bank Street's values are purposefully interwoven throughout the practices and structures of the program. "We are an institution that is trying to model what we think is really good practice for our students," explains one Bank Street administrator. These values are also expressed in a set of principles underlying the teaching of teachers that emphasize a contextualized, socially just, and equitable approach to education, grounded in teachers' deep knowledge of child development and learning, as well as their commitment to ongoing inquiry and development for themselves. These principles are foundational to Bank Street's coursework, fieldwork, and the practices and routines of its faculty, teacher candidates, and graduates.

The living laboratory within Bank Street's Childhood General Education program demonstrates how Bank Street puts its values into action. The laboratory consists of coursework, advisement, supervised fieldwork both on-site in Bank Street's preK–8 School for Children and in partner schools across the city, and key assignments and assessments; it is shaped by a focus on child and adult development in family and community contexts, experiential learning, and equity and social justice. By emphasizing inquiry and respectful, collaborative relationships among faculty and teacher candidates, candidates are enabled to adopt student-centered inquiry practices.

Moreover, Bank Street's learning process helps teacher candidates make meaning of and grow from their coursework and student teaching. This process involves building on candidates' experiences; using inquiry to observe and record their experiences; critically analyzing those experiences using rich tools developed in a variety of disciplines; and finally reflecting on their experiences to develop insights that candidates can apply in future, different contexts. Bank Street courses model the types of learning environments that allow teacher candidates to deeply engage with content. Teacher candidates apply the same experiential, developmentally appropriate, and equity-oriented pedagogies in their own classrooms that they experience as students themselves in Bank Street's living laboratory.

In Bank Street's deeper learning laboratory, teacher candidates are the subjects within the immersive experience as learners. But they are also researchers who investigate and analyze the elements and conditions that support the acquisition of deeper learning competencies. Even the way that Bank Street candidates encounter course programming reflects program values, as one striking attribute of Bank Street's program is its flexibility and individualization. Bank Street allows for variation in the duration and sequence of the program, giving candidates the opportunity to develop in ways that fit their learning styles and personal needs. This feature of the program models how the teacher candidates will eventually learn to adapt their instruction based on their students' needs.

Montclair State University's Portrait of a Teacher also serves multiple roles, both organizational and pedagogical, in helping the program prepare its students to teach for deeper learning. With its large size and multitude of pathways available to undergraduate, graduate, and post-bachelor students, the Portrait is a critically important touchstone. It provides a clear, comprehensive, and coherent vision to guide the policies and practices of all these pathways. Like Bank Street's principles, this document emphasizes knowledge of development, learning, and learners as the core foundation, along with expertise in curriculum, content pedagogy, and assessment to enact universally accessible, culturally responsive teaching. The Portrait adds expectations about collaboration and leadership to teachers' roles.

Pedagogically, the Portrait is used to guide the admission of candidates as well as their assessment throughout the program. It is also employed in the evaluation of cooperating teachers and supervisors and integrated into Montclair's Standards for Initial Teacher Programs. Dr. Tamara Lucas, dean of the College of Education and Human Services, noted that "by the last semester teacher candidates are assessed on all components of the Portrait," making it a central focus of practice as well as a big-picture guide for pathways' policies.

The four "design principles" that guide and shape instruction at High Tech High network schools—equity, personalization, authentic work, and collaborative design—serve to connect the pedagogy and structures for its K–12 schools and the teacher education program. The principles ground all of the coursework and supervisory review of candidates in the credential program, creating a framework for apprentices and intern teachers that supports and presses them to establish classrooms that operationalize those principles. This framework allows for collaboration and communication between students and teachers in a small and personalized setting that supports the development of real-world, student-led projects through which both students and candidates can access a rich and engaging curriculum.

Faculty who teach in the preparation program, many of whom are current or recent teachers at High Tech High schools, train teachers using the same instructional and pedagogical approaches they employ with K–12 students. In this way, comparable structures exist between High Tech High's K–12 schools and the intern program. The mirroring of the school's principles in the intern program can be seen in other ways as well, ranging from the size of classes, to the frequent contact with advisors and mentors, to the use of project-based learning. All of these are important elements for preparing teachers to personalize learning in equitable ways that help students develop deeper learning skills and competencies.

Trinity's commitments to preparing educators to teach for deeper learning and equity are encapsulated in the program's Core Beliefs About

Principled Practice. The MAT program instantiates these core values, which emphasize pedagogical and content knowledge, ethics, leadership, and cultural responsiveness, through coursework and clinical experiences. The program also relies upon a set of Core Beliefs on the *Development* of Principled Practice. This second set of core beliefs, which guide the design of the preparation programs, focuses on the importance of apprenticeship, engagement in inquiry, a continuum of practice, and a professional learning community.

Together these two sets of beliefs provide guidance on what candidates should be learning and doing to become the teachers Trinity aims to prepare. They shape the structure of the one-year MAT program and the collaboration between the university and its professional development school (PDS) sites, their faculty, and administrators. In both coursework and field experiences, which are tightly integrated, Trinity candidates experience these core beliefs in practice as faculty and mentors model what they teach. Candidates work closely with mentors and faculty in the community. Teaching itself is taught as a matter of learning about the self and continuing to learn about the world, about developing cultural competence and a sensitivity to students' needs, as much as it is about imparting knowledge to others. Trinity's core beliefs thus impact the program in all its aspects, right down to the learning experiences of teacher candidates.

In San Francisco's Teaching Residency, the program's stated mission is similarly tied to practice. The program is explicitly rooted in learning to teach for social justice, which creates a discourse that infuses every course. The SFTR program is further guided by its Vision of Transformative Teaching. This vision places students at the center of learning and creates the expectation that educators will facilitate engaging learning experiences that are grounded in rigorous academic content and differentiated to meet students' diverse needs. It also prioritizes educators' learning about the local context and family and community engagement as well as teacher leadership for equity and social justice. The Vision of Transformative Teaching is expressed through program structures. It is tied to and guides candidate recruitment, coursework, clinical experiences, and supervision, as well as the SFTR's induction program offered to program graduates.

The program also makes staffing decisions in alignment with these commitments. Dr. Peter Williamson, who played a key role in selecting instructors for SFTR courses when he was at the University of San Francisco and now plays a similar role as the faculty cirector of Stanford's Teacher Education Program's secondary program, explained how the vision of good teaching shapes each university's choice of instructors, which then informs course content:

> We're looking for deep knowledge of the content and a strong teaching record in higher ed as well as in K–12 schools. We're also looking for certain pedagogical dispositions, such as a focus on developing child-centered classrooms, dialogic classrooms, constructivist classrooms. We're looking for instructors who are mindful of social learning theory as a key tenet in curriculum development and who are using social learning theory as a framework for the whole curriculum; who can help novice teachers to see themselves as literacy instructors, whether they are teaching math or science; and who can help novice teachers see themselves not as social workers there to save children but rather as people who are there to be allies of children and teach in solidarity in them.

Finally, the University of Colorado at Denver also weaves its program's values into its structure, content, and practice, and makes hiring decisions like those articulated by San Francisco's Teaching Residency program. The CREDE standards articulate a vision of student learning as a joint productive activity in communities of learners, and the essential questions that guide the anchor experiences for all the pathways shape an equity-oriented approach to this vision for learning in all courses and clinical work.

The program's conceptual framework is constructed as a cycle of learning, and this cyclical model is used to guide the faculty as they design learning experiences in their courses. This framework also guides the teacher candidates as they design learning experiences for their clinical settings. Whether the students are K–12 students or teacher candidates, teaching and learning are conceptualized as a cycle that is grounded in learning theory, discipline-specific and culturally responsive pedagogies, the centrality of collaboration and inquiry, and social justice and equity values. The program makes an intentional effort to hire faculty whose expertise includes both research and practitioner knowledge, working across a common boundary at universities, with a clear commitment to social justice teaching in urban settings.

Values around teaching, learning and development, leadership and instruction, and equity and social justice are instantiated in every aspect of the seven programs and drive program structure, content, and practice. Not only are they explicit in vision statements and conceptual frameworks, but the values are clearly expressed in action, as they are lived out in teaching standards, instruction, and assessments; in coursework and clinical experiences; and in decisions around program features and personnel. They drive a powerful and coherent experience for candidates that is rooted in the deep structures of institutional activities and ways of being.

LEADERSHIP THAT PRIORITIZES TEACHER PREPARATION

The second common structural component across these programs is the institutional leaders' prioritization of teacher preparation, generally, and teacher preparation for deeper learning, specifically. At most of the institutions we studied, teacher preparation is one mission among many. High Tech High is largely focused on operating schools, with teacher preparation interwoven with its main mission. Bank Street is unique in that teacher preparation is the focal point for the entire institution and so is prioritized by design.

At Bank Street, deep commitment to progressive teacher education was the reason for the institution's founding and has been a long-standing reason for the ongoing success of its programs. It is worth noting that, even when political winds were blowing in different ideological directions, Bank Street's leaders and faculty did not waver in their commitment to its unique child-centered approach. Similarly, High Tech High is deeply committed to its project-based, experiential approach and founded the teacher education program to support that specific kind of teaching.

At the five institutions where programs are embedded in a multifaceted organization, leaders from the college president to the dean to the teacher education director have provided vital support for teacher preparation as a critically important institutional function, with appreciation for the programs' special focus on empowering and equitable learning. Leaders work to elevate the importance of teacher education across different academic disciplines and with multiple partners, both on and off campus, and to provide the conditions necessary for success.

Alverno, Montclair State, and Trinity all illustrate how leaders can make teacher preparation a priority at the institutional level. Alverno College has long prioritized teacher education, and during the thirty-five-year presidency of Sister Joel Read, it became a national leader in innovative educational design and assessment for the entire college as well as for teacher education. Emphasizing student-centered, competency-based education for all its students along with a strong equity mission, Alverno has especially prized teacher preparation as a means to carry this kind of education to children and youth in K–12 schools in the Milwaukee area.

Today Alverno's program also prioritizes opportunities for learning and collaboration among faculty, which allows them to design their courses to provide candidates with appropriately challenging deeper learning opportunities. The small size of Alverno's faculty gives faculty members the chance to work together to ensure that they each develop personalized, engaging classroom experiences for teacher candidates that complement the students' experiences in their colleagues' classes. Yet even this small, tight-knit group benefits from deliberate efforts to foster collaboration, such as the allocation of weekly time for shared work within and across disciplines. The college does not schedule classes on Friday afternoons so that faculty can meet with their departments or participate in "workshops on curriculum, teaching, learning, and assessment."[1]

Alverno's School of Education also provides additional time for instructors to meet on Tuesday afternoons so that they can discuss the content of their classes and design their upcoming coursework to connect to other courses and field experiences. In addition, the dean meets with adjunct faculty to describe the content and sequence of courses so they understand candidates' depth of knowledge and can design their classes to build on students' prior learning experiences at Alverno.

Montclair State's College of Education and Human Services is housed within a large public university with multiple schools and colleges, yet among the university's many missions, teacher preparation receives an impressive level of support. The university's president describes teacher education as "the heart of this university," and the university matches actions to sentiment. In 2005, when MSU started capital improvements on campus, the first new building to be erected was the current state-of-the-art building that houses the College of Education and Human Services. The dean of the College of Education, Tamara Lucas, who is herself a teacher educator and has been with the university in a variety of roles for over twenty years, talked about how important this type of public endorsement is to the work of teacher preparation, even taking into consideration the history of Montclair State as a normal school: "It's amazing, really, especially given that . . . in many places, teacher education is not valued."

Montclair State has built support for teacher preparation by integrating faculty from other units into the work. Through the Center of Pedagogy— described more fully later in this chapter—Montclair State brings together faculty from the College of Education and Human Services with those from the arts and sciences, and also incorporates faculty from the local public schools, an arrangement program leaders refer to as "the Tripartite." As stated on the center's website, "anyone who is involved in the education of educators is a member of the Center of Pedagogy," and all three aspects of the Tripartite play a role in shaping teacher preparation policies and practices.

Trinity University's MAT program enjoys similarly strong support and respect from Trinity leadership. One key reason for this is the fact that the MAT program is considered one of the primary vehicles for faculty and students to reach out to the local San Antonio community. Both the last two presidents of Trinity as well as the board of trustees have prioritized community involvement, and this has translated into their advocacy for the program.

At Trinity, as at Montclair, the program's evolution has opened up opportunities for faculty across disciplines to engage with future teachers. In 1989, Trinity made the shift from the four-year education major to a five-year Master of Arts in Teaching (MAT) program, meaning that Trinity students intending to become teachers could major in any degree program at the university before going on to earn their MAT. With this change, faculty across the university began to view any Trinity student as a potential teacher, resulting in shared responsibility among academic departments for preparing teacher candidates. This is a rare and highly desirable feature in an academic world where education is often seen as separate and unequal by faculty in other disciplines. Additionally, because the education department advises prospective teacher candidates from all the undergraduate majors, faculty have strong knowledge of the various undergraduate academic programs. As one faculty member reflected: "The MAT founders who moved this from a bachelor's to a master's were very intentional [in saying] . . . you will not be able to look out into your Trinity classroom and say that's an education student or that's not. They should be like any other Trinity student."

At CU Denver, Education School leaders are strong advocates of teacher education. Both Dean Rebecca Kantor and Associate Dean Barbara Seidl are teacher educators themselves. They articulate clearly that "teacher education is everyone's business," and they have acted on this commitment by moving the program to the center of the university's work in education, and by expecting faculty participation and providing incentives for research faculty to teach, lead, and conduct research in the program. Unlike the system at many universities, teacher education program leadership work "counts" as programmatic teaching in dossiers that tenure-track faculty present for tenure and promotion, an important demonstration of institutional commitment that shapes how faculty can deploy their time and effort.

The San Francisco Teacher Residency demonstrates a unique form of cross-cutting leadership. It has benefited from strong support for teacher education from the presidents and deans of both Stanford University and the University of San Francisco. It has also benefited from the solid backing and vocal advocacy of SFUSD's superintendent, Richard Carranza, who invested in the growth of the program, and the United Educators of San Francisco, which has been a strong partner in designing the program, as well as lobbying for resources and helping recruit and recognize excellent mentor teachers.

Beyond the support of each partner individually, SFTR must coordinate the efforts and priorities of these multiple partners from different institutional settings—two universities and a school district, plus the teachers association—in order to maintain the program's operation. Therefore, an essential leadership structure is the residency program's advisory board. The board meets at least quarterly and includes two representatives from each of the program's four partners. Board members have included the SFUSD's director of human resources and assistant superintendent, leadership from the Professional Learning Division along with the president and vice president of United Educators of San Francisco, and teacher education directors from the universities. The advisory board approves SFTR's budget and hires the executive director. Each partnering organization has one vote on the board.

SFTR's partnership structure enables the program to closely align candidates' coursework (taken at either USF or STEP) and clinical practice in a way that is deeply linked to the local context in which candidates are serving SFUSD. This is no easy feat, in that it involves coordination not only among the two university teacher preparation programs, but also the school district, the union, and SFTR staff. However, a shared belief in the value of this alignment, and in the importance of context-specific teacher preparation, was what gave rise to the program in the first place and has since driven purposeful structures to facilitate it. SFUSD's director of Human Resources described the importance of the advisory board as creating the space to "have a forum to have conversations about what we are we trying to do with this program, and how are we meeting the needs of the district, how are we meeting the needs of the union, and all of the partners who are part of it."

STEP's clinical director added that the board provides the space to build relationships that demonstrate a "commitment on the part of both universities to make this thing fly."

For preparation for deeper learning to flourish, leadership support is essential. This commitment is expressed at the institutional level, at the unit level, and across multiple partners on and off campus. The expression of this commitment manifests not only through institutional and program priorities, but also through concrete investments in structures and resources that allow the programs to thrive.

DEDICATED RESOURCES

The development of structures to support teacher preparation depends on the intentional and focused dedication of institution and program resources. Deans and other leaders make investments to create the time and space for faculty learning communities that promote effective collaboration, engage in critical and constructive feedback, and plan instruction to meet candidates' needs. Programs develop structures that enable deep clinical practice by funding enough high-quality faculty and supervisors to provide intensive support of candidates; adequately compensating strong mentor/ cooperating teachers; enabling shared efforts of faculty, supervisors, and mentor teachers; creating incentives for university- and school-based faculty who model strong teaching and invest time in clinical sites; and providing support and training for mentor/cooperating teachers and other school staff at those clinical sites.

At CU Denver, for example, university resources have been used to create and staff a high-level Office of Community Partnerships, which funds the course releases for tenure-track faculty to participate in program leadership. Administrative leadership of the program, a task that in many universities is relegated to nontenured clinical staff, is shared by diverse teams from across the program. This means that the often sharp, status-riddled distinctions between tenure-track "research" faculty and nontenure-track "clinical" faculty are blurred considerably, as people in both positions play both teaching and administrative roles. This, in turn, shows how a program's commitment to the goals of high-quality teacher training, backed by resources, can shape even long-held norms.

CU Denver's Teacher Education Leadership team is backed by resources that shape faculty roles in support of teacher preparation, and research faculty are "bought out" of some of their teaching responsibilities to make their participation possible. The team brings staff together from across program pathways representing different interests and program dimensions and includes both tenure-track and clinical faculty as well as PDS representatives. The team's job is to ensure cohesion, alignment, quality, and responsiveness to changing needs and conditions, as well as to act as a liaison between the program's diverse pathways. Together, research and clinical faculty have developed regularized coursework and common syllabi, assignments, and assessments that are used across the pathways, challenging yet another norm—the university's highly prized culture of academic freedom and faculty autonomy, which creates barriers to developing and sustaining shared practices across the community. This step to ensure program alignment, cohesion, and integration across coursework and clinical work has, perhaps unsurprisingly, shaken up hierarchies. Fortunately, strong and consistent leadership and the considerable status accorded the program within the School of Education and Human Development has enabled the program to weather occasional divisions among the faculty, and to continue renewing the program's vision while revising coursework and clinical experiences and aligning them for cohension among the pathways.

A key use of resources is these programs' commitment to hire enough supervisors and faculty to create small advisory groups that guarantee significant in-classroom coaching and small-group problem solving. Learning to teach in the ways we've described here is a challenging, sophisticated process that requires significant support to overcome candidates' preexisting views developed during their apprenticeship of observation, as well as the problems of enactment and complexity that we described in chapter 2.

As we noted above, Alverno leadership prioritizes time for faculty collaboration. It also invests in the resources necessary to structure faculty time and clinical loads to promote deeper learning experiences. Faculty are responsible for observing between four and twelve candidates each semester, but generally have no more than six. Faculty receive two teaching credits for every three students they oversee. Alverno's low faculty/student ratio and faculty's frequent observations of supervisees, which represent a significant allotment of program resources, allow faculty to know the details of each candidate's placement intimately, so they can ensure that candidates observe and practice deeper learning approaches in their fieldwork and student teaching.

Similarly, Bank Street creates a high-touch experience with supervised fieldwork, advisement, and conference groups. All Bank Street faculty serve as advisors, and advising represents 40 percent of faculty load, with a typical two- or three-credit class representing 15 percent. Faculty advisors supervise cohorts of five to seven teacher candidates, observing each candidate in his or her fieldwork setting for half a day at least once a month and meeting the student for planning and debriefing more frequently. In addition to the one-on-one meetings between advisors and teacher candidates, each advisor meets with his or her small group of advisees weekly. This "conference group" meeting provides a place for teacher candidates to discuss the issues they face as educators in their field placements.

Of course, the creation of this experience requires significant commitments of time, money, and faculty energy, and the dean of Bank Street described the many logistical challenges of coordinating faculty schedules, course schedules, and the location of teacher candidates' placements. Given the cost and difficulties of this model, this substantial investment by Bank Street reflects the college's belief in the centrality of the supervised fieldwork and advisement experience in preparing teacher candidates.

The investment of resources to promote strong clinical experiences is reflected at Trinity in its hiring of a number of faculty who work closely and collaboratively with PDS sites. One program leader noted of the institutional commitment that Trinity makes to support its faculty in doing work in schools: "The faculty are out in the schools more than in the university." Faculty support mentor teachers and other faculty in the PDS sites in order to ensure that candidates have a rich learning environment and high-quality internship placement; they also advise Trinity undergraduates in pre-MAT field placements as well as the graduate MAT candidates.

In these ways, the structures at Trinity shape both the role of faculty and the on-the-ground workings of the program in schools. Trinity faculty provide professional development for all teachers on the PDS campuses, not just candidates. In fact, the university commits $20,000 to both the elementary and secondary programs per year to support professional development, including allowing the MAT program to pay for substitutes when teachers attend professional development, letting candidates and mentors work together, funding summer training, and providing for other enrichments and learning, including in-kind resources making Trinity's campus available for various activities and events.

At Montclair, faculty receive budget support from university leaders for community engagement and collaboration. Maintaining a committed and experienced faculty is recognized as essential to the program's mission, and funding has been specifically earmarked for faculty professional development. Budget support has also helped the program to maintain administrative coherence through the creation and continued sustainability of the Center of Pedagogy, the unique organizational structure that provides a common framework for all teacher preparation pathways. The center, established in 1995, coordinates all aspects of teacher education as well as Montclair's partnership network, grant-funded initiatives, and faculty professional development. To support this holistic approach, the center engages faculty and staff from the College of Education and Human Services, the arts and sciences, and Montclair's network of partner schools through the "Tripartite." The center houses a number of administrative programs and offices, including the Montclair State University Network for Educational Renewal (MSUNER), the Office of Admissions and Retention, the Office of Clinical Internships, the Teacher Education Advocacy Center, and the Newark Montclair Urban Teacher Residency. A full-time director and deputy director oversee the work of the center.

Beyond support structures for clinical practice, the San Francisco Teaching Residency—like other teacher residencies around the country—directs resources to support teacher candidates directly, as well as to provide them with a high-quality program that extends beyond preservice preparation to two years of on-the-job mentoring. SFTR strategically combines support for candidates' tuition assistance, living stipends, health insurance, food stamps, and (for program graduates) housing assistance from the universities themselves, federal programs such as AmeriCorps, federal and state health and food assistance programs, and district investments in housing and mentoring.

These benefits are offered in exchange for a commitment to teach in the district for at least three years following the completion of the residency year, which is a key lever for successfully recruiting and retaining residents in San Francisco schools. These various types of financial support allow SFTR graduates to enter the teaching profession with stronger preparation and less debt than other new teachers in the district, and many residents identify this strong financial support as a key reason for choosing SFTR over other pathways into teaching.

Like the other programs, the two universities associated with SFTR also invest resources in their cooperating teachers and supervisors. Stanford's supervisors, for example, oversee four to six supervisees, meeting with them in small groups and visiting them one-on-one for classroom support. Cooperating teachers receive a $2,500 stipend, paid for by the district, to compensate them for the significant time they spend mentoring and supporting a resident teacher for a full year. SFTR also supports the professional learning of cooperating teachers, striving to provide them with deeper learning opportunities similar to those they are providing to residents. The program expects cooperating teachers to participate in three professional development days with SFTR instructors over the course of the school year, for which the program provides paid substitutes.

SFTR coaches visit residents at their sites on a regular basis, meet with residents and cooperating teachers regularly, and lead weekly hour-long small-group supervisory meetings for all of their residents together. They also work with residents as they become novice teachers once they have finished the preparation program. They are all former San Francisco teachers. The residency has allocated resources to keep the caseload for full-time coaches at about fourteen, though it varies with the mix of residents and novice teachers. The resources allocated to support mentors and supervisors is an important draw for experienced San Francisco educators to participate in the program and increases the quality of the preparation.

Training teachers to provide deeper learning experiences for their students requires investments in the people who prepare the teachers. This includes the program faculty, the supervisors, and the mentor or cooperating teachers at the school sites. Each of the programs, with the support of key leaders, has made intentional investments that allow faculty from within the teacher preparation program to collaborate regularly to ensure alignment of program values with program experiences, provide faculty with time and compensation to work closely with candidates, staff the program adequately to maintain low ratios between preparation staff and candidates, and invest in the partnerships with the K–12 schools and districts that serve as clinical sites to ensure alignment in priorities and practices.

PARTNERSHIPS WITH K–12 SYSTEMS AND SCHOOLS

Programs engaged in teacher preparation for deeper learning also develop strong, reciprocal partnerships with K–12 schools, above and beyond what is typical in teacher preparation. This is perhaps the most critical element of structural support needed in this work, since candidates cannot readily learn to practice in ways they have never experienced or seen—and the twenty-first-century abilities the programs want them to teach are not typically taught well in most schools. Thus, as in medicine's teaching hospitals, sites need to be developed where state-of-the-art practice is visible, and candidates can learn that practice firsthand while connecting it to their theoretical training.

In education, this kind of partnership work got its start decades ago in university laboratory schools—often private schools on college campuses where best practices were instantiated, largely for the children of professors, and teachers were trained in those practices. However, in the 1980s and '90s, the Holmes Group of Education Deans, located in flagship state universities, broadened this concept to the creation of public school partnerships in professional development schools where strong relationships and practices could be developed for diverse learners. These schools are sites for training student teachers, developing veteran teachers, and collaboratively improving both K–12 and higher education curricula through research and shared initiatives to improve practices for both student and teacher learning.

CU Denver, Trinity University, and Montclair State University were early adopters of this approach and are participants in the National Network for Educational Renewal that maintained support for the Holmes Group's work during the 1980s and '90s. These universities have strong relationships with their professional development schools, some going back many years. Bank Street and Alverno also have a variety of both long-standing and more recent partnerships, many of them quite deep. The newer efforts of SFTR are following suit with the development of partner schools as teaching academies, while High Tech High's program is centrally grounded in school-based work.

These reciprocal program/district partnerships allow for mutually beneficial joint efforts. Not only do they ground preparation for deeper learning, but they also facilitate school improvement. Partnerships are another route through which programs live out their values around equity and social justice, as programs choose clinical sites in high-poverty communities and structure placement opportunities to give teacher candidates experience teaching diverse learners. Although the professional development schools model is prevalent, the structures and commitments of partnership vary according to program priorities and local contexts. Most programs create partnership school networks that are also supported by program staffing and organizational structures, including integration of candidates and university faculty into local schools as well as integration of K–12 faculty into programs as instructors, mentors, and supervisors. Overall, it is these partnership structures that make possible the introduction and dissemination of practices aligned with deeper learning and consistent with educational equity, not only for candidates, but also for leaders, mentors, and other teachers.

High Tech High has its own built-in laboratory with its eleven charter schools and like-minded schools that partner with the teacher education program because they want to develop schoolwide project-based learning approaches and focus on equitable access to this kind of learning.

Bank Street's School for Children was originally designed and still functions much like the early lab schools, although it admits a more diverse group of city children. It is right on-site with the college, which also has deep partnerships all over New York City, many of them led by principals who trained in Bank Street's teacher education program, its Principals Institute, or both. These are often staffed almost entirely with Bank Street teachers and thus illustrate those practices in every classroom. Midtown West, where our vignette about Ted Pollen's classroom (see chapter 5) took place, is such a school.

Trinity's program is characterized by a close collaboration between Trinity faculty and the faculty at the PDS sites, made possible by Trinity's institutional commitment to supporting their faculty's work in schools. Part of this support is shown in the weight that teaching and work with local schools carries in the tenure and promotion process at Trinity, and this translates into faculty connections with mentor teachers and PDS faculty as well as candidates. The partnership relationships, like any close relationship, were developed over time and with significant effort. Dr. Patricia Norman, associate professor and coordinator of the elementary MAT program, describes the development of the relationship with a PDS site in terms of her own work:

> I spend more time here at the PDS campus than at Trinity. I taught an undergraduate class at the elementary school this fall. [The PDS principal] and I work closely together planning staff development. I feel like we are great thought partners. Being in classrooms to support interns and teachers allows me to be another set of eyes and ears for [the PDS principal]. The first year that [the school] became a PDS was a tense transition, in part because the school didn't have a say in this new role. I engaged in a lot of relationship building in the first year to earn their trust. For me, the good news is that there is evidence that trust has been established. When the university recently announced a new partnership with the district, a teacher asked me, "Pat, are you going to the new school?" in a worried tone. I don't think that would have happened a year ago. These are encouraging signs that we are developing a trusting culture and strong partnership.

Another deliberate aspect of building relationships with partner schools comes in the area of staffing. Trinity employs two PDS coordinators, each hired from a local school district (North East Independent School District) to work at their respective middle and high school PDS sites. The university funds these two positions. The school district is compensated around $60,000 ($30,000 for each coordinator) to provide a halftime release for them. This unique model shows how a university can engage school faculty to serve in a teacher preparation program, but is also an example of how program staff can be simultaneously engaged in K–12 schools. The

PDS coordinators work with mentors and Trinity interns at their placement sites, and play an important role, due to their deep connections to the schools, in the selection of Trinity mentor teachers.

CU Denver also uses a PDS model of collaboration with K–12 schools, and deep, substantive relationships between a set of professional development schools and the university faculty have been nurtured over the past twenty years. Those schools see the relationship with CU Denver as mutually beneficial, with two-way, equal-status sharing as partners in the preparation of new teachers and in the schools' own improvement efforts. At PDS schools, candidates, clinical teachers, site teams, and the broader school faculty engage in ongoing professional learning and a commitment to improvement of practice. The educators at the PDS schools and the university teacher education faculty agree that the growth and achievement of the K–12 students at the partner schools is the top priority. Toward that end, they collaborate to (1) prepare the next generation of teachers to teach those students well, (2) generate new knowledge through collaborative research, and (3) foster the learning of experienced teachers and inquiry-based school improvement. As is the case in many teacher preparation programs, teacher candidates in the traditional CU Denver undergraduate and graduate pathways have a range of clinical experiences at the professional development schools during their tenure in the program, sometimes changing grade levels within a school and other times switching schools.

As with Trinity's PDS model, CU Denver's is supported by staffing structures and collaborative expectations that form links between the work of the program and the work of K–12 schools. It is also both symbolically and tangibly important that the program's leadership resides in the Office of Partnerships and is led by the director of community partnerships, Cindy Gutierrez, as this both signals the high value placed on embedding learning and garners considerable program resources to support this work.

At each clinical site, key personnel share the responsibility of supporting the learning of teacher candidates and ensuring the coherent implementation of the PDS initiatives. These include a site supervisor (employed by the district to oversee teacher preparation on behalf of the school) and a site professor (employed by the university to supervise the clinical experience). Thursdays are designated as "all-hands-on-deck" days. Site supervisors and site professors are available to each other to coordinate, to informally and formally observe and meet with the teacher candidates individually and as a cohort (from five to twelve candidates at the sites), to meet with the clinical teachers, and to support facets of school improvement and professional development at the site. Both the district and the university commit additional resources to support the site supervisor and site professor positions, both of which are part time, yet are pivotal to the strength of the relationships, coordination, alignment, and more.

As in many university programs that employ this apprenticeship model, CU Denver's clinical teachers are essential to the day-to-day modeling and instruction for teacher candidates. Clinical site teams do the "care and feeding of the clinical teachers" and schedule events where all of them come together at least twice a semester, though usually monthly. In these sessions, the site teams work to build capacity and consistency across candidate experiences. Topics include working to ensure that there is evenness in "air time" for teacher candidates to engage in practice leading instruction, problem solving around shared challenges, offering strategies and tools to use with clinical teachers, and other organically generated topics. There is an online community for clinical teachers as well, which offers them a platform through which to share ideas and get input from peers at other PDS sites.

The relationship between SFTR and its partner schools, known as "teaching academies," also follows a professional development schools model. The goal for the teaching academies is to set up strong partnerships to create environments in which residents receive high-quality training, the school staff receives high-quality development, and the school benefits from the support of SFTR, Stanford, and USF.[2]

SFTR partners with these schools because they serve high-need student populations and because they are supportive, collaborative working environments where the staff and administration are committed to preparing the next generation of teachers. Wherever possible, SFTR seeks to identify teaching academies that illuminate deeper learning practices, showing an investment not only in resources to support partnerships, but in efforts to find the schools where those partnerships can best serve residents' learning. As described in chapter 4, the SFTR supervisors and coaches find themselves working as closely with veteran teachers in the academies as with the preservice candidates, as is true in other universities' PDS sites.

The theme of mutually beneficial partnerships is strong across these examples, though the partnerships can look different in their forms and structures. Montclair State follows many of the practices described above, and has also made efforts to formalize partnerships with districts that mutually invest in them. These partnerships are managed through the Montclair State University Network for Educational Renewal (MSUNER), a key structure that engages and coordinates more than thirty partner districts. It is because of these close relationships that Montclair can partner in teacher preparation on such a large scale and continuously improve its program to better fit the needs of the schools in Newark and other partner school districts, while simultaneously investing in and supporting the improvement of those same schools and classrooms.

For MSU, "partner district" is more than a title, and "partnership" means that schools are seen as much more than buildings to house teacher candidates as they complete field placement hour requirements. Districts must go through an application process that includes a site visit by MSU faculty to ensure that teaching practices in the school align with their conception of deeper learning. Once a district becomes a part of the network, it has access to an array of resources. Every district that joins the network pays dues, makes a commitment to its mission and goals, promises to give Montclair teacher candidates priority in placements, and commits to the learning and growth of its own faculty as well as MSU teacher candidates. One MSU faculty member describes the relationship in this way:

> [It] involves us having a dynamic relationship with a school or district where our mentor teachers are really seen as teacher educators. . . . There is a reciprocal relationship between us and the school, meaning [that] we are not just asking them to provide cooperating teachers for us, but there is a dynamic relationship where we see ourselves as growing teachers together. That includes their teachers, as well as ours. That is one of the hallmarks of our work.

Montclair places teacher candidates from all program pathways in partner schools within MSUNER for field experiences and student teaching. Within these network placements, teacher candidates are assigned a cooperating teacher, who is encouraged to use the coteaching model.

To maintain and grow partnership relationships, the university embraces the importance of leadership at all levels and works closely with district leaders and principals to facilitate learning opportunities for mentor teachers and teacher candidates. This multilevel support system of university, district, and school leaders helps support a cohesive experience for Montclair teacher candidates, particularly when it comes to clinical experiences aligning with Montclair values and coursework. MSUNER allows mentor teachers access to collaboration that also builds their skills. Field supervisors, who work closely with mentor teachers, see part of their responsibility as modeling for mentor teachers how to help teacher candidate learn and grow. Teachers and leaders participate in a wide variety of professional development opportunities, and they are eligible to receive small grants to work on specific short-term projects.

School-based clinical faculty members serve on university committees and task forces that focus on the renewal and development of teacher preparation.[3] Over eleven thousand teachers and leaders in the network have access to professional development activities that MSU education faculty, as well as arts and sciences faculty, provide through MSUNER. Tenured teachers within the network are recruited to become clinical faculty members by taking three required mini-courses focused on coaching and mentoring, teaching for critical thinking, and culturally responsive teaching. Over half of all cooperating teachers are designated clinical faculty members.

Because of the local context, the process of partnership building at Alverno College looks quite different. In Milwaukee, Wisconsin, where Alverno places many of its teachers, the school district has a centralized student teaching placement policy. When teacher candidates are placed in Milwaukee Public Schools, the district decides not only which schools can be placement sites for Alverno teacher candidates, but also which teachers can act as mentor teachers. Therefore, Alverno cannot build a partnership or PDS network that looks like those of other programs. Yet, despite this challenge, Alverno works creatively to ensure that candidates are exposed to classrooms that practice deeper learning pedagogy. To do this, Alverno works closely with Milwaukee school leaders and teachers to support candidates' learning, cultivating relationships with schools throughout the Milwaukee area that provide rich clinical and student teaching placements.

Alverno's creative problem solving illustrates the college's commitment to having candidates experience and practice deeper learning pedagogies and dispositions in diverse placements. This work is also "system building" in that Alverno's approach seeks to influence those teachers and schools that struggle with deeper learning and move them closer to practices that create deeper learning environments for all students. Alverno also develops relationships with schools in nearby Milwaukee suburbs to support teaching placements.

One way Alverno does this is by identifying principals from the college's school leadership pathway program who support deeper learning instruction. Developing relationships with these principals can lead to opportunities for clinical placements for Alverno teacher candidates.

Alverno also provides professional learning experiences to schools in order to build relationships with its alumni, mentor teachers, and community, with the aim of creating schools and classrooms that are more personalized and equitable. For example, Alverno partnered with a nearby district where it places candidates for fieldwork to help the district develop an ability-based curriculum similar to Alverno's. As the director of curriculum and instruction in the district explained, "Now we have identified these five attributes. We are in the process of building ways to demonstrate those abilities throughout and building that into our curriculum." This partnership supports deeper learning instruction for the students in the district and provides a deeper learning placement for Alverno's teacher candidates, showing how a program can work even within the restrictions of a local setting to accomplish partnership goals.

Strong, reciprocal relationships between teacher preparation programs and the local K–12 schools and districts where teacher candidates do their clinical work (and where many ultimately teach) are essential for ensuring that candidates have opportunities to practice the deeper-learning-aligned instruction they are learning in the programs, and also to promote these practices among a broader group of teachers at those sites. Even in places where those relationships do not exist, programs like Alverno's find creative solutions to ensure candidates have a coherent experience between coursework and clinical practice that prepares them to teach for deeper learning.

If teachers are to be prepared systemically rather than idiosyncratically for deeper learning, it is important to attend to the deep organizational structures that support these features and practices. The programs featured here practice what they preach, creating and sharing values and then taking steps to live them out. Leaders have prioritized teacher preparation for deeper learning at the institutional and program levels, across campuses and with outside partners. Leaders and programs have also dedicated resources to create spaces for deeper learning among faculty and candidates and to back other program goals with investments of time and money. Programs have undertaken the effort to build partnerships with K–12 schools, creating experiences that are vital in supporting teacher preparation for deeper learning. All of these organizational and infrastructure-building efforts which make this work possible, are the results of deliberate choices and sustained effort by faculty and administrators, and an important part of the overall picture of how programs enact teacher preparation for deeper learning.

CHAPTER 11

POLICIES FOR TEACHER PREPARATION AT SCALE

Deeper learning will do little for our economy and democracy unless it is accessible to every student. All too often, low-income students have had to subsist on a pedagogical diet of basic skills instruction, with few opportunities to develop the academic mindset and self-directed learning habits they need for future success. Seeking both excellence and equity in public education will require American school systems to shift in dramatic ways. . . . And most importantly, the roles of teachers must be transformed.

—Alliance for Excellent Education, 2011

As we have discussed, learning to teach successfully for the social demands of the twenty-first century requires learning how to support developmentally grounded approaches that are both personalized to individual learners' needs and contextualized in learners' experiences; apply knowledge so that it can be transferred to real-world problems; enable collaboration in productive communities of practice; and create equitable practices that produce more socially just opportunities and outcomes among students.

The programs we studied do several things that are critically important to this kind of powerful preparation but are relatively rare among teacher education programs nationally. First, rather than a set of fragmented courses representing individual professors' notions of what should be taught, these programs created a *coherent set of courses and clinical experiences* focused on a *vision of teaching* featuring a sophisticated set of practices promoting deeper learning and educational equity.

Second, in lieu of traditional lecture and textbook learning, instructors in these programs *model powerful practices* in their own teaching, showing prospective teachers how to teach in the ways that people learn best—through applications of learning to real problems, in collaborative communities of practice, with coaching, feedback, and opportunities to apply the feedback to performances of understanding that steadily improve.

Third, rather than expecting candidates to connect theory to practice themselves after taking a batch of fragmented courses and then experiencing a short stint in a disconnected classroom, the programs have created a *strong theory-practice connection* by organizing well-planned, *closely supervised clinical experiences interwoven with well-designed courses*. In these extended clinical experiences—frequently located in *partnership schools* that work closely with the university—powerful teaching practices are also modeled, and candidates have the opportunity to get to know diverse learners and families well, plan and teach curriculum, assess and support student learning, and reflect continually on how to improve their practice so as to deepen learning.

Fourth, rather than grading students primarily based on papers and tests in theoretical classes, these programs engage in *performance assessments* that help candidates bring together and practice what they are learning, and help instructors see what their candidates can do as well as what they know. This enables instructors, supervisors, and cooperating teachers to ensure that candidates' learning is focused and appropriate supports are provided.

The programs teach and support their candidates in the same ways that they expect their candidates to work with children. These features—a coherent vision and set of integrated experiences, modeling of effective practices that provide concrete examples and tools for candidates, strong clinical experiences, and performance assessments—are similar to those found in earlier studies to produce more effective teachers.[1]

The obvious question is what it would take to get these practices more widely represented across the entire enterprise of teacher education. There are several critically important policy levers that can influence the quality of teacher education and, ultimately, of the teaching force itself. These include *standards* that define the goals of teaching and teacher education and *processes for evaluating* those standards; the *incentives* and *opportunities* that are constructed for programs to improve their quality and for candidates to seek out and gain access to high-quality preparation; the *funding* available for programs and candidates; and the *labor market forces* that determine whether high-quality individuals will choose to enter teaching, where they will teach, and whether they will stay.

In this chapter, we examine these levers and how they might operate; we conclude with recommendations for a policy framework that can support high-quality teacher education and increase the odds that all teachers will have access to the knowledge they need to teach well. Our recommendations address:

1. *Strengthening teaching standards* in each state so that they reflect the knowledge and skill base described here that enables teaching for deeper learning and equity.
2. *Adopting performance assessments* reflecting these standards as a condition of initial teacher licensure to leverage candidate learning and program change.
3. *Establishing performance-based accreditation* of teacher education programs, so that the focus of program approval is on what candidates know and can do, rather than how many courses or credits they have taken.
4. *Investing in professional development school partnerships* that function like teaching hospitals in medicine to ensure state-of-the-art clinical training for candidates.
5. *Seeding residencies in high-need communities,* a key equity move to end shortages with high-quality, high-retention pathways that prepare candidates to teach diverse learners well and to stay in teaching.
6. *Underwriting candidate training* for those who enter high-needs fields or locations, as other countries routinely do, so that high-quality candidates can choose teaching without going into debt.
7. *Adequately funding teacher education as a clinical practice profession* that requires intensely supervised processes of learning to teach in practice.

DEFINING HIGH-QUALITY PRACTICE

The seven teacher education programs we studied suggest that teachers who succeed at developing deep understanding of challenging subjects for diverse students exhibit some common practices. As they construct developmentally appropriate learning opportunities that apply knowledge in real-world, culturally connected contexts, they enable students to learn in productive communities of practice that support equitable outcomes in a number of ways:

- They engage students in meaningful tasks within the disciplines, as they conduct historical inquiries; analyze literature; write and publish poetry, books, newspapers; investigate scientific questions; and use mathematics to solve real-world problems.
- The tasks they design provide choices and different entry points into the work, building on student strengths and interests as they reach for new understandings and skills, with scaffolding, feedback, and opportunities for revision as students take each step.

- They develop "two-way pedagogies" to find out what students are thinking and feeling by listening and observing carefully, inviting student experiences into the classroom, and connecting to families, so that they can plan around student interests and needs.
- They assess students to support their learning and fine-tune their teaching. They reinforce and build on students' accomplishments, creating a growth mind-set.
- They help develop student confidence, motivation, and effort by developing their social-emotional skills, assuring that students feel connected and capable in school.

Graduates of these programs use knowledge about learners and learning, subject matter, curriculum, and teaching to combine pedagogical content knowledge and pedagogical learner knowledge in ways that ultimately meet at the intersection of subjects and students. They know how to vary their practice in different contexts, depending on their instructional goals, the demands of challenging content, and the needs of particular students and classes. They practice what John Dewey called "manner" as method: their clear commitment to student success supports the risky quest for knowledge.

New teachers are able to engage in these sophisticated practices because of how they learned to teach: seeing these practices in their teacher education classes and partnership school settings; learning the underlying theories connected to strategies, so they can develop classroom activities based on how children learn and develop socially, emotionally, and cognitively; having opportunities to plan curriculum, enact it, and evaluate learning; developing dispositions to meet all students' needs and understanding how to act on these intentions from their time spent in communities; knowing how to reach out to parents; and learning how to take up equity and social justice issues in their work with schools as well as with children.

The Role of Professional Standards

One way to change practice in professions is by enacting strong standards for professional licensing and program accreditation that reflect these practices and are universally enforced. Standards are now a strong lever in medical, legal, and other areas of professional education. However, when Abraham Flexner conducted his famous 1910 study of medical education that eventually led to its overhaul, there were no serious standards for the field. Programs ranged widely—from a three-week course of study in which doctors memorized a list of symptoms with associated "cures" to Johns Hopkins University's purposeful coursework in the sciences of medicine coupled with clinical training in the school's newly invented teaching hospital.

In his introduction to the Flexner Report, Henry Pritchett, president of the Carnegie Foundation for the Advancement of Teaching, noted that, although there was a growing science of medicine, most doctors did not get access to this knowledge because of the great unevenness in medical training. He observed that "very seldom, under existing conditions, does a patient receive the best aid which it is possible to give him in the present state of medicine, . . . [because] a vast army of men is admitted to the practice of medicine who are untrained in sciences fundamental to the profession and quite without a sufficient experience with disease."[2] Similarly, few students—especially in the neediest schools—receive the quality of education it is possible to deliver today, in substantial part because so many of their teachers have not had the opportunity to learn what is known about how to teach them effectively.

Flexner's identification of successful models was the stimulus for the reform of medical education, which occurred over the next two decades through the use of licensing and accreditation standards to ensure that doctors would get the best training the field had to offer. Now, doctors all over the world are trained with a common introduction to the sciences of medicine and clinical training through internships and residencies in teaching hospitals.

Fortunately, teaching standards exist that can help leverage this kind of reform. The teaching practices described earlier and the teacher education practices associated with them are exceptionally strong instantiations of the professional standards that have emerged since the National Board for Professional Teaching Standards was created in 1987 and began certifying veteran accomplished teachers in the 1990s. The National Board built on research about learning and teaching—and the wisdom of highly respected practitioners—in developing standards articulating what expert teachers should know and be able to do.

The standards—and the associated performance assessments, which include teacher plans, classroom videotapes, commentaries about practice, and evidence of student learning—support a view of teaching as complex and responsive to students' learning pathways. By examining teaching in the light of learning, the Board put teacher effectiveness at the center of practice. Many studies have since found that the Board's assessment process identifies teachers who are more effective than others,[3] and that teachers' participation in the assessment process stimulates changes in their practice.[4]

Although more than one hundred thousand teachers have been certified through the Board's assessment, this voluntary process has reached only about 3 percent of the teaching force.

Applying these kinds of standards and assessments in the licensing process for beginning teachers could have much more systemic effects. The National Board's standards were carried into initial teacher licensing standards by the Interstate New Teacher Assessment and Support Consortium (INTASC), a consortium of state education agencies and higher education institutions. These were recently revised to incorporate the implications of new student standards across the states.

The INTASC standards have been adopted or adapted by more than forty states and integrated into licensing and accreditation standards for candidates and programs. California's Standards for the Teaching Profession, which are central to the organization of the curriculum and supervisory rubrics used by SFTR and High Tech High, evolved from the INTASC standards, as did the standards in Colorado, New York, New Jersey, Texas, and Wisconsin, which informed other programs' curriculum frameworks. Leaders of programs we studied, such as Alverno, Bank Street, Stanford, and Trinity, were involved in both the development of the standards and their adaptation in state contexts. These standards are reflected in important ways in the vision statements and expectations for candidates we reviewed in chapter 10.

The standards developed by the National Board and INTASC take into explicit account the need for teachers to respond to a student body that is multicultural and multilingual and that learns in diverse ways. They define teaching as a collegial, professional activity that responds to considerations of subjects and students. In addition, the move toward *performance-based* standards placed the focus on what teachers should know, be like, and be able to do rather than listing the courses that programs should offer or that teachers should take in order to be awarded a diploma, license, or certificate. This shift toward performance-based standard-setting is in line with the approach to licensing taken in other professions, which have used licensing tests and accreditation practices to clarify what competence means, placing more emphasis on the abilities professionals should develop than on the hours they spend taking classes.

Evaluating the Standards Through Performance Assessments

As important as statements of standards are for focusing a field on common goals, much more is needed to change actual practice. In our study, we found that recent efforts to develop performance assessments for evaluating the effectiveness of beginning teachers had become a powerful force for change. All of the programs we studied were using a portfolio assessment process to examine candidates' planning, teaching, and analysis of student work during their program of studies, and most were using a version of the edTPA,[5] which evolved in a genealogical line from the National Board Portfolio, via the Connecticut BEST portfolio,[6] and then via the Performance Assessment for California Teachers (PACT).[7] Key leaders at several of the programs we studied were involved in developing one or more of these assessments.

These assessments, like that of the National Board, have been found to predict teachers' effectiveness in promoting student learning.[8] Initial data suggest that performance assessments also pose fewer barriers to entry into the profession for teachers of color than many other teacher tests whose disparate pass rates by race/ethnicity have often reduced the diversity of the teacher workforce.[9] Most important, the assessments shape candidate learning and program design in noticeable ways.

The assessments require teachers to document their plans and teaching for a unit of instruction; adapt the lessons for English learners, students with disabilities, and other students requiring particular attention; videotape and analyze the lessons, offering commentary about their teaching decisions; and collect and evaluate evidence of student learning, outlining what should happen to support the learning of different students in the future. Studies have found that these performance assessments help beginning teachers develop a more learner-centered practice, and shape practice in ways that continue after the assessment experience has ended.[10]

THE STANDARDS AND ASSESSMENTS IN ACTION. The way that assessments can shape practice is well illustrated at Alverno College, which uses performance assessments throughout candidates' coursework and fieldwork to help them develop and demonstrate the eight core abilities and the additional competencies outlined by the teacher education program. For example, after candidates' first field placement, they complete a portfolio and interview assessment. This assessment requires candidates to connect evidence of their teaching practice to two INTASC standards and two Alverno education abilities.

Before students advance to student teaching, they complete another portfolio and interview assessment. For this assessment, candidates prepare evidence of their readiness to student teach from their prior coursework and field experiences. Candidates must demonstrate that they have developed the dispositions and mind-sets teachers need to help all students develop deeper learning competencies. As part of the assessment, candidates meet with K–12 practitioners (e.g., principals and teachers) to discuss their portfolio and the challenges of teaching. This interview assessment serves as a gateway into student teaching. If students do not successfully complete this interview, they are counseled out of teaching and into a more appropriate course of study at Alverno.

The edTPA occurs for candidates at the end of their program, before they are recommended for a license. Dr. Mary Diez, an Alverno faculty member who helped the college develop its famous ability-based system starting in the 1980s, was a cochair of the INTASC standards committee in its first iteration and in its later revision, helped advise on the design of the first INTASC portfolio. She also later helped develop the edTPA and bring it to the college to pilot before there were any state expectations requiring the portfolio.

The dean and Alverno faculty emphasized how the edTPA has helped the faculty collaborate to improve the preparation of teachers. edTPA requires teacher candidates to create and analyze a unit of learning that includes planning, instruction, and assessment. Across the structured analysis, candidates must demonstrate proficiency in supporting their students' academic language development and the capacity to reflect on their practice to improve it.

To determine the value of edTPA during its five-year use, Alverno faculty scored their students' portfolios in addition to having them externally scored. After seeing congruence between the scores, the faculty examined the edTPA results, including the subscores, to determine patterns of strengths and weaknesses in their students, and then strategized about how they could update their courses to address the needs they identified. The dean explained:

> One of the things that we did as a faculty is we examined edTPA results and subscores, [and] then looked at where we can backtrack in our courses to look at the areas where our students are doing very well. We found out our students are doing really well in planning . . . and they did pretty well in instruction. Assessment was the piece that was most challenging for them. And apparently that is true across the United States. So then we could back up and say, "All right, where are there things we can do in our courses to help students think more deeply, whether it is to revise the prompts that we have for reflections or to move an assignment, or something else?"

One Alverno faculty member who teaches candidates' first fieldwork course described how edTPA helped her to improve her students' reflections. Before candidates completed the assessment, she provided them with a blank page to reflect on the first lesson they gave during their fieldwork and found that students generally did not engage in deep and critical inquiry of their lesson. However, after Alverno adopted edTPA, the instructor explained:

> I took questions and reworded them from edTPA and put those as prompts for their self-assessment. . . . Oh my gosh, what better responses! It was so good and much deeper thinking about the elements. . . . It's not just about completing that lesson, especially the first two they have ever done. But really digging into the meaning of the preparation, their environment . . . The kind of thinking that is required in the edTPA really is a good kind of thinking for practitioners. So it also gives our students a way to really start thinking in preparing for the edTPA, because we're using some of the same language. And that deeper thinking about what they've done: that has been a good guide for us to enhance what we are already doing.

And in actually completing edTPA, Alverno students were learning about assessment and improving their assessment skills. One candidate remarked:

> In the final field placement, we had to do a mock edTPA . . . And in that edTPA, you have to teach two or three connected lessons, and you have to set a context, your planning, and your assessment strategies for the lesson. So, you have to choose assessments that are going to be beneficial to the needs of the students, . . . not just "okay, I'm going to give you this assessment," but why are you giving this assessment? What is it going to help you to see? And how is it going to help you teach the students what they need to know?

In this way, the edTPA helped to support teacher candidates' learning, enabling both candidates and the program to become more learner-centered in areas like assessment and language development.

Similarly, in the San Francisco Teacher Residency, as in all California programs, candidates must pass a state-approved teacher performance assessment in order to earn their California teaching credential. Options have included the California Teacher Performance Assessment (CalTPA), developed by the California Commission on Teacher Credentialing , or the PACT, a teacher performance assessment developed by a consortium of

California programs, including Stanford and the University of California campuses, and used at more than thirty institutions of higher education and two other educator preparation programs in the state, including High Tech High.[11] (Since our study, many programs, including STEP, have moved to the edTPA, which is the national version of PACT.)

The PACT and CalTPA are both aligned with the California Standards for the Teaching Profession (CSTP)—developed from the INTASC standards—and they are structured similarly, with prospective teachers completing several performance tasks centered around a particular lesson—the "culminating teaching experience" in CalTPA, or the "teaching event" in PACT—which is videotaped and analyzed.[12] Candidates must complete planning, instruction, and assessment tasks, as well as reflections on the lesson and student learning from it. They must also provide evidence that their planning and instruction are developed with knowledge of the teaching context; focus on and analyze the work of individual students in assessing the lesson; and describe how the lesson met the needs of English learners.

When the assessment was first used, many programs, like Alverno's, found that their candidates did less well in assessing students and supporting their academic language development. STEP, along with several other California programs, expanded and refined its instruction about assessment and the teaching of English language learners in response to the PACT data, as confirmed by other measures.[13]

A survey of PACT completers also found that a large majority agreed that the assessment improved their practice as well as measuring it. Sixty percent agreed that "I learned important skills through the process of completing the [PACT] Teaching Event." In addition, 64 percent agreed that the PACT had improved their assessment of student learning, and 72 percent agreed that the PACT had improved their ability to reflect on their teaching.[14]

Beyond the positive impacts on individual teacher candidates, performance assessments like the PACT also improve teacher preparation in other ways. The assessments are scored by trained raters, which include faculty members, supervisors, cooperating teachers, and principals. This act of scoring—which involves rigorous training and the use of rubrics, calibration, and audit procedures—is itself a powerful form of professional development for the scorers. As one teacher education faculty member commented: "This [scoring] experience . . . has forced me to revisit the question of what really matters in the assessment of teachers, which—in turn—means revisiting the question of what really matters in the preparation of teachers."

A cooperating teacher commented: "[The scoring process] forces you to be clear about 'good teaching'; what it looks like, sounds like. It enables you to look at your own practice critically, with new eyes."[15]

Another noted: "It helped me as a teacher. Principals should learn it for their efforts to help new teachers."

And an induction program coordinator said, "I have a much clearer picture of what credential holders will bring to us and of what they'll be required to do. We can build on this."

Instituting high-quality performance assessments can help hone a practice that is more focused on learners and learning and that is based in a vision of teaching for deeper learning, as well as greater equity.

ACCREDITING PROGRAMS BASED ON PERFORMANCE. A second use of stronger standards would be in the accreditation process for preparation programs. Accreditation, designed a century ago as a process in which institutions describe their work in relation to common questions or standards (typically at great length) and display it in brief site visits, has value as a means for guiding self-assessment and reflection. However, in most states and nationally, it has not been a powerful tool for setting a floor on the quality of teacher education or for moving the field forward on a common path toward more powerful practices.

While all states approve programs and a few require or encourage national accreditation, neither process has incorporated and enforced clear requirements for the kinds of practices we have described here: demonstrated coherence around a vision of practice grounded in what we know about deeper learning and productive development; modeling of powerful teaching practices in university coursework, along with the provision of concrete strategies and tools for practice; demonstrated connections between theory and practice and between coursework and clinical work; extended, well-planned, carefully supervised clinical training in sites that also instantiate these practices.

Even when these practices are present in some universities' programs, those same universities often operate other, weaker programs that do not offer the same features. Despite the fact that the achievement of goals is not universal across programs, accreditors commonly approve the program provider, allowing low-quality programs a free pass.

Two needed changes in accreditation, then, are the much clearer incorporation of these features of successful programs into the requirements for approval, and the application of these standards universally to all programs. In California, for example, new standards for teachers require more extensive and better supported clinical experiences for both interns and student teachers, as well as stronger preparation for all teachers—including those who enter through alternate routes—in:

- content pedagogy focused on deeper learning
- classroom management focused on educative and restorative practices, including social-emotional learning
- how to teach diverse learners, including English learners and students with disabilities
- how to work effectively with parents
- how to reflect on and continuously improve one's own practice[16]

In our fieldwork we witnessed one result of these new standards in High Tech High's internship program. Based on California's Commission on Teaching Credentialing (CTC) Standards expressed in a set of new Teaching Performance Expectations, interns are required to receive 120 hours of preservice training that includes preparation to teach English learners before entering the classroom, in addition to ongoing work thereafter. Thus, as we described in chapter 9, before interns begin teaching they take a required six-week Foundations of English Language Development course, praised by candidates as an extremely helpful starting point for the work they were just beginning. High Tech High also offers interns a hands-on course taking up critical equity issues and supports interns in designing curriculum before they enter the classroom—strategies that are embedded in the standards.

However, to enforce standards universally, it is critical to know whether the standards have indeed been met, a challenging feat when the evidence consists of reams of paper describing self-reported practice and a short visit that is guided by the institution being reviewed. Because of this challenge, there is currently a move across professions—ranging from medicine and engineering to occupational health and safety—toward a form of performance-based accreditation, which relies on evidence that graduates have the required knowledge, skills, and dispositions (usually demonstrated through surveys about their training and observations of their practice) rather than programs' ability to complete hundreds of pages of reporting about program activities.

These approaches are also beginning to take hold for teacher education accreditation. For example, in California, a newly launched accreditation system will take into account candidate pass rates on the new performance assessments that examine what candidates can *do* to support student learning, rather than merely what courses they have taken; results from graduate surveys about whether they have experienced strong learning opportunities like those we have described (both as they graduate from preparation and two years later, after they have been teaching); and results from surveys of mentors and employers. The new system will examine the conditions of clinical work—including the kinds of supports, coaching, and learning opportunities provided—as well as the specific content of courses, including candidates' views of their quality. Already, some programs have changed substantially or ceased operating as a result of the standards.

OPPORTUNITIES FOR IMPROVING PROGRAM QUALITY

Policies that are effective combine the right mixture of pressure and support for change in ways that increase the capacity for good practice among the institutions that are the targets of the policy. While stronger, more widely enforced standards for preparation programs and more useful and authentic assessments of teaching skills can provide information as well as productive pressure for change, investments are also necessary.

One set of prerequisites involves incentives for the creation and institutionalization of school-university partnerships needed to make strong clinical practice possible. Also needed are targeted incentives for seeding the creation of high-quality teacher education programs, such as teacher residencies, in the low-income urban and rural areas where well-prepared teachers are most needed and least available.

Investing in School-University Partnerships

As noted earlier, the invention of the teaching hospital was a key element in the capacity of the medical profession to dramatically improve practice. The analog of the teaching hospital has been fully implemented in Finland, where all teachers are prepared in partner schools that are tightly connected to universities.[17] The teachers in these partners schools are especially selected for their expertise and capacity to mentor; they also engage in research on practice with the teacher candidates and the university professors. The school-based teachers have appointments in the university. University faculty also work directly in the schools. Theory and practice are tightly linked. These efforts are funded by the national government, through the universities.

This work has been launched in teacher education in the United States, although generally without governmental support. To allow their candidates to see and experience the pedagogies supporting deeper learning, all of our programs had developed strong professional development school partnerships, many of them a direct result of the National Network for Educational Renewal (NNER), a group of university teacher education programs that have dedicated themselves to the simultaneous renewal of schools and the institutions that prepare teachers. Taking up the charge developed by the Holmes Group of Education Deans (1986), the NNER member institutions established professional development school (PDS) partnerships. CU Denver was one of the earliest members in the early 1990s. The Montclair State University Network for Educational Renewal (MSUNER), part of the national network, was also launched in the 1990s as a partnership between Montclair State and thirty-one member school districts.

Much like teaching hospitals in medicine, professional development schools connect the faculty of the school with university partners in an ongoing process of improving the education provided to the preK–12 students attending the schools and, at the same time, provide high-quality clinical settings in which future teachers learn to teach and become part of a professional community. Often the schools also develop curriculum or other innovations and conduct research that ultimately advances knowledge and practice beyond their borders.

In many of the programs we studied, universities were deeply involved in educational reforms in existing schools or in starting new schools to exemplify the equitable deeper learning practices they were trying to teach. Since settings that are beacons of excellent education for low-income students of color simply do not exist in large numbers, they must be created if practice is to change on a wide scale. Seeking diversity by placing candidates in schools serving low-income students or students of color that suffer from the typical shortcomings many such schools face can unfortunately "strengthen preservice teachers' stereotypes of children, rather than stimulate their examination, and ultimately compromise teachers' effectiveness in the classroom."[18] For this reason, a growing number of universities have actually created new schools and developed partnerships that support and help transform existing schools to demonstrate state-of-the-art practices and to serve as training grounds for teachers.

These kinds of relationships, which simultaneously transform both schools and teacher preparation, are critical to long-term reform, because it is impossible to teach people how to teach powerfully by asking them to imagine what they have never seen or to suggest they "do the opposite" of what they have observed in the classroom. It is impractical to expect to prepare teachers for schools as they should be if teachers are constrained to learn in settings that typify the problems of schools as they have been—where isolated teachers provide examples of idiosyncratic practice that rarely uses well-implemented deeper learning strategies designed to teach a wide range of learners well. No amount of coursework can, by itself, counteract the powerful experiential lessons that shape what teachers actually do.

In highly developed professional development school partnerships, faculty from the school and university work together to develop curriculum, improve instruction, and undertake school reforms. They work together teaching children and prospective teachers, making the entire school a site for learning and feedback for all of the adults, as well as the students. Many such schools actively pursue an equity agenda, confronting the inheritances of tracking, poor teaching, inadequate curriculum, and unresponsive systems.[19] Student teachers are encouraged to participate in all aspects of school functioning, ranging from special education and support services for students to parent meetings, home visits, and community outreach to faculty discussions and projects aimed at ongoing improvement in students' opportunities to learn. This kind of participation helps prospective teachers understand the broader institutional context for teaching and learning and begin to develop the skills needed for effective participation in collegial work around school improvement throughout their careers.

Studies of highly developed PDSs have found that new teachers who graduate from such programs feel better prepared to teach and are rated by employers, supervisors, and researchers as stronger than other new teachers. Veteran teachers working in such schools describe changes in their own practice as a result of the professional development, curriculum work, and mentoring that are part of the PDS. Studies have documented gains in student performance tied to curriculum and teaching interventions resulting from PDS initiatives.[20] Having centers of support for continuous professional learning is essential for turning around schools that serve the students most often left behind because their teachers are left behind.

Although many school-university partnerships have emerged across the nation as sites for student teaching and the development of good practice, these often exist tenuously, on soft money or at the margins of institutions, and many have come and gone due to the vicissitudes of changing budgets. Without ongoing support, it is difficult to sustain collaboration between schools and universities when funding streams are targeted separately to each sector for specific purposes that typically do not include partnerships. The PDS models we observed relied on university and district funds, as well as outside grants, to support faculty working in these schools and professional development opportunities for all their teachers.

And while some programs had been successful in designing long-lasting models, the capacity to expand this practice was limited by funding.

Some states have sought to address these problems. For example, in the 1990s, North Carolina created legislation to fund professional development school partnerships launched by each university in the state. It encouraged all colleges to require and support a full year of clinical training for candidates, preferably in partnership schools. North Carolina's package of reforms supporting stronger teacher education and recruitment, along with higher and more equitable salaries, was related to the sharp rise in student achievement the state experienced.

Maryland required and funded professional development schools as part of its teacher education redesign initiative, using both state funds and federal grants targeted to teacher education and professional development. By 2004, every college or university in the state had launched PDS sites, which served 92 percent of all teacher candidates in "extensive internships"; these sites also offered a very substantial level of professional development for veteran teachers and teacher educators as well as novices. In an evaluation, early indications suggested that these initiatives were associated with stronger competence and retention of beginning teachers, which, the state noted, were in turn associated with reduced costs for induction and attrition.[21]

But both North Carolina and Maryland eventually lost these streams of funding, and while some universities continued their school partnerships, many did not. State and federal funding for such initiatives would help to institutionalize needed reforms of preparation and improve key outcomes of teacher education—teacher entry, initial competence, and retention— at the same time. Federal supports for professional development schools would emulate the long-standing federal role under the Medical Manpower Act and the Health Professions Education Assistance Act, which have supported grants for training innovations and reimbursements for teaching hospitals through both federal funding systems and third-party reimbursement formulas.

Seeding Residencies in High-Need Communities

One of the critical factors to solving teacher shortages is creating high-quality programs that prepare and retain well-trained teachers where they are most needed. In districts that meet shortages by hiring teachers who have not completed adequate preparation, turnover is higher, as novices without training leave after their first year at more than twice the rate of those who have had student teaching and preparation.[22] Similarly, teachers who are left to sink or swim on their own leave teaching at much higher rates than those who receive supportive mentoring in their first years on the job. Under these circumstances everyone loses: Student achievement is undermined by high rates of teacher turnover and teachers who are inadequately prepared for the challenges they face. Schools suffer from continual churn, undermining long-term improvement efforts. Districts pay the costs of both students' underachievement and teachers' high attrition.

Two of the programs we studied were from a new breed of program designed to address these perennial problems: the San Francisco and Newark Montclair teacher residencies. CU Denver also operates a residency with Denver Public Schools. Building on the medical residency model, these universities partner with districts to recruit residents who are career switchers or recent college graduates who want to teach in high-need urban or rural schools. These residencies have created professional development school partnerships, wherever possible with reform-oriented schools that exemplify deeper learning and equity.

The residents apprentice alongside an expert teacher in one of these teaching schools for a full academic year. They take closely linked coursework from a partnering university that leads to a credential and a master's degree at the end of the residency year. They receive living stipends and tuition support as they learn to teach, plus two years of early career mentoring after they start teaching. In exchange, they commit to teach in the district for three to four years beyond the residency. This model fosters tight partnerships between local school districts and teacher preparation programs. Residencies recruit teachers to meet district needs—usually in shortage fields. Then they rigorously prepare them and keep them in the district.

A San Francisco study found that 97 percent of all residents were still in teaching somewhere, and 80 percent were still teaching in the district after five years. This compares to only 38 percent of other newly hired teachers who entered the district five years earlier. Retention rates are similar in the more recently founded Newark Montclair residency program, where 86 percent of residents were still teaching after three years.[23]

The full-year clinical residency and the close work with schools and districts are powerful tools for learning to teach—and are present in other programs: Trinity, Stanford, and Bank Street have for many years used this kind of yearlong student teaching model in partner schools. Although candidates do not get the financial benefits—accompanied by service requirements—that go along with district-sponsored residencies, the preparation model is the same. High Tech High's internship/apprenticeship models also embed learning to teach in school classrooms, with coursework wrapped around those experiences.

The benefits of this interrelationship between the school and university are so pronounced that Montclair is introducing many of the features of its residency program into some of its other teacher education programs at the undergraduate and graduate levels. CU Denver has also begun to infuse into its other, more traditional programs some of the innovations that have accompanied its residency program, including a highly interactive internet platform that serves as a hub for materials, assignments, and ongoing discussions. This platform also allows teacher candidates to present videorecorded lessons and to receive feedback and one-on-one mentoring.

Initial research suggests that residencies also bring greater racial and ethnic diversity into the teaching workforce. Nationally, about twice as many candidates in teacher residency programs are teachers of color as in the entering teaching force generally. In Newark, nearly half of residents are candidates of color, and in San Francisco, the proportion is two-thirds. Across the country, residents have significantly higher retention rates and are found to be effective, highly sought after teachers.[24] In San Francisco, for example, 100 percent of principals surveyed reported that they find residents more effective than beginning teachers from any other source.

This model offers a promising approach to addressing recruitment and retention issues in high-needs districts and in subject areas with chronic teacher shortages. At the same time, it creates fundamental systemic change and builds a more stable, well-prepared teaching profession, especially in the most challenging districts. Residencies are a promising long-term solution to meeting district hiring needs, allowing districts to play a direct role in training their future workforce. Districts benefit by filling vacancies with better prepared, more diverse teachers who stay longer to serve as leaders in their schools and community. And students benefit from well-prepared teachers who provide continuity and leadership in their schools.

Given that the teacher residency model—when well designed and well implemented—creates long-term benefits for districts, for schools, and ultimately and most importantly, for the students they serve, a key question is how this model could be scaled up across the country. With recent federal and philanthropic support, there are now at least fifty residency programs nationwide, and legislation has been enacted in California, Louisiana, and Texas to provide state support for expanding residencies.

In addition to these initiatives, federal grants, like those used in medicine to create "centers of excellence" and develop community-based health facilities, could be offered to create or expand new model teacher preparation programs within cities or rural areas where the problems are most severe.

The costs of such an initiative would be modest. To create two hundred such programs, each training fifty teachers annually, for example, by allocating $1 million per year to each program, the annual cost would be only about $200 million to produce ten thousand well-trained teachers a year who stay in teaching—a small fraction of the cost of poor education and high attrition that high-needs districts normally experience. Given the high retention rates of such programs, this kind of initiative could eliminate the hiring of unqualified teachers in urban centers and many rural areas within half a decade.

The models that emerge might include not only new forms of professional development schools used to develop state-of-the-art practices; they might also include new applications of distance technology, new forms of collaboration by the private and public sectors, and new kinds of partnerships among networks of schools, districts, and universities.[25] A critical goal would be to study models that prove successful so as to stimulate further reform.

STRENGTHENING THE ATTRACTIONS TO TEACHING

Ensuring universal high-quality preparation depends not only on creating stronger programs, but on enabling candidates to gain access to them. One major reason that many candidates do not get adequate preparation is that they cannot afford either the tuition or the opportunity costs of being without employment for a period of time. Furthermore, these costs are harder to bear when a recruit is entering a profession that does not promise large salaries later to compensate for loans taken earlier. US teachers are paid 30 percent less on average than other college graduates,[26] and in most states, the average teacher heading a family of four qualifies for several forms of government assistance.[27] The children of teachers can themselves be on food stamps at home and free lunch at school. US teachers' wages have declined relative to those of other college-educated workers since the early 1990s, when they were at their most competitive—and when teacher attrition was much lower than it is today.[28]

Exacerbating inequalities, the salaries that teachers can expect are often lowest in the urban and poor rural school districts serving the most disadvantaged students with the greatest educational needs. And the supports teachers will receive in the critical first years of teaching—both mentoring and physical supports like adequate classrooms, materials, and supplies—are much less available in poorer districts, which then suffer greater turnover and must recruit greater numbers of teachers. They often do this, ironically, by sponsoring backdoor routes and fast tracks to teaching that only speed up the revolving door of candidates spinning through classrooms and back out of the system.

Whereas many countries fully subsidize an extensive program of teacher education for all candidates, the amount of preparation secured by teachers in the United States is left substantially to what they can individually afford and what programs are willing and able to offer given the resources of their respective institutions.[29] Although many US institutions are intensifying their programs in order to prepare more effective teachers, they lack the systemic policy supports for candidate subsidies and programmatic funding that their counterparts in other countries enjoy. And, where districts lack mentoring and induction supports, programs are continually called upon to increase the production of new recruits, who are then squandered when they land in and quickly leave an unsupportive system that treats them as utterly dispensable.

Despite the promise of professional standards for teaching, during times of teacher shortages, like the present, many states allow the hiring of individuals who have not met the standards. Unlike professions such as law and medicine, where practitioners cannot practice without having passed the bar or the medical licensing examination, nearly every state offers emergency permits or substandard licenses that allow individuals to enter without having completed—or sometimes even started—their preparation.

With most states experiencing shortages in 2017–18, more than one hundred thousand classrooms in the United States were staffed that year by instructors who were unqualified for their jobs.[30] About 90 percent of open teaching positions were created by teachers who had left the profession the year before. Meanwhile, states across the country have faced steeply declining enrollments in teacher education, which fell 35 percent between 2009 and 2015 as salaries and working conditions deteriorated. This affects students, who experience cancelled courses, larger class sizes, and unqualified teachers—many of whom leave quickly, creating churn and instability that further depresses student learning. It also wastes funds in districts, which may pay over $20,000 to replace each teacher who leaves.[31]

These shortages are most severe in low-income, high-minority schools, although in some key subjects—such as math, science, world languages, special education, and English language development—every kind of district has been hit by a lack of qualified applicants. Not only are underprepared teachers less effective on average,[32] they are also two to three times more likely to leave teaching than fully prepared teachers,[33] creating a revolving door that makes solving shortages an uphill climb. Teacher attrition—twice as high in the US as in high-performing countries like Finland and Singapore—makes meeting the demand for teachers rather like filling a leaky bucket.[34]

Managing Alternatives

The low salaries of teachers coupled with the debt of teacher training posed challenges we encountered in our study. The situation has been difficult in all of the states, but particularly so in Wisconsin, where in 2011, Governor Scott Walker proposed and the legislature passed Wisconsin Act 10, which reduced the compensation, retirement, health insurance, collective bargaining, and sick leave of public sector employees. Wisconsin teachers lost the right to collectively bargain over benefits, working conditions, and all aspects of pay. As salaries slipped and teacher education enrollments went down, a growing share of Milwaukee teachers entered the profession through alternative pathways, which provide abbreviated preparation with on-the-job training and support.[35] As a point of note, in Wisconsin, only Milwaukee—the state's one largely minority city—is allowed, by state law, to hire underprepared teachers.

As a consequence, Alverno College stretched to find ways to prepare teachers who had started teaching before they were fully trained. (This was also true of two other programs we studied.) The college created two graduate pathways: "on-the-job" and "preservice." The on-the-job program is for candidates who are currently working in a school as a paraprofessional or through an alternative credential program. The preservice graduate program is meant for career changers or others who have completed college. Most of the graduate courses are offered every other weekend or weeknights to ensure that students can earn an income during their preparation.

Among these candidates are teachers with Teach for America (TFA), a program that recruits recent college graduates to a two-year term in teaching through alternative routes in which they train on the job. At the time of our study, TFA was providing about 130 teachers in Milwaukee. While having teachers enter the classroom without undergoing the full sequence of coursework or a strong student teaching experience is "not our first choice," as an Alverno faculty member explained, the faculty wants to make sure that the preparation for the on-the-job candidates is "as good as it can be," because "they are teaching our children." The faculty found that supporting these candidates required more work from them:

> To create learning opportunities for people who have lots of chances to practice with kids, and fewer opportunities to be exposed to highly experienced mentors, . . . we have to be out in their schools more. We have to give demonstration lessons. We might be doing a video of them where they are bringing it in and using their own practice with kids as an opportunity to self-assess and see strengths in each other's practices . . .. Some of it is crisis control, like "What do you need to know tomorrow to go back into that classroom?" But it's also "and why?" It's not just, "do this and it will work miracles." It's "try this because . . ."

The TFA coordinator for Milwaukee described how one instructor re-designed her course for first-year teachers to help them with their crises and their feelings of being "overwhelmed and experiencing a lot of sadness because it is hard," creating a setting where corps members could "vent and complain" but also "build a team [to] move to solutions as a group." She also noted that Alverno faculty will reach out to her when they notice that a corps member needs more support and often co-observe in their class-rooms with TFA coaches to ensure that the corps member receives coher-ent feedback from both coaches. She sees the thirty or so graduates from Alverno staying in teaching at higher rates, beyond the two-year commit-ment after which most other TFA recruits leave, and using more student-centered practices in the classroom, "reflecting what they know about their students as learners. I see them planning intentional structures in their classrooms, fold[ing] different parts of content together: writing into sci-ence, reading into math, social justice across the curriculum . . . getting student voice involved."

For similar reasons, CU Denver created five pathways that vary in their size, structure, pace, and timing of preparation experiences to attract stu-dents from a wide range of backgrounds and experience. The pathways are specifically designed to accommodate differences in students' previous educational experiences and in their current life circumstances. In addi-tion to traditional undergraduate and graduate programs, CU Denver has developed a teacher residency program with the Denver Public Schools, an alternative certification program that includes Teach for America members, and a program for first-generation undergraduates (NxtGEN) who need fi-nancial and other supports to navigate college and licensure.

As is true at Alverno, TFA candidates at CU Denver take the same courses as other candidates and receive a more supported preparation that teaches them more student-centered practices than is true for many other TFA corps members. CU Denver's commitment to a common set of values and practices has been expressed in the CU Denver faculty's collaborative development of a well-articulated vision and common experiences that span the pathways.

Of particular note is the way that the university has sought to deal with the scarcity of resources for preparation—which often limit teacher diversity, since college students of color have difficulty affording the costs of teacher preparation—by creating the NxtGEN pathway. Launched in 2015 to attract and prepare first-generation college goers, many of whom are low-income students, students of color, and immigrants, the program is helping to diversify the student body at CU Denver in hopes that this will carry over to the Denver teaching force.

Rather than encouraging these valuable recruits to enter teaching underprepared, the unique arrangement blends full-time undergraduate coursework with a twenty-hours-per-week paraprofessional position in the Denver Public Schools, providing candidates with the financial wherewithal to pursue a college degree. Director Paula Chopra remarked that the NxtGEN students are overcoming the challenges first-generation, low-income, and immigrant college students often face and have developed their own positive identity as a group. In the words of Associate Dean Seidl, "Students [who often have] less social and cultural capital have actually developed more because of being part of the NxtGEN program."

These equity-focused strategies for creating paths to entry that protect students extend to High Tech High, which developed an apprenticeship model in addition to its internship model. Untrained teachers with no prior experience are placed as apprentices in the classrooms of veteran teachers, functioning like student teachers until they have demonstrated they are ready to take on their own class. Interns are experienced teachers undertaking the preparation program who have the capacity to learn these new pedagogies while teaching students responsibly. They, too, are closely mentored and supported. Thus, students are not endangered by this immersion approach to learning to teach—an important equity move.

Underwriting Costs for Teacher Candidates

Strong preparation for teaching enhances teachers' efficacy, increasing the likelihood they will remain in the profession: Comprehensively prepared teachers are half as likely to leave as those who enter the profession without training.[36] Nonetheless, given the rising costs of higher education, many prospective teachers understandably choose pathways that allow them to earn a salary while undergoing training, rather than taking on debt they must repay while earning a low salary. Evidence shows that college students' willingness to enter a lower-paying field is tied to the level of debt candidates must carry.[37]

Fortunately, there are ways to offer prospective teachers high-quality preparation without asking them to take on large student loans. The federal or state government can provide service scholarships or loan forgiveness programs to attract candidates to the fields and locations where they are needed most. These are paid back with several years of service in public schools. This approach is routinely used in medicine to recruit doctors for specialties and communities where they are needed.

The most successful approaches, like the North Carolina Teaching Fellows program, completely underwrite a student's education in exchange for a commitment to teach in the state for at least four years. Studies have found that the program has high rates of retention, with 75 percent still there after five years, and graduates are among the most effective teachers in the state.[38]

Funding Teacher Education

The programs we studied were able to provide high-quality coursework and greater attention to their candidates, including well-supervised clinical placements of significant duration, because their universities were willing to make strong commitments to this work and because they often raised additional funding from foundations and/or from external government grants—such as the federally funded Teacher Quality Partnerships.

But their situations are not typical of programs across the country. Most state funds for teacher education innovation have dried up, and federal funds have been dramatically reduced since 2000. Teacher education funding has often been inadequate, as universities historically have treated such programs as "cash cows," and states have typically allocated lower reimbursement ratios for programs of teacher education than they have for higher education programs in other professions, such as nursing, engineering, and medicine. Teacher preparation has often been treated as a liberal arts department that does not require the intensive clinical placements and supervision that high-quality programs depend upon.

Funding has been more threatened over the last decade as states cut budgets for public colleges and universities during the Great Recession that began in 2007. In some states, funds intended for teacher education programs are sent to the universities in ways that do not ensure they will actually be spent on those programs, and much of the intended funding can "leak out" of the pipeline before it reaches them. Thus, one area in which state action is needed is the establishment of funding ratios comparable to those for other clinically based professional programs, and the targeting of those funds so that they are spent on preparing teachers. While funding alone won't create innovative programs, the kinds of intensive attention these programs provide require a base of funding to enable personalization and strong clinical supports. Focusing more programs in this direction also requires the development of new relationships that connect schools and universities committed to deeper learning.

CREATING A POLICY FRAMEWORK

Whereas the pendulum politics driving US education tends to launch and undo policies on a regular basis, some other nations have taken a more systemic approach to the development of teacher knowledge and skill that makes well-trained teachers more widely available to all students. For example, many European and Asian nations we might consider peers or competitors routinely prepare teachers more extensively, at little or no cost to candidates and often with a stipend or salary while they train; pay them as much as entrants to competing occupations; ensure a thoughtful induction process; and provide them with more time for joint planning and professional development.[39] They demonstrate that it is possible to develop an infrastructure for preparing high-quality teachers who can stay in teaching and continue to improve.

Finland—which is the size of our median state—is perhaps the leading pioneer in teacher education. For more than thirty years, as part of a major reform of its education system, Finland has trained all of its teachers in two-year master's degree programs that feature strong content preparation and pedagogical preparation especially focused on learning to teach diverse learners, including those with special needs, and to develop a reflective, research-oriented approach to teaching. Finnish universities sponsor "model schools" as well as other partnership schools where extended clinical experience takes place. All teachers complete a master's thesis that involves them in research on practice. Programs aim to develop "highly developed problem solving capacity" that derives from teachers' deep understanding of the principles of learning and allows them to create "powerful learning environments" that continually improve as they learn to engage in a "cycle of self-responsible planning, action and reflection/

evaluation."[40] Spots in teacher education are highly competitive, and the government invests substantial funding in both teacher education and in research on teaching and teacher education. Salaries for teachers are equal across schools, with the exception of additional incentives for teachers who teach in hard-to-staff regions of the country.[41]

Since Finland took these steps, many other countries—including Australia, France, Germany, Hong Kong, Ireland, the Netherlands, New Zealand, Singapore, and Chinese Taipei (Taiwan), as well as several provinces in Canada—have moved most teacher education to the graduate level, adding in-depth pedagogical study and intensive clinical study in schools to strong preparation in the disciplines.[42]

The programs we studied had taken many of these same steps. However, they live in a hostile policy environment that guarantees that their work will be the exception and not the rule. One of the things the US can learn from other countries is how to build a policy infrastructure to make these opportunities available to all. This is especially critical given the dramatic inequalities in students' access to well-prepared and well-supported teachers, strongly correlated with race and class, which exacerbate all of the other deep and long-standing inequalities in the American educational system.

Such a policy infrastructure would invest adequately in high-quality teacher preparation, ensure that it is affordable for candidates, directly address issues of teacher shortages, develop and enforce standards for teaching grounded in what is known about development and learning, and increase the attractions to teaching as a career. In many ways, this would resemble the work that other countries—often the size of a US state—have done.

What States Can Do

To educate all our students to succeed in today's complex society requires that teachers have a greater repertoire of knowledge and skills than ever before, along with deep commitment to an equitable and socially just education system. States have considerable power to enable teachers to acquire these abilities and to support a well-prepared and equitably distributed teaching force. Past experiences demonstrate the strong influence a coherent policy agenda can have: For example, during the late 1980s, Connecticut and North Carolina enacted some of the most ambitious teacher legislation of any states. Both states, which serve large low-income and minority student populations, coupled major statewide increases in teacher salaries and greater funding equity across districts with intensive initiatives to improve preservice teacher standards, preparation quality, licensing, accreditation, and beginning teacher mentoring. Within a decade, both states posted large student achievement gains and substantial closing of their achievement gaps.[43] Massachusetts pursued similar reforms in the 1990s, with comparable effects. California is pursuing a like-minded agenda today.

As we have noted, the elements of a state agenda to accomplish preparation for deeper learning and equity should include:

- Incorporating features of the teaching knowledge and skills we've described here into the *standards* that inform licensing and accreditation.
- Developing or adopting *performance assessments* that reflect these standards as a means for licensing candidates.
- Moving to *performance-based accreditation* that takes these and other related candidate performances—along with other evidence of preparedness—into account in determining the capacity of programs to produce competent professionals, and eliminating those programs that cannot demonstrate this capacity.
- *Funding teacher preparation* like other clinical professions—at least at the level of nursing education—so as to support strong, well-supervised clinical practice and the development and maintenance of partnership schools that instantiate deeper learning practices in equitable ways.

Moreover, such an agenda would ensure that all teachers can afford to receive this stronger preparation and stay in the profession by:

- Offering *service scholarships and forgivable loans* that are paid off with four or five years of teaching service in the state's high-need fields or in high-priority schools serving large proportions of low-income students.
- Supporting *high-retention pathways* into teaching in high-need districts, such as teacher residencies.
- Raising teachers' *compensation* to a level that is competitive with what other college graduates receive while equalizing resources across districts, so that they can equitably compete in the labor market for good teachers. Compensation might include strategies beyond wages, like loan forgiveness, child care, health benefits, or housing supports.

The Federal Role

The federal government has a key role to play in expanding the supply of teachers and stimulating high-quality programs. There are strong precedents for this role in the field of medicine. Since 1944, the federal government has subsidized medical training and facilities to meet the needs of underserved populations, to fill shortages in particular fields, to improve the quality of training, and to increase diversity in the medical profession. The federal government also collects data to monitor and plan for medical manpower needs. This consistent commitment has contributed significantly to America's world-renowned system of medical training and care.

In teaching, the federal role can lead and leverage state actions by:

- Strengthening *incentives for program improvement*—including funding for teacher residencies that allow for strong clinical models, integration of new knowledge about learning and teaching, and strategies that enhance equity in the classroom. The competitively awarded Teacher Quality Partnership grants in Title II of the Higher Education Act—which funds a range of innovations, including teacher residencies—could play a major role in improving teacher education if funded at the originally authorized $300 million (rather than the current level, which is about a tenth of this amount). In addition, Title III of the Higher Education Act supports investments in minority-serving institutions and could be expanded and targeted to teacher education in these important settings. Since three-fourths of teachers of color serve in the schools with the highest proportions of students of color, and evidence suggests that these teachers enhance achievement for such students, the pipelines that enable their high-quality preparation are essential to the success of these teachers and children.[44]
- Providing matching grants to states for funding to well-designed *partnership schools*, just as the federal government underwrites teaching hospitals in medicine, so that this critical feature of high-quality preparation becomes universal and sustainable.
- Addressing teacher shortages in the highest-need locations and perennial shortage fields with *forgivable loans and scholarships* that cover the full costs of preservice preparation, repaid with four or five years of service. This is analogous to the federal role in medicine and would serve as a foundation for the civil rights guarantee the federal government should make to children most in need.

The federal initiatives outlined here could be undertaken for less than 1 percent of the $250 billion a year tax cut enacted in 2017, and within only a few years, they would build a strong teaching force that could last decades. Moreover, these proposals could save far more than they would cost. The savings would include the several billion dollars annually now wasted because of high teacher turnover as well as the costs of special education, grade retention, and remedial programs required because too many children are poorly taught. Long-term benefits, such as higher graduation rates and employment, would also be realized if all students had access to teachers who could help them become well-educated citizens in a knowledge-based society.

Although teacher education is only one component of what is needed to enable high-quality teaching, it is essential to the success of all the other reforms urged upon schools. For without thoughtful teachers who can ensure successful learning experiences for students who learn in different ways, there is nothing that governments can do to improve student learning.

The benefits of investing in strong preparation for all teachers will repay the costs many times over. With carefully crafted policies that rest on professional standards, invest in serious preparation, and make access to knowledge a priority for all teachers, it is possible to create a teaching profession that can meet the demands posed by a knowledge-based twenty-first-century society that must achieve equity as well as an active and educationally empowered citizenry.

APPENDIX A

Methodology

The Learning Policy Institute conducted this study between fall 2015 and fall 2017. To identify programs to serve as case study sites, the research team asked experts in the field of teacher preparation, as well as those who have experience working with new teachers, to identify programs that train teachers to use deeper learning pedagogies with strong equity tools in their teaching. The research team identified seven sites in which to conduct in-depth case studies through a rigorous and iterative process that included background research on the design and outcomes of each of the nominated programs (reviewing accreditation reports, program descriptions, survey and other data about candidates' and employers' perceptions), plus initial conversations with program leaders and faculty. The final sites were selected to ensure geographic and program diversity by size, type of program (undergraduate and graduate; traditional and alternative), and sector (public and private).

Prior to each site visit, we completed additional background research and interviews. We first reviewed each program's website, course catalogs, syllabi, admissions forms, publicly available data, and any available research, evaluations, or publications about the program. We sought out survey results from graduates, mentors, and employers; data about graduation, entry, and retention rates; and other outcome-related data. In addition, we spoke with program leaders and administrators to further develop our background knowledge about each site. Based on our review of this information, we worked with administrators at each site to schedule interviews and observations with key individuals and for activities that appeared to contribute to candidates' deeper learning preparation.

In spring 2016, the research team participated in data collection site visits spanning two to three days at each participating teacher preparation program. During these visits, the research team used semistructured protocols to interview key stakeholders from the selected programs, including faculty (deans, instructors, supervisors), mentors, current teacher candidates, and program graduates, as well as district leaders/liaisons, community organizations, and other key stakeholders involved in program development and support. Interviews lasted approximately forty-five to sixty minutes each and covered topics such as program characteristics and design, specific courses and their content, the design and conduct of clinical work and its connection to coursework, perceptions of critical features contributing to success and challenges, the development of local partnerships, political context and other factors that support or hinder implementation, and perceptions and evidence of effectiveness (such as course evaluation results and individual experiences).

The visits also included multiple observations of teacher preparation coursework and clinical work, including observations of program candidates' and graduates' classroom teaching. Moreover, we developed and administered an online survey of teacher candidates about the extent to which their program prepared them to teach for deeper learning. During our visits we also collected additional program documents and effectiveness data for review.

Across the seven sites, researchers interviewed 232 individuals through one-on-one interviews and focus groups and conducted a total of 46 observations of teacher preparation courses and K–12 classroom teaching at the partner school sites. A total of 477 program candidates received the survey; 294 completed it in 2016–17 for a response rate of

62 percent, with response rates ranging from 52 percent to 100 percent across the seven sites. Researchers also reviewed job placement and candidate, graduate, and employer data from each program, as well as lesson plans, assignments, and any relevant program documents. We conducted additional telephone interviews, document requests, and fact checking during the course of our analyses and writing.

Our analyses used triangulated evidence from the interviews, observations, survey results, and documents. To analyze the data we collected before, during, and after our visit, we engaged in a multistage approach. Upon the completion of our qualitative data collection at each site, we conducted a holistic review to identify key topics and emergent themes and determine preliminarily which were specific to particular sites and which were cross-cutting. Next, we re-reviewed and coded our transcribed interviews, observation notes, and documents to determine the frequency of the themes within and across programs and the ways in which they were demonstrated or expressed. We analyzed our survey data to produce frequency distributions and means for responses to each of the questions asked. After that, we continued to refine our analysis through an iterative process of comparing the interview, survey, and observation data to the themes that we first identified. We sought to triangulate our findings across multiple data sources, seeking confirmatory and disconfirmatory evidence, and to develop illustrations of the key points that emerged.

We analyzed the programs separately and produced detailed case study reports about each. These seven reports were reviewed by key informants in each of the programs, who contributed helpful suggestions to adjust and amplify our analyses. Each was also peer reviewed by independent scholars, whom we thank in the acknowledgments for each case. These cases are published and available as e-books through major online booksellers.

This book reports our cross-case analyses of the seven programs, which focused on identifying and illustrating themes that cut across the programs and how those themes emerged and were expressed in contextually specific ways. As in our analyses of the individual cases, we relied on evidence from interviews, observations, survey results, and documents. Members of the research team reviewed each other's interpretations and cross-checked the evidence to ensure that program data were fairly and accurately represented.

APPENDIX B

Program Curriculum Designs

ALVERNO COLLEGE
Undergraduate Early/Middle Childhood Education Program Requirements

Course	Title
FSS-125 or LA-230	First Semester Seminar Liberal Learning for Transfer Students
AC-151	Initial Social Interaction Assessment
CM-120	Communication Seminar 1
QL-122	Quantitative Literacy in the Modern World
FA-110	Fine Arts
HUM-150	Humanities
CM-125	Communication Seminar 2
QL-156	Mathematical Connections
CM-225	Communication Seminar 3
HFA-210	Humanities and Fine Arts Elective
SC-117	Physical Science
ADV-229	Intermediate-Level Event
BSC-215	Small-Group Behavior
GEC-300	The Globally Effective Citizen
HFA-310	Humanities and Fine Arts Elective
Elementary Education/Early Child Beginning	
ED-116	Human Relations Workshop
ED-201	Field Experience 1: Exploration in Teaching, Learning, and Assessment
PED-150 or PSY-110	Human Development Life Span Development
Praxis I/Core	
Elementary Education/Early Child Intermediate	
ED-215R	Field Experience 2: Engagement in Teaching, Learning, and Assessment
ED-220	Interview Assessment
ED-225	Literacy in Early Childhood
ED-325A	Literacy in Middle Childhood—Elementary
ED-338	Early Childhood Curriculum and Field
ED-396	Introduction to Exceptional Learner
ED-399	Formal Introduction to Advanced Work
HS-308	US History 1607–1900

MT-243	Fundamental Concepts / Mathematics 1
MT-244	Fundamental Concepts / Mathematics 2
ED-344	Field Experience 3: Teaching Math / Elementary Classroom
Elementary Education/Early Child Advanced	
ED-315	Field Experience 4: Immersion in Teaching, Learning and Assessment
PST-329	Praxis II Prep Seminar
Praxis II	
ED-412	Critical Issues in School and Society
Foundations of Reading Test	
ED-420	Portfolio/Interview Assessment
ED-475	Student Teaching Seminar
Student Teaching	
ED-435EC	Directed Observation / Teaching Early Childhood
ED-445MC	Directed Observation / Middle Childhood

Source: *Alverno Course Catalog*, https://catalog.alverno.edu/weekday-college/majors/education
-undergraduate-level/education-elementary-early-childhood/index.html.

BANK STREET
Childhood General Education Course Requirements

Childhood General Education		
Course requirements: This course listing does not indicate a suggested sequence. Course selection and sequencing is planned in consultation with the program director or advisor.		
Course	**Title**	**Credits**
EDUC 500	Child Development	3
or EDUC 800	The Social Worlds of Childhood [Prerequisite: EDUC 500 or EDUC 501 or permission of instructor]	3
EDUC 505	Language Acquisition and Learning in a Linguistically Diverse Society	2
EDUC 530	Foundations of Modern Education	3
or EDUC 531	Principles and Problems in Elementary and Early Childhood Education	3
EDUC 535	Science for Teachers (Grades N–6)	2
or EDUC 551	Science Inquiry for Children in the Natural Environment	3
EDUC 540	Mathematics for Teachers in Diverse and Inclusive Educational Settings (Grades N–6)	2
	Choose one of the following reading/literacy and language/literature pairs:	
EDUC 563	The Teaching of Reading, Writing, and Language Arts (Grades K–3)	3

(continues)

Course	Title	Credits
and EDUC 565 or	Children's Literature in a Balanced Reading Program (Focus on Grades 3–8)	3
EDUC 564	Language, Literature, and Emergent Literacy (Focus on Grades N–3)	3
and EDUC 568	Teaching Literacy in the Elementary Grades (Grades 2–6)	3
EDUC 590	Arts Workshop for Teachers (Grades N–6)	2
or EDUC 591	Music and Movement: Multicultural and Developmental Approaches in Diverse and Inclusive Settings (Grades N–6)	2
	Choose one of the following curriculum pairs:	
EDUC 510	Curriculum in Early Childhood Education (Grades N–3)	3
and EDUC 866 or	A Developmental-Interaction Approach to Teaching Geography in the Upper-Elementary Grades [Prerequisite: EDUC 510 or EDUC 514]	1
EDUC 514	Curriculum in Early Childhood Education: Developing Learning Environments and Experiences for Children of Diverse Backgrounds and Abilities	3
and EDUC 866 or	A Developmental-Interaction Approach to Teaching Geography in the Upper-Elementary Grades [Prerequisite EDUC 510 or EDUC 514]	1
EDUC 511	Curriculum Development Through Social Studies (Elementary and Middle School)	3
and EDUC 606 or	Block Building and Dramatic Play as an Integral Part of the Early Childhood Curriculum	1
EDUC 513	Social Studies as the Core of the Integrated Curriculum for Children with Special Needs (Grades 1–6)	3
and EDUC 606 or	Block Building and Dramatic Play as an Integral Part of the Early Childhood Curriculum	1
EDUC 517	Geography in the Social Studies Curriculum (Upper-Elementary and Middle School Years)	3
and EDUC 606	Block Building and Dramatic Play as an Integral Part of the Early Childhood Curriculum	1
EDUC 604	Family, Child, and Teacher Interaction in Diverse and Inclusive Educational Settings	2
EDUC 803	Developmental Variations [Prerequisite: EDUC 500, EDUC 501, or EDUC 800, or permission of instructor]	2
EDUC 808	The Study of Children in Diverse and Inclusive Educational Settings Through Observation and Recording [Prerequisite: EDUC 500 or EDUC 800 or permission of instructor]	3
	Elective credits as needed to complete the requirements of the program	0–2
EDUC 956	Childhood General Education Supervised Fieldwork/Student Teaching/Advisement	12

Course	Title	Credits
EDUC 990	Extended Field Experiences with Diverse Learners (for students completing fieldwork as student teachers)	0
or EDUC 991	Integrative Seminar in High Needs Educational Settings: Extended Field Experiences (for students completing fieldwork as head or assistant teachers) [with some exceptions])	1
STMD 100	State-Mandated Training on School Violence Prevention	0
STMD 105	State-Mandated Training on Child Abuse Identification and Reporting	0
STMD 110	State-Mandated Training in Dignity for All Students Act	0
	Total credits	**45**

Source: Bank Street College Graduate School of Education, *Catalog 2015–2016* (New York: Bank Street College of Education, 2015), 12, https://d2mguk73h8xisw.cloudfront.net/media/filer_public/filer_public/2015/08/26/gs_catalog_2015-16_1127.pdf.

CU DENVER

University classes in CU Denver's teacher preparation program are organized into three main categories: foundational core courses, content methods courses, and internship courses. These categories apply across the various pathways, although the sequencing and modality of courses may differ. Candidates take core foundational courses that provide them with a strong grounding in an understanding of schooling for equity in urban communities, learning theory, and pedagogical approaches. Candidates also complete a series of methods courses aligned to their content area and grade level (elementary or secondary). Internship courses encompass candidates' field experiences in schools.

University Course Sequence for Undergraduate and Graduate Pathways

	Core Courses	Content Methods	Internships
Undergraduate	• Social Foundations and Cultural Diversity in Urban Education • Classroom Communities • Data Decisions and Diverse Learners • Pedagogy	*Elementary* • Methods Block I (3 courses): Elementary Literacy Instruction and Assessment; Math Instruction and Assessment; Elementary Science Methods • Methods Block II (2 courses): Social Studies Through Children's Literature and Writing; Teaching Elementary Mathematics *Secondary* (varies depending on content area) • Secondary Literacy Instruction and Assessment (all) • Theory and Methods of Teaching (math, English, science, foreign language, history) • Adolescent Literature; Assessment in Math Education; Inquiry Science Pedagogy and Practices; Language Acquisition; Social Studies Methods	• Early Internship • Internship and Learning Community I • Internship and Learning Community II • Internship and Learning Community III *Note*: Candidates gradually increase their time in the placements/internships as they progress through the program. Time spent in clinical placements ranges from 1,000 to 1,200 hours, depending on undergraduate major.

(continues)

	Core Courses	Content Methods	Internships
Graduate	• Social Foundations and Cultural Diversity in Urban Education • Classroom Communities • Understanding Students in Urban Contexts • Exploring Diversity in Content and Pedagogy I & II	*Elementary* • Methods Block I (3 courses): Elementary Literacy Instruction and Assessment; Math Instruction and Assessment; Elementary Science Methods • Methods Block II (2 courses): Social Studies Through Children's Literature & Writing; Teaching Elementary Mathematics *Secondary* (varies depending on content area) • Secondary Literacy Instruction and Assessment (all) • Theory and Methods of Teaching (math, English, science, foreign language, history) • Adolescent Literature; Assessment in Math Education; Inquiry Science Pedagogy and Practices; Language Acquisition; Social Studies Methods	• Internship and Learning Community I • Internship and Learning Community II • Internship and Learning Community III *Note*: Candidates gradually increase their time in the placements/internships as they progress through the program. Time spent in clinical placements totals over 900 hours by the end of the program.

Sources: CU Denver Program Overview; Overview of Undergraduate and Graduate Programs, School of Education and Human Development.

The assignments in all of these courses align to the Essential Questions, Anchor Learning Experiences, and Program Level Assessments described in the chapters. The description of the core and subject-specific pedagogy courses below illustrate this alignment. They all require that candidates learn from their actual teaching experiences by using specific tools that engage them in reflecting, and adjusting continues throughout the program. Although the content methods courses expect candidates to have a firm grasp on the content they will teach, they also provide deeper learning experiences that enable candidates to increase their content knowledge. Here, too, the stream of knowledge and learning processes flow directly from how candidates are *prepared* to how they will eventually *teach* students.

Pedagogy 1: Exploring Diversity in Content and Pedagogy	The purpose of this course is to explore multiple aspects of complex curriculum and instructional processes, including (1) standards-based instruction; (2) instructional design; (3) formative and summative assessment, and (4) differentiation in curriculum and instruction so that meaningful instruction becomes accessible to all students.	Anchor Experience #5: Lesson Level Planning, Instruction & Assessment; students prepare for and engage in PLA #2 in this course.

STEM Secondary Pedagogy Capstone	This course provides secondary STEM education students with a capstone learning experience that integrates knowledge of STEM content, students, and school context into socially just and culturally responsive practices through the design and implementation of a unit in their internship classroom.	Anchor Experience #6: Unit Level Planning, Instruction & Assessment; students prepare for and engage in PLA #3 in this course.
Humanities Secondary Pedagogy Capstone	The course provides secondary English/language arts, foreign language, and social studies education students the opportunity to integrate knowledge of humanities content, disciplinary literacy, students, and school context into socially just and culturally responsive practices through the design and implementation of a unit in their internship classroom.	Anchor Experience #6: Unit Level Planning, Instruction & Assessment; students prepare for and engage in PLA #3 in this course.

HIGH TECH HIGH
Intern Program Course Descriptions—2015–2016 School Year

HTH 101. How People Learn: Principles of Educational Psychology
In this course, candidates learn major theories, concepts, principles, and research related to adolescent development and human learning. The course focuses on the physical, personal, intellectual, social, and ethical development of adolescents. Candidates learn how to create learning opportunities in their subject area to support student development, motivation, and learning.

HTH 102. Introduction to Teaching Methods and Content Standards
In this course, candidates will learn the skills and acquire the tools necessary to prepare for the beginning weeks of the school year. The course will focus on developing learning communities that promote student effort and engagement. Candidates explore ways to create an effective classroom environment, establish rapport with all students, and develop relationships with students' families.

HTH 103. Equity and Diversity: Social and Cultural Foundations
This course develops candidates' concept of culture and its implications for teaching and learning. Candidates learn about the background experiences, skills, languages, and abilities of diverse student groups, and how to apply appropriate pedagogical practices that provide access to the HTH curriculum and create an equitable community within the classroom. Candidates study different perspectives on teaching and learning, examine various theories of education, and identify the inequalities in academic outcomes in American education. The course will focus on how teacher and student expectations affect student achievement.

HTH 104. Classroom Management and Assessment (Field Experience)

This course is a comprehensive, rigorous introduction to classroom management, lesson planning, and assessment. This course provides candidates with the opportunity to work with their assigned mentor teacher and complete all requirements for their field experience report.

HTH 105. Teaching Methods, Curriculum Design, and Classroom Settings

This course provides candidates with instruction and practice for planning and delivering curriculum in their specific content area (math, English, science, humanities, art, Spanish), and in using appropriate instructional technology in the content area. Candidates will review and analyze the state content standards in their specific content area as part of this course.

HTH 106. Teaching Practicum I

This course provides candidates with the opportunity to apply and practice the learning theories covered in HTH 101 in a classroom setting in their subject area. The course provides opportunities to identify and solve subject-specific problems inherent in clinical teaching, lesson planning, and classroom organization and management. This course runs concurrently with HTH 105 (Teaching Methods).

HTH 107. Professional Portfolio Development I

This course introduces candidates to the portfolio development process. Candidates learn about the Teaching Performance Assessment requirements and the final exit interview, and how they relate to the Teaching Performance Expectations. The course helps candidates identify the types and quality of teaching artifacts that should be collected and presented in the portfolio.

HTH 108. Technology in Portfolio Development

This course is designed to assist and guide candidates in the use of technology to complete and assemble their professional teaching portfolio. The course combines training in the use of appropriate technologies and portfolio advisement for each of the portfolio domains, which candidates will be expected to present electronically.

HTH 109. Teaching Reading and Writing Across the Curriculum

This course prepares candidates to teach content-based reading and writing skills to all students. Candidates review and analyze the *Reading/Language Arts Framework for California Public Schools*, and learn to use effective strategies and methods aligned to the framework. The course provides practical experience in content-based reading and writing,

HTH 110. Teaching Practicum II

This course provides candidates with opportunities to connect learning theories with subject-specific pedagogical practices in the classroom. Candidates work with their mentor teachers in their subject area. This course runs concurrently with HTH 109 (Teaching Reading and Writing Across the Curriculum).

HTH 111. Technology in Instruction

This course will focus on the application of teaching and learning strategies that integrate technology into the learning process. Candidates will learn to use technology tools to prepare teaching materials, to develop curriculum, deliver instruction, evaluate student performance, and assist in course management.

HTH 112. Philosophy of Education: Teaching Performance Expectations
In this course, candidates review the full range of Teaching Performance Expectations identified in the *Standards for Quality and Effectiveness for Teacher Preparation Programs*. Candidates will research prominent educational philosophies and learning theory, and will articulate in writing their own philosophy of education.

HTH 113. Preparation to Teach English Language Learners
In this course, candidates learn about issues pertaining to the special needs and considerations of English learners in secondary classrooms. The course emphasizes understanding English language proficiency assessment and placements, and how to address a range of fluency and proficiency levels in a single classroom.

HTH 114. Teaching Practicum III
This course provides candidates with the opportunity to apply and practice the learning theories covered in their teacher training sessions in a classroom setting in their subject area. The course provides opportunities to identify and solve subject-specific problems inherent in clinical teaching, lesson planning, and classroom organization and management. This course runs concurrently with HTH 113 (Preparation to Teach English Language Learners) and HTH 116 (Assessment and Evaluation).

HTH 115. Healthy Environments
This course is designed to teach methods and best practices in the physical education and health curricula. Candidates review and analyze the California Physical Education and Health Frameworks and supplemental readings to develop their understanding of a comprehensive physical and health education system that will prepare adolescents for a lifelong commitment to physical activity and health.

HTH 116. Assessment and Evaluation
This course is designed to teach candidates how social, emotional, cognitive, and pedagogical factors impact students' learning outcomes. Candidates learn how a teacher's beliefs, expectations, and behaviors affect student learning. The course provides a professional perspective on teaching that includes an ethical commitment to teach every student effectively and to continue to develop as a professional educator.

HTH 117. Professional Portfolio Development II
This course provides candidates with the opportunity to assemble their professional portfolio. Each candidate will work with a portfolio advisor to examine the materials they have collected during their supervised fieldwork to determine which will be the best examples to use as evidence of their professional growth.

Source: High Tech High *Course Catalog*. For the current version, see https://www.hightechhigh.org /teachercenter/district-intern-program/.

MONTCLAIR
Undergraduate and Graduate Course Sequence

	Pre-professional	Content Methods	Clinical Experience
Undergraduate	• General Psychology I • Child Development I • Child Development II • Psychology of Exceptional Children and Youth (Early Childhood) • Perspectives EC/EL Education • Philosophical Orientation to Education • Math in Elementary Schools • Public Purposes of Education: Democracy and Schooling	*Early Childhood* • Arts and Creative Expression in Childhood • Mathematics in Elem Schools I • Working with Diverse Families • Problem solving in Science/Technology/ Math • Building Programs/Community in Inclusive EC • Initial Inquiry Literacy Dev. • Language and Literature for Young Children/Children's Literature for a Multicultural Society *Elementary* • Explorations: Science, Math, and Technology in EL Classrooms • Math in Elementary Schools II • Social Studies and the Arts in EL Classrooms • Cultural and Social Contexts of Families and Communities • Working with Diverse Families • Initial Inquiry Literacy Dev. • Reading: The Content Areas *Secondary* (varies depending on content area) • Teaching for Equity and Diversity • Inclusion in Middle and Secondary Schools • Educating English Language Learners • Language and Literacy Across the Curriculum • Assessment of Learning • Integrating Technology Across the School Curriculum	• Content Integration and Assessment in Inclusive EC Classrooms (Early Childhood) • Integrating EL Curric./Assess. for Equity/Diversity (Elementary) • Clinical Experience I: Inclusive EL Classrooms • Seminar I: Inclusive EL Classrooms *Student Teaching* • Clinical Experience II: Inclusive EL Settings • Seminar II: Inclusive EL Classrooms Time spent in clinical placement averages 690 hours depending on undergraduate major. • Fieldwork • Teaching for Learning • Methods Course • Teaching for Learning II • Student Teaching

	Pre-professional	Content Methods	Clinical Experience
Graduate	• Perspectives on Early Childhood and Elementary Education in a Diverse Society • Sociocultural Contexts of Disability and Inclusive Education • Methods of Research • Learning and Development in Children with and without Disabilities • Strengthening Partnerships with Families of Children with Disabilities • Literacy Strategies for the Inclusive Elementary Classroom • Observation and Assessment of Elementary Age Children with Disabilities • Principles and Practices in Inclusive Elementary Education *Secondary* • Teaching, Democracy, and Schooling • Technology Integration in the Classroom	*Elementary* • Social Studies and the Arts: Understanding Democracy in Elementary Classrooms • Integrating Science and Technology in Early Childhood and Elementary Classrooms • Mathematics Education in Elementary School *Secondary* (varies depending on content area) • Sociocultural Perspectives on Teaching and Learning • Meeting the Needs of English Learners • Inclusive Classrooms in Middle and Secondary Schools • Teaching for Learning I • Fieldwork • Content-Area METHODS course(s) • Student Teaching • Teaching for Learning II	• Curriculum Development and Assessment in Diverse Elementary Classrooms • Clinical Experience I in inclusive Early Childhood and Elementary Settings • Seminar I: Inclusive Early Childhood and Elementary Classrooms • Clinical Experience II in Inclusive Early Childhood Settings Time spent in clinical placements totals over 690 hours by the end of the program.

SAN FRANCISCO
Teaching Residency

STEP Secondary

The Master of Arts and the California preliminary single-subject teaching credential require a minimum of 45 quarter units of graduate work. These courses are distributed over a four-quarter sequence. The distribution of these units is determined by course schedule, accreditation requirements, and a specially designed tuition plan.

To fulfill program and credentialing requirements, the plan must include *all* of these courses and units:

Summer	Fall (incl. Pre-Fall)	Winter	Spring
EDUC289: *Centrality of Literacies in Teaching and Learning* **Units: 3**	**EDUC240:** *Adolescent Development & Learning* **Units: 3**		
EDUC246A: *Secondary Teaching Seminar* **Units: 4**	**EDUC244:** *Classroom Management & Leadership* **Units: 3**	**EDUC26C:** *Secondary Teaching Seminar* **Units: 4**	
EDUC262-8A: *Curriculum & Instruction* **Units: 3**	**EDUC246B:** *Secondary Teaching Seminar* **Units: 3**	**EDUC262-8C:** *Curriculum & Instruction* **Units: 3**	**EDUC246D:** *Secondary Teaching Seminar* **Units: 2–7**
	EDUC262-8B: *Curriculum & Instruction* **Units: 3**	**EDUC388A:** *Language Policies & Practice* **Units: 2**	**EDUC285:** *Supporting Students with Special Needs* **Units: 3**
	EDUC299: *Equity & Schooling* **Units: 3**		
	EDUC284A: *Designing Equitable Groupwork* **Units: 1**	**EDUC284B:** *Designing Equitable Groupwork* **Units: 1**	**EDUC262-8D:** *C&I Elective* **Units: 4** Or other elective **Units: 1–5**
Total: 10 units	**Total: 18 units**	**Total: 10 units**	**Total: 10 units**

Source: Stanford Graduate School of Education, *Stanford Teacher Education Program: Secondary Handbook 2017*, https://ed.stanford.edu/sites/default/files/step/page/step_secondary_handbook_2017-2018_1.pdf.

UNIVERSITY OF SAN FRANCISCO
San Francisco Teacher Residency Program

Program Details

SFTR residents work under the guidance and supervision of an expert teacher while training to become teachers of record. Residents spend five hours a day, five days a week, in an SFUSD classroom during the residency year. The entire cohort meets once a week for SFTR's practicum seminar, which places emphasis on the San Francisco context and focuses on the needs and issues specific to SFUSD students. Residents take late-afternoon and evening classes at USF to work toward their credential and master's degree.

Course Sequence

For more information and course descriptions, see https://www.usfca.edu/education/programs/masters-credential-programs/san-francisco-teacher-residency/program-details.

Term	Multiple Subjects	Single Subject
Summer 2016	• TEC 643: Education of Exceptional Children • TEC 600: Teaching, Learning & Technology • TEC 618: Teaching for Diversity & Social Justice • *SFTR Orientation & Practicum*	• TEC 643: Education of Exceptional Children • TEC 600: Teaching, Learning & Technology • TEC 618: Teaching for Diversity & Social Justice • *SFTR Orientation & Practicum*
Fall 2016	• TEC 602: MS C&I: Visual & Performing Arts • TEC 610: Learning & Teaching • TEC 611: Education of Bilingual Children • TEC 621: MS C&I: Early Literacy • *Practicum:* TEC 616: Student Teaching I • TEC 635: BCLAD Language & Culture of Emphasis	• TEC 610: Learning & Teaching • TEC 622: SS C&I: Academic Literacy • TEC 615-01/615-02: SS C&I (Science/Math) • *Practicum:* TEC 660: Student Teaching I • TEC 635: BCLAD Language & Culture of Emphasis
Intersession	• Option to take MS C&I: Visual & Performing Arts	• N/A
Spring 2017	• TEC 612: MS C&I: Reading & Language Arts in the Intermediate Grades • TEC 630: MS C&I: Social Studies • TEC 613: MS C&I: Math & Science *Practicum:* • TEC 605: MS Student Teaching II • TEC 606: MS Student Teaching III • TEC 607: MS Student Teaching III— Bilingual Authorization • TEC 642: Health Education (1) • TEC 636: BCLAD Methods & Materials in the Language of Emphasis	• TEC 611: Education of Bilingual Children • TEC 632 or 633: Curriculum & Instruction II • TEC 625: Teaching Adolescents) *Practicum:* • TEC 655: SS Student Teaching II • TEC 656: SS Student Teaching III • TEC 657: SS Student Teaching III— Bilingual Authorization • TEC 642: Health Education • TEC 636: BCLAD Methods & Materials in the Language of Emphasis

(continues)

Term	Multiple Subjects	Single Subject
Summer 2017	• TEC 663: MAT: Curriculum Currents & Controversies • TEC 664: MAT: Curriculum Development & Design	• TEC 663: MAT: Curriculum Currents & Controversies • TEC 664: MAT: Curriculum Development & Design
Or later *(up to two semesters' leave of absence)*	• TEC 663: MAT: Curriculum Currents & Controversies • TEC 664: MAT: Curriculum Development & Design	• TEC 663: MAT: Curriculum Currents & Controversies • TEC 664: MAT: Curriculum Development & Design

TRINITY UNIVERSITY

Candidates complete 30 credit hours in the one-year master's program and, over the duration of their eight-month teaching internship, they participate in over 1,000 hours of clinical experience.

Trinity MAT Coursework and Sequence

Elementary Course Requirements	Secondary Course Requirements
Summer	**Summer**
EDUC 5350 Curriculum Inquiry and Practice	EDUC 5350 Curriculum Inquiry and Practice
EDUC 5351 Teaching Inquiry and Practice	EDUC 5351 Teaching Inquiry and Practice
Fall	**Fall**
EDUC 5339 Teaching Diverse Learners	EDUC 5339 Teaching Diverse Learners
EDUC 5360 Pedagogics: Early Childhood—Grade 6	EDUC 5370 Pedagogics: Secondary
EDUC 5661 Clinical Practice: Early Childhood—Grade 6	EDUC 5671 Clinical Practice: Secondary
Spring	**Spring**
EDUC 5263 Graduate Intern Seminar: Early Childhood—Grade 6	EDUC 5273 Graduate Intern Seminar: Secondary
EDUC 5352 School Leadership, Supervision and Evaluation	EDUC 5352 School Leadership, Supervision and Evaluation
EDUC 5763 Advanced Clinical Practice: Early Childhood—Grade 6	EDUC 5773 Advanced Clinical Practice: Secondary

Source: Trinity University, Master of Arts in Teaching Course Sequence. For more information, see https://new.trinity.edu/academics/departments/education/master-arts-teaching/course-sequence.

APPENDIX C

Survey Results

TABLE 1 Percentage of Candidates Reporting That Their Program Trained Them to Engage and Support Students in Learning

The top number indicates the percentage of candidates who reported that their program trained them "adequately" or better and the number in parentheses beneath it indicates the percentage of candidates reporting that their program trained them "well" or "very well."

	Alverno (10)*	Bank Street (24)	High Tech High (21)	Montclair (137)	SFTR (31)	Trinity (30)	CU Denver (41)	All Sites (294)
Plan instruction based on how children and adolescents develop and learn	100% (80%)	100% (96%)	90% (72%)	99% (86%)	94% (77%)	100% (97%)	83% (56%)	95% (81%)
Relate classroom learning to the real world	100% (90%)	100% (96%)	100% (100%)	97% (83%)	97% (68%)	100% (93%)	95% (66%)	98% (82%)
Teach students from diverse ethnic, linguistic, and cultural backgrounds	100% (90%)	100% (79%)	100% (95%)	98% (87%)	94% (77%)	100% (86%)	98% (95%)	98% (87%)
Identify and address special learning needs with appropriate teaching strategies	100% (100%)	100% (83%)	95% (86%)	98% (80%)	94% (61%)	100% (90%)	85% (54%)	96% (77%)
Teach in ways that support English learners	90% (50%)	83% (67%)	100% (90%)	88% (58%)	94% (64%)	100% (80%)	95% (80%)	95% (67%)
Understand how factors in the students' environment outside of school may influence their life and learning	100% (100%)	100% (96%)	100% (85%)	97% (84%)	100% (87%)	100% (90%)	98% (85%)	98% (87%)
Use instructional strategies that promote active student learning	100% (90%)	100% (96%)	100% (100%)	99% (90%)	100% (90%)	100% (93%)	93% (66%)	98% (88%)
Teach students from a multicultural vantage point	100% (70%)	100% (83%)	100% (96%)	96% (79%)	100% (74%)	100% (80%)	93% (80%)	97% (80%)
Encourage students to see, question, and interpret ideas from diverse perspectives	100% (80%)	100% (92%)	100% (95%)	98% (84%)	100% (78%)	100% (87%)	90% (66%)	98% (83%)
Support students' social, emotional, physical, and cognitive development	100% (90%)	96% (91%)	95% (86%)	100% (91%)	97% (75%)	100% (93%)	88% (68%)	97% (86%)
Choose teaching strategies for different instructional purposes and to meet different student needs	100% (90%)	100% (96%)	100% (91%)	100% (91%)	97% (81%)	100% (97%)	90% (59%)	98% (83%)

*The number in parentheses under the program name represents the number of candidates in the program who responded to the question.

TABLE 2   **Percentage of Candidates Reporting That Their Program Trained Them to Plan Instruction and Design Learning Experiences for Students**

The top number indicates the percentage of candidates who reported that their program trained them "adequately" or better and the number in parentheses beneath it indicates the percentage of candidates reporting that their program trained them "well" or "very well."

	Alverno (10)*	Bank Street (24)	High Tech High (21)	Montclair (137)	SFTR (31)	Trinity (30)	CU Denver (39)	All Sites (292)
Develop curriculum that helps students learn content deeply so they can apply it in new situations	100% (100%)	100% (96%)	95% (85%)	99% (82%)	100% (71%)	100% (94%)	82% (64%)	97% (82%)
Design effective project-based instruction in which students conduct inquiries and produce ideas, solutions, or products	90% (80%)	100% (92%)	95% (90%)	95% (75%)	74% (39%)	100% (76%)	82% (51%)	92% (71%)
Help students learn to think critically and solve problems	90% (90%)	100% (92%)	95% (85%)	99% (86%)	100% (81%)	100% (93%)	99% (54%)	97% (82%)
Develop curriculum that builds on students' experiences, interests, and abilities	100% (90%)	100% (87%)	90% (85%)	96% (82%)	97% (52%)	100% (94%)	90% (64%)	96% (78%)
Create interdisciplinary curriculum	90% (80%)	100% (92%)	95% (86%)	95% (70%)	74% (42%)	100% (83%)	79% (46%)	91% (69%)
Help students learn to communicate orally, in writing, graphically, and using technology	100% (90%)	100% (80%)	95% (76%)	99% (81%)	94% (55%)	100% (90%)	90% (56%)	97% (76%)
Use technology to support instruction in the classroom	100% (90%)	88% (34%)	90% (80%)	98% (80%)	87% (48%)	100% (90%)	82% (49%)	93% (70%)

*The number in parentheses under the program name represents the number of candidates in the program who responded to the question.

TABLE 3   **Percentage of Candidates Reporting That Their Program Trained Them to Assess Student Learning**

The top number indicates the percentage of candidates who reported that their program trained them "adequately" or better and the number in parentheses beneath it indicates the percentage of candidates reporting that their program trained them "well" or "very well."

	Alverno (10)*	Bank Street (24)	High Tech High (20)	Montclair (137)	SFTR (31)	Trinity (30)	CU Denver (39)	All Sites (291)
Give productive feedback to students to guide their learning	100%	100%	100%	96%	97%	100%	92%	97%
	(90%)	(92%)	(90%)	(79%)	(65%)	(90%)	(74%)	(80%)
Help students learn how to assess their own learning	90%	100%	95%	96%	84%	100%	92%	95%
	(90%)	(87%)	(95%)	(77%)	(55%)	(73%)	(59%)	(74%)
Use a variety of assessments, including observations, papers, portfolios, or performance tasks, to determine strengths and needs to inform instruction	100%	96%	95%	99%	97%	100%	92%	97%
	(100%)	(88%)	(85%)	(86%)	(71%)	(93%)	(77%)	(84%)

*The number in parentheses under the program name represents the number of candidates in the program who responded to the question.

TABLE 4   **Percentage of Candidates Reporting That Their Program Trained Them to Create and Maintain Effective Environments for Student Learning**

The top number indicates the percentage of candidates who reported that their program trained them "adequately" or better and the number in parentheses beneath it indicates the percentage of candidates reporting that their program trained them "well" or "very well."

	Alverno (10)*	Bank Street (24)	High Tech High (20)	Montclair (137)	SFTR (31)	Trinity (30)	CU Denver (39)	All Sites (291)
Engage students in cooperative group work as well as independent learning	100% (90%)	100% (96%)	100% (95%)	99% (89%)	94% (90%)	100% (93%)	92% (79%)	98% (89%)
Help students become self-motivated and self-directed	100% (90%)	100% (87%)	100% (85%)	96% (76%)	77% (52%)	100% (77%)	90% (64%)	94% (74%)
Set norms for building a productive classroom community	100% (100%)	96% (84%)	100% (95%)	98% (85%)	90% (90%)	97% (94%)	92% (79%)	96% (87%)
Develop students' questioning and discussion skills	100% (90%)	100% (96%)	100% (95%)	99% (79%)	97% (74%)	100% (87%)	92% (74%)	98% (82%)
Develop a classroom environment that promotes social/emotional development and individual and group responsibility	100% (80%)	96% (83%)	100% (90%)	100% (86%)	97% (74%)	97% (94%)	92% (77%)	98% (84%)

TABLE 5   **Percentage of Candidates Reporting That Their Program Trained Them to Engage in Effective Teaching Practices**

The top number indicates the percentage of candidates who reported that their program trained them "adequately" or better and the number in parentheses beneath it indicates the percentage of candidates reporting that their program trained them "well" or "very well."

	Alverno (10)*	Bank Street (24)	High Tech High (20)	Montclair (137)	SFTR (31)	Trinity (30)	CU Denver (39)	All Sites (291)
Collaborate with colleagues to address students' needs and to improve instruction	100% (80%)	100% (88%)	100% (90%)	96% (80%)	94% (71%)	97% (90%)	95% (72%)	96% (80%)
Work well with families as partners to better understand students and to support their learning	100% (60%)	100% (88%)	100% (75%)	91% (70%)	87% (55%)	100% (90%)	92% (64%)	93% (71%)

*The number in parentheses under the program name represents the number of candidates in the program who responded to the question.

TABLE 6 **Percentage of Candidates Reporting That They Experienced the Following Strategies in Their Coursework**

The top number indicates the percentage of candidates who reported that their program trained them "adequately" or better and the number in parentheses beneath it indicates the percentage of candidates reporting that their program trained them "well" or "very well."

	Alverno (10)*	Bank Street (24)	High Tech High (20)	Montclair (137)	SFTR (31)	Trinity (30)	CU Denver (38)	All Sites (290)
Project-based instruction	100%	100%	100%	96%	68%	90%	89%	92%
	(100%)	(92%)	(95%)	(75%)	(40%)	(63%)	(58%)	(71%)
Culturally responsive practices (that bring student experiences and/or community knowledge)	100%	100%	100%	96%	81%	100%	97%	96%
	(80%)	(92%)	(90%)	(80%)	(55%)	(87%)	(84%)	(80%)
Differentiation of instruction to meet different student needs	100%	96%	100%	97%	97%	97%	95%	97%
	(100%)	(84%)	(85%)	(83%)	(65%)	(90%)	(73%)	(81%)
Collaborative learning and group work	100%	100%	100%	99%	100%	100%	95%	99%
	(100%)	(96%)	(100%)	(90%)	(77%)	(94%)	(82%)	(90%)
Presentations of student work that include products, papers, or oral discussions/defenses	100%	100%	100%	98%	87%	97%	97%	97%
	(80%)	(79%)	(100%)	(87%)	(48%)	(76%)	(79%)	(80%)
Opportunities for students to research and investigate ideas or events	90%	96%	100%	94%	87%	97%	92%	93%
	(80%)	(82%)	(95%)	(75%)	(50%)	(70%)	(63%)	(72%)
Opportunities for students to revise their work in response to feedback	90%	92%	100%	94%	90%	97%	92%	94%
	(70%)	(84%)	(95%)	(73%)	(61%)	(80%)	(68%)	(74%)
Opportunities for students to raise questions, discuss, and debate ideas	90%	96%	100%	99%	97%	100%	89%	97%
	(70%)	(92%)	(95%)	(83%)	(65%)	(87%)	(63%)	(80%)
Opportunities for students to engage in performance-based assessments that require them to show what they have learned in applied projects, papers, or tasks	90%	96%	100%	99%	87%	100%	92%	96%
	(80%)	(87%)	(90%)	(84%)	(65%)	(94%)	(71%)	(81%)

*The number in parentheses under the program name represents the number of candidates in the program who responded to the question.

TABLE 7   Percentage of Candidates Reporting That They Experienced the Following Strategies in Their Field Placement

The top number indicates the percentage of candidates who reported that their program trained them "adequately" or better and the number in parentheses beneath it indicates the percentage of candidates reporting that their program trained them "well" or "very well."

	Alverno (10)*	Bank Street (24)	High Tech High (19)	Montclair (136)	SFTR (31)	Trinity (30)	CU Denver (38)	All Sites (288)
Project-based instruction	90% (80%)	88% (79%)	100% (89%)	89% (67%)	58% (43%)	90% (55%)	82% (53%)	85% (65%)
Culturally responsive practices (that bring student experiences and/or community knowledge)	90% (60%)	88% (67%)	100% (95%)	97% (76%)	87% (68%)	100% (80%)	89% (55%)	94% (74%)
Differentiation of instruction to meet different student needs	100% (90%)	96% (71%)	100% (100%)	96% (84%)	90% (81%)	97% (94%)	89% (68%)	95% (83%)
Collaborative learning and group work	90% (80%)	96% (92%)	100% (100%)	97% (87%)	94% (77%)	97% (93%)	92% (74%)	96% (86%)
Presentations of student work that include products, papers, or oral discussions/defenses	90% (80%)	96% (79%)	100% (100%)	93% (75%)	84% (65%)	100% (83%)	84% (61%)	92% (75%)
Opportunities for students to research and investigate ideas or events	90% (80%)	92% (75%)	100% (100%)	90% (69%)	81% (58%)	97% (65%)	84% (58%)	90% (69%)
Opportunities for students to revise their work in response to feedback	90% (70%)	79% (71%)	100% (100%)	93% (72%)	81% (68%)	93% (70%)	76% (61%)	89% (71%)
Opportunities for students to raise questions, discuss, and debate ideas	90% (70%)	96% (82%)	100% (100%)	97% (81%)	90% (71%)	100% (83%)	82% (58%)	94% (78%)
Opportunities for students to engage in performance-based assessments that require them to show what they have learned in applied projects, papers, or tasks	90% (80%)	96% (83%)	100% (100%)	95% (82%)	87% (65%)	100% (83%)	87% (63%)	93% (78%)

*The number in parentheses under the program name represents the number of candidates in the program who responded to the question.

TABLE 8   Percentage of Candidates Reporting That Their Program Prepared Them for Teaching

The top number indicates the percentage of candidates who reported that their program trained them "adequately" or better and the number in parentheses beneath it indicates the percentage of candidates reporting that their program trained them "well" or "very well."

	Alverno (8)*	Bank Street (20)	High Tech High (16)	Montclair (126)	SFTR (30)	Trinity (27)	CU Denver (35)	All Sites (263)
	100%	100%	100%	99%	100%	100%	91%	99%
	(100%)	(95%)	(94%)	(89%)	(93%)	(96%)	(60%)	(88%)

*The number in parentheses under the program name represents the number of candidates in the program who responded to the question.

NOTES

CHAPTER 1

1. Anna Brown, "Key Findings About the American Workforce and the Changing Job Market," Pew Research Center, October 6, 2016, http://www.pewresearch.org/fact -tank/2016/10/06/key-findings-about-the-american-workforce-and-the-changing -job-market/.
2. Joergen Oerstroem Moeller, "Struggle to Prepare the Workforce for a Fast Changing World" (article prepared for the 6th Asian-Europe Foundation Conference, Singapore, October 9–13, 2017), https://yaleglobal.yale.edu/content/struggle-prepare -workforce-fast-changing-world-0; Bureau of Labor Statistics, *Occupational Outlook Handbook* (Washington, DC: US Department of Labor, 2006); World Economic Forum, *The Future of Jobs: Employment, Skills and Workforce Strategy for the Fourth Industrial Revolution,* World Economic Forum Report, January 2016.
3. National Research Council, *Education for Life and Work: Developing Transferable Knowledge and Skills in the 21st Century* (Washington, DC: National Academies Press, 2013).
4. Southern Education Foundation (SEF), "Low Income Students Now a Majority in the Nation's Public Schools," Research Bulletin, SEF, January 2015, http://www .southerneducation.org/getattachment/4ac62e27-5260-47a5-9d02-14896ec3a531 /A-New-Majority-2015-Update-Low-Income-Students-Now.aspx.
5. Linda Darling-Hammond et al., *Powerful Teacher Education: Lessons from Exemplary Programs* (San Francisco: Jossey-Bass, 2006).
6. K. Brooke Stafford-Brizard, "Building Blocks for Learning: A Framework for Comprehensive Student Development," Turnaround for Children, 2015, https://www .turnaroundusa.org/wp-content/uploads/2016/03/Turnaround-for-Children -Building-Blocks-for-Learningx-2.pdf.
7. Maria Montessori, *The Discovery of the Child* (Madras: Kalkshetra Publications Press, 1948).
8. For further discussion, see, for example, Jeannie Oakes, Martin Lipton, Lauren Anderson, and Jamy Stillman, *Teaching to Change the World,* 5th ed. (New York: Routledge, 2018).
9. Roland G. Tharp and Ronald Gallimore, *Rousing Minds to Life: Teaching, Learning, and Schooling in Social Context* (Cambridge, UK: Cambridge University Press, 1988); Michael Cole, Yrjo Engestrom, and Olga Vasquez, eds., *Mind, Culture, and Activity: Seminal Papers from the Laboratory of Comparative Human Cognition* (Cambridge, UK: Cambridge University Press, 1997).
10. For a review, see Carol D. Lee, "2008 Wallace Foundation Distinguished Lecture—The Centrality of Culture to the Scientific Study of Learning and Development: How an Ecological Framework in Education Research Facilitates Civic Responsibility," *Educational Researcher* 37, no. 5 (2008): 267–79.
11. Jal Mehta, "Deeper Learning Has a Race Problem," *Education Week,* June 20, 2014.
12. David Jonassen and Susan Land, eds., *Theoretical Foundations of Learning Environments* (New York: Routledge, 2012), vi.

13. John D. Bransford, Ann L. Brown, and Rodney Cocking, eds., *How People Learn: Mind, Brain, Experience, and School* (Washington, DC: National Academies Press, 1999); John D. Bransford and M. Suzanne Donovan, "Scientific Inquiry and How People Learn," in *How Students Learn: History, Mathematics, and Science in the Classroom*, eds. Suzanne Donovan and John D. Bransford (Washington, DC: National Academies Press, 2005), 397–420.

14. Kurt W. Fischer and T. R. Bidell, "Dynamic Development of Action and Thought," in *Handbook of Child Psychology*, vol. 1, *Theoretical Models of Human Development*, ed. Richard M. Lerner (Hoboken, NJ: John Wiley & Sons, 2006), 313–99; Arnold M. Rose, *Human Behavior and Social Processes: An Interactionist Approach* (New York: Routledge, 2013).

15. Jacqueline Ancess, *Beating the Odds: High Schools as Communities of Commitment* (New York: Teachers College Press, 2003); Deborah Meier, *The Power of Their Ideas: Lessons for America from a Small School in Harlem* (Boston: Beacon Press, 2002); Linda Darling-Hammond, Nicole Ramos-Beban, Rebecca Padnos Altamirano, and Maria E. Hyler, *Be the Change: Reinventing School for Student Success* (New York: Teachers College Press, 2015); Diane Friedlaender et al., "Student-Centered Schools: Closing the Opportunity Gap," Research Brief, Stanford Center for Opportunity Policy in Education, June 2014.

16. Linda Darling-Hammond et al., *Powerful Learning: What We Know About Teaching for Understanding* (San Francisco: John Wiley & Sons, 2015).

17. Darling-Hammond et al., *Powerful Teacher Education*.

18. Organization for Economic Cooperation and Development (OECD), *Education at a Glance 2015: OECD Indicators*, https://www.oecd-ilibrary.org/education/education-at-a-glance-2015_eag-2015-en.

19. John Dewey, *The Sources of a Science of Education* (New York: Horace Liveright, 1929/Read Books, 2013), 12, 20–21.

20. Bransford, Brown, and Cocking, eds., *How People Learn*.

21. Darling-Hammond et al., *Powerful Teacher Education*.

22. James D. Anderson, *The Education of Blacks in the South, 1860–1935* (Chapel Hill: University of North Carolina Press, 1988).

23. Deborah A. Harmon, "Culturally Responsive Teaching Though a Historical Lens: Will History Repeat Itself?" *Interdisciplinary Journal of Teaching and Learning* 2, no. 1 (2012): 12–22.

24. Pedro Noguera, Linda Darling-Hammond, and Diane Friedlaender, *Equal Opportunity for Deeper Learning*, Deeper Learning Research Series (Boston, MA: Jobs for the Future, 2015).

25. Geneva Gay, *Culturally Responsive Teaching: Theory, Research, and Practice* (New York: Teachers College Press, 2000), 29; see also Gloria Ladson-Billings, "Toward a Theory of Culturally Relevant Pedagogy," *American Educational Research Journal* 32, no. 3 (1995): 465–91; Etta R. Hollins, Joyce Elaine King, and Warren C. Hayman, eds. *Preparing Teachers for Cultural Diversity* (New York: Teachers College Press, 1997).

26. Luis Moll, Cathy Amanti, Deborah Neff, and Norma González, "Funds of Knowledge for Teaching: Using a Qualitative Approach to Connect Homes and Classrooms," in *Funds of Knowledge*, eds. Norma González, Luis C. Moll, and Cathy Amanti (New York: Routledge, 2005), 71–88.

27. David F. Labaree, "School Syndrome: Understanding the USA's Magical Belief That Schooling Can Somehow Improve Society, Promote Access, and Preserve Advantage," *Journal of Curriculum Studies* 44, no. 2 (2012): 143–63.

28. David B. Tyack and Larry Cuban, *Tinkering Toward Utopia* (Cambridge, MA: Harvard University Press, 1995), 85.

29. Alliance for Excellent Education, "A Time for Deeper Learning: Preparing Students for a Changing World," Policy Brief, May 2011, 3, https://all4ed.org/reports-factsheets/a-time-for-deeper-learning-preparing-students-for-a-changing-world/; Barnett Berry, "Teacher Leadership and Deeper Learning for all Students," Center for Teaching

Quality, 2016 https://www.teachingquality.org/wp-content/uploads/2018/03/Deeper Learning_CTQ.pdf; Pedro Noguera, Linda Darling-Hammond, and Diane Friedlaender, "Equal Opportunity for Deeper Learning: Executive Summary," Deeper Learning Research Series, Jobs for the Future, 2015.

30. Alliance for Excellent Education, "A Time for Deeper Learning," 1.
31. US Department of Education, National Center for Education Statistics, "Fast Facts: Back to School Statistics," https://nces.ed.gov/fastfacts/display.asp?id=372.
32. Southern Education Foundation, "Low Income Students Now a Majority."
33. US Department of Education, National Center for Education Statistics, "English Language Learners in Public Schools," in *The Condition of Education 2017*, NCES 2017–144, https://nces.ed.gov/fastfacts/display.asp?id=96.
34. US Department of Education, National Center for Education Statistics, *The Condition of Education 2017*, NCES 2017-144, https://nces.ed.gov/pubsearch/pubsinfo.asp?pubid =2017144.
35. Elizabeth G. Cohen and Rachel A. Lotan, *Designing Groupwork: Strategies for the Heterogeneous Classroom*, 3rd ed. (New York: Teachers College Press, 2014).

CHAPTER 2

1. Kenneth Zeichner, "Ability-Based Teacher Education: Elementary Teacher Education at Alverno College," in *Studies of Excellence in Teacher Education: Preparation in the Undergraduate Years*, ed. Linda Darling-Hammond (Washington, DC: American Association of Colleges for Teacher Education, 2000), 1.
2. For example, see "The North Carolina Recent Graduate Survey Report 2012–13," North Carolina A&T State University, May 2014, http://www.ncat.edu/ced/aboutus /accreditation/report/Exhibits/1.4.I.a-NCAT-final-201213.pdf; "Ohio Educator Preparation Provider Performance Report," Hiram College, 2017, http://www.hiram .edu/wp-content/uploads/2018/04/2017EPPReport.pdf.
3. Linda Darling-Hammond et al., *Powerful Teacher Education: Lessons from Exemplary Programs* (San Francisco: Jossey-Bass, 2006).
4. This section draws on Linda Darling-Hammond and John Bransford, eds., *Preparing Teachers for a Changing World: What Teachers Should Learn and Be Able to Do* (San Francisco: John Wiley & Sons, 2007).
5. Dan C. Lortie, *School Teacher: A Sociological Inquiry* (Chicago: University of Chicago Press, 1975), 61.
6. Mary M. Kennedy, "The Role of Preservice Teacher Education," in *Teaching as the Learning Profession: Handbook of Policy and Practice*, eds. Linda Darling-Hammond and Gary Sykes (San Francisco,: Jossey-Bass, 1999), 54–85.
7. Sharon Feiman-Nemser and Margret Buchmann, "Describing Teacher Education: A Framework and Illustrative Findings from a Longitudinal Study of Six Students," *Elementary School Journal* 89, no. 3 (1989): 365–78.
8. Kennedy, "The Role of Preservice Teacher Education."
9. Donald A. Schön, *Educating the Reflective Practitioner: Toward a New Design for Teaching and Learning in the Professions* (San Francisco: Jossey-Bass, 1987).
10. See, for example, P. Chin and T. Russell, "Structure and Coherence in a Teacher Education Program: Addressing the Tensions Between Systemics and the Educative Agenda," in *Proceedings of the Annual Meeting of the Canadian Society for the Study of Education*, Montreal, May 1995; Jon J. Denton and Lorna J. Lacina, "Quantity of Professional Education Coursework Linked with Process Measures of Student Teaching," *Teacher Education and Practice*, 1982: 39–64.
11. Magdalene Lampert, *Teaching Problems and the Problems of Teaching* (New Haven, CT: Yale University Press, 2003), 2.
12. See, for example, Arthur Levine, "Educating School Teachers," Report #2, Education Schools Project, September 2006, http://edschools.org/.
13. Darling-Hammond and Bransford, *Preparing Teachers for a Changing World*, 391–93.
14. UCan, "Alverno College," n.d., http://members.ucan-network.org/alverno.

15. Alverno College, *In Her Own Words* (Milwaukee, WI: Alverno College, n.d.), 13, unpublished document.
16. Nancy Nager and Edna Shapiro, "A Progressive Approach to the Education of Teachers: Some Principles from Bank Street College of Education," Occasional Paper Series 18 (2007): 1, https://educate.bankstreet.edu/occasional-paper-series/vol2007/iss18/1/.
17. Bank Street College of Education, "History," n.d., https://www.bankstreet.edu/about-bank-street/history/.
18. Jaime G. A. Grinberg, *Teaching Like That: The Beginnings of Teacher Education at Bank Street* (New York: Peter Lang, 2005).
19. Lucy Sprague Mitchell, as cited on the Bank Street College website, https://www.bankstreet.edu/about-bank-street/leadership/cabinet/mission-credo/.
20. Nager and Shapiro, "A Progressive Approach to the Education of Teachers."
21. Bank Street College Graduate School of Education, *Catalog 2015–2016* (New York: Bank Street College of Education, 2015), https://d2mguk73h8xisw.cloudfront.net/media/filer_public/filer_public/2015/08/26/gs_catalog_2015-16_1127.pdf.
22. Linda Darling-Hammond and Maritza Macdonald, "Where There Is Learning There Is Hope: The Preparation of Teachers at the Bank Street College of Education," in *Studies of Excellence in Teacher Education: Preparation at the Graduate Level*, ed. Linda Darling-Hammond et al. (Washington, DC: *AACTE Publications*, 2000), 1–95.
23. Lucy Sprague Mitchell, "A Cooperative School for Student Teachers," *Progressive Education* 8 (1931): 251–55.
24. Ira Lit and Linda Darling-Hammond, *The Threads They Follow: Bank Street Teachers in a Changing World* (Stanford, CA: Stanford Center for Opportunity Policy in Education, 2015).
25. UC Denver School of Education and Human Development, "Employer Survey Report," Spring 2015.
26. New Jersey Department of Education, "Montclair State University, Unit-Level Report," 2014, http://www.state.nj.us/education/educators/rpr/preparation/providers/2014/Montclair/EPP.pdf.
27. "Teacher Preparation Performance Summary," Montclair State University, 2016.
28. San Francisco Teacher Residency, "Vision of Transformative Teaching," n.d.
29. San Francisco Teacher Residency, "Program Overview," n.d., http://www.sfteacher-residency.org/programs/.
30. San Francisco Teacher Residency, "Impact," 2016, http://www.sfteacherresidency.org/impact/.
31. National Center for Teacher Residencies, *Measuring UTRU Network Program Impact* (Chicago: National Center for Teacher Residencies, 2015).
32. Julia Koppich, "Trinity University," in *Studies of Excellence in Teacher Education: Preparation in a Five-Year Program*, ed. Linda Darling-Hammond (Washington, DC: American Association of Colleges for Teacher Education; New York: National Commission on Teaching and America's Future, 2000), 1–48, http://files.eric.ed.gov/fulltext/ED468995.pdf.

CHAPTER 3

1. Linda Darling-Hammond and John Bransford, eds., *Preparing Teachers for a Changing World: What Teachers Should Learn and Be Able to Do* (Hoboken, NJ: John Wiley & Sons, 2007).
2. John D. Bransford, Ann L. Brown, and Rodney Cocking, eds., *How People Learn: Mind, Brain, Experience, and School* (Washington, DC: National Academies Press, 1999).
3. John Dewey, *The Child and the Curriculum* (Chicago: University of Chicago Press, 1902).
4. Darling-Hammond and Bransford, *Preparing Teachers for a Changing World*; Linda Darling-Hammond et al., *Powerful Teacher Education: Lessons from Exemplary Programs* (San Francisco: Jossey-Bass, 2006).

5. Barbara Biber, "What Is Bank Street?" (lecture originally given at the Bank Street College of Education Convocation Luncheon, November 27, 1973), 1–2, https://www.bankstreet.edu/archives/bank-street-thinkers/ what-bank-street/.
6. Darling-Hammond and Bransford, *Preparing Teachers for a Changing World*, 92–93.
7. Bank Street College Graduate School of Education, *Catalog 2015–2016* (New York: Bank Street College of Education, 2015), 74, https://d2mguk73h8xisw.cloudfront .net/media/filer_public/filer_public/2015/08/26/gs_catalog_2015-16_1127.pdf.
8. Bank Street College Graduate School of Education, *Catalog 2015–2016*.
9. Bank Street College Graduate School of Education, *Catalog 2017–2018* (New York: Bank Street College of Education, 2017), 97, https://d2mguk73h8xisw.cloudfront .net/media/filer_public/filer_public/2017/08/31/gs_catalog_2017-2018_1515.pdf.
10. Bank Street College Graduate School of Education, *Catalog 2015–2016*, 74.
11. Bank Street College Graduate School of Education, *Catalog 2015–2016*, 80.
12. Bank Street College Graduate School of Education, *Catalog 2015–2016*, 84.
13. Zoltan Sarda and Amy Reising "Health/Child Development/Adolescent Psychology," Syllabus, High Tech High, San Diego, CA, 2013, 1.
14. Sarda and Reising, "Health/Child Development/Adolescent Psychology."
15. Luis C. Moll and N. Gonzalez, "Engaging Life: A Funds of Knowledge Approach to Multicultural Education," in *Handbook of Research on Multicultural Education*, 2nd ed., ed. James A. Banks and Cherry A. M. Banks (San Francisco: Jossey-Bass, 2004), 699–715.
16. For more information about San Francisco Board of Education Parent Advisory Council, see http://pacsf.org/.
17. High Tech High Course 107.
18. CU Denver, *2014–2015 Graduate Catalog*, http://catalog.ucdenver.edu/preview _course_nopop.php?catoid=16&coid=107801.
19. CU Denver, *2014–2015 Graduate Catalog*, http://catalog.ucdenver.edu/preview _course_nopop.php?catoid=16&coid=107824.
20. Lee S. Shulman, "Knowledge and Teaching: Foundations of the New Reform," *Harvard Educational Review* 57, no. 1 (1987): 1–22.
21. Shulman, "Knowledge and Teaching," 9.
22. Deborah Ball and David Cohen, "Developing Practice, Developing Practitioners," in *Teaching as the Learning Profession: A Handbook of Policy and Practice*, ed. Linda Darling-Hammond and Gary Sykes (San Francisco, CA: Jossey-Bass, 1999).
23. Liping Ma, *Knowing and Teaching Elementary Mathematics: Teachers' Understanding of Fundamental Mathematics in China and the United States* (New York: Routledge, 1999).
24. Lee S. Shulman, "Those Who Understand: Knowledge Growth in Teaching," *Educational Researcher* 15, no. 2 (1986): 4–14, 9–10.
25. Bank Street College Graduate School of Education, *Catalog 2015–2016*, 77.
26. Bank Street College Graduate School of Education, *Catalog 2015–2016*, 75.
27. Bank Street College Graduate School of Education, *Catalog 2015–2016*, 74.
28. For more information on the STEP program and the redesign it underwent, see Linda Darling-Hammond, X. Newton, and R. C. Wei, "Evaluating Teacher Education Outcomes: A Study of the Stanford Teacher Education Programme," *Journal of Education for Teaching* 36, no. 4 (2010): 369–88.
29. Grant P. Wiggins and Jay McTighe, *Understanding by Design* (Arlington, VA: ASCD, 2005).
30. Wiggins and McTighe, *Understanding by Design*.
31. Georgine Loacker and Glen Rogers, *Assessment at Alverno College: Student, Program, Institutional* (Milwaukee, WI: Alverno Collge, 2005).
32. Loacker and Rogers, *Assessment at Alverno College*.
33. Thomas Dee and Emily Penner, "The Causal Effects of Cultural Relevance: Evidence from an Ethnic Studies Curriculum" (working paper, National Bureau of Economic Research, 2016), http://www.nber.org/papers/w21865.
34. Melissa Daniels, "Equity, Cultural Diversity, and English Learners," Syllabus, High Tech High, San Diego, CA, 2015, 1.

35. Roland G. Tharp, *Teaching Transformed: Achieving Excellence, Fairness, Inclusion, and Harmony* (Boulder: Westview Press, 2000).
36. Brigid J. Barron and Linda Darling-Hammond, "How Can We Teach for Meaningful Learning?" in *Powerful Learning: What We Know About Teaching for Understanding*, Linda Darling-Hammond et al. (San Francisco: Jossey-Bass, 2008).
37. Barron and Darling-Hammond, "How Can We Teach for Meaningful Learning?"
38. Elizabeth G. Cohen and Rachel A. Lotan, *Designing Groupwork: Strategies for the Heterogeneous Classroom*, 3rd ed. (New York: Teachers College Press, 2014).
39. Ross W. Greene, *Lost at School: Why Our Kids with Behavioral Challenges Are Falling Through the Cracks and How We Can Help Them* (New York: Simon and Schuster, 2009).
40. National Center for Teacher Residencies, *Measuring UTRU Network Program Impact* (Chicago: National Center for Teacher Residencies, 2015).

CHAPTER 4
1. Linda Darling-Hammond and Maritza Macdonald, "Where There Is Learning There Is Hope: The Preparation of Teachers at the Bank Street College of Education," in *Studies of Excellence in Teacher Education: Preparation at the Graduate Level*, Linda Darling-Hammond et al. (Washington, DC: AACTE Publications, 2000), 1–95.
2. San Francisco Teacher Residency, "Eligibility and Resources," 2015, http://www.sfteacherresidency.org/eligibility-resources/.
3. Alverno College School of Education, *Handbook for Initial Licensure Teacher Education Candidates Part I* (Milwaukee, WI: Alverno College, 2016).
4. Alverno College Educational Research and Evaluation, "Follow-up Surveys of Alverno Prepared Teachers and Their Employers," April 25, 2015, 7.
5. Uri Bronfenbrenner, *The Ecology of Human Development: Experiments by Nature and Design* (Cambridge, MA: Harvard University Press, 1979).
6. University of Colorado Denver, *2014–2015 Undergraduate Catalog*, http://catalog.ucdenver.edu/content.php?filter%5B27%5D=-1&filter%5B29%5D=&filter%5Bcourse_type%5D=-1&filter%5Bkeyword%5D=&filter%5B32%5D=1&filter%5Bcpage%5D=54&cur_cat_oid=14&navoid=2639&print=1&coid%5B0%5D=94541&display_location=filter_template&expand=1.
7. Alverno College School of Education, Field Descriptions, LTM Field Placement Early Adolescence/Adolescence, https://catalog.alverno.edu/courses/ltm/ltm.pdf.
8. Alverno College School of Education, Field Descriptions.
9. Alverno College School of Education, Field Descriptions.
10. Alverno College School of Education, Field Descriptions.
11. Harvey F. Silver, Richard W. Strong, and Matthew J. Perini, *The Strategic Teacher: Selecting the Right Research-Based Strategy for Every Lesson* (Franklin Lakes, NJ : Thoughtful Education Press, 2007).
12. Donald Schön, *The Reflective Practitioner: How Professionals Think in Action* (New York: Basic Books, 1986).
13. TEDD organizes teacher candidates' learning into a staged approach that includes exposure to representations of practice, engagement in approximations of practice, and opportunities to enact and analyze practice. (See the TEDD website at www.TEDD.org.)
14. "Teacher Inquiry—Supporting the Classroom Community Plan in Action Anchor Experience," *Teacher Education—Professional Year Handbook*, University of Colorado Denver, School of Education and Human Development, http://www.ucdenver.edu/academics/colleges/SchoolOfEducation/CurrentStudents/Resources/program_docs/Teacher_Education_Handbook_17_18.pdf.
15. YouthTruth, "Products & Services," http://www.youthtruthsurvey.org/products-services/.
16. Alverno College, *Student Assessment-As-Learning*, http://lampout1.alverno.edu/saal/, 3.
17. Alverno College, *Student Assessment-As-Learning*, 19.

18. Texas Classroom Teachers Association, "Goodbye PDAS, Here Comes T-TESS," https://tcta.org/node/14211-goodbye_pdas_here_comes_t_tess; Texas Teacher Evaluation & Support System, *Teacher Handbook*, November 10, 2016, https://teachfortexas.org/Resource_Files/Guides/T-TESS_Teacher_Handbook.pdf

19. Committee on Assessment and Teacher Quality, National Research Council, *Testing Teacher Candidates: The Role of Licensure Tests in Improving Teacher Quality* (Washington, DC: National Academies Press, 2001); Walter Haney, George Madaus, and A. Kreitzer, "Charms Talismanic: Testing Teachers for the Improvement of American Education," *Review of Research in Education* 14 (1987): 169–238.

20. Performance Assessment for California Teachers, "What Is PACT?" n.d., http://www.pacttpa.org/_main/hub.php?pageName=Home.

21. For more information about edTPA, see https://scale.stanford.edu/teaching/edtpa.

22. As the PACT grew into edTPA and is being replaced by it, Stanford is now transitioning to edTPA and USF is transitioning to the new state TPA.

23. Bank Street College Graduate School of Education, *Catalog 2015–2016*, 12.

24. San Francisco Teacher Residency, "SFTR Cooperating Teachers 2015–2016" (job description), July 2015, http://2nzvmtmxyesbi7fm3pk4v9h7.wpengine.netdna-cdn.com/wp-content/uploads/2015/09/SFTR-CooperatingTeacher-JobDescription-2015-16.pdf.

25. Eden Kyse et al., *NMUTR Year 4 Evaluation Report* (Montclair, NJ: Montclair State University, 2016).

26. June Jordan School of Equity website, https://jjse.org/.

CHAPTER 5

1. Linda Darling-Hammond and John Bransford, eds., *Preparing Teachers for a Changing World: What Teachers Should Learn and Be Able to Do* (Hoboken, NJ: John Wiley & Sons, 2005), 95. This volume is based on the results of a commission of the National Academy of Education.

2. All candidates' names are pseudonyms.

3. Lev Vygotsky, *Mind in Society: The Development of Higher Psychological Processes*, ed. M. Cole, V. John-Steiner, S. Scribner, and E. Souberman (Cambridge, MA: Harvard University Press, 1978).

4. Barbara Biber, "What Is Bank Street?" (lecture originally given at the Bank Street College of Education Convocation Luncheon, November 27, 1973), 3, http://www.bankstreet.edu/archives/bank-street-thinkers/ what-bank-street/

5. John Dewey, *The Child and the Curriculum* (Chicago: University of Chicago Press, 1902).

6. Bank Street College Graduate School of Education, *Catalog 2015–2016* (New York: Bank Street College of Education, 2015), 20, https://d2mguk73h8xisw.cloudfront.net/media/filer_public/filer_public/2015/08/26/gs_catalog_2015-16_1127.pdf.

7. Bank Street College Graduate School of Education, *Catalog 2015–2016*.

8. C. Wiggins, EDUC 808, "The Study of Normal and Exceptional Children Through Observation and Recording," Bank Street College of Education, 2016.

9. Alverno College, "Follow-up Surveys of Alverno-Prepared Teachers and Their Employers," April 25, 2015, 4, internal document.

CHAPTER 6

1. Mark K. Singley and John Robert Anderson, *The Transfer of Cognitive Skill* (Cambridge, MA: Harvard University Press, 1989); Linda Darling-Hammond and John Bransford, eds., *Preparing Teachers for a Changing World: What Teachers Should Learn and Be Able to Do* (New York: John Wiley & Sons, 2007).

2. Norma González, Luis C. Moll, and Cathy Amanti, eds., *Funds of Knowledge: Theorizing Practices in Households, Communities, and Classrooms* (New York: Routledge, 2006); Luis Moll and Norma González, "Engaging Life: A Funds of Knowledge Approach to Multicultural Education," *Handbook of Research on Multicultural Education* 2 (2004): 699–715.

3. International Baccalaureate (IB) is an educational nonprofit organization founded in 1968 that is recognized worldwide for providing a high-quality course of study for students from the primary grades through high school. Schools around the world who wish to participate in IB must be authorized by a central body in order to offer courses. Source: http://www.ibo.org/about-the-ib/.

4. Barohny Eun, "From Learning to Development: A Sociocultural Approach to Instruction," *Cambridge Journal of Education* 40, no. 4 (2010): 401–18.

5. "Who Is June Jordan School for Equity ?" June Jordan School for Equity, https://jjse.org/. See also California Department of Education DataQuest, https://data1.cde.ca.gov/dataquest/cbeds3.asp?cYear=2016-17&Grads=on&Uccsu=on&cSelect=3868478--San%5EFrancisco%5EUnified&cChoice=DstProf2&cLevel=District&cTopic=Profile&myTimeFrame=S&submit1=Submit.

6. Kristina Rizga, *Mission High: One School, How Experts Tried to Fail It, and the Students and Teachers Who Made It Triumph* (New York: Nation Books, 2015).

7. Bank Street College Graduate School of Education, "COS: Council of Students," 2016, https://www.bankstreet.edu/graduate-school/student-resources/council-students/.

8. Domonique Williams, "Talking About Race in the Classroom" (blog), Bank Street College Graduate School of Education, January 18, 2016, https://www.bankstreet.edu/blogs/graduate-admissions/2016/01/18/talking-about-race-in-the-classroom/.

9. Ira Lit and Linda Darling-Hammond, *The Threads They Follow: Bank Street Teachers in a Changing World* (Stanford, CA: Stanford Center for Opportunity Policy in Education [SCOPE], 2015).

10. Norma Gonzalez et al., "Funds of Knowledge for Teaching in Latino Households," *Urban Education* 29, no. 4 (1995): 443–70.

11. Enid Lee, Deborah Menkart, and Margo Okazawa-Rey, *Beyond Heroes and Holidays: A Practical Guide to K–12 Anti-Racist, Multicultural Education and Staff Development* (Washington, DC: Network of Educators on the Americas, 1997); Sarita Srivastava, "Troubles with Anti-racist Multiculturalism: The Challenges of Anti-racist and Feminist Activism," in *Race and Racism in 21st Century Canada: Continuity, Complexity, and Change*, ed. Sean P. Hier and B. Singh Bolaria (Toronto: University of Toronto Press 2007), 291–311; P. Rothenberg, "Multicultural Curriculum Transformation: Beyond Tacos and Egg Rolls" (Peace Through Diversity Lecture Series, University of South Florida, Tampa, February 2006).

12. Sidonia Jessie Alenuma-Nimoh, "Reexamining the Concept Multicultural Education: Recommendations for Moving Beyond 'Eating the Other Multiculturalism,'" *Journal of Intercultural Disciplines* 15 (2016): 128.

13. Christopher Emdin, *For White Folks Who Teach in the Hood . . . and the Rest of Y'all Too: Reality Pedagogy and Urban Education* (Boston: Beacon Press, 2016), 27–28.

14. Janie Griswold and Rob Riordan, "Another Innovation from High Tech High—Embedded Teacher Training," *Phi Delta Kappan* 97, no. 2 (2015): 26–27.

15. Zoltan Sarda and Amy Reising, "Health/Child Development/Adolescent Psychology," Syllabus, High Tech High, San Diego, CA, 2013, 1.

CHAPTER 7

1. Alverno College, *In Her Own Words* (Milwaukee, WI: Alverno College, n.d.), 4–5, unpublished document.

2. This section draws on Linda Darling-Hammond and Kim Austin, "Lessons for Life: Learning and Transfer," from the course The Learning Classroom: Theory into Practice, https://www.learner.org/courses/learningclassroom/session_overviews/learn_transfer_home11.html.

3. John Dewey, *Experience and Education*, 60th anniversary ed. (West Lafayette, IN: Kappa Delta Pi, [1938] 1998), 49.

4. Lauren B. Resnick, *Education and Learning to Think* (Washington, DC: National Academies of Science, 1987), cited in *How People Learn: Brain, Mind, Experience, and*

School, ed. John Bransford, Ann L. Brown, and Rodney R. Cocking (Washington, DC: National Academy Press, 2000), 74.

5. See, for example, a meta-analysis of 225 studies by Scott Freeman et al., "Active Learning Increases Student Performance in Science, Engineering, and Mathematics," *Proceedings of the National Academy of Sciences* 111, no. 23 (2014): 8410–15, http://www.pnas.org/content/111/23/8410.

6. Jean Piaget, "Part I: Cognitive Development in Children: Piaget Development and Learning," *Journal of Research in Science Teaching* 2, no. 3 (1964): 176–86.

7. William T. Greenough, James E. Black, and Christopher S. Wallace, "Experience and Brain Development," *Child Development* 58, no. 3 (June 1987): 539–59.

8. Bransford, Brown, and Cocking, *How People Learn*, 119.

9. Linda Darling-Hammond et al., *Powerful Learning: What We Know About Teaching for Understanding* (San Francisco: Jossey-Bass, 2008); Darling-Hammond and Austin, "Lessons for Life."

10. Bransford, Brown, and Cocking, *How People Learn*.

11. Grant P. Wiggins, and Jay McTighe, *Understanding by Design* (Arlington, VA: ASCD, 2005).

12. Bank Street College Graduate School of Education, *Catalog 2015–2016* (New York: Bank Street College of Education, 2015), 8, https://d2mguk73h8xisw.cloudfront.net/media/filer_public/filer_public/2015/08/26/gs_catalog_2015-16_1127.pdf.

13. Daniel L. Schwartz, Xiaodong Lin, Sean Brophy, and John D. Bransford, "Toward the Development of Flexibly Adaptive Instructional Designs," in *Instructional-Design Theories and Models: A New Paradigm of Instructional Theory* 2, ed. Charles E. Reigeluth (Hillsdale, NJ: Lawrence Erlbaum Associates, 1999): 183–213, cited in Bransford, Brown, and Cocking, *How People Learn*, 59.

CHAPTER 8

1. John Dewey, "My Pedagogic Creed," in *The Curriculum Studies Reader*, 4th ed., ed. David J. Flinders and Stephen J. Thornton (New York: Routledge, 2013), 29–35.

2. Lev S. Vygotsky, *Mind in Society* (Cambridge, MA: Harvard University Press, 1978).

3. Roland G. Tharp and Ronald Gallimore, *Rousing Minds to Life: Teaching, Learning, and Schooling in Social Context* (New York: Cambridge University Press, 1991).

4. Roland G. Tharp, Peggy Estrada, Stephanie Dalton, and Lois Yamauchi, *Teaching Transformed: Achieving Excellence, Fairness, Inclusion, and Harmony* (Boulder, CO: Westview Press, 2000); Stephanie S. Dalton, *Pedagogy Matters: Standards for Effective Teaching Practice* (Santa Cruz, CA: University of California Center for Research on Education, Diversity & Excellence, 1998).

5. Linda Darling-Hammond et al., "Implications for Practice of the Science of Learning and Development," *Applied Developmental Science*, in press.

6. For a review, see Linda Darling-Hammond et al., *Powerful Learning: What We Know About Teaching for Understanding* (San Francisco: Jossey-Bass, 2008).

7. Linda Darling-Hammond, Kim Austin, Suzanne Orcutt, and Daisy Martin, "Learning from Others: Learning in a Social Context," in The Learning Classroom, Annenberg Learner, https://www.learner.org/courses/learningclassroom/.

8. Tharp et al., *Teaching Transformed*, 33.

9. Fred M. Newmann, Walter G. Secada, and Gary G. Wehlage, *A Guide to Authentic Instruction and Assessment: Vision, Standards and Scoring* (Madison, WI: Wisconsin Center for Education Research, 1995), 5; Fred M. Newmann, *Student Engagement and Achievement in American Secondary Schools* (New York: Teachers College Press, 1992).

10. Etienne Wenger, *Communities of Practice: Learning, Meaning, and Identity* (Cambridge, UK, and New York: Cambridge University Press, 1998).

11. Vygotsky, *Mind in Society*.

12. John Seely Brown, Allan Collins, and Paul Duguid, "Situated Cognition and the Culture of Learning," *Educational Researcher* 18, no. 1 (1989): 32–42.

13. Jean Lave and Etienne Wenger, *Situated Learning: Legitimate Peripheral Participation* (Cambridge, UK: Cambridge University Press, 1991); Wenger, *Communities of Practice*; Etienne Wenger, Richard Arnold McDermott, and William Snyder, *Cultivating Communities of Practice: A Guide to Managing Knowledge* (Cambridge, MA: Harvard Business Press, 2002).

CHAPTER 9

1. US Department of Education, *For Each and Every Child—A Strategy for Education Equity and Excellence* (Washington, DC: DOE, 2013), 15.
2. Leib Sutcher, Linda Darling-Hammond, and Desiree Carver-Thomas, *A Coming Crisis in Teaching?* (Palo Alto: Learning Policy Institute, 2016); Charles T. Clotfelter, Helen F. Ladd, Jacob L. Vigdor, and Roger Aliaga Diaz, "Do School Accountability Systems Make It More Difficult for Low-Performing Schools to Attract and Retain High-Quality Teachers?" *Journal of Policy Analysis and Management* 23, no. 2 (2004): 251–71, https://doi.org/10.1002/pam.20003.
3. Jal Mehta, "Deeper Learning Has a Race Problem," *Education Week*, June 20, 2014, http://blogs.edweek.org/edweek/learning_deeply/2014/06/deeper_learning_has_a_race_problem.html.
4. Mehta, "Deeper Learning Has a Race Problem."
5. Jal Mehta, "A Pernicious Myth: Basics Before Deeper Learning," *Education Week*, January 4, 2018.
6. Mehta, "A Pernicious Myth."
7. Mehta, "A Pernicious Myth."
8. Grant P. Wiggins and Jay McTighe, *Understanding by Design* (Arlington, VA: ASCD, 2005).
9. Barbara Biber, *Early Education and Psychological Development* (New Haven, CT: Yale University Press, 1984).
10. "Eligibility and Resources," San Francisco Teacher Residency, http://www.sfteacherresidency.org/eligibility-resources/.
11. "SFTR Launches with Largest-Ever Cohort," press release, San Francisco Teacher Residency, 2016, on file with author.
12. HTH 107.
13. HTH 101-C.
14. Glenn Eric Singleton and Curtis Linton, *A Field Guide for Achieving Equity in Schools* (Thousand Oaks, CA: Corwin Press, 2006).
15. Paul Fleischman, "Honeybees," in *Joyful Noise: Poems for Two Voices* (New York: Harper & Row, 1988).
16. Eileen Horng, Xinhua Zheng, Ira Lit, and Linda Darling-Hammond, *The Preparation, Professional Pathways, and Effectiveness of Bank Street Graduates* (Stanford, CA: Stanford Center for Opportunity Policy in Education, 2016).
17. Carolina Soto, "Culturally Responsive Practice—Shared Funds of Knowledge with Our Community" (blog), Bank Street Graduate School of Education, January 23, 2017, https://graduate.bankstreet.edu/admissions-financial-aid/admissions-blog/culturally-responsive-practice-shared-funds-of-knowledge-with-our-community/ .
18. Bank Street Graduate School of Education, "Center for Culturally Responsive Practices at Bank Street College of Education (CCRP)," https://www.bankstreet.edu/ccrp/.
19. Jessica Cardichon and Linda Darling-Hammond. *Advancing Educational Equity for Underserved Youth: How New State Accountability Systems Can Support School Inclusion and Student Success* (Palo Alto, CA: Learning Policy Institute, 2017), https://learningpolicyinstitute.org/product/advancing-educational-equity-underserved-youth-report.
20. San Francisco Unified School District, School Health Programs Department, "ExCEL After School Programs," 2007, http://www.healthiersf.org/ExCELafterschool/About/ExCELBrochure0708.pdf; http://www.sfusd.edu/en/programs-and-services/after-school-programs.html.

CHAPTER 10

1. Alverno College faculty, *Ability-Based Learning Outcomes* (Milwaukee, WI: Alverno College, n.d.), viii.
2. For more on professional development schools, see Richard W. Clark, *Effective Professional Development Schools* (San Francisco: Jossey-Bass, 1999); Linda Darling-Hammond, *Professional Development Schools: Schools for Developing a Profession* (New York: Teachers College Press, 1994); Linda Darling-Hammond and Joan Baratz-Snowden, *A Good Teacher In Every Classroom: Preparing the Highly Qualified Teachers Our Children Deserve* (San Francisco: Jossey-Bass, 2005); Holmes Group, *Tomorrow's Teachers: A Report of the Holmes Group* (East Lansing, MI: Holmes Group, Inc., 1986); Holmes Group, *Tomorrow's Schools of Education: A Report of the Holmes Group* (East Lansing, MI: Holmes Group, Inc., 1990); Holmes Group, *Tomorrow's Schools of Education: A Report of the Holmes Group* (East Lansing, MI: Holmes Group, Inc., 1995); Marsha Levine and Roberta Trachtman, eds., *Making Professional Development Schools Work: Politics, Practice, and Policy* (New York: Teachers College Press, 1997); Hugh G. Petrie, *Professionalization, Partnership, and Power: Building Professional Development Schools* (Albany, NY: SUNY Press, 1995); Dorene Ross et al., "Research from Professional Development Schools: Can We Live Up to the Potential?" *Peabody Journal of Education* 74, nos. 3 & 4 (1999): 209–23; Lee Teitel, "Two Decades of Professional Development School Development in the United States. What Have We Learned? Where Do We Go from Here?" *Journal of In-Service Education* 30, no. 3 (2004): 401–16; Roberta Trachtman, "The NCATE Professional Development School Study: A Survey of 28 PDS Sites," in *Designing Standards That Work for Professional Development Schools. Commissioned Papers of the NCATE PDS Standards Project*, ed. Marsha Levine (Washington, DC: National Council for the Accreditation of Teacher Education, 1998); Nancy Winitzky, Trish Stoddart, and Patti O'Keefe, "Great Expectations: Emergent Professional Development Schools," *Journal of Teacher Education* 43, no. 1 (1992): 3–18.
3. National Education Association, "Teacher Residencies: Redefining Preparation Through Partnerships," NEA Report 2014, http://www.nea.org/assets/docs/Teacher -Residencies-2014.pdf.

CHAPTER 11

1. Donald Boyd et al., "Teacher Preparation and Student Achievement" (NBER Working Paper No. W14314, National Bureau of Economic Research, 2008), http://ssrn.com /abstract=1264576; Linda Darling-Hammond, *Powerful Teacher Education: Lessons from Exemplary Programs* (San Francisco: Jossey-Bass, 2006).
2. Abraham Flexner, *Medical Education in the United States and Canada: A Report to the Carnegie Foundation for the Advancement of Teaching*, Bulletin No. 4 (New York: Carnegie Foundation for the Advancement of Teaching, 1910), http://archive.carnegie foundation.org/pdfs/elibrary/Carnegie_Flexner_Report.pdf.
3. For a review, see National Research Council, *Assessing Accomplished Teaching: Advanced-Level Certification Programs* (Washington, DC: National Academies Press, 2008).
4. David Lustick and Gary Sykes, "National Board Certification as Professional Development: What Are Teachers Learning?" *Education Policy Analysis Archives* 14 (2006); Mistilina Sato, Ruth Chung Wei, and Linda Darling-Hammond, "Improving Teachers' Assessment Practices Through Professional Development: The Case of National Board Certification," *American Educational Research Journal* 45, no. 3 (2008): 669–700.
5. For more information about edTPA, see https://scale.stanford.edu/teaching/edtpa.
6. Ellen R. Delisio, "Portfolios Help Teachers Reflect on What Makes Good Teaching," Education World, 2011, http://www.educationworld.com/a_admin/admin/admin 201.shtml.
7. Performance Assessment for California Teachers, "What Is PACT?" http://www .pacttpa.org/_main/hub.php?pageName=Home.

8. Linda Darling-Hammond, *Evaluating Teacher Effectiveness: How Teacher Performance Assessments Can Measure and Improve Teaching* (Washington, DC: Center for American Progress, 2010); Mark Wilson, P. J. Hallam, Raymond Pecheone, and Pamela Moss, "Evaluating the Validity of Portfolio Assessments for Licensure Decisions," *Education Policy Analysis Archives* 22, no. 6 (2014); edTPA, *Educative Assessment and Meaningful Support: 2014 edTPA Administrative Report* (Stanford, CA: edTPA, 2015); Dan Goldhaber, J. Cowan, and Roddy Theobald, "Evaluating Prospective Teachers: Testing the Predictive Validity of the edTPA" (CALDER Working Paper No. 157, 2016); Stephen Newton, *Preservice Performance Assessment and Teacher Early Career Effectiveness: Preliminary Findings on the Performance Assessment for California Teachers* (Stanford, CA: Stanford Center for Assessment, Learning, and Equity, 2010); Dan Goldhaber and Emily Anthony, "Can Teacher Quality Be Effectively Assessed? National Board Certification as a Signal of Effective Teaching," *Review of Economics and Statistics* 89, no. 1 (2007): 134–50.

9. Darling-Hammond, *Evaluating Teacher Effectiveness*; edTPA, *Educative Assessment and Meaningful Support: 2016 edTPA Administrative Report* (Stanford, CA: edTPA, 2017); Goldhaber, Cowan, and Theobald, "Evaluating Prospective Teachers."

10. Ruth R. Chung, "Beyond Assessment: Performance Assessments in Teacher Education," *Teacher Education Quarterly* 35, no. 1 (2008): 7–28; Linda Darling-Hammond, Stephen P. Newton, and Ruth Chung Wei, "Evaluating Teacher Education Outcomes," 369–388.

11. For a number of years, both USF and STEP used the PACT. However, as all the other USF candidates were using CalTPA, SFTR residents were shifted to this assessment as of 2015–16. Like most institutions that initially used the PACT, STEP has recently replaced the PACT with the edTPA, an updated, national version of the PACT.

12. California Commission on Teacher Credentialing, "California Teaching Performance Assessment," http://www.ctc.ca.gov/educator-prep/TPA-files/CalTPA-general-info.pdf; Performance Assessment for California Teachers, "A Brief Overview of the PACT Assessment System" (white paper, PACT, 2008), http://www.pacttpa.org/_files/Main /Brief_Overview_of_PACT.doc.

13. Darling-Hammond, Newton, and Wei, "Evaluating Teacher Education Outcomes."

14. Raymond L. Pecheone and Ruth R. Chung, "Evidence in Teacher Education: The Performance Assessment for California Teachers (PACT)," *Journal of Teacher Education* 57, no. 1 (January/February 2006): 22–36.

15. Darling-Hammond, "Evaluating Teacher Effectiveness."

16. California Commission on Teacher Credentialing, *California Teaching Performance Expectations* (Sacramento, CA: California Commission on Teacher Credentialing, 2016), https://www.ctc.ca.gov/docs/default-source/educator-prep/standards/adopted-tpes -2016.pdf?sfvrsn=8cb2c410_0.

17. Linda Darling-Hammond et al., *Empowered Educators: How High-Performing Systems Shape Teaching Quality Around the World* (San Francisco: John Wiley & Sons, 2017).

18. Margaret A. Gallego, "Is Experience the Best Teacher? The Potential of Coupling Classroom and Community-Based Field Experiences," *Journal of Teacher Education* 52, no. 4 (2001): 314.

19. Irma N. Guadarrama, John M. Ramsey, and Janice L. Nath, eds., *Professional Development Schools: Advances in Community Thought and Research* (Greenwich, CT: Information Age Publishing, 2005).

20. For a summary see Linda Darling-Hammond and John Bransford, eds., *Preparing Teachers for a Changing World: What Teachers Should Learn and Be Able to Do* (San Francisco: John Wiley & Sons, 2005), 415–16.

21. Maryland State Department of Education, 2004.

22. Richard Ingersoll, L. Merrill, and H. May, *What Are the Effects of Teacher Education and Preparation on Beginning Teacher Attrition?* (Consortium for Policy Research in Education, University of Pennsylvania, CPRE Report #RR-82, 2014).

23. *Newark Montclair Urban Teacher Residency Evaluation* (Montclair, NJ: Center for Research and Evaluation on Education and Human Services (CREEHS), Montclair State University, 2017).
24. Roneeta Guha, Maria E. Hyler, and Linda Darling-Hammond, "The Teacher Residency: An Innovative Model for Preparing Teachers," Learning Policy Institute, September 15, 2016.
25. Linda Darling-Hammond and Gary Sykes, "Wanted, a National Teacher Supply Policy for Education: The Right Way to Meet the 'Highly Qualified Teacher' Challenge," *Education Policy Analysis Archives* 11 (2003): 33.
26. OECD, *Education at a Glance 2017: OECD Indicators*, https://read.oecd-ilibrary.org /education/education-at-a-glance-2017_eag-2017-en#page377.
27. Ulrich Boser and Chelsea Straus, *Mid- and Late-Career Teachers Struggle with Paltry Incomes* (Washington, DC: Center for American Progress, 2014), https://cdn.american progress.org/wp-content/uploads/2014/07/teachersalaries-brief.pdf.
28. Sylvia Allegretto and Lawrence Mishel, *The Teacher Pay Gap Is Wider Than Ever: Teachers' Pay Continues to Fall Further Behind Pay of Comparable Workers* (Washington, DC: Economic Policy Institute, 2016), https://www.epi.org/publication/the-teacher -pay-gap-is-wider-than-ever-teachers-pay-continues-to-fall-further-behind-pay-of -comparable-workers/.
29. Darling-Hammond et al., *Empowered Educators*.
30. L. Sutcher, L. Darling-Hammond, and D. Carver-Thomas, *A Coming Crisis in Teaching? Teacher Supply, Demand, and Shortages in the US* (Palo Alto, CA: Learning Policy Institute, 2016); Linda Darling-Hammond, "Where Have All the Teachers Gone?" Learning Policy Institute, September 20, 2017, https://learningpolicyinstitute.org /blog/where-have-all-teachers-gone.
31. Sutcher, Darling-Hammond, and Carver-Thomas, *A Coming Crisis*.
32. Linda Darling-Hammond, "Research on Teaching and Teacher Education and Its Influences on Policy and Practice," *Educational Researcher* 45 no. 2 (2016): 83–91.
33. A. Podolsky, T. Kini, J. Bishop, and L. Darling-Hammond, *Solving the Teacher Shortage: How to Attract and Retain Excellent Educators* (Palo Alto, CA: Learning Policy Institute, 2016).
34. Sutcher, Darling-Hammond, and Carver-Thomas, *A Coming Crisis in Teaching?*
35. Erin Richards and Matt Kulling, "School Districts Scramble to Find Teachers for Open Positions," *Journal Sentinel*, August 17, 2015, http://archive.jsonline.com/news /education/school-districts-scramble-to-find-teachers-for-open-positions-b99556824 z1-322096631.html.
36. Linda Darling-Hammond, Ruth Chung, and Fred Frelow, "Variation in Teacher Preparation: How Well Do Different Pathways Prepare Teachers to Teach?" *Journal of Teacher Education* 53, vol. 4 (September/October 2002): 286–302; Ingersoll, Merrill, and May, *What Are the Effects of Teacher Education*.
37. Jesse Rothstein and Cecilia Elena Rouse, "Constrained After College: Student Loans and Early-Career Occupational Choices," *Journal of Public Economics* 95, no. 1–2 (2011): 149–63.
38. Gary T. Henry, Kevin C. Bastian, and A. A. Smith, "Scholarships to Recruit the 'Best and Brightest' into Teaching," *Educational Researcher* 41, no. 3 (2012): 83–92.
39. Darling-Hammond et al., *Empowered Educators*.
40. Irina Buchberger and Friedrich Buchberger, "Problem Solving Capacity of a Teacher Education System as a Condition of Success? An Analysis of the 'Finnish Case,'" in *Education Policy Analysis in a Comparative Perspective*, ed. F. Buchberger and S. Berghammer (Linz, Austria: Trauner, 2003), 10.
41. Darling-Hammond et al., *Empowered Educators*.
42. Linda Darling-Hammond, Velma Cobb and Kavemuii Murangi, *APEC Education Forum: Teacher Preparation and Professional Development in APEC Members* (Washington, DC: US Department of Education, May 1995), 1–16; Darling-Hammond et

al., *Empowered Educators*; Per-Olof Erixon, Gun-Marie Frånberg, and Daniel Kallós, "The Role of Graduate and Postgraduate Studies and Research in Teacher Education Reform Policies in the European Union," in *Proceedings of the Conference on the Role of Graduate and Postgraduate Studies and Research in Teacher Education Reform Policies in the European Union* (Umeå, Sweden: European Network on Teacher Education Policies, 2001).

43. Linda Darling-Hammond, "Teacher Education and the American Future," *Journal of Teacher Education* 61, no. 1–2 (2010): 35–47.

44. Desiree Carver-Thomas, *Diversifying the Teaching Profession: How to Recruit and Retain Teachers of Color* (Palo Alto: Learning Policy Institute, 2018).

ACKNOWLEDGMENTS

The authors are extremely grateful to the many individuals who supported this work. We thank first the teacher candidates, graduates, faculty, staff, district and community partners, and leadership from the seven teacher preparation programs for generously sharing their time, experiences, and expertise. Without them, this book would not have been possible. In particular, the following individuals provided incredible wisdom and support as they organized and hosted our visits during the 2015–16 school year, compiled stacks of background documents, and shared reams of data: Patricia Luebke and Desiree Pointer-Mace from Alverno College; Shael Polakow-Suransky and Cecelia Traugh from Bank Street College Graduate School of Education; Rebecca Cantor and Cindy Gutierrez from the University of Colorado Denver; Ben Daley, Janie Griswold, and Julie Holmes from High Tech High; Tamara Lucas and Jennifer Robinson from Montclair University; Peter Williamson from the Stanford Teacher Education Program and Jonathan Osler, formerly with the San Francisco Teacher Residency; and Shari Albright, Patricia J. Norman, and Angela Breidenstein from Trinity University.

Several scholars served graciously as external peer reviewers of the seven case studies, from which this book draws. We greatly benefited from their vast expertise, thoughtful insights, and sometimes-tough questions: Rachel Lotan, Emeritus Professor at Stanford Graduate School of Education, and Thomas Levine, Assistant Professor at the University of Connecticut Neag School of Education, for their review of the Alverno case; Jon Snyder, Executive Director at the Stanford Center for Opportunity Policy in Education, and Anna Richert, Professor of Education at Mills College, for their review of the Bank Street College case; Lauren Anderson, Associate Professor of Education at Connecticut College, for her review of the CU Denver case; Cynthia Grutzik, Dean, College of Education at San Francisco State University, Ellen Moir, Founder and Chief Executive Officer of the New Teacher

Center, and Emily L. Davis, Senior Director at the New Teacher Center, for their review of the High Tech High case; Etta Hollins, Kauffman Endowed Chair for Urban Education, College of Education, University of Missouri, Kansas City, and Monica Williams Shealy, Dean, College of Education, Rowan State University, for their review of the Montclair case; Joyce King, Benjamin E. Mays Endowed Chair for Urban Teaching, Learning and Leadership at Georgia State University, and Saroja Warner, Director, Workforce Initiatives at the Council of Chief State School Officers, for their review of the San Francisco Teacher Residency case; and Misty Sato, University of Canterbury and Pia Wong, Professor at the College of Education at California State University, Sacramento, for their review of the Trinity case.

We are also grateful to Ira Lit, Associate Professor at Stanford's Graduate School of Education, for his contributions to the Bank Street research, and to our LPI colleagues, Julie Adams and Larkin Willis, for their help in writing and editing sections of the book. The assistance, support, enthusiasm, and patience of editors Douglas Clayton and Jayne Marie Fargnoli at Harvard Education Press helped us move our work to the story this book tells.

Finally, we greatly appreciate the generosity of the Carnegie Corporation of New York, which provided major funding for the study, as well as to the S. D. Bechtel, Jr. Foundation, the William and Flora Hewlett Foundation, and the Sandler Foundation, which provided additional support for LPI's research in this area. We are enormously grateful to all of them.

ABOUT THE AUTHORS

LINDA DARLING-HAMMOND is the president and CEO of the Learning Policy Institute. She is also the Charles E. Ducommun Professor of Education Emeritus at Stanford University, where she founded the Stanford Center for Opportunity Policy in Education and served as the faculty sponsor of the Stanford Teacher Education Program, which she helped to redesign. Darling-Hammond is past president of the American Educational Research Association and recipient of its awards for Distinguished Contributions to Research, Lifetime Achievement, and Research-to-Policy. Among her many publications are a number of award-winning books, including *The Right to Learn, Teaching as the Learning Profession, Preparing Teachers for a* Changing *World*, and *The Flat World and Education.*

JEANNIE OAKES is senior policy fellow at the Learning Policy Institute; Presidential Professor of Education Equity Emeritus at UCLA; and the former director of education at the Ford Foundation. She is past president of the American Educational Research Association and a member of the National Academy of Education. Oakes's research examines the effect of social policies on the education of low-income students of color and also investigates equity-minded reform. Her books include *Keeping Track: How Schools Structure Inequality, Becoming Good American Schools: The Struggle for Civic Virtue in Education Reform, Learning Power,* and *Teaching to Change the World.*

CHANNA M. COOK-HARVEY is Director of Social and Emotional Learning at Folsom Cordova Unified School District. She was previously a senior researcher at the Learning Policy Institute where she led work on performance assessments and social-emotional and academic learning. She has been a high school English teacher, literacy coach, and principal, and has taught courses and supervised teacher candidates in the Stanford Teacher Education Program.

RONEETA GUHA is a senior researcher who coleads the Learning Policy Institute's Deeper Learning Team. She served as the codirector of this LPI study on teacher preparation programs that support deeper learning. She also manages several state and national projects promoting the use of authentic assessments in education, including the California Performance Assessment Collaborative, the Reimagining College Access initiative, and the State Performance Assessment Learning Community.

AKEELAH HARRELL is a program manager at Jobs for the Future and a member of the Building Economic Opportunity Group. Harrell has previously served as a consultant for the Learning Policy Institute and as an academic advisor at the Harlem Center for Education in New York City.

MARIA E. HYLER serves as the deputy director of the Learning Policy Institute's Washington, DC, office and is a senior researcher on staff. Hyler coleads LPI's Educator Quality team and represents the institute on several initiatives focused on teacher and leader preparation, development, and leadership. Before taking her position at LPI, Hyler served as an assistant professor of teacher preparation and professional development in the Department of Teaching and Learning, Policy, and Leadership at the University of Maryland, College Park.

CHARMAINE N. JACKSON MERCER is a program officer in the Education Program at the William and Flora Hewlett Foundation. Previously, she served as director of the Washington, DC, office and senior researcher for the Learning Policy Institute. Her prior experience includes serving as vice president of policy and advocacy at the Alliance for Excellent Education, directing policy and research at Communities for Teaching Excellence in Los Angeles, and working in federal government.

TARA KINI is the director of state policy at the Learning Policy Institute. Kini has two decades of experience working in public education as a civil rights attorney, classroom teacher, and teacher educator. Previously, she was a senior staff attorney with the civil rights law firm Public Advocates, taught English and history in Bay Area public schools, and served as a faculty supervisor with UC Berkeley's teacher education program.

ANNE PODOLSKY is a doctoral student at Stanford University. She was previously a researcher and policy analyst at the Learning Policy Institute, for which she continues to consult. She focuses on improving educational opportunities and outcomes, especially for students from underserved communities. She is an Illinois State Board of Education–certified teacher and a member of the State Bar of California.

STEVEN K. WOJCIKIEWICZ is the director of the Pacific Alliance for Catholic Education at the University of Portland and a consultant with the Learning Policy Institute. Wojcikiewicz has previously served as an associate professor of teacher education at Western Oregon University; an assistant director for educational issues at the American Federation of Teachers in Washington, DC; and vice president of policy for Deans for Impact in Austin, Texas. He started his career as a social studies teacher in Tulsa, Oklahoma.

INDEX